DON'T

SEE ME CRY

DON'T LET HER SEE ME CRY

A MOTHER'S STORY

HELEN BARNACLE

BANTAM BOOKS

SYDNEY • AUCKLAND • TORONTO • NEW YORK • LONDON

DON'T LET HER SEE ME CRY
A BANTAM BOOK

First published in Australia and New Zealand in 2000
by Bantam

This new edition published 2001

National Library of Australia
Cataloguing-in-Publication entry

Barnacle, Helen.
    Don't let her see me cry.
    ISBN 1 86325 308 4.
    1. Barnacle, Helen. 2. Psychologists — Victoria —
    Biography. 3. Narcotic addicts — Rehabilitation — Victoria
    — Biography. 4. Narcotic addicts — Victoria — Biography.
    5. Women prisoners — Victoria — Biography. I. Title.
362.29309945

Transworld Publishers,
a division of Random House Australia Pty Ltd
20 Alfred Street, Milsons Point, NSW 2061

Random House New Zealand Limited
18 Poland Road, Glenfield, Auckland

Transworld Publishers (UK) Limited
a division of The Random House Group Ltd
61-63 Uxbridge Road, Ealing, London W5 5SA

Random House Inc
1540 Broadway, New York, New York 10036

Cover photograph by Neale Duckworth
Edited by Jo Jarrah

Typeset in 12/10.5/14 Bembo by Midland Typesetters, Maryborough, Victoria
Printed and bound by Griffin Press, Netley, South Australia

20 19 18 17 16 15 14 13 12

This project has been assisted by the
Commonwealth Government through
the Australia Council, its arts funding body.

Australia Council for the Arts

To Ali

You have taught me so much, and when I searched for
a reason to go on living, you were there.

Pseudonyms have been used and other details altered where necessary to protect the identity of people and organisations mentioned in this book.

Contents

Acknowledgements

The process of writing this book has been one of the most stimulating, emotional and yet rewarding experiences in my life. Before I mention those who assisted directly with the book, I'd like to thank just a few who have touched my life, some only briefly, but who have all contributed to my survival along the difficult path I once chose.

To Ron, my very special brother, thanks for enduring feeling helpless for so many years and never losing faith in me.

Dame Phyllis Frost and Father Brosnan succeeded in lobbying the relevant minister to change the rule that babies could only remain with their mothers in prison until one year of age. Their perseverance allowed me four precious years in prison with Ali, instead of seven years without her. It is difficult to express the depth of gratitude that I feel, except to say that at least partially due to their efforts, Ali and I today have a deep connection and a lot of fun together.

My singing teachers, Murray and Anna Madardy, made my singing lessons a spiritual journey.

Our other special friends along the road are Corliss Searcey, Kurt Searcey, Greg Sneddon, Maud Clark, Sue Wong, Pete, David, Jan and Annie (singers/friends from TRAMM), Elizabeth

Meikle, Cheryl Cornish, Tony Longo, Ian Freckleton, Elva Murray, Peter Rostran and Danni Sinclair. There are many others I haven't named here, but to whom I am grateful.

Many people have helped me in the writing process. My thanks go especially to the following:

The Australia Council for awarding me a fellowship which provided the financial means as well as the time and space required to complete this project, and the Jessie Street Trust for awarding me a grant in 1996 which enabled me to buy new computer equipment.

The staff of Random House Australia, particularly Fiona Henderson, whose enthusiasm for the story inspired me to work even harder. Thanks to every staff member of Random House who I have had contact with and who have all been so respectful and delightful to work with.

My agent Fiona Inglis of Curtis Brown Literary Agents. Fiona was the first 'outsider' to read my initial draft manuscript. Without the editorial assistance and advice she provided in the early stages, the manuscript may never have reached a publisher. Thanks for your time and for being so genuine, constructive and trustworthy.

To my editor Jo Jarrah, thanks for your endless questions and the ability to know just what would work best. For helping me to turn jumbled thoughts and sentences into a coherent, flowing story, for the respect and care you showed towards some incredibly sensitive material, for your constant and endless encouragement which enabled me to feel positive about my work, and for making the whole editorial process feel like this work has been blessed, thank you.

Thanks to Amanda George and Ron for their assistance in reading early drafts. Ron, thanks for your continued support and for taking the time to help with ideas and changes to the manuscript. Thanks to Amanda for much reading, constructive criticism and positive reinforcement, but most of all for our friendship.

For all the women in prison—yesterday, today and tomorrow—I'd like to say:

>I love these women
>I am these women.

Prologue

I'm busted, locked up.

'Please get me out. I can't stay here!' I beg my lawyer.

He looks back at me unemotionally.

'You've got to get me out of here! It's nearly Christmas. I can't spend Christmas in jail!' I repeat. My boyfriend had organised for him to come to the prison to discuss my recent unsuccessful bail application. Although he's a junior, he's from a high profile organisation. I thought he was being paid to get me out, not to tell me I had to stay in.

'I'm sorry. There's nothing more I can do,' he replies.

'What do you mean? Can't you hear me? I'm going to go mad in here!' I plead with him, thinking with dread of the bleak dormitory that had suddenly become my home. My eyes search the prison visit centre where our meeting is taking place, as if looking for a way out of the oppressive pressed-tin walls and barred windows that surround us. The shiny, swirly patterned linoleum glares up at me from under my feet.

'You're going to have to stay here until we get your first trial out of the way. They won't give you two lots of bail,' the lawyer says, eyes disinterested. He might as well be speaking a foreign language. He doesn't seem to understand my despair.

It's 31 October 1979 and I'm on remand at Fairlea Women's Prison in Melbourne, facing two separate lots of drug charges. I had been busted for the first time a few months earlier, in June, on a charge of possessing heroin. I was out on bail awaiting the trial when the police decided I was involved in another, much bigger case, and they subsequently charged me with conspiracy to import heroin, along with four others who had been charged a few months before I was.

Deep down I feel like I'm too good a person, too nice, to be in jail, but the police and the courts don't see it that way. Guilty? Of sticking a needle in my arm—yep, that's me. But I've never been able to figure how that makes me a criminal. I know I'm self-destructive and selfish, but that doesn't make be 'bad', does it? I've never thieved, burgled or assaulted anyone. I've always felt it was important not to abuse or invade other people's spaces, and in all my years of drug use I've never crossed that line. I'd hang out from heroin withdrawals rather than steal someone else's property. I've never even cheated on a boyfriend. The only thing I'm continually dishonest about is my heroin use, and other than the shame associated with being labelled a 'heroin addict', I'm proud of the way I treat other human beings.

I do sell smack to other drug-using friends to maintain my own habit, and straight people consider that 'bad', but not my friends and I, even though it is illegal. That's the problem, of course. Anyway, I just can't accept—won't accept—that me, Helen Barnacle, is in jail. I shouldn't be here, I keep saying to myself. I may not have much self-esteem left, but there's something unshakable still inside.

I try pleading with my lawyer again: 'There must be something you can do to get me out. Jails are for bad people, violent people,' although that last statement is untrue—most women are in jail for non-violent crimes. The lawyer just shakes his head once more. I can't believe how unmoved he is, with that vacant, unfeeling look on his face. I'm not a violent person, but I'm feeling so agitated that for a moment I want to smash his clean-shaven, middle-class baby face right now! I grip my knees tightly with my hands and my jaw clenches.

As I sit staring at him, I realise how much I want him to show at least a tiny bit of understanding about what's happening to me. I don't bother to say it out loud, though. He's young, probably quite new to the business, but I'm young too, just twenty-five years old, and feel he should understand.

So quickly my life is changing, spinning completely out of my control. Random thoughts chase each other in and out of my brain, like some nightmare merry-go-round ... my unhappy adolescence, my mother's death six months earlier, my estrangement from my father, my brother's futile attempts to help, the violent abuse of the drug world, my transition from dux of primary school to drug addict/criminal, my singing career down the drain, the shame and alienation. And the beloved baby daughter growing inside me—what is to become of her?

All of a sudden my world seems to belong to people who don't know me at all—police, prosecution lawyers, judges. Worse, they seem to feel only hatred and contempt for me. I have never felt so lost, alone and frightened in my life.

Who *am* I? I keep asking myself. Why am I here and how on earth did it come to this? A last plea to myself, or to anyone else who cares to listen.

Only the coming years would provide any answers. During them I experience the birth of my daughter and devastating separation from her, my own descent into suicidal depression, and the loss of many friends to drug overdoses. But at that moment in October 1979 when my heart wept with sadness and my body was limp with despair, the cell door closed, and there was just me, the concrete and the stainless steel. A gaping, solitary space. The only thing I would be able to hang on to was my baby girl,

Ali. One day I would hold her in my arms for good. Motherhood would teach me about unconditional love and I wouldn't let go.

But that moment was still years away ...

Part I
Life

1

The fairytale of childhood

For most of my childhood I lived in MacGregor Street, Parkdale, in a three-bedroom weatherboard war-service home with Mum, Dad and my brother Ron, who is three years older than me. The house was painted a cacky blue–green colour, which I guess my parents must have thought was attractive—or maybe the paint was just on special! Parkdale is twenty-four kilometres south of Melbourne, nestled along the coast of Port Phillip Bay, and in 1953, when I was born, it mostly consisted of vacant paddocks. The land was being subdivided to build houses which could be bought by ex-servicemen. The mortgage repayments were very low, so life was relatively inexpensive. I guess this was some sort of concession for them having fought in the war.

My father had served in the navy during the Second World War, and my mother with the air force. I think if my dad hadn't married and had children he would have remained in the navy as he loved the travelling and life at sea. Most of our neighbours were in the same situation and, after returning from the war, had married and were starting families. It was quite a close-knit community with common interests, and Ron and I had plenty of friends our own age. Several families used to play tennis at the local courts every Sunday, and my father was involved in the local football club. We loved footy (Australian Rules) and in our family you had to barrack for Collingwood. We often went to the games, Ron and I screaming out in support of the mighty 'Woods'. My father and several other locals established the Mordialloc Youth Club, which offered young people a variety of sports, gymnastics and calisthenics. Quite often several neighbouring families would organise a weekend picnic and we'd all drive to a bush location with our thermoses and picnic baskets. We'd play games like cricket or shuttlecock or, if we were somewhere like Lake Eildon, we'd go swimming. During the Christmas school vacation we'd sometimes go on camping holidays to places like Phillip Island, Wilsons Promontory or Rosebud—always near the beach or a river as Ron and I loved swimming, and for a short time were involved in the Parkdale Lifesaving Club.

From as early as I can remember, my best friend was Libby. She was the same age as me and, although we attended different schools, we remained best friends until the last couple of years of primary school, at least from ages five to ten. After that we spent more time with friends from our respective schools. Libby had an older sister who was about the same age as my brother. Her family lived in the street behind ours, in a house that backed onto the Thompsons'. To get to her place all I had to do was go down a few houses to the Thompsons' and walk through the gap in their back fence. The Thompsons and Libby's family were good friends. I loved going to Libby's house because her mum, who didn't have to work like my mum, would often bake yummy cakes and you could smell them as you approached. Her place seemed to have a more homely atmosphere than ours, mostly because her mum was always there. My poor mum was always at work, which meant that Ron and I had lots of chores to complete before she arrived home in the afternoons. We weren't complaining, though, because our life was good too—it was just a bit different to those families where the mums didn't work.

Our dad leased a little lock-up barber shop on the other side of Nepean Highway, closer to the main shopping centre in Parkdale. He was a qualified men's hairdresser, but I don't know that the business was very prosperous because our mum always had to work. Her job in a commercial laundry was quite strenuous, and she had to be on her feet all day. It was a large factory and sometimes during school holidays I'd work there too. I always remember it as being hot, sweaty work, but I'd be paid a small amount for folding towels, so I thought it was terrific. Most school holidays we'd go to our cousins' farm at Hamilton, in the Western District of Victoria, where Mum came from and where most of her six brothers and sisters still lived. At other times we'd go to Mum's other sister's farm in Pakenham, about an hour south-east of Melbourne. Ron and I loved our holidays on the farm and our cousins taught us to ride their horses.

Mum worked at the laundry for about fifteen years before going to a factory that made parts for cars. Mum didn't have any qualifications, so she was restricted in her choices. Back then, in the 1950s and '60s, most families in our suburb had a telephone but we didn't, so if Ron or I were out and wanted to get a message to Mum at home, we'd ring Ivy and Cobber, our neighbours over the road, and they'd pass it on to her. Our clothes were pretty crappy compared to the other kids as well. Mum made a lot of my dresses, but sometimes we were given hand-me-downs from relatives, which I quite liked as they were usually better quality than what we could afford.

Every weekend I'd be around at Libby's, and there were always wonderful cooking smells emanating from the kitchen. 'Any "licky" today, Mrs Bott?' I'd ask as I walked through the back door into the warm, inviting kitchen. 'Licky' was what we called the leftover cake mixture. Then we'd go to the cubby house behind their outside toilet. It offered privacy for any plans we wanted to hatch, and we had lots of secrets stored there. That's where we'd have important discussions or sometimes hold 'meetings'. At other times we'd make perfume from rose petals, or play on our pogo sticks. When we weren't in our cubby house we'd go on bike-riding adventures, or play tennis or netball. The best times were when Libby slept over at my house or I slept at her place. I don't think we ever fought—I only remember having lots of fun in the adventure world created by our young, imaginative minds.

When Ron and I were still quite young and in primary school, my father leased a bigger retail premises in Parkdale to run another barber's shop. Unlike the previous shop, it was located in the main shopping centre and included an attached dwelling, so we moved there for about six years and rented out our house in MacGregor Street. The new shop didn't make much money either, so our mum continued to work at the laundry in Mentone, a neighbouring suburb. She used to get pissed off with Dad when she arrived home after working hard in the factory all day to find the till relatively empty. Money seemed to be the main thing they argued about, but rarely in our hearing. However, it was while we were living behind this shop that Ron and I first began to notice the tension between them. They tried not to display it in front of us, but sometimes at night we could hear their raised voices arguing behind the closed door of their bedroom. It didn't concern us too much, though; we were generally pretty happy kids, although we never hung around together. We both had lots of friends and were always outside playing somewhere. We only came home for meals.

On my first day at primary school, having turned five only weeks earlier, my mum went off leaving me crying in the shelter shed, but by morning playtime the tears were gone. I settled into school easily and I loved the friendships and stimulation it provided. From about fourth grade I developed a new friendship with Kym, who was in the same class as me. She and I always achieved high grades and we were both energetic, imaginative and enjoyed playing outdoors. We adored each other and spent most of our out-of-school time together too, because when my family moved to the residence behind our shop in Parkers Road, we were only one street away from Kym's house, where she lived with her mum. Although her father was still alive, he only returned home to visit occasionally as he'd been seriously injured in the war and required full-time nursing care.

Kym and I never went home from school until we absolutely had to. Instead we would stay behind after classes were finished to play on the monkey bars at the back of the school, somersaulting and spinning around forward and backward, round and round. I loved the feeling of the wind against my body as I'd spin round faster and faster. I felt strong, invincible and without a care in the world.

Kym was learning ballet and loved to sing, and I was learning calisthenics and also loved music, so we often had little concerts where she and I were the star attractions, singing and dancing our little hearts out in front of an invited audience of children and adults from the neighbourhood. We worked out the song and dance routines ourselves and thought we were 'shit hot'. We'd be busy rehearsing for weeks on end: 'No, Kym, I think you should move on your left leg and open your arms up more,' I'd advise her. 'Can you do the splits on your right leg instead of your left?' You'd think I was an expert—I guess I never doubted that I was. Then it would be Kym's turn to advise me on one of my many items. We'd go on like this for hours, never seeming to tire of our fantasy world. When we weren't at home playing, we were at school having fun, or I was at calisthenics which I'd begun at the age of four.

I'd been born with a knee problem which meant that I couldn't stand with my legs straight together, one knee always pushing in front of the other. The doctor told my mother that I should do some kind of sport or physical activity to try to correct this, so my mum joined me up at a calisthenics club down the road from my father's shop. Under Mrs Wilson's tuition I grew to love calisthenics so much that I couldn't imagine life without it. I also became very good at it and won the 'Most Improved' award at the end of my first year there. Our sub-junior team went off to calisthenics competitions all over Melbourne and we were quite successful. I also joined the club at the Mordialloc Youth Club so that I could have lessons more than once a week.

When I was about ten or eleven, I left Mrs Wilson's group and the Youth Club to join another, more competitive club in Mordialloc where I did solos as well as teamwork, again achieving great success. Mrs Graham was the teacher there and her winning teams were well known around the competition circuit. My mum didn't have a driver's licence and couldn't drive a car, so we had to walk quite a few kilometres to calisthenics classes. Mum stayed and watched as I was too young to walk home in the dark on my own. She used to take the girls' money and mark off the attendance sheets for the teacher, and she enjoyed being part of it all. I attended one or two nights a week, with another class on Saturday morning and tuition for my solo work in the afternoon, but Mum didn't have to come with me on Saturdays as it was daytime and I could ride my bike. I loved sharing this part of my life with Mum who, because she always watched us rehearsing, was able to give me useful tips. On calisthenics days I would wake up in the mornings with a big smile and literally bounce out of bed with glee. It was like living in a fairytale.

At calisthenics classes we had a pianist, Mrs Rattigan, who accompanied us with classical music that was so beautiful it reached into my heart. Sometimes after my own class was finished, I'd talk Mum into staying behind to watch the older girls rehearsing. Mrs Rattigan was a short, happy, robust woman and I'd sit beside her, chatting away in the breaks and otherwise watching her fingers move over the keys. The music intrigued me and I was fascinated by the names of the composers on the sheet music.

I loved Beethoven's 'Moonlight Sonata'. As Mrs Rattigan played I'd close my eyes and imagine a clear sky with the moon and stars shining down onto water. It was like I could touch it and my heart would open and fill with the beautiful sounds. At times I thought my heart would burst with joy. Often I didn't know how long I'd been daydreaming until the music stopped and I'd find myself back in the hall watching the calisthenics class. Sometimes I didn't know which I loved more, the calisthenics or the music.

What Mrs Rattigan told me about Mozart and Beethoven excited me so much I immediately wanted to find out more about them. The Parkdale library just happened to be across the road from the barber's shop, so on the very next Friday night, which was the night I always went to the library, I walked in and asked the librarian for help. We looked up the names of these composers and, after finding books about them on the shelves, I returned home to lie in bed, night after night, reading about their lives.

Because I found school stimulating and interesting, I was often one of the teacher's favourites. I had the same teacher, Mrs Andrews, in both fourth and fifth grades. She was a jovial woman, full of life, who played an old squeeze-box (piano accordion). She loved music, so that's what we did most. I don't remember how much schoolwork we did, although we must have done enough because I wasn't behind when I reached sixth grade. Every day she'd play the squeeze-box and we'd sing along ... old English and Irish folk songs, and all sorts of old favourites. I didn't mind at all and discovered I had a good voice. Mrs Andrews would get me out the front of the class singing on my own.

'Come on, Helen, out the front and sing "Cockles and Mussels",' she'd say. I'd walk out there, no self-consciousness then, and my voice would effortlessly release its unique sound: 'singing cockles and mussels alive, alive-oh'. It seemed natural to be out the front leading the class.

As we progressed during the school year Mrs Andrews taught me about singing in harmony, and I'd sing along in counterpoint to the rest of the class. I was fascinated by the way the voices blended together to make an even fuller and more beautiful sound. I think Mrs Andrews opened my heart to music because I began to think not just of singing, but of learning an instrument ... maybe the piano? My mind was constantly full of little melodies and I'd often be humming or singing to myself as I walked or rode to school. I wanted to be able to play the melodies myself. I wanted to be able to create the music, so I finally asked my mum if I could learn piano.

'We'll see when you're a bit older,' she said, and for the moment I had to be satisfied. At least she hadn't said 'no'. My dad had a good singing voice, but neither he or Mum had had any musical training. I remember my dad singing at parties in our street when the neighbours all got together. After they'd had a few beers Ivy, who lived across the road, would always ask Dad to sing.

'Come on, George,' she'd say. 'How about a song?' She loved hearing him sing to the record of 'How Great Thou Art'. 'I'll put the record on,' she'd say, placing it on the turntable.

'Yeah, come on, George,' all the others would chime in,

urging him on. With the amount of beer they'd all consumed, he didn't really take much persuading. Dad enjoyed singing too, so off he'd go, singing along to the record. Then they'd all join in, continuing to drink until they ground themselves to a halt. I always thought 'How Great Thou Art' was a strange choice of song for a party as it's such a sober, slow one, but it would get them started and then they'd move on to Bing Crosby and Slim Dusty. I'd never liked country and western music, and their renditions put me off even more!

Most people were regular drinkers—it was considered a social thing—and there was never any shortage of beer in the neighbourhood because everyone made their own home brew, which meant it was inexpensive. We kids would go home to bed when we got sick of listening to them droning on, but it was funny to watch them all having a good time. They were a nice bunch of people who had formed close friendships with each other, although I always thought our mum kept to herself a bit more than the others, probably because she was at work all week. Ivy, Alice (next door) and Doris (a few houses down) met several afternoons a week for a drink (home brew), a smoke and a chit-chat before their husbands got home from work. They all had kids of their own, although families weren't usually large, and most of the focus was within the local community, concentrated around the footy and youth clubs. It was almost as if there was no world outside our local suburbs. The only time people seemed to leave the vicinity was for a weekend picnic or to visit relatives.

As well as music I also loved just about every sport offered at school. I participated in team inter-school competitions for rounders and, later, softball, volleyball and netball. Because of my achievements my parents had high expectations of me, taking as a given that I'd be at the top end of my school year and would gain a place in my calisthenics competitions.

Although they always expected my reports to be positive, I never felt any pressure because I never thought about it—everything seemed to come naturally and I enjoyed being successful. I remember my father always boasting about me on the phone to his relatives and I guess it made me feel proud that I'd gained his approval, unlike Ron, who didn't enjoy school much. Ron made up for it at sports, though, and was a very good high-jumper. He also learned gymnastics and boxing at the youth club, and Dad would take him to his classes.

I think it used to shit Ron that I was good at everything, especially when our father would hold me up as an example—and was I ever a show-off! Dad was very proud of my success and he made sure everyone knew about it. I think I was his favourite. It must have made Ron feel a bit insignificant, although he and Mum were close. Our parents insisted that Ron come to my calisthenics competitions, which he hated, and I had to go and watch his boxing bouts. It was weird seeing him up there beating the hell out of another young boy, but all our activities were experienced as a family. Most of the time Ron's fights were okay because he was good and always won, but I remember one night when his opponent didn't turn up, they paired him up with an older, bigger boy, and we had to sit there watching him getting beaten up, his head lurching from his shoulders every time this big guy hit him. He was staggering around the boxing ring, looking like he was barely conscious, until eventually they stopped the fight. It was awful and so unfair, I felt sick in the stomach, which was a shock because I didn't think I cared. I have no idea what my mum thought.

It's only since we've grown older that Ron has told me he actually hated boxing. I think our dad thought it would be good for him ... you know, toughen him up, so that he'd grow into a 'real' man. Dad was typical of most men of that era; they thought their sons had to be tough and able to fight—after all, they'd not long since returned from the war. Unfortunately, Ron was always pretty skinny as a young kid and I think Dad felt he had to build him up. Dad seemed to talk a lot about when Ron would 'fill out', and it appeared important to him, although I never got the impression that Ron saw it as significant.

Ron and I were typical siblings and as young children we hated each other, like other siblings in the neighbourhood. It was common practice to try to get away from your brother or sister as much as possible. We'd argue about anything and every-thing, from who was using the bathroom first, to who had to peel the potatoes for dinner, or who had to go to the shop to buy some milk—and generally drove Mum mad. I was the 'good' little girl, which really pissed Ron off, and he was the 'not so good' little boy, but because he was three years older and phys-ically bigger than me, he could bully me to some extent.

I remember one time we were out in the back yard playing. It was when the sewerage was being connected and the whole yard had been dug up into long ditches where the pipes were going to be laid. It created a great place for adventure games. We were hiding in ditches at opposite ends of the yard and every so often one of us would stand up and throw hard balls of dirt at the other, hoping to connect. After a few goes Ron threw a big one at me just as I was stepping out of my ditch and— 'bang!'—it hit me on the forehead. I yelled in pain, 'Ouch! That hurt!' Moments later I noticed blood running down the side of my face onto my hand, and there seemed to be a lot of thick red blood on the dirt at my feet.

'Shit!' Ron yelled, obviously shocked at the sight of all that blood. He came running towards me to get a closer look.

'That was a rock, not dirt, you stupid idiot!' I screamed at him, sobbing by now. All he could see was the deep gash to the right-hand side of my forehead and he reached for a hanky to try and stop the blood. He looked a bit concerned, but I knew that he wasn't worried about me as much as he was about getting into trouble once I dobbed on him, and I sure intended to do that.

'What are you going to say to Mum and Dad?' he asked.

'That you threw a rock at me, you shithead! What do you think?' I spat at him in a nasty voice, glad to have one over him. I knew that bargaining time was about to commence and I had the upper hand.

'Don't say that—I didn't mean it,' he squirmed. 'Can't you say you walked into the netball pole?' I had a netball goal ring in the back yard where I'd practise shooting goals for the school team.

'Yeah, sure . . .' I said.

'Please?' he persisted. 'I'll be in big trouble if they know I threw a rock at you.' He was almost begging me not to dob him in. I was quite enjoying my position of power, except that my head was beginning to throb badly. In the end my sense of fairness won. For once I knew he hadn't meant to hurt me and, besides, I needed to get inside and inspect the damage.

'Okay,' I said, walking off. 'But you owe me.' With that I went inside to get cleaned up. For ever after I think our parents believed that I really had walked into the netball pole.

I remember really getting him back one day, though. I don't recall why, but we were fighting as usual, and I had somehow managed to get him down on his back on the lounge-room floor. I had my hands around his neck, nearly choking him. I didn't want to ever let go except I knew that, if I didn't, he'd choke to death and then I'd be in trouble, although the idea of him not being around held strong appeal. It's the only time I can remember ever winning a fight with him. I think he used to try and ignore me as much as possible, especially when his mates were around; I always felt like a bit of a dork in front of them because I was the little sister—'little Barny' they called me.

It was while we were living at the shop, when I was about ten, that my mother finally gave in to my nagging about learning piano. She found me a teacher who lived in our street, so once a week I'd walk to Mrs Hill's house for my lessons. I loved it and no-one ever had to ask me to practise, although I didn't have my own piano initially. As I was progressing well, Mrs Hill suggested that I think about sitting for piano exams. Mum and I searched the second-hand dealers for a reconditioned piano for me to practise on. She wasn't prepared to spend much money on it because she wasn't sure whether I'd keep it up, but I already knew I would. I began with 'Preliminary' and worked my way up through the grades. Because I was interested and confident, I had no trouble and received excellent results.

When Ron and I were still young, aged about eleven and eight, our father decided to get involved in greyhound racing. Once we'd moved back to our house in MacGregor Street, he converted the old backyard chook pen into kennels for our many dogs. We'd had chooks for a while when Ron and I were little— I can remember our dad killing one occasionally for us to eat— but we hadn't kept any for years and the pen was just an empty shed. We started off with just one dog, but it did well, so we acquired many more over the years. Ron and I loved having the greyhounds as they were beautiful, loyal dogs and we enjoyed the social outing of going to the races. It was our job to walk them in the mornings and it would take a while because they had to be walked several kilometres. I think that was one of the few times when Ron and I didn't fight or argue. When we returned it was my job to put lanoline on the pads of their feet so they didn't crack from all the walking on roads and footpaths.

My favourite dog over the years was Fury and Ron's was Smokey. Fury only won one country race but we both loved him dearly. If any stranger came near us he would growl like you wouldn't believe. Smokey was a champion and held the record at a city track for a while. Dad even allowed her to come inside the house the night she broke the record. I think she was Dad's favourite. Twice a week we'd go to the races, Olympic Park on Monday nights and Sandown Park on Thursday nights, and on other occasions we'd go to the country tracks. We had photos of our dogs' successful races hanging from the picture rail right around the lounge-room walls, although most of them were of Smokey. We had a series of greyhounds over a period of about five years; some we owned, some we just trained for other owners, but none of them achieved the success that Smokey did. Mum was always the administrator of the family finances and eventually, after several years of unsuccessful racing, she put pressure on Dad to get rid of them. I can only imagine how much it must have cost to keep the ever-increasing number of dogs— more than their combined income could afford, no doubt. Dad was always looking for another champion, but it never did happen.

We lived behind the barber shop for about six years before selling the business, and then both our parents worked at the laundry, Mum in the factory and my father delivering the laundry to customers. We returned to our home in MacGregor Street. It was only a kilometre away, just on the other side of the highway, so it didn't make much difference to our lives. Because both our parents worked full-time and had low mortgage repayments, we were lucky that their dual income provided us with extras like calisthenics and music lessons for me, and gymnastics and boxing for Ron. Later, Ron dropped gymnastics and boxing to go yachting at the local club, eventually crewing for many of the guys there. He never had his own yacht, though; it was probably beyond our family's income.

It wasn't until I was about twelve that I felt my first signs of unrest. Instead of being my usual happy, carefree self, I began to feel uncertain and anxious. At home things were beginning to change between our parents, although they did their best to hide their problems. There seemed to be a growing animosity between them, but they never sat down and talked to us about how they were feeling or what was going on in their relationship. Increasingly Ron and I would hear them arguing behind the closed door of their bedroom, and late at night we'd often sneak as close as we dared to try and listen. Mum would never say anything about it, like it just never happened.

Our father became less and less communicative, and over the next couple of years ceased his community involvement in the footy and youth clubs. We also stopped visiting relatives and our involvement in the weekend picnics, tennis games and parties ended, although Ron and I continued all our activities and our friendships with the local kids. As a family we became isolated from the others. Mum continued to talk to Ivy and the other women occasionally, but I'm not sure if she ever told them about her troubled relationship with Dad. Over time our neighbours also came to expect a lack of communication with Dad. Ron and I would sometimes go over and talk to Ivy and Cobber about how it felt at home. We trusted and liked them—they seemed to understand and always welcomed us. Our once happy household had turned into a desolate island full of tension and uncertainty. Our father, previously a social being, seemed to have shut down and off.

It was around this time that I remember going into Ron's bedroom one afternoon to find him writhing in pain on his bed. Mum was already in there and had called a doctor. It was awful to see him in such excruciating pain. A few days later, after completing some tests, the doctor diagnosed a stomach ulcer and Ron was put on tablets which Mum always described to me as 'nerve tablets'. I can always remember Ron's tablets sitting on the kitchen table. He remained on them right through his teenage years, and during this time he also developed a nervous tic in his face.

It had become strange in our house, and questions from Ron or I weren't welcome. We both felt afraid of our new style of father, his aloofness; it always felt like he might blow up, like a time bomb about to go off, even though he was never physically violent. But Mum just brushed us off without giving us any adequate answers. Ron's response to our new environment was to become nervy but quiet, whereas my response was to move from one extreme to the other. I would be quiet and submissive for days on end, then I'd suddenly explode, becoming loud and agitated, demanding answers as to why Dad was treating us that way. As I grew older I became increasingly angry at his treatment of Mum, which I found disrespectful. She didn't deserve to be treated with disdain, and I couldn't understand why she became increasingly submissive towards him. Our mum never said much, and certainly she couldn't be described as an emotional person, but she was a good person and we always knew she loved us. Our family was becoming fragmented.

Not long after this, when I was about thirteen and Ron sixteen, our relationship began to change from sibling rivalry to something that contained some compassion. Because we never knew or understood what was going on between our parents, I felt like I needed to have Ron around. I was having problems communicating with my father, who often wouldn't talk to me. It seemed that the more I began to change from being a girl to a young woman with a desire for independence, the more he tried to control me—and the more I would defy him, which made him even angrier. This caused Ron and I to collude in an effort to try and work it out. I trusted Ron was looking out for me, even if it wasn't displayed in overt affection and emotion. I felt 'safe' having him there.

Around this time our parents had an extension built onto

the back of the house. It was meant to be a spare room but, almost immediately after it was built, Mum moved out there and it became her bedroom, although she continued cooking the meals, doing the washing and cleaning, and paying the bills like nothing had changed. Increasingly our dad seemed to be shutting off from Mum both emotionally and verbally. There was no yelling at her; it was more like he'd turned into an iceberg, and between them there was an eerie silence splattered with moments of plain, damn rudeness. After dinner every evening he'd sit staring at the television. I was becoming confused and agitated at his treatment of Mum. I couldn't understand what she'd done wrong to deserve it. When she put his dinner on the table in front of him, he'd either grunt or completely ignore her, and we'd all have dinner in silence. After a while it really gave me the shits and I started to let him know.

'Aren't you going to say thank you?' I'd demand angrily. Mum would just turn her back and walk away, and Ron would look down and start eating. They never challenged him or stood up for themselves. I found it so exasperating. I couldn't understand how she could just keep her mouth shut and take it.

When I was alone with her I'd ask her: 'Why do you let him treat you like that?'

'It's easier than arguing with him. I just want to keep the peace, and it doesn't help that you keep arguing with him either.'

'But I can't stand it—he shouldn't treat you like you don't exist.'

'It doesn't bother me. I'd rather it this way than fighting with him,' she told me.

'That's bullshit!' I'd yell, before storming off, becoming more and more angry, confused and frustrated. It was so different to the family life we'd enjoyed up until the last couple of years. It wasn't only Mum he'd turned on either. He didn't have a good word for anyone. He criticised their friends and the way they lived, Ron's friends, my friends—no-one was good enough.

I couldn't accept that Mum wanted it this way, oscillating between silence and explosions, although I have to say it was only Dad and I who caused the sparks to fly. Ron respected Mum's wish to keep the peace, supporting her in her silence. This seemed to draw them closer together as Mum approved of Ron's behaviour and was grateful to at least have his support. And so the two of them were increasingly quiet and I became increasingly angry and loud, although there were times when I was exactly the opposite. There seemed to be no middle ground, no room for negotiating or compromising. I was either frightened and submissive or exploding with rage. It sort of made me the odd one out, in a way, although I always thought it was Dad's behaviour that was bad, and he was certainly becoming increasingly excluded from any discussions.

Gradually, though, both Mum and Dad came to see me as the problem. Dad wouldn't even communicate with me, and I could only guess that it was my loud, demanding ways that caused him to dislike me. In such a short time I'd changed from being his favourite child to one he wanted to dominate. He achieved this with aloofness and condescension. At a time when developmentally I needed support to appropriately detach from my parents and become a more independent person, I found myself becoming insecure and unable to express or understand my feelings or needs. From Mum's point of view I was a problem because she'd decided to submit to Dad in an effort to keep the peace, and I wasn't happy to participate in this new arrangement. Secretly I wished she would leave him. I needed someone to talk to and there weren't any real options within the family; Ron, as confused as I was, was busy supporting Mum in whatever way she required, and Mum herself was busy being the 'peacekeeper'. Even though Ron and I discussed the situation we were really just two confused kids who felt powerless to change anything. They say every family has a scapegoat and it looked like it was becoming me!

2

The shadow in
the fairytale

The emotional effects of my home life had not yet impacted on my school life or other activities outside of home, and when I left Parkdale Primary School aged 12, I was dux of the school. At this point in my life I was still a relatively happy and fulfilled kid. In my hand I had a scholarship cheque to assist with the costs of high school. I'm sure my mum was grateful for this as money wasn't abundant. In February 1966, a few weeks after I'd turned thirteen, I was excited to be wearing my new school uniform and off to my first day at Mordialloc–Chelsea High School. Ron was already a pupil there, and my mum told me to ride my bike with him for the four-kilometre ride to school. In actual fact I rode behind him and his mates because I think it embarrassed them having me tagging on, but I was happy to step into line and ride well behind them because I didn't really want to be seen with them either!

Kym and some of my other friends from Parkdale Primary School and calisthenics were enrolled at this school too, but I was in awe of it all. The first thing I sensed was that the place was BIG. There were about four times as many students here as there had been in primary school and they were drawn from suburbs stretching from Parkdale to Chelsea which, on the train line, are five stations apart. Everyone at Parkdale Primary had lived in Parkdale. I felt a bit lost among the multitude of double-storey red-brick buildings. I also had to contend with prefects, senior students whose job it was to enforce rules like wearing your hat and blazer to and from school. Everything seemed so very different to what I'd known. Instead of having one classroom and one teacher assigned to us, we had to learn to navigate our way around the different classrooms, and we had a different teacher for each subject. I had gotten so used to being a 'good' student—and therefore a bit of a teacher's favourite—that I found the new set-up slightly daunting. Here I wasn't treated as special, which I missed. The comparatively short time periods spent with individual teachers meant you didn't get to know them like you did in primary school, and this made me feel a bit insecure. However, because I was a good student, I continued to manage quite well, at least outwardly.

I didn't tell anyone, but during this first year at high school a restlessness started to develop inside me and at the end of the year I only came about sixth out of all the first-year students, Kym and another girl from calisthenics finishing ahead of me. It shocked me, but no-one else appeared to find it disappointing. It seemed too minor and silly to talk to anyone about, but it was my first experience of feeling a failure, or at least of not living up to my own high expectations of myself, and it subtly began to undermine my confidence. I began to think that Kym and the others were more intelligent than me, and I had a sense of being left behind, which in hindsight sounds silly as only five of them achieved higher scores than me. It's difficult to explain, but I felt it was something over which I had no control, and that at primary school I must just have been lucky to have done so well. I thought that my friends were going to improve and I was going to deteriorate and that eventually it would be proven that I wasn't intelligent at all. I could feel my grasp on things slowly loosening and I couldn't get a handle on why . . .

I can only guess now that my growing insecurity about my family and the breakdown in my central relationships had begun to have an impact on my sense of self outside the family. Confusion took up residence in my mind where confidence and dreams of success had once lived. Of course I didn't say anything to anyone at home about how I was feeling, because it didn't seem like a safe haven any more. My mum had gone so quiet, although she still came to calisthenics with me. I think she saw it as an escape from home as much as she did a chance to participate in my life. She became an island for both Ron and me, even though I didn't agree with her submission to Dad. She must have found her relationship depressing, but she was always fair in her treatment of us. My dad seemed to have stopped communicating, at least positively, anyway. He just stared at the television endlessly, night after night, not saying a word, but often seething with anger. When my friends came around they learned to just ignore him, which was easy because he rarely spoke. Mum made up for it, though, always welcoming anyone Ron or I brought home. Increasingly Dad became irrelevant and excluded but, unfortunately, in our world then, no-one seemed to ask for help. Mind you, I don't believe he saw that he needed help either, and I'm sure it would have been seen as a shameful thing.

I don't think Dad was ever physically violent to Mum, he just spat derogatory comments at her on a daily basis. He didn't really have conversations with any of us any more, although he still ordered us to do things or admonished us when we hadn't done our chores satisfactorily. Sometimes he'd act okay when a neighbour like Ivy dropped over to give us a phone message, but other times he'd just ignore her too. He certainly didn't participate with anyone socially, those occasions having long since been relegated to the past.

My father had a series of low-paying jobs after he left the laundry, with short periods of unemployment in between. He seemed to be willing to try anything, and had a variety of delivery jobs—spare parts for cars, bread—as well as a couple of stints as a door-to-door salesman. Eventually Mum got him a job at the car-parts factory where she was working at the time. Ron and I had often overheard Mum and Dad arguing about money, and certainly they had always bought the cheapest food and clothing. It wasn't that Dad was unintelligent—quite the opposite, in fact—but during the depression he'd had to help out at the boarding houses that his mum had run, and I think that the combination of the depression and the war had limited his career opportunities. I'd have to guess that in terms of his employment, he felt unfulfilled. Maybe this had contributed to his emotional shutdown, or perhaps you could've called it 'depression'. No-one ever referred to it that way, so it's only in hindsight that I can make an assessment.

Also around this time Mrs Hill, my piano teacher, was getting quite old. She decided to retire from teaching music and moved away from Parkdale, so my mother organised for me to see another teacher who lived locally. I walked from my home to the new teacher's house for my first lesson. As soon as she answered the door, though, I was filled with doubt and apprehension. Struggling to overcome my anxiety, I politely introduced myself. Her response was to sigh in a sort of annoyed tone, like I'd interrupted something important. She looked to me like a hook-nosed witch and, unlike Mrs Hill, who was always warm and welcoming, she was grumpy and cold and her house felt dark and damp. Without any friendly preliminaries or an attempt to get to know me, she commenced the lesson.

'Play one of your recent third-grade exam pieces,' she com-manded. My heart immediately filled with pride as I confidently opened my music book and readied my fingers on the keys, convinced that this would change her impression of me. I knew I could play well because I'd received an honours result in the exam. I didn't have to read from the sheet music because I knew all my pieces off by heart, and I moved and swayed as my heart guided me through the light and shade of this music that I loved. Once again I was lost inside its beauty until I reached the end and lifted my hands from the keys. I awaited her praise expectantly.

'Hmm . . .' she grunted. 'I think we'll get started on some scales and exercises.' She made no comment about my playing and I immediately thought she didn't like me. I started playing each scale she requested, but when I didn't hold my hands in the right position she'd whack me over the knuckles with a ruler. After a few months with my new teacher, I began to think I wasn't very good at playing piano after all, just like at school, where I'd begun to question my intelligence. I found this treatment particularly difficult after the kindness of Mrs Hill, but for some unknown reason I didn't complain, perhaps because my mother never complained about anything. There seemed to be an unspoken rule in our family that you never complained about illness, didn't take time off unless you were just about dying, and you didn't complain. I was also aware that my parents didn't have much money, so I knew I was lucky to be having piano lessons at all. Besides, I was still fascinated by the lives of the composers whose music I was learning to play, and I wanted to continue.

Over the next couple of years, though, instead of saying something about my unhappiness with the new music teacher, I found myself doing less piano practice and not looking forward to lessons. My exam marks began to reflect this lack of enjoyment, which was obviously expressed in my playing. I began to walk slowly and dejectedly to my piano lessons, eventually, when possible, finding excuses not to attend. Gradually, as my little fingers danced across the keys on the piano, my heart didn't reach inside the music any more and I no longer searched for books about my favourite composers' lives. Music became relegated to the background in my life and, increasingly, practice became a chore.

At the beginnning of 1967, my best friend Kym accepted a private-school scholarship which her mother encouraged her to take. She didn't really want to change schools but she did it to please her mother, and so I lost that closeness I'd had with my soul buddy of many years. Still, I had plenty of friends at school so I was not alone. I continued to do well and won a government scholarship, which assisted with the costs of my education. I was also good at sport, no doubt because of my years of calisthenics. At fourteen and in my second year at high school, I was form captain, popular and successful, with no outward signs of my inner anguish evident yet.

However, in my third year at high school a few cracks began to show outwardly. Although Kym was unhappy at the private school and returned to our local school, I didn't hang around with her as much as I'd done before. I'd made a new friend, Julie, who had moved to Parkdale with her father. He ran a local milk bar and they lived behind the shop like we once had. I don't know what had happened to Julie's mother, but she didn't live with them and Julie never talked about her. Julie was more interested in boys than schoolwork and I was intrigued by her. She seemed so worldly in comparison to me and my other friends. All I knew was school, calisthenics and piano, and I felt naive alongside her, but I was willing to learn and I listened and watched intently.

My parents soon received their first negative feedback about me. Usually it was Ron who received negative comments from teachers, because he simply didn't enjoy school and almost never did his homework. He and his mates were quite disruptive in class and had a bit of a reputation as nuisances. They weren't really considered troublemakers, but often had to stay behind for detention. At 'parent and teacher' nights, Mum and Dad would be told, 'He doesn't pay attention ... he doesn't complete his homework ... he's disruptive in class.' This was standard feedback in relation to Ron, but there'd never been anything like that about me—until now. I can still remember the first time the negative feedback was about me. My geography teacher told Mum I wasn't doing my work, that I wasn't concentrating and was always chatting with Julie in class. He felt I was wasting my potential. He also said that we were distracting other students and suggested that Julie was having a bad influence on me. Why do people always have to find someone to blame? Personally, I felt defensive that this obviously perceptive teacher had been able to see something was wrong—I'd been trying so hard to hide my growing insecurities. He was probably the first person to realise something was amiss but, unfortunately, my parents didn't take much notice. They weren't even talking to each other most of the time, although they tried their darndest to present a happy face to the world, like turning up to 'parent and teacher' nights together.

Sometimes my dad would be nice as pie when one of my friends came to my place after school, but this didn't happen often. Most of the time I went to my friends' houses to play, and the remainder of the time I spent at calisthenics. I'd even started assisting the calisthenics teacher with the younger kids. No-one outside our family was ever going to know there was anything wrong inside the cacky blue–green exterior that was our home, although a couple of friends saw Dad attack me verbally, and put me down in front of them. But they learned to ignore him, just as I did. It's common knowledge that abusive males are most often sociable and pleasant in public, outside the family domain, and our family fitted that picture well.

As a fourteen-year-old I knew my world was changing because my heart felt heavy. I didn't wake up smiling any more, but I didn't understand why and I also didn't know how to talk about it. My mother never complained about anything and I modelled my behaviour on hers. Like the day Ron and I came home from school and discovered at bedtime that Mum had moved into the extension at the back of the house, with nothing said and no explanation given. There was always this unspoken rule: don't ask any questions.

It was around this time that I remember Mum collapsing on the kitchen floor one day. She remained there unconscious for some time.

'Mum! What's wrong?' I screamed as I ran to her. I thought she was dead. It seemed a long time to me before she responded. I was so afraid as I kneeled on the floor beside her body, bending over her, willing her to regain consciousness. 'Wake up!' I kept saying to her, shaking her, not knowing what else to do.

Ron and my father eventually came running in and they took over. I must have been yelling out to them. After what seemed an eternity, Mum's eyes blinked open for a moment. She looked dazed and unsure. She stood up shakily, walked over to the couch and sat down to catch her breath and steady herself. I was still standing by the sink in the kitchen, afraid to take my eyes off her, trying to reassure myself that she was in fact alive.

'I'm okay, don't worry,' she sighed. 'I'll be all right in a few minutes.' She was trying to take deep breaths and I could tell she was still having difficulty. After a little while her breathing became more regular. She got up, went back to the kitchen sink and resumed peeling vegetables like nothing had happened. To this day I don't know if it was to do with blood pressure, hormonal problems or whatever. She never talked about it and I don't even know if she saw a doctor. No-one ever told us kids anything, and when I subsequently asked her what was wrong she just shrugged it off. I started to feel as though I must be imagining things; it was like we were living in a vacuum.

The one good thing that came out of our troubled home life was that Ron and I became increasingly close. Not in any overt, emotional way—that just didn't happen in that family—but on a subconscious level I sensed him becoming more like a parent than a brother, and I trusted him. He seemed to be growing into a responsible and caring person. He now had his driver's licence and was approaching adulthood himself. He also seemed to be handling the family situation better than I was, although with a stomach ulcer from the age of fifteen, I reckon he must have been holding a lot inside. It was probably more a case of him just not showing what he felt, like Mum, although he certainly appeared to be coping better. With Ron the stress of our home life began to manifest in physical symptoms that could be medically treated, like his ulcer and nervous tic; with me, it was more consistently visible, evidenced by my increasingly erratic—and subsequently self-destructive—behaviour, although the source was psychological for both of us.

I think I felt more pressure from Dad because when I was younger he'd always boasted of my successes. It felt like the more I needed to shake him off as I grew into a teenager, the more he wanted to control my life. Ron had never met Dad's needs in the same way, so possibly he never experienced that strong desire to break free. Unfortunately, the more Dad clung and tried to gain control over me, the more I rebelled and disrespected his behaviour. This made him angry and frustrated or, alternatively, impatient and emotionally distant. I wasn't listening to him any more and his response was to make derogatory statements such as accusing me of having sexual activity with boys for years before I even became sexually active. I'd received so little sex education, I was too afraid to have sex in case I became pregnant! When I was about twelve years old Mum had taken me to a 'mother and daughter' film at my school; when I turned thirteen and began menstruating, she handed me a packet of pads and told me to use them. I had to read the instructions to find out how to strap them on (this was the 1960s, remember)!

As I continued to grow both physically and emotionally and my need for independence developed, my father and I became more and more distant. By now I was fifteen years old and wanting to go out socially with friends from school. I had also become keen on a boy, Nikki, who was in my year. I had to get permission from Dad to go out anywhere socially at night. Because of the silent treatment he meted out to me, I would have to start asking on Monday whether I could go out on the following Friday or Saturday night. I grew accustomed to the fact that it was going to take me days to get an answer from him, if I could get one at all. He almost always let me stew on it all week, only responding, usually with a 'yes' the night prior to my proposed date.

'Can I go out with Nikki on Saturday night? His band is playing at a dance and his father will be taking us there,' I'd tentatively ask. No answer. He'd just sit there and stare at the television as though I wasn't there. I'd take a breath, trying to stay calm, and ask again.

'Dad,' I'd say, a little louder this time, 'can I go out with Nikki on Saturday night?' Nikki, who was also learning piano, had a portable electric piano and was in a band that was managed by his father. We were interested in each other, the music being a common bond. This was the first time my interest in a boy had been reciprocated, but I had to get through to my dad before it could go anywhere.

After dinner the following night I'd be in the lounge room again, standing only a couple of metres from my dad's chair, wringing my hands and looking alternately at the side of his face and the ceiling while he maintained his focus on the television.

Again, he wouldn't answer me. I'd try a few more times before
deciding to give up until the next night, when I'd have to build
up the courage to ask once more. I felt humiliated standing there
like a dickhead while he ignored me. Sometimes Mum or Ron
would also be in the room, watching television, but they'd never
intervene. I've no doubt this gave Dad an immense sense of
power, holding the family to ransom through silence.

Wednesday night would arrive and off I'd go again. His
aloofness made me frightened of him, but at the same time this
'bottling up' of emotions resulted in my periodic verbal explosions at him.

'Dad, can I go out with Nikki on Saturday night? His band
is playing.' I started to feel like a tape recorder, except my
stomach was churning with nerves at having to repeat the same
question night after night. I knew it must piss him off having to
hear it over and over, but still he wouldn't answer me. Some
nights I felt scared, some nights frustrated and angry, but mostly
I was growing increasingly disrespectful of him. It was just really
unfair. The structure of our family was unquestionably patriar-
chal, and Dad was king, circumstances never seemingly placing
my mum within earshot of any feminist voices.

'Why won't he just answer me?' I'd ask her later, when she
came into my room. She'd just shrug her shoulders; she had no
answers either. That's a great help, I'd think to myself.

Then Thursday night: 'Dad, can I go out with Nikki on
Saturday night?' No answer, or occasionally he'd snap out something disdainful that had nothing to do with the question. I'd
repeat it another half dozen times before giving up and retiring
to my room and my books. I can't imagine why I kept it up for
so long, except that it's probably an indication of how powerless
I felt in that environment and also, perhaps, of how much I'd
loved him when I was a young child. I was damned if I could
figure out what was going on in his head and, as it continued,

my sense of humiliation increased until, over time, I became very nervous and frightened to ask anything. It's hard to explain how it made me feel, but the image in my mind of him at that time is that he was like a bolt of white lightning, icy-looking and jagged. Lightning can hit at any time and can injure—or even kill—you, then it disappears as quickly as it came. But you never know when it will return. Sometimes it doesn't hit, it just threatens. I learned what fear felt like, and it made me insecure because I didn't know how to deal with it.

Finally my mother stepped in and took control of the situation. I don't know whether she ever spoke to Dad about it, she just did it. 'Don't ask him any more,' she said to me one day when she could no longer bear him ignoring me. At least she understood, because he ignored her most of the time too, but of course she didn't have to ask his permission like I did! She'd fixed her own problems with him by moving out to the back of the house and rarely speaking to him. 'If you want to go out, ask me,' she finished off.

'Thanks, Mum,' I replied, grateful not to have to approach him again.

From that point on I only communicated with her, which led to years of silence between my father and me. We never went out socially as a family any more and we didn't even visit relatives, which was something we'd often done when Ron and I were younger. Both Mum and Dad came from large families and each had six or seven brothers and sisters.

This really was a turning point in the family. Mum took control of our upbringing and my father was now excluded from these decisions. I discovered later that around this time Mum began to talk to Ron about the option of leaving Dad and getting a place for just the three of us. I was about fifteen then. Ron had completed high school and commenced a marketing cadetship. He was working part-time at a petrol station, so he was willing to assist Mum financially. Ron only told me this twenty years later, and since then I've dreamt of how different life might have been had Mum gone through with it. Apparently she backed down, even though Ron had organised a unit for us to live in. She told Ron that she felt she'd invested so much of her working life in the family home, both financially and physically, she didn't want to leave it, although she had no intention of reconnecting emotionally with Dad. I believe her decision had an enormous impact on my own emotional well-being, with far-reaching consequences for the path my life would take. If it's ever possible to trace one's direction back to a life-changing crisis, I think that was mine. It became a negative turning point, even though I now only had to ask Mum's permission for any-thing. You had to live in that house to understand the turmoil that dwelled within it although I came to realise, years later, that many families from that generation suffered through lack of communication.

During that same year I was beaten in calisthenics compe-titions by girls who had never beaten me before. I was shocked and frightened, and became very self-conscious. With my con-fidence waning, my performances were increasingly mediocre. I felt like I could topple over at any minute. One night at my regular calisthenics class I was in the middle of a back bend when I literally fell sideways and crumpled in a heap on the floor. Pain shot down my back and leg. The teacher and my mum helped me up, but I had difficulty walking. X-rays showed that I had a disc injury near the base of my spine. Over the next year or so I went to a gymnasium for daily workouts specially tailored to build up the muscles surrounding my spine so that they could provide additional support. I also had to have osteopathic and heat treatments three times a week. Although I worked hard to regain my previous flexibility, the truth is, my calisthenics career, at least at the level I was accustomed to, was over. My frustration

and disappointment at the lack of improvement in my back esca-
lated, while my self-confidence plummeted.

During my fourth year at high school things continued to
slide and the home environment deteriorated even further. My
brother and mother became closer. Ron had become instrumental in keeping the peace, but I wanted no part of it and everyone's
silence and lack of emotion irritated me. It seemed so dishonest,
no-one saying what they felt. My frustration increasingly erupted
in spasmodic verbal outbursts, often at the dinner table at night
and always directed at my father. It was often triggered by his
discourtesy towards Mum, although more and more our arguments were about my disrespectful behaviour towards him. I'd
changed too. I was becoming more irresponsible and careless, my
outbursts now littered with swearwords. I'd also discovered the
joys of drunkenness, although I didn't do it at home. My behaviour wasn't appreciated by anyone and I knew it wasn't making
Mum's lot any easier, but I couldn't help it. I was a volcano
waiting to explode the silence. I could feel anger burning up
inside me and it was like a fetus growing into a monster to which
I was about to give birth. I had no doubt I would—it was only
a matter of when.

Sure enough, that moment soon arrived. While attending
the gym for workouts and back treatments, I met a young guy
who became interested in me and who asked me out socially. I
wasn't going out with Nikki any more, although we'd remained
friends. This guy's name was Peter and he seemed really nice. I
wasn't hugely attracted to him, but I was interested and his attentions felt good to my waning self-esteem. We went out to the
pub after gym a couple of times. (I was never caught for under-
age drinking; I think being tall made me look older.) We even
started kissing and cuddling, the sort of entry into romance that
all young people go through. In fact it was quite sedate in comparison to some of my friends, but because I never actually talked

to my father any more, he must have had other ideas about what was going on between Peter and me.

One night after we'd been to the gym and then the pub, Peter drove me home and parked the car outside my house. We embraced and started kissing passionately. We'd been sitting there for a while when all of a sudden the passenger side door of the car flew open and I felt a hand grab me.

'Get inside!' my father's angry voice demanded as he pulled me from the car.

In shock about his intervention in my enjoyment, I called out, 'It's okay, Peter,' as my father tried to drag me across the nature strip and down the sideway into the house. 'I'll see you at the gym!' I didn't know what else to say and, besides, my father was much stronger than me physically. When he finally pushed me through the doorway, I took off ahead of him, disgusted with his behaviour.

'Fuck off!' I yelled at him as I rushed through the kitchen door, slamming it behind me. 'What do you think you're doing?'

'You get back here!' he roared, trying to catch up to me. He was gaining fast but I made it through the next door and again slammed it behind me.

'Fuck off! You've got no right to treat me like this! You don't even know what I'm doing!' I screamed at him. And of course, that was at least part of the problem: my activities were being left to his imagination. We banged our way through the house, his anger escalating, until he followed me into my bedroom and threw me onto my bed like a wet rag. Then he was on top of me, arm raised in the air about to attack and beat the living daylights out of me. I was cringing, trying to protect myself from the inescapable blows he intended to inflict on me, when I heard my mother crying out and Ron came storming through the door. Ron grabbed the madman from behind and pulled him off me before he had a chance to land any serious blows. All I can remember seeing, when I thought it was safe to look up, was Mum standing in the doorway of my bedroom, her face white with shock. I was in a state of shock myself as I hadn't done anything wrong that I was aware of. It's not like I'd even had sex with Peter, but I'm sure Dad assumed I was out there slutting around, particularly as he'd also made deprecatory remarks about my consumption of alcohol. He seemed to think promiscuity and drunkenness went hand in hand.

Anyway, Ron got him out of my bedroom and I never heard another thing from any of them. I realised things were out of control at home and that I needed to get out. It seemed that if Mum wasn't going to leave, I'd have to, although I was still at school. Any remaining skerrick of respect I may have had for my father disappeared that night. Needless to say, Peter never asked me out again either, but we still talked to each other at the gym.

I never did make much of an emotional connection with my mum, although she remained supportive of me in her quiet way. Even when she was upset about my behaviour, I knew she still loved me. She always continued to take an interest in my music and calisthenics, even after I'd given up piano lessons and dropped to the 'B' grade calisthenics team. How I've wished over the years that we'd been able to talk about intimate things, about how I felt about different boys I went out with, about sex, about her own feelings, her relationship with Dad, whether she was depressed about the direction her life had taken. I can't even remember her laugh. When I think of her I think of quietness, a thinker, a generous person but a sad one. I felt that she gave up any hopes for her own fulfilment in order to give Ron and me better opportunities, spending a lifetime working in factories in order to do so. She must have had her own problems, but I wasn't aware of them because she never talked about them.

Only eight weeks into my fifth year at high school, just after I'd turned sixteen, all the outward appearances of coping caved in. I couldn't maintain the false persona any more and I gave birth to the monster whose first name was 'anger'; its family name was 'frustration'.

I had an argument at school with the headmistress, who was also my modern history teacher. I'd never liked her, and I had no interest in the subject. I didn't see the point in studying times from the past. I just wanted to wash away the last few years of my own life. The only thing that was relevant to me was the present, and I was having enough trouble understanding that without delving into the past, so I definitely didn't want to study that subject. I became disruptive in the class and wound up in the headmaster's office, stubbornness written across my face, anger fuelling me. I hadn't really been that bad, mostly just chatting and distracting other friends, although I have to admit I also wasn't listening, concentrating or doing any classwork or homework.

'I want to drop modern history,' I said to him in the presence of the headmistress, who was glaring at me. I looked across at her in disgust. We'd had a personality clash for a couple of years already and the climax was about to take place.

'No, you shouldn't do that,' he replied. 'You're too good a student.' Of course, my reputation as a good student preceded me, and I'd also been elected sports prefect at the beginning of the year, so although I wasn't very familiar with him, he was aware of my achievements.

'But I've already passed my fifth grade piano exam, which I've sat externally, so I'll still have the same amount of subjects, even without modern history,' I replied. It's a rational argument, I thought to myself. The school didn't offer music at fifth-year level.

'I'm sure you can work it out,' he countered. 'Go home and think it over.'

'I can't. I hate modern history!' I responded dramatically. I'd had no lessons in dealing with conflict at home, so I wasn't good at communicating how I felt. In fact all I was aware of standing there in that office was that I was outnumbered, and I needed to get out as quickly as possible.

'Go away and think about it. It can't be that bad,' he said. He raved a bit more about my achievements and the respect I'd gained at school—'Blah ... blah ... blah ...' They both stood their ground and wouldn't allow me to drop the subject. Because of their superior status, I felt like I had no say, just like with my father—no-one was listening.

Fuck you!, I thought to myself. At sixteen years old I walked out of that school and I never returned. I'd gradually spent less and less time with my friends outside of school too. In hindsight, I don't think the issue was really about the modern history subject at all. I think I'd already decided I was leaving school—all I needed was an opportunity to create enough drama to be able to do it. It's a shame I didn't know about negotiating, compromising or communicating my feelings.

I went home and told my mother. She couldn't understand what was going on with me either, except that she was aware that I was unhappy. I'd communicated that much to her, but she also seemed unable to help. She didn't seem to want to take any responsibility either, and certainly not about me leaving school because she knew it was going to cause another major drama with my father. I longed for her to speak up and protect me from him, but she would never challenge him. How I wish I could have talked to her about how insecure I'd become, about my loss of confidence, my fear of failure, how I thought that my intelligence had deserted me and I was going to fail my subjects. I wish I could have expressed what a lost and frightened little girl I really was. How I wished she could do something to help me. How I wished she would take responsibility for me, or take control of me, because I sure was out of control, and the only direction I was following was out of that school, which to me was better than facing the prospect of failing.

'I need to see a psychiatrist or something. I don't know what's going on with me,' I told her.

'No, neither do I,' she answered, 'but you're not going to sit around here doing nothing. You'll have to get a job.' I immediately saw that as a window of opportunity, so we discussed my employment options further. I was so impulsive and had no long-term plans—I was merely looking for a quick fix. Eventually she put forward a solution that was acceptable to both of us.

'Well, okay, you can leave,' she said, 'but only if you get an apprenticeship. You need to have something behind you.' She wasn't keen on the idea of me working in factories all my life. The only sort of apprenticeship I knew about was ladies' hairdressing. I thought back to childhood when I used to play with my dolls and do their hair. I'd always enjoyed that.

'No worries,' I replied. And with that we organised for me to commence a hairdressing apprenticeship at the local salon. I already knew I was never going to be a hairdresser, but I was determined to fulfil my mother's conditions for leaving school.

My father was beside himself about me leaving school. He and Mum had loud arguments about it for about a week. But our relationship was already too damaged and mutually disrespectful for me to care about his reaction. It was scary watching him in a rage though, all puffed up and red in the face. After his anger had subsided and he'd given up trying to take control—no-one took any notice of him any more—he went back to his usual silent treatment, not speaking to me at all.

I had planned on going to university to study music and physical education, but what the hell! My back injury had incapacitated me in terms of the standard of calisthenics I was able to perform, so I felt I might as well chuck school in too! With the back injury I'd lost quite a bit of flexibility and, even though

I was still receiving treatment, I experienced continuing pain. Just before my injury I had been about to take part in a national competition, for which I had been working so hard all those years. It was April 1970, I was sixteen years old, and my childhood dreams were in tatters.

3

School is out

I only had about a week off between leaving school and commencing work. No-one in our family was ever going to be
a slouch! I walked to work each day and washed hair, swept
floors and generally learnt how to tint, bleach, cut, curl and do
anything you like with hair. I also attended hairdressing school
one day a week where I was top of the class in theory, which I
found quite interesting, yet indifferent to the practical subjects.
In fact I found hairdressing school a real chore, but you had to
pass to become qualified and I'd promised my mum at least that
much.

I was feeling okay working at the salon. It was stable, if
unexciting, and the other workers were easy to get along with—
in fact they were a really nice bunch of people. I became especially friendly with Sheryl, who had also gone to Mordialloc
High School. She was only a year older than me and lived two
streets away, so we began to socialise together. After I finished
work in the afternoons I'd catch public transport to the gym
for my treatment and workouts, and turn up home later in the
evenings, which suited everyone. I still went to calisthenics,
but now I was only competing with the 'B' grade team. It was
impossible for me to move out of home yet because, as a first-year

apprentice, I only earned $13 a week. I also didn't really feel mature or independent enough to take that step; to some degree I still relied on Mum and Ron.

The first year passed uneventfully, and to all appearances I was doing okay. I resumed piano lessons, this time with a young man called Chris who had played piano for a while at the Mordialloc calisthenics club. I wasn't taking it very seriously and didn't practise all that much, but I enjoyed it because Chris was funny and a bit irresponsible himself. He'd recently been dishonourably discharged from the navy, where he'd done his musical training. At least the lessons were filled with laughter. I also accepted an offer to teach calisthenics at the Mordialloc Youth Club, which was quite a commitment for a sixteen-year-old. Although I enjoyed the teaching role, it wasn't the same as performing and I still longed to be up there competing in 'A' grade. I was increasingly dissatisfied competing at a lower level and I found I began to lose interest. It didn't help that I was in constant pain.

Coinciding with the acknowledgment that my performing career was over, I started going to the pub after gym quite often, exhibiting the same kind of behaviour that had led to my throwing school away. I was feeling like a failure at calisthenics and, with no sign of improvement in sight, I drowned my deterioration in alcohol and an increasingly carefree—or, should I say, irresponsible—attitude. As the year came to a close, I decided not to take up the teaching position the following year, and Chris moved to Sydney so I stopped bothering with the piano as well. I was throwing away responsibilities and commitments one by one.

At the hairdressing salon I soon met another new friend, Sue, who started work there during my second year. We must have been looking for each other because we hit it off straight away. Sue was a couple of years older than me and she was wild and loud and had her licence and a car. She was such a contrast to my repressed family. She made me laugh and not think about all the things I'd just thrown away: my schooling, calisthenics and a possible teaching career, piano lessons ... Her boyfriend, Dennis, had been found guilty of theft and was serving an eighteen-month jail sentence, so Sue was at a bit of a loose end. She was glad to find someone to party with and help ease the emotional pain of being separated from him. Some weekends we'd drive to Ararat prison, in country Victoria, to visit Dennis. He and I got along well, too, but he was stuck in there and couldn't join us.

Over the next year I stopped going to the gym and ceased the treatment for my back. I put on about two stone (nearly 13 kilograms) in weight, and discovered the 'joys' of an ever-increasing consumption of alcohol. Sue and I would go off together almost every night after work and drink ourselves into a stupor, then we'd stay at the little bungalow she rented in Sandringham, another suburb along Port Phillip Bay, only ten minutes from Parkdale. Staying at Sue's also eased the problem of living at home. Occasionally I'd return to the gym, trying desperately to improve my back problem and hang on to my fading dream of competing in the national competition, but I knew now that it really was only a dream. Realistically I was never likely to compete again, at least in solo work, but I yearned for that feeling of success that calisthenics had once given me. Alcohol was becoming an antidote to an increasingly empty feeling: it was fun and introduced me to a raging social life, but it was only moderately successful in blocking out some of my problems. I was still rational or intelligent enough to know that the path I was on wasn't going to allow me to achieve a great deal and, until the last couple of years, I'd always been an 'achiever'. I began to construct a new fantasy in my mind, of becoming a singer, and to this end I commenced singing lessons.

Otherwise life consisted of work and the pub. Fre[...]
Sue and I would roll in to work in the mornings after o[...]
couple of hours' sleep. I'm sure that half the time we were pro[...]
ably still drunk. Although I now rarely stayed at home, I maintained contact with Mum who, as always, was welcoming. Sue
and I would go to my place a couple of nights a week and Mum
would cook us a meal before we headed off to the pub.
Somehow she knew we needed nourishment. We'd tell her
about our raging and our many escapades, and we never felt
judged by her. She welcomed Sue into my life and appeared to
be happy that we were out having fun. Maybe it was a relief to
her that I wasn't living at home. Whenever we were there Dad
would either be outside or in his usual place in the lounge room
watching television. We just ignored him. He hadn't spoken to
me at all since I'd left school, not even to argue. We'd stay in
the kitchen with Mum, who seemed to enjoy our company. Sue
understood what Dad was like as I'd discussed it with her and
she'd witnessed it for herself. It didn't affect our interactions with
Mum and generally we enjoyed our little visits. I think it was
important for both Mum and me to maintain a connection.

At this stage Ron was still living at home, but he was rarely
there. He was doing well with his marketing cadetship at Repco
(a large car-part manufacturer) and seemed to have found a voca-
tion that was meaningful and enjoyable. In fact he now seemed
to be the success story in the family, having completed high
school and moved on to further study and a career. He and I
had minimal contact during these years, mainly because I was
rarely around the family. He continued with his part-time job at
the petrol station, as earning money had become a priority for
him. I think he was hellbent on moving out of 'working class'
life. He had maintained his yachting activities as well as developing an interest in driving racing cars; he started in the Formula
Ford category and later was to win the championship.

...lso interested in car racing so he diverted
...attending the racetrack with him (Mum
...of Ron's racing). Increasingly Dad
...'s activities and was proud of his suc-
...inner! Ron's and my roles were now
...seemed as if I didn't exist. Dad's relationship with
...remained much the same, although I'm sure it was easier
for her to deal with now that I was out of the way; the tension
that existed when I was living there had largely dissipated.

At the pub one night Sue and I met a group of guys who
liked to go surfing at the weekends, so we started hanging around
with them. They were protective of us and we felt quite safe.
Whenever we weren't seeing Dennis for a weekend visit we'd
take off in Sue's car with a bottle of whiskey, a bottle of brandy
and a bottle of Coke. We'd head to Phillip Island, where we
used to sleep on the beach, and by the time we got there we'd
be pissed. Eventually I started going out with one of the guys,
another Peter, who was a boiler-maker a year or two older than
me. At seventeen, just before my eighteenth birthday, I became
sexually active. I met his mother and we got along fine too, so
much so that I found chatting with Peter's mum more interesting
than talking to him! Peter's dad was an alcoholic and later, his
mum gave up on the marriage and divorced him. Peter was also
a big drinker and had already lost his licence for drunk driving.
In a way he was heading nowhere fast, just like me, but we all
had jobs so we thought we were okay. As soon as I turned
eighteen I got my driving licence and bought a cheap old bomb
of a car on hire purchase, my mum going guarantor for me.

Sue and I continued drinking at the pub most nights after
work and afterwards we'd continue on partying at one of the
guy's places or at Sue's, at least until Dennis's release from jail
became imminent. Dennis was a lovely guy and I grew to love
him dearly as a friend. Sue and he continued their relationship

after his release and it wasn't long before they were planning their marriage. Of course this put an end to Sue's capacity to party, while I was just getting into the swing of things and was ready to pick up the pace, not slow it down. I took off with another group of people, including some of the guys I'd met with Sue, and became fully submerged in the pub scene in Frankston, which is another beachside suburb of Melbourne, about forty minutes drive from the city. If you were travelling on the train line south from Melbourne, you'd reach the pub in Moorabbin first, then Parkdale a few stations further, then about eight stations later you'd be in Frankston. In actual fact, I just changed locations from Moorabbin pubs to Frankston.

The scene was the same—young people, mostly employed but wanting to rage, and not very responsible. At least that was the crowd I hung around with. There was a bit more of a drug scene at Frankston too, with both illicit drugs and prescribed drugs such as Serepax, Valium, Rohypnol, and weight reduction drugs like Duramine, which contained pseudoephedrine, a major ingredient in amphetamines (speed). I soon learnt that if you took a few Duramine along with the normal evening's alcohol, you could stay up all night raging. The speed in the Duramine, being a stimulant, seemed to counteract the alcohol, which is a depressant; it also helped me to lose some of the weight I'd stacked on since giving up calisthenics. My relationship with Peter fizzled out after about three months, but I maintained occasional contact with his mum for many years—we even wrote to each other when I was in prison.

Around this time I happened to be at home one night when my mum was having a bath. After she'd dressed and come out of the bathroom, she called me out the back to her room. 'Could you have a look at this? The soap just bounced off this lump under my arm,' she said with an anxious expression on her face. She lifted her arm to show me, and I could also feel it through her singlet. She never shared any of her illnesses with anyone that I knew of, so it was unusual for her to involve me, although I guess I was older now. In this 'just get on with it' family, no-one seemed to pay much attention to any type of sickness. That she shared this information with me was probably an indication of just how scared she must have felt but, of course, I wasn't perceptive enough to sense her fear.

'What do you think it is?' I asked her in the kind of tone you might use to ask about someone's head cold.

'I don't know . . . I think I'd better go to the doctor tomorrow.' For her to go to the doctor meant she thought it could be serious.

The next day she made an appointment and the doctor immediately ordered a biopsy, which had to be done at the local hospital. After about a week she received the results. She said they 'weren't good', which I guessed meant malignant, and she was immediately admitted to hospital to have the lump surgically removed. Subsequent pathology confirmed that the tumour had been cancerous. Soon after the operation the doctors gave her the 'all clear', telling her that they'd removed it all before it could spread any further through her body. Ron, Dad and I breathed a sigh of relief, although not a collective one, and Mum resumed work. Work had never been a voluntary choice for her as our parents had always seemed to be under financial pressure with my dad's erratic employment history and unsuccessful businesses. I also think, though, that her work and the people she met there had long since become a lifeline, providing social interaction that was much more satisfying than her relationship with Dad at home.

Life continued on and I kept up my singing lessons. I'd always had a good voice and had fantasised about being a famous singer. I still had a bit of ambition in me, although in reality it was probably more just a dream that I held on to in order to convince myself I was still worth something, that I could achieve great success. My musical knowledge and ability to play piano were proving useful and my singing teacher was enthusiastic and complimentary at lessons, but the truth is, I lacked the confidence I'd possessed in abundance only a few years earlier. I was full of doubt and insecurity. I did manage to win a couple of pub competitions singing ballads and Carol King-style songs but, really, it was a struggle to fit singing in along with my job and socialising, and I didn't feel like it was going anywhere much. Despite my pub successes, I didn't actually believe that I was all that good. I knew my voice was okay, but it was contained; I seemed to have learned the art of repression and couldn't let it loose, no matter how much I wanted to. Because of my low level of confidence, the performing and entertaining aspects of my singing were even more lacklustre than my voice. In some ways singing just made me feel worse. Besides, I needed more ... more of anything, and alcohol was only moderately successful at covering up my inner sense of failure. I was impulsive and needed instant results. I felt like there was a void inside me and I didn't know what to put in there to fill it.

I was becoming increasingly restless. Chris, my former piano teacher, was moving to Sydney. He'd promised to try and help me break into the club scene there. As singing seemed to be my only prospect for achieving success—at least at something I was interested in—I decided to follow him. It was the beginning of a pattern my life would follow for many years: whenever I felt restless and unfulfilled, I'd pack up and go. I discussed it with Mum and, once I'd made the decision, I began to feel excited at the prospect of living in a new city. It also resolved the problem of my living arrangements. While Dennis was in jail I had been able to stay at Sue's place, but that was no longer possible. I'd been having to sleep at home again, although I always tried to stay over at friends' houses if I could. I knew having me at home was a problem for Mum. I seemed to have become the 'big mouth' of the family, unlike Ron and Mum, who chose to maintain the silence instead of voicing their conflicts. I actually felt their behaviour was dishonest, but they weren't going to support mine because it was equally—or, arguably more—destructive. The truth was, I just didn't fit in at home, but I hadn't officially moved out even though I only stayed there occasionally. Sydney seemed like a good solution all round.

In preparation for my move interstate I wrote to the Victorian Hairdressing Association to put forward a case for completing my apprenticeship early; I'd finished the school component and only had to complete the experiential part in the salon ... boring. I used my back injury as an excuse, telling them that it prevented me from being able to work in the industry. In due course they accepted my proposition and sent me a certificate, although I knew I'd never work as a hairdresser. I didn't tell Mum that, though. With these things tied up, I was ready to go.

Dad drove Mum and me to the bus terminal in the city and still, today, the expression on my mother's face as the bus drove away is etched into my memory. As she stood there waving on that lonely, empty street, watching the tail end of the bus disappear, she looked as sad and lost as I felt. I stared out the window at this woman who I loved and respected but barely knew. She looked so alone, even though my father was there. I guess she was accustomed to feeling alone with him.

'I wonder what she thinks about me? I wonder if she's disappointed?' I asked myself under my breath. I was aware that I'd probably never know the answers to these questions, of any of my mother's thoughts. I wondered if there was anyone that she ever talked to about her feelings or problems. Maybe she did talk to a couple of her friends from work or from our neighbourhood, like

Ivy or Val, I thought to myself as the bus turned the corner and she disappeared from my sight.

After arriving in Sydney I settled in with Jan and Danny, a married couple that Mum knew. Mum had worked with Jan at the laundry in Melbourne years before, and Ron and I had known her since we were little. When we were living at the barber shop, Jan used to live in a bungalow only a block away from our place. She and Mum used to walk to and from work together, although Jan was about twenty years younger than Mum. Jan had had a pretty tough life but she was good fun, and Ron and I had loved going to her place or down the beach with her when we were kids.

Jan was able to get me a factory job assembling electrical components, so every day we'd go off to an industrial estate in North Ryde where Jan worked in a factory that made lifts and escalators. I easily settled into life with her and Danny as I'd always been a quiet kid outside the family. No-one from the community would have ever predicted that I was going to evolve into such a self-destructive person. I guess it's like those stories you often hear about young people who suicide: everything appears to be going along well, they're successful at school, no outward signs of disintegration, then—boom!—they suicide. I think young people who are labelled 'quiet' are often misunderstood. Teachers at high school always used the terms 'quiet' and 'mature' in relation to me when in fact it was just that I hadn't exhibited the turmoil going on inside me.

I made contact with my ex-piano teacher, Chris, who was only young himself, probably in his mid to late twenties, and who had already become quite well known around the music and club scene. He was a very talented pianist and never had trouble finding work. He was also very confident and good at marketing himself. He took me to a few of the big leagues clubs, and Jan and Danny, through a friend of theirs, took me to the

Rose Bay Yacht Squadron where they allowed me to sing a bracket of songs, without payment, to assist me in gaining exposure. But my anticipated musical career didn't seem to have any direction and, possibly due to my lack of belief and self-confidence, it floundered. It was, after all, more a dream than a commitment. I can't imagine why I didn't think to get an agent, but I guess I was pretty naive and I had no-one familiar with the music industry advising me. Chris, as it turned out, had really been more interested in me sexually than in my music career. I felt confused and disappointed in him because I'd thought he was genuine. I stayed around a few more months, about six in all, before deciding to return to Melbourne.

Once back in Melbourne, it didn't take me long to find a factory job, this time assembling components for radio equipment. It was an assembly line and you had to be fast. I felt quite proud that I was placed at the quickest end of the line—obviously my expectations in regard to success had diminished. I quickly picked up where I had left off.

Living at home was no longer an option; Mum, although supportive, made it clear that I wasn't welcome to live there. She wouldn't have seen me out on the streets, though, so she said I could stay there for a little while until I found something suitable. After only a couple of weeks Ron located a little self-contained flat behind a house in Bonbeach, which is only a few train stops before Frankston. It belonged to some friends of his from work and they became my landlords. Ron was now working for a large international advertising organisation and was doing extremely well. Although we didn't see much of each other, we always maintained contact, at least once a month, by phone. I had moved my piano into the flat, still intending to have a career in music, and I practised diligently for a couple of hours every afternoon after I got home from work. I also commenced singing lessons with a new teacher. Nothing much else was happening musically though—I seemed to be waiting to be discovered, which was unlikely because the only place I sang was in the bungalow at Bonbeach!

Most nights I went to one of the pubs in Frankston, only a few kilometres from where I lived, and I resumed my consumption of Duramine tablets and alcohol. Frankston was the kind of place I was looking for and I met many people like me, although a lot had even less direction than I did as they were unemployed and perhaps more entrenched in a drug-using/drinking lifestyle. I felt quite at home in this suburb full of adolescent angst where the topics of discussion were what kind of music we liked, and what kind of drugs and/or alcohol we were about to consume.

There were two popular pubs that regularly presented great bands of the '70s like Chain (a favourite of mine), Billy Thorpe and the Aztecs, and the Masters Apprentices. I mostly met my friends at the pub, where we collaborated in a strong desire to be out of it. We all had our individual reasons, no doubt, but we never talked about our personal or emotional problems, preferring to blame society for our restlessness. The common element between us was a feeling of 'not fitting in', or a lack of desire to conform to what the majority expected of us. It was probably just common adolescent rebelliousness but without the stability and direction that a healthy family can provide our behaviour tended to be extreme at times. Most nights we checked out the two pubs that had bands, staying at whichever one seemed to be 'happening' on that particular evening. Usually it was The Vines, which targeted young people and had a large room for live bands. Drugs were easy to acquire there.

My first contact with the syringe came one night when I went to a party with Andy, a young Frankston guy I liked. Although he was only seventeen, a few months younger than me, he was already an experienced drug user. We arrived at a slightly rundown weatherboard house which from the outside looked like any other average Frankston house. There was nothing unusual about the place until you opened the front door and stepped inside. My eyes opened wide in amazement; I'd never seen anything like it. There were people everywhere, mostly lying around in various poses on the floor, which was dotted with syringes, spoons and other injecting paraphernalia. We walked through the lounge room, Andy saying hello to people he knew along the way, only to find more groups of people at various stages of hitting up in the hallway and bedrooms. Many were slumped forward, their heads nodding, while others with their heads still erect were having difficulty keeping their eyelids open.

Andy and I had dropped some acid at the pub earlier in the evening and we were tripping, but it wasn't very strong. Besides, acid, or LSD as it was also known, wasn't a favourite of mine. Because it's an hallucinogen, it often spins you totally out of touch with reality, producing some very weird—in fact sometimes abnormal—behaviour. When you wake up the next day, you often have no idea where you've been, or what you've done. It usually came as a tiny tablet (stuck to sticky tape so it didn't get lost) which you'd swallow. Sometimes it was fun hallucinating, seeing things that weren't even there, and in the '70s acid was often described as a psychedelic drug. But sometimes you could have a bad trip, and once you were on it there was no way out, the hallucinations lasting for 6–8 hours. Sometimes I found tripping more anxiety producing than enjoyable, but if it was around and my friends were dropping it, I'd join in, because it wasn't any fun being an outsider when everyone else was tripping.

Since arriving at this house and watching people hitting up, I was getting restless and eager to have a go too. They all looked so content and out of it. I turned to Andy. 'I want to try some,' I said without hesitation.

'No you don't,' he replied, trying to be protective.

'Yes I do,' I pleaded with him.

He was determined to maintain his stance. 'No, Helen, don't. It'll only cause you trouble. Believe me, it's not worth it,' he said as he mixed up a hit for himself.

You bloody hypocrite, I thought to myself as I watched him go through the ritual. He put the powder in a spoon, added a few drops of water, heated the mixture up with a match until the powder dissolved, then sucked the liquid up into the syringe. Next, he wrapped a tourniquet around the upper part of his arm, causing his veins to pop up, and I watched as he put the needle right into the middle of a vein and slowly pushed the plunger down on the syringe until there was no liquid left inside. Then he pulled the needle out of his arm, stemmed the bleeding by pressing hard with his finger, leaned back against the wall and slumped into a relaxed position, eyelids heavy, his head nodding forward as though he couldn't hold it up, just like everyone else.

'Wow ...' he said after the initial 'rush' was over, 'that's good gear.'

By this time I was absolutely committed to trying the drug. I assumed it was heroin, but it could have been morphine or pethidine—who knows? It didn't really matter to me. I just wanted some and I was determined to get my own way. I wanted to feel like he looked.

'Please, Andy, I really want to try it,' I said, hoping that he mightn't be so resistant now that he was stoned. I pleaded and pleaded, and finally he gave in. He started to mix me up a hit while I put a tourniquet, which is really just a belt, around my upper arm.

'Pull the belt tight and start pumping your arm,' Andy instructed me. 'Keep clenching and unclenching your fist—it'll help bring your veins up.' While I was concentrating on getting my arm ready, he was heating the powder and water mixture in a spoon. When he had the syringe filled, he moved his focus to my arm in search of a vein. It didn't take long to find one. I was nervous but excited in anticipation of my first hit, my stomach squirming like when a doctor gives you a needle. My eyes were transfixed as I sat on the floor watching Andy slowly inject the substance into my protruding vein. He instructed me to loosen the belt from around my arm and I let it fall onto the floor. Immediately I felt what everyone calls the 'rush' go straight to my brain.

'Wow!' I exclaimed as my eyelids became heavy.

From the moment the drug entered my bloodstream I loved it. It was different to LSD, alcohol, marijuana, hash or speed. It was the best feeling I'd ever experienced, even though I had to run to the bathroom to vomit. It's common to vomit when you first start using. When I returned, I sat back down on the floor beside Andy.

'Are you okay?' he asked me from his slumped position.

'Yeah, I'm fantastic,' I replied, 'thanks so much.' It's hard to describe it, but everything suddenly seemed okay. I was okay. I felt warm inside instead of troubled and searching. I felt full of love. I loved Andy . . . I loved the world . . . It was a momentous occasion and the memory of this initial feeling became imprinted on my brain. In the coming years I would try desperately to reclaim it over and over again.

At about this time I met another new friend while I was hanging around Frankston. While Rhonda was happy to drink lots of alcohol, she drew a rigid line when it came to drugs. Peter, one of her brothers, was already heavily into drugs and was causing the family a lot of grief. I met him, too, and paired up with him for a while, initially as a drug-experimenting friend. There were also some romantic overtones to our relationship as I found him attractive, although in the end it didn't go anywhere because he was acting increasingly weird. He and I dropped a lot of acid together—'clearlight', it was called—and we were out of it most nights. After a few months of regular tripping on LSD I kept seeing lampposts jumping out in front of me while I was driving. It totally freaked me out, especially when I realised the hallucinations and flashbacks were coming even when I wasn't dropping trips. I didn't enjoy feeling so out of touch with reality and I began to steer clear of both LSD and Peter, much to Rhonda's delight. Although Peter was her brother and she loved him, Rhonda was also a bit frightened of him. He was hallucinating so often that his behaviour had become increasingly scary for her family; it was like experiencing someone in the middle of a psychotic episode—it rendered you helpless and unable to reach them.

Personally I felt okay about being stoned and 'out of it', but not being in reality was too freaky and I began to avoid the hallucinogenic drugs like acid. These kinds of drugs also made it incredibly difficult to hold down a job. Because they were stimulants, you just couldn't get to sleep, sometimes for days on end. That was okay if you were unemployed, but I was still committed to earning an income. I never seriously considered being on unemployment benefits. I just wanted to feel warm and fuzzy, and the narcotics like morphine, pethidine and heroin achieved that. They are depressants, not stimulants, and even though you might be semi-conscious, or even unconscious for a while after a hit, you basically just felt like there wasn't a worry in the world. Let's face it, you can't get up to much trouble when you're unconscious! And when you regained consciousness, the warm feeling inside was wonderful. Even though you mightn't be very active, and in that way heroin can be an isolating drug rather than a social drug, it certainly fulfils its potential as a painkiller. It's no coincidence that so many people with abusive family backgrounds use it.

Several times over the next few years, Peter was admitted to a psychiatric institution following psychotic episodes which, it appeared, had been induced by his constant use of acid. Rhonda and I visited him often and I was shocked at the high level of medication, mostly sedatives, that he was on. He seemed an incredibly inferior version of his former self, when he'd been physically strong, intelligent and enthusiastic. He seemed somehow 'broken'. After witnessing the extent of the psychological damage dropping acid had caused him, I was pleased with myself for giving it up. It made me feel as though I was in control of my life. It's all relative and, when you're underachieving, it's always handy to look at someone worse off than yourself ...

Not long after this Rhonda quite suddenly became very sick. After she collapsed one day, it was discovered that she had kidney failure, and she had to live on a dialysis machine until a kidney became available for transplant. She coped well, but her partying and drinking life was over. In between work, visiting Rhonda in hospital and partying, I was becoming increasingly exposed to the drug scene and mixing with the people involved. I was also extricating myself from my family, only very occasionally dropping in to see my mother. Every so often I'd be at a party where there was heroin, and I'd always have a hit when it was available. I hadn't started seeking it out myself yet, though. I was just happy to be around it, knowing I could get some now and then.

I soon met another group of people who were in Australia on a working holiday from New Zealand. They were mostly guys and a couple of young women around my age, although some were a few years older, in their early twenties. At times there were up to a dozen of us hanging around together. They lived in a couple of rooming houses in St Kilda, about seven kilometres south of Melbourne. They also liked to drink a lot and smoke dope (marijuana), so I became a part of their group. A couple of them had access to heroin, so I scored and used a little bit more, but still only socially (meaning occasionally at weekends). I didn't tell Rhonda about my heroin use as I knew she would freak out, especially since she now had other priorities, like trying to stay alive while she awaited a kidney transplant. It was distressing to watch the deterioration in her health, but there was little I could do except to keep visiting her and offering whatever support I could. She was too sick to get around much and was forced to move back to her parents' home where they could look after her when she wasn't in hospital.

One weekend my New Zealand friends dropped in to the bungalow where I lived in Bonbeach. We were hanging around in the street, leaning over our cars, bored and wondering what to do, trying to think of a pub that would be open on a Sunday.

'Let's go to Sydney,' Tam, one of the guys, suggested.

'What a great idea!' I exclaimed. 'Yeah, I'd love to!' I was ready to take off anywhere.

'Yeah, I've been to Sydney before,' Fred, another of the guys, said. 'It's fun up there. I wouldn't mind returning.'

'Yeah, so have I. I'd love to go back. Let's go,' I replied, looking at them enthusiastically. We discussed it a bit more and, within two weeks, two car-loads of us were on our way. We planned to get jobs as soon as we arrived, and to leave our return date open. The next day I gave notice to Ron's friends, who owned my bungalow, organised to move my stuff to the spare shed out the back at my parents' place (the now empty greyhound kennels), gave two weeks' notice at work, and was ready to go. When we left I had $50 in my pocket.

On the way we called in to see some other New Zealand friends of theirs who were living in Canberra. We partied up there for a few days, then hit the road again. By the time we reached Sydney we had very little money. Between the eight of us we scrounged together enough to rent a couple of rooms in a rundown boarding house in Darlinghurst, on the edge of Sydney's red-light district, Kings Cross. Fred was the first to find employment. He was a butcher and could always find a job quickly; he was also very likable and easygoing. This turned out to be very lucky as we had no money left and were getting very hungry. Fred was able to bring some meat home from the shop where he worked, which we ate each night for dinner between two slices of bread.

Fred and I and the cockroaches shared a room in the boarding house, although initially we didn't share a sexual relationship. I was now nineteen and Fred twenty-four, and for the first few months we had a close friendship but slept in single beds. It wasn't long, though, before Fred indicated he was interested in having more than friendship with me. He was an average sort of guy, not much taller than me and with medium-brown wavy hair and a moustache. Although I didn't feel all that physically attracted to him, we did have fun and got along well. He had a gentle manner and wasn't at all dominating or possessive like my father, which I admired.

Our room in the boarding house was pretty disgusting, really, and in the mornings we always awoke to cockroaches crawling around the bin looking for leftovers from our meat sandwiches. It felt grubby and I was hoping like hell to get a job soon so that we could move somewhere better. Within a couple of weeks I got a job as a barmaid at the Woollahra Hotel, a few kilometres east of Darlinghurst, where the manager was prepared to train me. Not long after this, Fred and I commenced a lover relationship. Really, it just seemed easier and more practical to share rent and other costs, although we did care for each other. We soon found better accommodation in a rooming house in Paddington, which was only five minutes from the pub where I worked, and ten minutes to Fred's job. Our room was a bedsitter with its own little kitchen area; it suited us fine and we settled in for a while. We were both pretty laid-back, neither of us expecting much more of the other than financial and emotional support, so while our relationship wasn't wildly exciting, it worked quite well.

Fred enjoyed experimenting with drugs and he also liked heroin, so we were quite happy to get stoned together and share the cost of scoring whenever we had the urge. Over time and almost without realising it, Fred and I began to seek out heroin much more regularly, so that we were on the borderline between social using and addiction, although in our minds it was still purely social. We'd just replace alcohol with heroin on most occasions. We certainly didn't perceive ourselves as heroin addicts—it was simply that we came to like it more than alcohol, pills or smoking dope. Although Fred enjoyed marijuana, it just made me feel paranoid, and I'd never liked cigarettes either— couldn't stand the smell of them or breathing in the smoke. As for pills such as Serepax, Mandrax, Rohypnol (downers) or, alter- natively, the diet pills (uppers), I'd never particularly taken to the sedatives, although I had hit the diet pills quite regularly earlier on. I just didn't like how I felt after using sedatives—they seemed to totally zonk you out so that you couldn't remember what you'd done.

One night when the opportunity presented itself, we decided to drop a trip each, something I hadn't done for a long time. We went to a local pub and later to Kings Cross, where we sometimes went to watch the drag shows, or just to wander around. It seemed to be a central location where the misfits of society gravitated. It was common to find marginalised people there. It provided a sense of community, somewhere for us to 'belong' where, because we all displayed a variety of 'different' behaviours, mostly outside of the law, we weren't judged. You could be a drug addict, prostitute, homosexual, transvestite or whatever wasn't the 'norm', and no extreme was too extreme. Acceptance was what you felt there.

Anyway, after a night of fun with our friends, we returned

home to our bedsitter at the rooming house. Fred had been 'tripping' all night, but mine hadn't seemed to kick in yet. We went to bed and immediately after I closed my eyes the hallucinations commenced. I opened my eyes, sat up in bed and looked across at Fred—and I could have sworn his head was doing 360-degree turns round and round on top of his shoulders, just like in that movie *The Exorcist*. I grabbed him by the shoulder and shook him.

'Fred! Wake up!' I said urgently.

'What?' he grumbled, still half asleep.

'Your head's turning round and round.'

'Oh . . . go back to sleep,' he replied, not at all interested.

I lay down and closed my eyes again, but I immediately started hallucinating again. I opened my eyes, sat bolt upright and looked over at Fred—his head was doing it again.

'Fred! Wake up! Your head is going round and round again. It won't stop!' I said as I shook him. No response.

'Fred! Sit up! You have to sit up so your head can stop turning!' I repeated, feeling a bit desperate and frightened now. Finally, after I'd shaken him for some time, Fred got up, exasperated. He came around to my side of the bed and pulled me up by my arms. By this time I couldn't look at him any more.

'Walk over here and look out the window. Look at something else and you'll see it's all right. You're still tripping,' he said, trying hard to console me. He knew there was going to be no sleep until my hallucinations stopped. We returned to bed, but every time I closed my eyes or looked at him, the hallucinations started again. Eventually, possibly from exhaustion, we both fell asleep.

The next morning I said to him, 'Good trip, hey?' I was laughing alone because he didn't seem to find it humorous.

'Yeah, sure,' he replied cynically. 'Won't be in a hurry to have another one, you fruit-loop!'

'Oh, you've got no sense of humour,' I teased him. But although I was laughing now, I'd been quite scared at the time, and this turned out to be almost the last occasion I took acid.

After a few months at the rooming house in Paddington we moved to Bondi, a few more kilometres east, and into a share house with some of our other New Zealand friends. We went to pubs and listened to bands, and sometimes at the Bondi pub I'd sing some songs with one of the New Zealand guys who played guitar. We hung out at Kings Cross on the streets and around the clubs and made a few new friends, mostly drug users. One of our friends had been living in Sydney for quite a while and had easy access to smack (heroin), so we could score whenever we wanted from a safe source. It was all pretty easygoing and without the desperation that accompanies physical addiction.

After living in Sydney for about eighteen months, and with my twenty-first birthday approaching, my mum offered to erect a marquee in their back yard for a party. I felt like she was really only doing it because they'd had a party at the Yacht Club for Ron's twenty-first three years earlier. Our parents had always felt it was important to treat us equally on a material level, not favouring one child over the other. Anyway, it sounded like a good excuse to return to Melbourne and catch up with friends, so we started organising our trip. The regulars at the Woollahra pub took up a collection for me and we had celebratory drinks before Fred and I left, although we were only going for the weekend. I felt happy and had a real sense of belonging at my job in the club bar at the pub; they were such lovely people who drank there, although I'd had difficulties with the manager, who was an arrogant, dominating male. When I first started work he was verbally aggressive, ordering me not to wear a particular perfume. It was patchouli oil, which was popular with us bohemians. I felt quite intimidated by him, but not enough to stop wearing it, and this caused another outburst from him. At one stage I thought he would sack me over it, but as time passed he dropped off giving me such a hard time. I was a good worker, after all, and popular with the locals who drank there.

Some of my Sydney friends were flying down to Melbourne for my birthday party, but four of us were driving as it was cheaper with a few of us sharing petrol costs. I had a little Renault 10 car that I was paying off and it was reliable. When we got to my parents' place I was relieved to feel there was no tension, especially between Dad and me, and we all immersed ourselves in blowing up balloons and putting up streamers. The strain between myself and my parents genuinely seemed to be put aside for the weekend, which was a relief because I hadn't been sure what to expect, having been out of home for some time by then. We were all focused on preparing for the party and having a good time, and none of our difficulties were discussed. I was certainly hoping not to have a blow up while I was there, so I was relieved to find my dad behaving like he used to when Ron and I were little, joining in and seeming quite jovial. It was nice to see his good qualities again.

The party night commenced and my old and new friends all started arriving. Sue and her husband, Dennis, turned up looking happy together, and I was pleased for them as I loved them both. Rhonda came with her brother Peter, although they had to leave early as Rhonda was pretty sick by then and on the waiting list for a kidney transplant. My father gave a speech and said nice things about me, and after those formalities it was down to partying in earnest.

There was a jukebox playing, so people were dancing and having a great time. Some of my Sydney friends had some smack with them, but I decided to stick to alcohol because I didn't want to cause any drama during this brief visit and my parents didn't know about my drug use. Fred eventually got so drunk that he tripped over one of the guy ropes anchoring the tent and landed flat on his face in the grass. He looked so funny lying spread-eagled on his stomach, and he didn't move again until the next morning. All my other friends from Sydney slept on the lounge-room floor in sleeping bags; there were bodies everywhere. After Fred had pulled himself up from the ground and come inside the next morning, we all laughed and joked about what a good party it had been. Even my parents joined in, seemingly relaxed. I guess it wasn't too different from the parties they used to have with our neighbours, most of whom had also turned up.

My parents' behaviour was so out of character compared to the way it had been for the last eight or so years, and I wondered why it couldn't have been more like this since I'd been twelve.

They were very generous that weekend and it still remains a happy memory. I have no idea why they behaved so differently, particularly my father. Perhaps they'd decided that twenty-first birthdays are a sign of reaching an important landmark in life, so they were determined to make a concerted effort.

We hung around for a while the next day, then took off for our return to Sydney where Fred and I remained for another six months or so. I continued to enjoy my job at the pub. I loved the company of the regular drinkers every afternoon when they arrived after work, as well as the sense of belonging which this job provided. I did a bit of singing at a local pub, although not for money, and quite a bit of drinking. We'd increased our drug use to every weekend and a couple of times during the week, but we could still afford it and we weren't using heroin to the point where it was out of control. In other words, we didn't have a habit.

We decided to go to New Zealand for a while so that I could meet Fred's family, who were spread around in various places on the south island. The plan was to travel a bit, see where Fred was born, then find work and settle in Dunedin, which was where Fred had spent most of his life. I was quite excited about it and, after a few weeks of organising, we found ourselves on our way to the airport.

We stayed about six months. I worked at 'Barton's the Butcher', in a small area of the shop that made take-away food, and Fred again worked as a butcher, although not at Barton's. We couldn't lay our hands on any heroin so it was a heroin-free time, although not drug-free. We still managed plenty of drinking and dope-smoking, despite my lack of interest in marijuana. It still only seemed to make me paranoid rather than happy. It was a good time, although after six months we were ready to return to Australia. We decided to make Melbourne our destination this time. I was now twenty-two, Fred twenty-seven.

4

I'm gonna be a singer

Not long after arriving back in Melbourne in 1976, Fred and I found a flat in St Kilda and decided to settle in for a while. Unfortunately, Mum wasn't very well. The doctors had recently discovered more cancer in her body, and it wasn't long before she was on her way to hospital to have one of her breasts removed. After surgery, however, she was only off work for about a month before being back in full swing. I don't think she ever felt comfortable with a lot of time on her hands—it probably made her think too much. I'm sure it must have been more comforting being in the company of her friends at work than in the silence of home. Mum was very likable and, although quiet, she made friends easily.

I remember having a discussion with her about the new bras she had to buy with one breast cup filled with some sort of padding, but I never thought to ask her how she *felt* about losing her breast. We only discussed the physical aspects of her operation. I don't think anyone in our family ever asked her how she was feeling. It was as though an emotional reaction to anything would be considered self-indulgent: it was neither expected nor valued.

At this point in my life—like at any other time, I guess—I

had no idea what she thought of me, and I didn't dare tell her about my drug use. I certainly didn't want to cause her any additional stress, although I was getting paranoid that she knew something. Mothers seem to have an uncanny ability to know about things you've never told them, although it's also true to say that paranoia goes hand in hand with the secrets and lies of illegal drug use. Because Fred and I were able to stay employed we found it reasonably easy to hide our 'other' life. Also, I didn't see that much of my mum, visiting only once every two or three weeks. I didn't allow myself to think too much about whether she'd noticed any changes in me. My father wouldn't speak to me, so I'd never hang around long, the purpose of my visits being to reassure Mum that I was okay.

After Fred and I had been back in Melbourne for a month or so, I began looking at newspaper advertisements for singers. It seemed that every time we moved location, I found renewed motivation to explore opportunities to become a singer, although I was aware it would probably only ever be a part-time involvement unless I got real lucky or became more persistent and committed. I was no longer having singing lessons.

I finally responded to a newspaper advertisement to audition as a singer for a band called TRAMM. There were five singers as well as about eight musicians in the band and I went along and sang a few songs for them. This was my first audition for a band and, surprisingly, I sang confidently. Afterwards they sat down and talked to me for a while, particularly the other singers, and it felt comfortable. They seemed impressed with my voice so I was offered the job on the spot. There were three guys and two women singers plus the band with a brass section—about fourteen in all, although it varied. With me included, there were three females. Annie, who was tiny and blonde, took the soprano lines, while Jan and I alternated with the low and middle range harmony lines. Jan was a brunette and me a redhead—perfect variety!

We sounded pretty good actually, because there were some excellent musicians and fabulous singers in the group, especially Peter and David. They mostly did the lead singing, although we all had a chance to sing lead in a song. Peter and David were also great entertainers and we did the pub circuit, wedding receptions and other special occasion gigs. At twenty-two years old I really thought this was my big break. Secretly, though, the doubts persisted, and I found the others a bit daunting. They were so talented, I couldn't regard myself as having the same ability as them. At the same time I felt excited and positive. Although the shadow of heroin addiction was still following me, I really believed that I was going to find that elusive confidence. What I also found in this band were some very special friends. I didn't realise until years later how important their friendship was going to be.

About six months after Fred and I had returned to Melbourne, our increasing dependence on scoring and using made it more difficult for us to live in denial. We were still adamant that we were merely 'social' heroin users. It's a common pattern among people addicted to drugs, to deny or lie about the extent of their drug consumption, much like an alcoholic, who kids himself and others about the amount he drinks, always trying to minimise it. It was our friend Danni who pointed it out to us one evening when we were at her place. Danni was about twenty, a couple of years younger than me. After scoring and hitting up together, we were all sitting back relaxing, 'on the nod' ('nodding off' is the term used to describe the immediate effect of having a hit, when the user's head keeps dropping forward), before she returned to working on the streets in St Kilda. In the 1970s St Kilda was a smaller version of Sydney's Kings Cross, with the same sort of nightclubs featuring drag shows and, on the street, prostitutes, transvestites and illicit drug users. I never understood how Danni did it, but she made a living out of prostitution ... well, at least enough to keep her and her boyfriend's drug addiction alive. Prostitution was something I could never seriously contemplate as a means to earning money. The thought of having strange men lying on top of me having sex was more than any drug could help me withstand—it wouldn't have mattered how much money they had offered me, or how big a hit I'd had, I just couldn't bear the thought of it.

Danni was one of the few people, along with Chipper, Sue, Stella, Rikki, Raelene and a few others, that Fred and I trusted to score with or from. We were all about the same age and I'd met all of them around the time I was seventeen or eighteen, when I'd first begun using, although I didn't hang around St Kilda much then. They usually worked as prostitutes to earn money to score their drugs, and they were mostly lesbian, although not Danni or Stella. Most of them had been sexually abused as children and had little in the way of family support. It struck me that they'd created their own family there on the streets and, for them, making men pay for sex appeared to restore some sense of balance in their lives; it saw them in control rather than helpless, the way they'd felt as abused children. I was closer to Danni than the others, but in subsequent years of drug use I became good friends with them all.

Anyway, while we were sitting back nodding off that evening, Danni made an astute observation. 'You two must have a habit,' she said knowingly. Danni had already been on the streets since she was twelve, and she knew the quantity we'd been using.

'No way,' the words tumbled out of Fred and me simultaneously.

'No, we don't have a habit,' I reassured her, 'not us ... no!' Never having had a habit before, we were still quite naive, and didn't know what to expect or what effect a habit could have on our lives.

'Well, be careful,' she said, like a wise woman.

Despite our protests, though, every morning the physical signs were becoming more obvious: the sweating, goosebumps, feeling like our skin was crawling until we'd had our 'breakfast', our first hit for the day. Breakfast had once consisted of toast and coffee, but not any longer. It was always such a relief to feel the heroin quickly move through our bloodstream that we'd immediately forget about the preceding nausea, anxiety and doubt. I'd also noticed that by lunchtime I had the telltale goosebumps and nausea of what's called 'hanging out', and would often have to rush home for a quick taste (hit). Fred and I both knew that Danni was right, but we weren't about to admit it.

Fred had a job as a boner at an abattoir in Dromana, quite a long distance away on the Mornington Peninsula, and I had a job as a receptionist/typist, having completed a six-week course when I returned from New Zealand. I was tired of boring factory jobs, so I now worked at a computer firm in St Kilda. St Kilda was the easiest place in Melbourne to score drugs, so my job location turned out to be very convenient, especially given that Fred had to spend two or three hours travelling to and from work every day. I was able simply to go round the corner and find my friend Danni, or one of the others who I trusted to score from. Sometimes I'd go looking for Danni, Stella or Chipper at lunchtime, other times I'd wait until after work. Of course it wasn't always that simple, don't get me wrong. It wasn't like going to the milk bar. In fact scoring was a pain in the arse as it could take anything from an hour to all day. Sometimes there was no-one around, or Danni would be having trouble scoring the heroin herself. There were times when none of us could score until well after midnight and trying to locate it increasingly consumed our 'social life'. By this time our escalating consumption of heroin was also more expensive than our 'straight' jobs could afford so, if we had discovered a good contact/dealer, we'd often buy a few grams and break it up into small amounts which we could sell as 'caps', $50 worth. The profit margin allowed for a couple of free caps for our own use. We needed to sell a gram or two per day to cover our own use. Given that we had quite a few friends in the drug scene, it was relatively easy, although time consuming, to sell six or eight caps a day.

I swear I don't know how I kept my job as I wasn't very motivated and only did exactly what was required of me, no more, no less, although I guess that's all you have to do. Each day I'd be starting to hang out by lunchtime and it became necessary to have a hit to see me through until the end of the day. After lunch I'd return to my desk at the front of the office. It was an organisation that dealt in computers—I wasn't even sure what they did with them and I didn't care either, as long as they paid me each week.

The office consisted of a reception area where I sat and, over on my right, a couple of individual offices for the representatives. I could see through their office doors, which were usually open. Generally their heads were down working, unlike mine, which was often down but not from working.

After my lunchtime hit I'd sit at my desk and nod off. I didn't mean to—it's just what happens for a while after a hit. It was a bit of a problem, really, because for about an hour or so it was hard to keep my eyelids open and my head tended to drop forward while I nodded off. Unfortunately, I'd often regain consciousness either in the midst of sliding off my chair onto the floor, or when my head slumped forward and hit the desk in front of me. You fuckin' idiot, you nodded off again!, I'd admonish myself. I'd sit myself up straight, dust myself off, take quick, furtive glances through the doors of the guys' offices to see if they'd noticed, then carry on as though nothing had happened. This started happening every day after lunch for about an hour until the initial stone wore off.

The boss of the computer firm was out on the road most of the time, thank goodness. He kept a diary at the front desk and it was part of my job to note any phone calls or messages for him in it. Sometimes I'd nod off in the middle of writing, and the pen would trail off leaving a line wherever my hand slid to. When I'd regained my composure, I'd have to white out the 'doodle' line and rewrite the message neatly. Some days the pages were almost covered with white-out and I'd giggle to myself looking at them. Everyone in that office was so neat and meticulous, I wondered if they ever suspected me of anything.

Increasingly, work and scoring became all that Fred and I had time for. My lunch hour and all our evenings were spent chasing heroin because, after being back in Melbourne only a few months, we now readily admitted we couldn't go without it. There was no way we'd get to work in the mornings without a hit. Relationships with people from the 'straight' world became strained, and gradually they disappeared from our lives. I guess they sensed the change in Fred and me, or maybe it was just that we didn't have time to see them any more.

I still found time to sing with TRAMM, though, and we'd rehearse one night a week and on Saturdays. Sometimes we'd have a gig at weekends. We played dance music along with some original material, and I enjoyed rehearsals and the company of the others. Peter, David, Jan and Annie had become good friends, although I didn't share my drug-taking stories with them as they weren't into that scene. Some of them were gay, but otherwise 'straight'. Fred sometimes came with me to gigs at the pubs, as did my old hairdressing friend Sue and her husband Dennis occasionally. About once every three months even Ron and my parents came to watch us; by then it was the only time I saw them. It was a part of my life they could feel proud of. It was the only part that I would allow them to see, the one in which I could maintain the facade that I was okay. They'd all long been waiting for me to be a singer so, to outside appearances, it seemed that I was still on the road to success. In reality, however, I was finding it more and more difficult to be in the band, living a double life.

One day Annie, one of the singers and a friend by now, said to me, 'Barny, you don't smile any more.'

I looked back at her hardly knowing what to say. 'Yeah, I do. What do you mean?'

'Are you okay?' she inquired kindly.

'Yeah, sure I am, honest …' I responded before turning away, not wanting to pursue the conversation any further. Of course I wasn't okay. Sometimes I couldn't score and I'd have to turn up to rehearsals hanging out, or late. Sometimes I was struggling to hide my foul mood and worries about scoring while trying to act interested in rehearsals. It was getting harder.

In 1975 our band was successful in getting a job in Perth over Christmas and, after discussion, we decided to go there for a month. I saw it as an opportunity to have a break from using smack, thus reducing my tolerance which had increased drastically, so I took holidays from work. Although I wasn't that keen, I knew it would be good for me as I'd be busy singing. The band was driving over in a van with all our equipment. Before we left, Fred and I hassled around to score so that I could have a last hit. I had planned to hang out across the Nullarbor Plain and by the time we reached Perth a couple of days later, I'd be over the worst of it.

I was late meeting the rest of the band because Fred and I had trouble scoring (there always seemed to be a drug drought around Christmas time), but they were getting used to me being increasingly unreliable. Once our bags and the equipment were packed into the van, we all climbed in and I waved goodbye to Fred as we drove out of Melbourne. He was going to try and have a break too. I was apprehensive about ceasing my drug use, but excited about the singing job. I just wanted to get the hanging out over and done with. Of course it was a very uncomfortable trip across the Nullarbor because I was sick. I pretended to have the flu, even though it was the middle of summer, and by the time we arrived in Perth I was beginning to come through the worst of it.

We settled into our accommodation and set up to play at a well-known club, Beethoven's, every night. We were increasingly playing disco-style music, which was popular in pubs and clubs at the time. At least I felt a bit more stable not running around trying to score every day. One day early in the gig we decided to be tourists, so we all went to Rottnest Island. It was just off the mainland, and we caught a ferry over there. Once on the island we hired bicycles and rode around for a while. It really was fun and I laughed with the others like I hadn't for a long time. I acknowledged that I was enjoying everyone's company, but while doing these 'ordinary' things it still felt as though something was missing. I'd felt like that since I was about fifteen ... always this sense of something missing from my life. Certainly not the anxiety of scoring, but I missed the instant high of the heroin entering my bloodstream and the emotional numbness it provided. I think since our family life had disintegrated when I was a teenager, I'd been in search of a replacement, something and somewhere that I felt accepted and as though I belonged. If I stayed constantly stoned I didn't feel like the failure that, deep down inside, I believed I was. I'd had so much potential when I was younger and I just wasn't confident that it was even there any more, let alone the possibility of fulfilling it. Heroin helped fill that gap inside and made me feel that I was okay.

We continued playing each night at the club and I kept trying to be interested in 'normal' life, joining the others socially as well as working together. Jan, David and I would go to the beach and different places around Perth before arriving for our gig at night. (Pete hadn't accompanied the band on this trip.) Secretly, though, despite having a good time, I was restless. As the days passed, I found myself missing the 'high' that comes with using heroin. I loved Jan and David and was enjoying their company, but there was still this nagging emptiness inside me. I knew if someone offered me some smack I'd be hitting up in an instant. I didn't know what the emptiness was, but I was increasingly finding it harder and harder, the longer I was away from my last hit. Straight life now seemed boring and with just one taste (of heroin), I knew I'd feel warm inside instead of lonely and isolated. When I used heroin I didn't feel like I needed anyone else in my life. At the same time it made me feel more loving and caring even though, in reality, it made me unreachable. Still, over in Perth I had no drug contacts, so I continued socialising with Jan and David. It might have helped if I'd been able to talk to them about my drug use, about what I was feeling, but I balked at the thought. There was no way I was going to expose that shameful part of my life to them; it would have made me feel 'dirty' in comparison, and I already felt inferior.

About a week into our Perth gig I discovered, after a phone call to Fred, that some old New Zealand friends were living there, so I rang them. 'What a stroke of luck!' I said to myself after hanging up the phone. They'd all been using regularly for a while and it happened that they were able to obtain heroin fairly easily at that time. That'll be the end of my socialising with Jan and David and the band! I could already feel the emptiness inside me being replaced by excitement at the thought of my first hit. I could feel the uneasiness I'd been feeling as a 'straight' person disappearing. With this drug I needed no-one; it made me feel stronger, more confident, and I was quick to organise to see these friends the next day so that I could score as soon as possible.

When I arrived at their house to a warm welcome, they'd already scored and they offered me a free hit. I couldn't believe my luck not having to pay for it! They even gave me some to take with me as they had access to a large amount of relatively pure smack just then. It turned out they were a bit stuck for contacts in Perth to sell it to, hence their phone call to Fred. He could certainly get rid of some of it among our friends and contacts in Melbourne. Needless to say, the remainder of my time in Perth was consumed by using, and it turned out to be one of the most plentiful Christmases ever in terms of availability of smack.

For the remainder of our month there I'd sing with the band at night, but during the day I would spend most of my time with my New Zealand friends, getting stoned at their house. By the time I arrived at the club to perform, I wasn't really on the ball and for the first time I became aware that I wasn't holding my harmony line. Some nights I'd look over at our sound person mixing our vocals and I could see our manager there, listening through the headphones. I hoped like hell he wasn't listening to my voice because I knew I was singing off the notes, but I couldn't seem to rectify it—it was like it was bigger than me. I'd never sung out of tune before and I was aware that it must have been because of my confused state of mind, one day thinking like a straight person, the next irrational, like the drug addict that I was. But I still wasn't prepared to give it up, especially when it was so plentiful and cheap.

It was also increasingly difficult to hide my stoned state from the others, especially Jan, with whom I shared a room. After our gig I'd return to our accommodation and have another hit, then nod off. I just had to hope she didn't notice. It was always the first hour or two after a hit that was so noticeable; once that had passed you usually just appeared and behaved much like a normal person, although with constricted pupils. Sometimes they looked like pinpricks, they were so tiny.

We finished the remaining three weeks of our gig in Perth, then prepared to return to Melbourne in the van. Jan and David had had enough of the 'group' thing and decided to fly back because it's a long, uncomfortable journey across the Nullarbor Plain, but I was okay because I'd bought enough smack to last me all the way back. In fact, because it was cheap and I had some spare money, I bought enough to last Fred and me for a few weeks after my return to Melbourne. During the journey home I'd hit up every six or so hours, at almost every toilet stop. I felt so lucky, or maybe 'elated' would be a better way to describe it. It's probably a bit like when a gambler wins the jackpot at the pokies! Because we now had an ongoing supply for a week or two, it gave me a fleeting sense of security. Undoubtedly, smack had become the priority in my life again. Damn it!

After the Perth dope ran out, life grew very tedious— working, scoring, working, scoring. Fred and I were feeling increasingly insecure about scoring enough to maintain our habits. With our tolerance burgeoning, our wages were nowhere near enough to buy the amount of smack we required to function normally, let alone to get stoned, unless we were able to sell small amounts to our drug-using friends and have enough left over to keep our own habits going. I'd just turned twenty-three and was feeling disgruntled and restless. Fred and I had a talk about our situation and decided to leave Melbourne to try and break free of the slavery to which our drug addiction bound us. We were also becoming known to the local police because we were on the streets of St Kilda so often. It was starting to feel a bit dangerous. I thought we needed to go far away, not just to Sydney where we still knew other heroin slaves. Eventually Fred suggested Darwin. He'd been there before and found it enjoyable, so why not? I loved hot weather and Darwin sounded almost like a tropical island. I didn't take much persuading. We'd try to come off our heroin habits and start over again, really give it a go, and return to a straight life. We felt we could do it if we got away from the rut in which we were stuck.

With the decision made, I gave notice at work—I still couldn't believe they hadn't sacked me—and I organised a meeting with the band and our manager, Steve, to tell them I was leaving. I'd been with the band nearly eighteen months and I knew this was going to be hard because I loved them all dearly, although I did think I was going to get booted out anyway. Saying goodbye to the band felt like also saying goodbye to my dream of becoming a singer because I didn't believe that any other band would want me, but I didn't let myself think too much about it as I didn't want to get emotional. Besides, I could always pick up some singing work in Darwin. If I was straight I'd probably get into it again.

We all met at one of the guy's places. I took a deep breath and decided to let it out as quickly as possible. 'Sorry, everyone, but I've decided to go interstate. Time to move on,' I said courageously, trying to cover my anxiety.

'Oh no! Barny, we'll miss you,' said Peter, who was one of the most beautiful people I had ever met. David and Peter were both gay and Jan and I went out with them socially every so often, partly because they were such good fun but also because we felt safe. We'd go to gay bars and dance the night away. Peter had actually left the band himself, but he was still involved with some of us, particularly Jan, David and I, and we'd formed strong friendships. Even though I hadn't shared my drug problems with anyone in the band, I still felt very close to them, and I respected every one of them. They were not only talented, but also incredibly compassionate human beings. I sat there looking at Peter, wondering why I'd never shared my problems with him. He wouldn't have rejected me. But it was too late now, it had all gone too far. Fred and I were hopelessly addicted and we needed to get away. It seemed like our only way out—one-way ticket to Darwin! I got through the meeting without getting too emotional and, with that taken care of, we were free to leave.

In February 1977 Fred and I packed up our stuff from our little rented flat in St Kilda and once again stored our furniture in the back shed at my parents' house. After hassling around we scored enough heroin for the long drive, with the plan of hanging out when we reached Darwin. We were determined to get off the rotten stuff for good. Some of Fred's non-using New Zealand friends were already living up there, so we intended to stay with them until we sorted ourselves out. We didn't even wait to collect the bond money on our flat, leaving that in Mum's capable hands. She would mail us a cheque as soon as the real estate agent paid it. She was also guarantor for my car, which we'd just sold, and was always willing to take care of any unfinished business that I left behind, although I was pretty good at closing things off as I'd moved so much.

I hadn't been seeing a lot of my parents and my father still rarely acknowledged me, but there was less pressure now that I hardly ever saw them. Occasionally they would come and watch the band playing. Ron now had a prominent position in one of the leading international advertising agencies with an office in Melbourne. He lived and worked around the St Kilda area too, so sometimes I would call into his work to see him and, I'm embarrassed to say, I'd usually ask him to lend me $50 while I was there. I'd like to think that I paid him back, at least now and then, but I'm really not sure!

5

Song of a drug addict

With our loose ends tied up, Fred and I drove out of Melbourne headed for Darwin, with a stopover in Sydney first. We still knew some people there, so by the next day we found ourselves back in Kings Cross, scoring more heroin because we'd already used all the smack, three days worth, that we'd bought for the entire trip to Darwin. We had planned to use a minimal amount for the drive, just enough to prevent us from hanging out, but once we were on our way it felt like party time.

'We can't be hanging out while we're driving, can we?' I'd asked Fred. He was trying to work out how much money we had between us.

'No, fuck it,' he'd eventually said.

We bought a few grams and hung around with some of our friends for a couple of days, then left. If we'd stayed around much longer, we both knew we'd never see Darwin. We were limited by the amount of money we'd been able to amass with our entitlements when we'd left our jobs, and we had to keep enough to reach Darwin and survive for the first couple of weeks. Once we were there we'd find jobs and, without the cost of heroin eating into our weekly budget, life would be much easier.

We were both sick of the merry-go-round of working to earn enough money to score and use, as well as having to sell some, just to survive. The more you use the more you need and the cost of maintaining a habit is more than a straight wage can supply, which added another factor for us to consider; we didn't want to become well known to the police, and if we'd hung around St Kilda much longer that's exactly what would've happened. They were already starting to recognise us.

'I wish we could just use at weekends,' I said somewhat wistfully to Fred as we drove out of Sydney.

'How many times have we tried that?' he replied.

'But if we just had a few hits, maybe it would be possible?' I pleaded with him, even though I already knew what his response would be. He was in a dejected state.

'I'm sick of it,' he replied, 'the hiding, trying to raise enough money ...' He trailed off. He was absolutely right, of course. 'The only way to do it is to stop altogether. It'll be okay after we get through the withdrawals. We just have to do it. That's why we're getting away, remember?' he added sarcastically, looking sideways at me as he drove on.

I sat there beside him in the front seat of his old green HR Holden, trying to get a grasp on what life was going to be like without the 'high' of heroin, even occasionally. I had to admit it was beyond me, but at least Fred seemed determined at that moment. For today, at least, I could rely on him. Of course, it changed daily—maybe tomorrow I'd be the one feeling stronger and more committed to stopping. It goes like that, one day I'd feel strong, then the next day he'd be stronger. The problem was that usually by the third or fourth day we'd both have a 'weak' day and end up scoring and using again. It's a bloody nightmare—can't live with it, can't live without it!

We drove inland through Orange, all the time heading north to the centre of Australia so that, eventually, we would go through Katherine right up to the top end. Being February it was the rainy season and we'd come across some flooded roads along the way; because we still had some smack left, though, it seemed like fun and we'd get out and take photos. When we were tired and neither of us felt like driving, we'd pull over and have a sleep in the car, but on the whole we'd try to keep moving on as much as possible. We didn't want to be on the road more than three days. There was no turning back now—we'd come too far.

Eventually we reached Darwin and our friends were pleased to see us, although a bit shocked. The last time we'd seen them was when we lived in Sydney and I'd worked in the pub. We'd even shared a house with them for six months before we returned to Melbourne, but then we'd only been using smack occasionally. We saw ourselves as 'social users', and I guess we were; we certainly weren't driven by the craving for heroin that had subsequently come to torment us. In Darwin we were moody and restless as we contemplated what lay ahead. I guess we were not as easygoing as when we'd mixed with them in Sydney, and we'd both lost a bit of weight as we'd often forget to eat. Nothing was as important as scoring and using and, besides, heroin suppresses your appetite, so you just don't feel hungry. After using heroin as a social drug in Sydney, our friends hadn't bothered with it since, so they were able to help us during our 'hanging out' by providing a 'clean' house. We were fortunate to have friends who didn't succumb to the temptation to score, and who also didn't know who to score from in Darwin.

Predictably, our supply ran out soon after we arrived and we had four or five days of vile physical withdrawals, sweating profusely, skin crawling, covered in goosebumps, vomiting and diarrhoea. Then, on about the fifth day, we began to feel slightly human again, although very weak and lethargic. The worst of the physical withdrawal was over. It took another week or so to build up a bit of strength, then we both went out searching for work and managed to find jobs almost immediately, me in a pub and Fred as a butcher. We bought an old caravan for next to nothing and put it out the back of our friends' house, which was in Casuarina, a suburb only about five kilometres east of Darwin city. This provided some privacy for us all as there were already four of them, two couples, living in the house.

Because we all got along well it worked out okay and the rent was affordable. Fred and I settled into our new jobs and a drug-free life. It was really quite all right, and I loved the hot weather and the transitory nature of the place. I'd go to the pool almost every afternoon for a swim. Having always lived near the beach, I loved the water, although at certain times of the year in the north you couldn't swim in the ocean because of sea wasps.

My mum and I stayed in touch by mail. She'd write one week and I'd write the next and, unfortunately, she soon had some more bad news. The doctors had found more cancer and she had to go to hospital for another operation. I sensed it must be serious, this being her third operation but, as usual, at least in her letters, she just carried on as though nothing was wrong. I felt a touch guilty for not being there, but I knew Ron would be looking out for her. She'd never tell any of us what was going on for her emotionally anyway. After this operation, the doctors once again told her it was 'all clear'. I don't know if she felt suspicious of their diagnosis given that she'd had three operations within a couple of years, but if she did she never let on.

My job involved working five or six nights a week at Lim's, a cocktail lounge which was part of one of the main pubs. It was good fun, although I preferred to work behind the bar rather than waiting on tables as that way I didn't have to deal with the sometimes drunk and difficult tourists. The lounge had bands playing regularly and sometimes I'd get up with them later in the night and sing a few songs, but that was about the extent of my singing. I always hoped it would lead to more, but I didn't actively go out and seek singing work. I missed it, but I wasn't motivated and it seemed easier to have a pub job, even if it didn't provide me with fulfilment. It did provide me with financial security on a week-to-week basis, and I'd never been one to plan further ahead than that—you never knew where you'd be the following week!

While we were in Darwin my relationship with Fred began to change. We'd been together three years and for the last two we'd been having problems with our addiction to heroin. I didn't understand what was going on, but I didn't feel the same attraction towards him. Maybe it's because I'm straight?, I asked myself over and over as I tried to sort through what I was feeling. I wasn't interested in him sexually any more, and Fred wasn't happy about it. Our relationship had begun more out of convenience than love, and while I had grown to love him dearly, for me it had always been more as a friend than a lover, although I was aware that he was still deeply in love with me. Even though I wasn't ready to give up what was left of the relationship, we were no longer intimate and sex had become almost irrelevant to my life. It was beginning to cause tension, though, because Fred wanted more than I was willing to give and, probably because we'd been straight for a month or two, his sex drive was returning. I couldn't say the same for me!

When you've been a heroin addict, it's amazing just how easy it is to suss out others with the same interest, so it wasn't long, about a month or so, before we met the local heroin-using population of Darwin. They were nice people and we gradually started hanging around with them more. Life seemed somehow boring without heroin. Once you've been addicted, the psychological craving remains long after the drug has physically left your body. The desire to have a hit became so overwhelming that we started scoring occasionally, then regularly, until—guess what?

Within a couple of months of our arrival in Darwin, it had again become a daily ritual. I think what we'd really been trying to escape in Melbourne was the chaos in our lives and fear of being busted, plus the fact that it's an all-consuming occupation just selling the drug and getting enough money together every day to feed your habit. I guess we still loved the drug too much to give it up and were willing to tolerate its associated difficulties. It really didn't feel like we had any control over our need to score.

Most days we both made it to work okay, but there were always those occasions when we couldn't score before I was due at work and I'd arrive late, hanging out, with some feeble excuse. I'd spend the next few hours trying to work with my eyes fixed on the door, waiting for Fred to arrive with the smack. With him would come my relief. When he finally got there, I'd quickly make an excuse to go to the toilet so I could have a hit and return to work feeling 'normal'. Soon, once again, it was getting harder to keep up the facade of normality. Heroin became our priority, and we still needed each other in terms of scoring and pooling our money in order to share the smack we bought. Smack is like any commodity: it's more economical to buy in bulk so, rather than only buying a single 'cap' at a time, between the two of us we could buy a gram or two by sharing our resources.

One night while I was waiting on tables at work, my left hip suddenly gave way and I crumpled over, unable to stand up. I couldn't use my left leg at all. I sat down for a while hoping it would magically fix itself, but it didn't improve. Eventually the boss told me to go home and I rang Fred. 'Can you come and pick me up from work? I can't walk, my hip has given way and it's getting really painful.'

After he arrived Fred and a couple of the others helped me out to the car. My hip felt like it was getting worse and the pain was certainly increasing. He took me to the hospital's casualty section where a doctor assessed me and ordered some X-rays. When they showed nothing unusual, the nurses sent me home, telling me to get some painkillers. On the way we bought the strongest painkillers we could find at the chemist and, once home, I propped myself up on the couch. Fred sat nearby watching me, but during the night the pain became unbearable and I continued taking painkillers until I started vomiting. By morning Fred was really worried and decided to take me back to casualty. I still couldn't walk, so they admitted me. By this time I was delirious with pain, so they pulled the curtains around me and a young doctor arrived at my bedside.

I remember thinking what a lovely face he had as he asked me numerous questions, eventually deciding to give me morphine every four hours for the pain. He needed to do a blood test and gently grabbed hold of my arm to prepare a vein for the syringe. I held my breath as I noticed the expression on his face change. He'd seen the track marks and scars. He looked up at me in shock.

'What are these needle marks from?' he asked.

'I use heroin,' I replied quietly, almost hoping he couldn't hear me, anxiously awaiting his reaction.

'Your arms are a mess. Why didn't you tell me about this before?' he said.

'I was too afraid, too ashamed, worried about how you'd react ...' I trailed off.

It took him a long time to find a suitable vein to put a needle into, but while he was searching we talked some more. He was so gentle, caring and nonjudgmental, I couldn't believe it. I expected that once the hospital found out about my heroin addiction, they might even refuse treatment. I'd heard similar stories from friends in Melbourne. I thought at the very least they'd refuse painkillers, particularly morphine. They usually think you're just bluffing the pain to get a free hit, but this doctor believed me and didn't seem to think any less of me for being a heroin addict.

By about the fourth or fifth day the pain began to ease, so they pulled the curtains back from around my bed and for the first time I noticed my surroundings and the other patients in the ward. They were trying not to stare at me, but were obviously curious. Eventually I was discharged from the hospital without ever finding out what was wrong with me, although the doctor suggested that maybe I'd had a 'dirty' hit which had lodged something near my hip. I went back to work at the pub and life returned to the same old routine that we had come so far to escape—working, scoring, selling, using.

After we'd been in Darwin for about six months, my relationship with Fred wasn't improving, so I asked him if he'd agree to some time out. I moved to a bedsitter not far from the pub where I worked. It wasn't what Fred wanted, but he was willing to give it a go and he helped me move. We continued to see each other pretty much daily so it wasn't really that different to living together except that we didn't sleep together any more, which took the pressure off me in terms of the sexual part of the relationship. As it was, we hadn't been spending a lot of time together given that Fred worked at the butcher shop during the day and I worked most nights. The only times we'd been seeing each other were when he'd call into the pub for a drink in the evening and when I got home in the early hours of the morning. In actual fact we simply continued the relationship, without any sex.

Fred and I had made particular friends with another couple, Paula and James, who had already discovered the proximity of Darwin to Malaysia or, more specifically, Penang, which was known to have very pure and cheap heroin. In fact the quality of the heroin in Darwin was much better than in Melbourne or

Sydney, and this was probably the reason why. Paula told us stories about trips she'd made to Malaysia to score, and we were fascinated—not with the place, but with the seeming abundance of heroin there. It was hard to imagine. She was already planning another trip to Penang but didn't have enough money to get there. She asked us if we were interested in contributing to her trip, saying she'd score some heroin for us too.

Fred and I just looked at each other. We didn't even need to go away and discuss it. The thought of plentiful amounts of relatively pure heroin was our wildest fantasy. In our flat in St Kilda we used to have a couple of beanbags as furniture, and we'd daydream that they were filled with caps of heroin rather than polystyrene balls. Each time we wanted a hit we'd just unzip the bag and pull out a cap. That was our dream . . . But this was reality and we were eager.

'Yes, we'd love some,' said Fred in response to Paula's offer. 'Between us, we've got a few hundred in the bank we could put towards your trip.'

'Fantastic!' Paula said with enthusiasm. 'On Monday I'll organise my ticket and go as soon as possible. It's only lack of finance that's been holding me up.'

As soon as the banks opened the following week, Fred and I withdrew our few hundred dollars in savings and handed them over to Paula so that she could leave almost immediately. Over there heroin was about a quarter of the price that we paid in Australia.

We were all feeling exhilarated thinking about the smack we were going to have. I literally bounced into work the next few days, I was so excited at the prospect of an ounce or two of heroin to keep us going for a while. We'd sell some of it to our local drug-using friends and maintain our habits with the remainder. We also planned ahead, deciding that before we ran out, one of the other three of us would go over and get some more, then another one, thus maintaining our supply. With four of us it shouldn't be too obvious, and we'd be able to maintain our habits quite economically for a while. We'd never been this organised.

I could feel myself getting more and more excited. I couldn't wait for my turn to go. It was all very fascinating, this talk of drugs in strange lands. It's funny how differently heroin addicts see their drug use compared to the police or some of the 'straight' community. We rarely thought much about the danger, or the fact that it was illegal, which of course made us 'criminals' even though we did everything behind closed doors or in laneways. You become desensitised to it, and just accept that's how it is. We'd only think about our desperate physical and psychological craving, and the fact that this drug could provide some happiness or, at the very least, satisfy our emotional neediness to some extent. It gave us a sense of belonging, a sense of community, and because the outside world seemed opposed to us, we became even more cohesive. The game, really, was about survival.

The only real anxiety we felt about the Malaysia adventure was Paula getting through customs on her return. A few weeks later the three of us were beside ourselves with anticipation driving out to the airport to meet her. After she cleared customs, she came through the doors to see us waiting there. She had a huge smile on her face so we knew we'd all been lucky. We hugged each other with exuberance, then walked casually to the car, not wanting to attract any attention just in case someone was watching.

'Let's hurry and get home,' Paula said as she plonked herself in the back seat. 'I need a hit real bad, I'm hanging out.'

'Where have you hidden it?' I asked her naively.

'It's up my arse, wrapped in plastic, and I'd really like to get it out,' she replied, screwing up her face.

'Doesn't it hurt?' I was intrigued to think that you could fit something like that up there. I shuddered at the thought of the pain. 'How big is it?'

'No, it doesn't hurt and it's really only a small parcel,' Paula explained. 'It hurts trying to push it up there, but once it's there, no worries.' She really didn't look like she was in pain.

'How are you going to get it out?' I asked her.

'How do you reckon?' she replied sarcastically. With that I didn't ask any more questions as I was starting to feel like a real dummy.

We arrived at her place and she immediately went to the toilet where I could only guess she was trying to use her bowel muscles to push the package out. Didn't bear thinking about, really. Besides, by now I was exclusively focused on what came next and that was to celebrate with a big hit! It took twenty minutes or so for the four of us to go through the ritual of mixing up a hit and injecting it, but then we sat there nodding off like we didn't have a worry in the world. I guess, right at that moment, we didn't.

A couple of months later we'd run out of dope and it was James's turn to go to Malaysia. A few more months on, it was mine. I'd never travelled outside Australia before, apart from the six months in New Zealand with Fred, so it was an exciting prospect even aside from the smack. I waved them all goodbye at the airport and up into the sky I went on my way to Singapore. I was both nervous and excited as I boarded the plane, but I didn't have anything to worry about on the flight over, except that by the time I arrived in Singapore I would be hanging out. I'd already decided I wasn't going to try scoring in Singapore because, as far as I knew, they shot you there for heroin-related offences, plus Paula didn't have a contact there, so I faced the fact that I was going to be sick. It wasn't worth the risk of looking for a street dealer.

I had to stay overnight at the YWCA until the next plane

left for Kuala Lumpur the following morning. It was an uncomfortable night, but it was made easier by the knowledge that, once I arrived in Kuala Lumpur, I'd be meeting a contact of Paula's, a guy called Rahim, who would be able to score some heroin for me. Apparently he was the manager of a cheap hotel there, so I'd be staying for a few days to have a look around, act like a tourist and enjoy getting stoned, then I'd fly to Penang where heroin is the same quality but cheaper, and I'd look for our contact to buy a larger amount, a few grams, that I'd take back to Darwin.

I arrived in Kuala Lumpur and took a taxi to the hotel. There Rahim took me to a vacant room which was to be my home for the next few days. He was Indian and, because of Paula's recommendation, I knew that he was okay. Once he had shown me into my room and closed the door behind us, I desperately asked him if he could score for me. I was hanging out badly by this time and he could see the urgency of my situation. Although he seemed a bit paranoid at the mention of illicit drugs, he agreed. I handed over some money and tried to relax, knowing that the wait was on but also confident that soon the pain would be over. He was friendly and I felt quite safe having him look after things. He even tried to feed me some fresh fruit, but I wasn't interested in anything except a hit. I tried my best to be patient, but the waiting always seems eternal when you're hanging out, and I couldn't relax until I felt that heroin hit my veins and loosen the knots and sickness in my stomach. I was also sweating profusely and had goosebumps all over my skin.

After a couple of hours I heard a knock at the door and then his most welcome voice. 'Helen, are you there?' he asked. I just about tripped over myself to open the door and let him in. I could tell by the suspicious way he was acting that he had the smack. He came in and sat down but he looked worried—after all he was a 'straight' person who probably thought more rationally about his freedom than I did. Of course if anything happened, I'd take the rap for it anyway. I couldn't understand why people worried so much although, I must say, all 'straight' (as in non-using) dealers are like that. It's as if they think their lives are more precious than ours, so they're always more cautious and careful, knowing the risks. Besides, their actions aren't driven by an all-consuming addiction to the drug.

I grabbed the plastic straws of heroin greedily. Rahim had also been able to get me a syringe, which was more difficult to buy there than in Australia. The conversation ceased until I had successfully mixed up and injected the smack. I could sense him watching me as I put a portion of the powder in a spoon then added a few drops of vinegar, which he'd also been able to supply, and a bit of water. This particular heroin, known as brown rocks, won't dissolve unless it has some vinegar or lemon juice in it, unlike the white powder heroin from Thailand, which only requires water. I held the mixture over a cigarette lighter flame to heat and dissolve the substance, then sucked it up into the syringe. I reached for a belt and wrapped it tightly around my upper arm, focused now on the task of finding a vein. I was lucky this time, finding one on my first attempt, and slowly I released the substance into my bloodstream. With that completed, I looked up triumphantly. Rahim appeared intrigued, and I realised we hadn't spoken for some time.

'Oh, that feels good,' I said. 'Thanks a million.'

Instantly I felt okay, relaxed and peaceful. The heroin was strong, much stronger than in Australia, and I only had to use a relatively small amount to get really stoned. No more hanging out on this trip—I was in heroin heaven and now I felt fantastic. I immediately forgot all the pain and sweating I'd just experienced.

Rahim turned out to be a nice guy. After I'd had my heroin

fix and a shower, I was in the mood for talking and he seemed genuinely interested in me.

'What sort of work do you do?' he asked me curiously.

'I work in a pub,' I told him.

'What wages do you earn?' he asked. He was interested in going to Australia for a trip himself; our wages were much better than in Malaysia and our living conditions were better too.

He seemed fascinated by my life in Australia, but had difficulty understanding my desperate need for heroin as he didn't use the stuff himself. I didn't tell him about my lack of confidence and self-esteem; it didn't seem the time or place to be delving into intimate details with a stranger. Besides, I didn't understand why I was like this either. I don't know why he was willing to score for people like Paula and me, although it was common knowledge that English, American and Australian girls were popular there. Maybe there was a bit of profit in it for him; wages were terrible in Malaysia. In the illicit drug world you soon learned not to ask questions.

Over the next few days we spent a lot of time together. In fact we got along really well and eventually sort of slid into a sexual relationship. I hadn't been sexually active for such a long time, heroin suppressing my libido, but I actually enjoyed the change. I guess in a way I felt like repaying him and sex seemed like a satisfactory arrangement. Besides, he was kind and loving and I enjoyed his company while in Kuala Lumpur. Before I left we arranged for me to return there on my way home from Penang, before continuing on to Singapore.

'I'll see you in ten days,' I said to him as I set out for the airport. I felt a bit sad leaving him, but at the same time I was excited to be seeing some more of the country; also, I had enough heroin to fill any emotional hole. Nothing like a hit to kill the pain! I didn't realise it at the time, but I was very disconnected from my feelings, knowing that I always had heroin to fall back on if things got too difficult, or if I was feeling too uncomfortable or confused. It seemed to fix everything.

It felt like a real adventure as I boarded the plane to Penang. Paula also had a contact there who I was supposed to find in an opium den. Because I wasn't hanging out and so didn't need to score, I was able to fully enjoy the rest of my trip. As I walked around Penang young guys would stop me in the street to ask if I wanted to buy hashish, opium, heroin or one of a numerous array of other drugs they reeled off in English. At first I couldn't believe how open these young people were about peddling drugs, but I was happy as I realised I would have no problem scoring. In the 1970s in Malaysia, drugs didn't have much of a media profile and didn't carry a death sentence. Heroin users travelling to Asian countries were as yet relatively unknown, so I felt fairly safe. I'd also been told that the police were quite corrupt: if you got busted, chances were you could pay your way out of trouble.

I went in search of the opium den where I was supposed to find my contact but, alas, I never found him or the den, even with the hand-drawn map Paula had given me. I don't seem to have any sense of direction and often find myself lost, although I'm usually all right with a map. I didn't worry too much because there was obviously no shortage of people to score drugs from. The main problem would be trying to suss out someone who wasn't a police informer. Apparently a lot of people there were paid police informers, but I was just going to have to trust my gut feelings on that one and hope that I was lucky. From what I'd learned from Paula, at least the quality of the heroin was always good.

It was September–October and during my ten days in Penang I got to know some locals and generally had a ball. One guy took me to Batuferringi, which is now the main tourist beach, and we spent a day and night there, sleeping out in the open. It was a beautiful tropical beach just like you see in travel brochures, but as a tourist I wasn't really doing much sightseeing. I had a hit every few hours, so I was stoned all the time. The young guy I was with smoked the heroin that he was scoring for me and was intrigued watching me go through the ritual of hitting up with a syringe, eventually trying it himself. He was impressed with the instant rush he got when it hit his bloodstream. Because smack was very cheap and very pure, there was little to stress about, unlike the usual problems of scoring back home. I wasn't really all that keen to return to Australia, although I knew I had to.

My new friend put me in contact with another guy who he said was trustworthy and wouldn't rip me off or dob me in to the police; he would also be able to acquire the heroin I needed to take back to Australia. I didn't have much choice but to trust him. My friend could only access smaller amounts. The three of us took the best part of a day to score my hundred grams, being taken here, there and everywhere, I think to avoid the police. Before the transaction was made I tried a sample to check the quality. No doubt it was very good. With my prize, and my time in Penang over, I flew back to Kuala Lumpur for my final few days with Rahim. We really did get along together very well, even though we knew it was impossible to take the relationship further. I knew I'd miss his kind, smiling face, and I was even enjoying our sexual relationship, something I'd ignored for so long, lack of desire being a side effect of heroin. I was also aware that I would probably never see him again because there were only so many trips you could make to Malaysia without raising suspicion. If I returned, it wouldn't be for some time. Paula, James, Fred and I had only planned one trip each, not looking any further ahead than that. So we were both sad when I left his cheap hotel.

During my stopover in Singapore I had to do the serious

business of hiding the heroin safely. To come from Malaysia to Singapore I'd just stashed it in my underwear, feeling certain that I wouldn't be searched. It seemed like a Melbourne to Sydney trip to me, and Paula had said that I needn't be concerned. However, my return to Australia was a worry and I wasn't looking forward to hiding the smack, even though Paula had assured me it wouldn't hurt.

Once in Singapore, I went to the privacy of my YWCA room and had my last hit before leaving. I then packaged the heroin up into a small, tube-like parcel and made sure it was well covered in plastic. I had to admit, Paula was right: it was a very small package. It took a bit of time and self-talk to work up the courage to give it a try, but I had a plane to catch so I couldn't muck around for too long. I tried a few pushes up my back passage and, let me tell you, she lied about this one! It hurt like hell, but the rest of her story proved true. Once it was safely up there I couldn't even feel it. I immediately turned my mind to trying to get it back out when I arrived home in Australia, but I couldn't bear the thought. I knew in the end my overwhelming desire to use the drug would win out and force me into prompt action. When I was satisfied that I had it well secured so that I wouldn't get caught, I went to catch my flight home.

At the airport I experienced my first rush of anxiety as the reality of what I was about to do hit me. It was like a charge of electricity surging through my body, but I didn't even consider pulling out. I was almost home and there was no way I was going to let the others down. Besides, I'd already decided this was going to be the only time I'd go through with this because I couldn't imagine ever having anything reside in my back passage again! I was comforted, though, by the thought that even if I was pulled in by customs and searched, they weren't going to find anything. Paula was right—it was the best hiding place.

I was mindful that I needed to look relaxed and 'normal', so I bought a book and some magazines and generally tried to look like a typical tourist. I'd bought a few souvenirs and presents for the others so I was pretty confident of pulling it off. I boarded the plane without any problems and read my book for most of the flight back until, a few hours later, the pilot announced that we were about to land; then my stomach lurched and I felt like I was going to have a bout of diarrhoea—well, I'm afraid that was out of the question! I tried hard to contain my nerves and apprehension, and instead just look forward to seeing Fred, Paula and James again. I knew how excited and anxious they'd be—in fact they'd be there waiting right now as the plane was landing.

When I got off the plane and walked into the customs area I knew I had to pretend that I was just another tourist returning from a trip overseas. It turned out to be easy as I wasn't left waiting long and was able to feign calmness without any problem. I walked through that gate with elation written all over my face.

The others were, of course, incredibly happy and relieved to see me and soon we were driving home. The only problem was, now I had to get the bloody package out. My friends kept me busy talking about my trip all the way home and when we arrived I went immediately to the toilet to see what I could do. I didn't want to keep them waiting and I knew I'd feel really stupid if I couldn't get it out! However, all my worries proved unfounded—with one big push, out came the prize. I sat on the toilet and wondered if that was what giving birth felt like ... but as the others were waiting impatiently in the lounge room, this was no time for pondering.

Soon we were all having a hit and nodding off.

6

The shadow of heroin addiction

I'd returned to Darwin with a huge habit, the biggest I'd ever had. We sold some of our smack to finance the next trip, which was Fred's, and used the remainder. We had all but run out by the time he left for Malaysia. Unfortunately, within days of him going a drought hit town—drug drought that is—and no-one could score. The whole town was hanging out and I was so sick I couldn't even make it to work. I had to phone them and make up an excuse. I couldn't even get out of bed without vomiting, and Fred wouldn't be back for another three weeks. It struck me that, far from getting off heroin, our habits had increased enormously since we'd arrived in Darwin. I was sick of it all; sick of my relationship with Fred not going anywhere, sick from hanging out, and sick of living in this hell. I was impatient and needed something to change, but I didn't know what.

Even though there was bound to be some heroin around before Fred got back, financially I had no hope of sustaining my raging habit for the next three weeks. Because Fred was away, I couldn't even reach him by phone. I was in my little flat perspiring, shaking and vomiting, and I'd never felt so alone or desperate. I'd never been so sick from hanging out. I decided to ring my brother in Melbourne—they say misery loves company and I just needed to share my problems with someone. I went to the public phone with some change and, for the first time, I told Ron about my heroin use. Until now I'd kept it a secret from all of my family. Although he was shocked, he was also supportive and I felt comforted emotionally and not as alone in the world, even if I was still sick. He was my brother, but more than that, he was a sort of parent. After we'd talked for a while he said kindly, 'If you want any help just ring me and ask, okay?' I'd never really thought of asking for help for my addiction. I don't think I'd ever seriously thought of giving up heroin, I usually just wanted the pressure of scoring, hiding and lack of money to go away. The fact was, that was probably also the truth then.

'Thanks, Ron. I was hoping you wouldn't turn against me,' I replied, feeling somewhat lighter to at least have the secret out in the open.

'I wouldn't say anything to Mum,' he went on. 'She's quite sick and there's no need to worry her unduly. It would probably only make her feel stressed and there's nothing she can do to help you anyway,' he added.

'Yeah, good idea,' I said to him. 'I wasn't planning on telling her anyway.'

'Don't forget to ring if you need anything.'

''Bye ... and thanks for listening to me,' I said as I hung up the phone and stood for a while in silence.

Although his support comforted me, it didn't change the fact that physically I was a wreck and I'd run out of money and heroin. There was no relief in sight. I continued on for another week, scoring small amounts which only just prevented me from hanging out, until totally fed up and sick yet again, I made another call to Ron. This time I asked him for help.

'Ron, I don't know what to do ... I feel terrible. I'm so

sick of using, scoring and hanging out. I need help! The relationship with Fred's not working out either. I don't even live
with him any more.' I knew I was sounding desperate, but I just
felt so miserable and destitute. I think my state of mind shocked
him a bit as he'd never seen the ugly side of heroin use; he'd
never seen any side of heroin use. I omitted to tell him that Fred
was in Malaysia scoring.

'Give me some time,' he said into the phone. 'I'll see what
I can find out about drug rehabilitation programs available here
in Melbourne. I'll ring you back as soon as I have some information, okay?'

'That'd be great,' I replied. 'I'll talk to you soon.'

Within a day or two Ron had bought my air ticket and
booked me into Gresswell, a government-funded drug rehabilitation centre in Melbourne which provided methadone to
addicts. Methadone is a legally prescribed drug that is opiate
based. Used as a substitute for heroin, it can stop you hanging
out within half an hour of taking it. I'd only ever tried it on the
black market as a means to stop hanging out when I couldn't
score. Gresswell's wasn't a residential program, but one where
you went every day to take your methadone in linctus form, so
you had to drink it rather than inject it. One of the reasons they
use the ingestion method was to get you out of the habit of
hitting up. They also offered counselling and support. Beyond
that Ron didn't know much about the program, but right now
it sounded okay to me. The methadone program had no set time
limit, each participant being assessed on an individual basis. Some
people remained on methadone for years, although I really only
wanted to stabilise on a dose, then gradually reduce until I was
drug-free. I thought it might take a few months if I went well.

I asked my friends in Darwin to let Fred know where I was
when he returned from Malaysia. Two days later I packed my
things and boarded the flight. It seemed to take a long time to

reach Melbourne, but eventually I found myself walking from the plane to meet Ron in the airport arrivals lounge. He gave me a big hug then we headed for the car park. Unfortunately, I was sweaty and sick from hanging out because the small amount I'd been able to afford to buy before I left had only held me for a couple of hours, so I felt like shit. The only positive side to the last few weeks was that my lack of access to the large amounts of good quality heroin my body had gotten used to meant my tolerance level had come back down. I needed to work up enough courage to ask Ron a tricky question. The fact was, I needed to score badly.

As we were driving from the airport, the desperate words tumbled out of my mouth: 'Ron, do you think we could stop in St Kilda so I can score a hit of smack? I'm already feeling sick and it's going to get worse during the night.' I felt embarrassed asking him, but the sweating and the thought of hanging out all night outweighed my anxiety at placing him in this position.

'Is that the only place you can get it?' he asked.

'Well, I haven't been in Melbourne for a long time, so it's the most likely place for me to find someone quickly,' I replied. 'I need to borrow $50 from you, too, please? I don't have much money on me,' I said, feeling like I was pushing my luck a bit. I had very little money with me because I'd given almost every-thing I had to Fred for his Malaysian trip, and I didn't want to tell Ron about it, not yet anyway.

'Yes, of course,' he said kindly. 'I don't want you to be sick all night. Just tell me where to drive to in St Kilda.'

When we reached Fitzroy Street, it only took me a few minutes to find a familiar face to score from. Things don't change much in the drug scene. Except for deaths, of which there are many, and imprisonment, which occurs frequently, many of the faces remain the same from one year to the next, just looking increasingly haggard as each year passes—at least for those lucky enough to survive the experience. I returned to Ron's car and we resumed the drive to Suzanne's, his girlfriend's place, where I was going to stay for at least a couple of weeks while I settled in. Ron had his own apartment in St Kilda but stayed most nights at Suzanne's, and he thought it would be better for me there. I was also too vulnerable to stay in St Kilda, where I would run into all my drug-using friends daily. Ron's compassion amazed me because I assumed this illegal drug world would freak him out. He only drinks alcohol occasionally and doesn't even smoke cigarettes! (Although, amazingly, I've never smoked cigarettes either; I always hated the smell. I was the only heroin addict I knew that didn't smoke.)

When we arrived at Suzanne's I immediately went to the spare room where I mixed up my hit. It didn't make me stoned but it was enough to stop the withdrawals for a while, allowing me to get some sleep. By the time we woke up and got ready to leave for the drug rehabilitation centre early the next morning, I was sick again. I couldn't wait to get there because I knew that, once the assessment was over and I got my dose of methadone, the physical pain would end. I longed for the relief.

After driving for forty-five minutes to Bundoora, about eighteen kilometres north-east of Melbourne, we arrived at Gresswell. It was part of a medical complex that included Mont Park, a public hospital, and Larundal, a public psychiatric hospital which had a forest wildlife reserve surrounding it. Soon after walking into the building I was called in by a worker to commence the assessment process. Ron went off to work then, promising to pick me up later. Because I was hanging out, the assessment really tested my patience. The questions seemed endless and I wasn't in much condition to answer them; at the same time I knew I had to in order for them to assess what dose to start me on. The larger the heroin habit, the more milligrams of methadone prescribed by the doctor. I knew I'd require a relatively high dose, but it was imperative that they find out precisely what I'd been using: if they prescribed too large a dose, a person could overdose or, alternatively, be very stoned, which wasn't the purpose of methadone at all. It was merely meant to substitute for the amount of heroin you'd been using which, in effect, would just make you appear 'normal'. If they prescribed too small a dose, you'd still experience withdrawal symptoms.

'When did you last have a hit?' the worker asked.

'Last night. Just a little one, though,' I replied.

'How much do you use?' she asked, 'and how often, how many hits a day?'

'Lots,' I responded, 'and several times a day, depending on how much is available.'

'How pure is the heroin?' She kept it up, and it felt like the questions were never going to stop.

'Very pure,' I replied, 'I've just come down from Darwin.' I assumed she would know something about the heroin there.

'When did you arrive?' she asked.

Who cares?, I thought to myself. I just wanted treatment.

It seemed like part of the process was to see how you looked when you were hanging out. I thought it was pointless, although I guess they wanted to make sure you weren't lying about being addicted to heroin. I was growing more impatient. I had to do a 'supervised urine', which meant a worker or nurse standing in the doorway of the toilet while I pissed into a jar. Fortunately, she turned her face the other way so she wasn't really watching me. Once I was on methadone I'd have to go there every day to pick up my dose and drink it in front of them, and twice a week I'd have to do supervised urines so they could check to see if I was using any other drugs. Once a week I'd have to stay for counselling. The value of methadone as a treatment drug was that, unlike heroin, it would 'hold' you (that is, prevent you from hanging out) for at least twenty-four hours. The staff there said that, once you were stabilised, it would even remain effective for up to forty-eight hours, which was useful to know just in case you ever missed a day's dose for some reason.

Finally, later in the afternoon, I got my dose of methadone and I soon began to feel like some sort of human being again. Ron arrived to pick me up and return me to Suzanne's house. I settled into not using, although my mind kept turning to Fred and the heroin he'd be bringing back; as his arrival date loomed closer, it became something I would have to deal with, even if only to collect my share of the money.

On the day Fred returned to Darwin, I rang him from Melbourne. Of course he was shocked when he found I wasn't there, but I told him how sick I'd been after he'd left and he understood how hard it must have been for me. We had to sort a few things out, like whether we were actually still in a relationship or not so, after a week and another couple of phone calls, he decided to come to Melbourne. He'd given Paula and James their share of the heroin and had retained our half, minus what he'd been using. I had mixed feelings about his arrival, more particularly about having all that relatively pure heroin around; I was less concerned about our relationship. I was really trying on the methadone, though, and I was determined not to use with him. I'd finished with heroin . . .

Fred arrived and I maintained my stance about not using. We decided to sell some of our heroin to a friend who would also use some and sell some; Fred kept the rest for his own use. At least I got my money back, even if it was only a few hundred dollars. It was something to live on until I decided what I was going to do next. Each day Fred would call in to see me at Suzanne's while she and Ron were at work. He'd mix up his hit right in front of me, but I didn't relent. I felt strong and I wasn't going to use, even though it was such pure smack part of me saw it as a missed opportunity. We didn't do much talking about our relationship, but in a strange sort of way I felt comforted having him there. It was nice to have someone around who was familiar with drug use, because Ron and Suzanne knew nothing about it. It was difficult to talk to straight people about addiction because they couldn't understand how out of your control it was, how the craving dictated your every move.

I was enjoying Fred's company, but each day when he came over he'd have a hit in front of me and for some reason I just tried to ignore it instead of asking him not to. Day after day I'd watch him go through the familiar process that had come to dominate our lives for the last three years. I could smell it when he heated up the mixture in the spoon. It made me feel sick and I dry retched as the smell filled my lungs. It was like when you have your first hit, then vomit almost immediately afterward. Vomiting on heroin doesn't have the negative connotations that straight people might associate with it. It's probably one of those things that only heroin users understand, but the smell of the heroin 'cooking' produced something like a body memory of my first hit. It was so hard not to give in, especially as Fred looked so peaceful as he nodded off after hitting up.

One day when Fred was around mixing up a hit as usual, I went to the toilet and sat there for a few minutes thinking about it, arguing with myself because I really did want to stay strong, I really did want to change my life. As I walked out of the bathroom and looked over to Fred, though, I knew I'd made the decision. I just couldn't bear watching him any more.

'Can you give me some? I want to have a hit,' I said, a tone of resignation in my voice.

'Are you sure?' he replied, although I could tell from the look on his face that he was relieved in a strange sort of way. He wasn't accustomed to using without me.

'Yep, I'm sure. Come on, just give me some before I think about it any more.' I was impatient now. If I didn't do it quickly

I might have changed my mind again; now that I'd decided, I just wanted to feel it in my veins. I could sense him watching me as I mixed up a hit and pierced a vein with the syringe. The rush was immediate; all those conflicting, confused thoughts—wanting to use, wanting to be straight—just disappeared, like water down a plughole.

'Oh ... yes,' I groaned as I sat there, my head falling forward. I regained consciousness about an hour later, opening my eyes slowly. It was the best I'd felt in a long time. Heroin has the ability to release all troubled thoughts from your mind, making you feel like everything is balanced again. The downside is that this feeling only lasts for about six hours, after which time the anxiety comes back. And if you don't score within eight hours, you'll be hanging out. But for the two to four hours after a hit, none of these niggling thoughts intrude. It's similar to an overweight person intending to go on a diet; they usually find the motivation for dieting soon after gorging themselves on food, comforted by their full stomach. It doesn't really matter what the addiction is, the thoughts and behaviour are similar.

'Shit, that feels good!' I said to Fred, who nodded his head in acknowledgment. It felt like a long time since I'd had that feeling, yet it had only been about three weeks. I had another hit that night and more the next day, and there I was on the merry-go-round again. I was twenty-three years old and nothing had changed.

I started sneaking other people's urine into Gresswell, hidden in a jar down the front of my pants to keep it warm; the workers would have been suspicious if the jar felt cold when I handed it to them. When I went to the toilet to do my compulsory urine sample, it was quite tricky to transfer it to the jar they'd issued while they were standing outside, but usually they only looked at you directly a couple of times while you were actually sitting on the toilet. I think most of the workers found the process of watching people having a pee almost as humiliating as we did, and so they didn't stare at us in the way that they were really supposed to. This meant that I could, with some difficulty, get the false urine into the Gresswell jar. It helped if I covered my jar with Glad Wrap, which I could pierce with my finger relatively easily.

I felt that I'd be punished if they discovered my 'dirty urines', and I didn't want to get kicked off the program. I don't really know that they would have gone that far, but I wasn't thinking very rationally and didn't want to test it. From their point of view it was dangerous to have people using heroin on top of their methadone dose as it increased the likelihood of overdose. Being on methadone also meant that I had to use a larger amount of heroin to feel the 'rush' and achieve a stoned feeling, both drugs being opiate based. Once you are stabilised on methadone, you build up a tolerance to the level of your particular dose; the result is that you merely feel 'normal' rather than experiencing the highs and lows that heroin induces. Also, because you drink the dose, you don't get the instant 'rush' of the drug into your bloodstream, but it does prevent you from hanging out for at least twenty-four hours after you've taken it, which is its advantage.

Of course, as always, a few weeks after Fred's return to Melbourne the heroin ran out and we were soon going to be short of money. We were forced to look at our current situation, something we'd managed to avoid up until then. I knew in my heart that we couldn't break free of heroin addiction while we were together, and so did he, even though we didn't want to admit it. For the first time, though, we talked seriously about our relationship and the situation we were in once again. Finally, we agreed to break up even though technically we'd ended the relationship months ago in Darwin. Fred decided he'd go home to New Zealand and get straight, and I was going to remain in

Melbourne on the methadone program. It was some sort of relief to have made a decision about our relationship, but I also felt heavy and sad, like I was losing a part of me.

About a week later, we drove out to the airport in Ron's car, neither of us saying much. We stood there in silence holding each other, almost afraid to let go, then I waved him goodbye as I watched him walk towards the departure lounge doors that closed behind him as he disappeared from sight. My heart felt like it had a heavy weight dragging it down and tears formed in my eyes. I wanted to release them and let them flow, but instead I took a deep breath and let out a big sigh. I felt that if I allowed myself to cry it would increase my feeling of sadness. I didn't realise that releasing tears could actually assist in dealing with these emotions. In my whole life I'd never seen my mother or father cry. Now that I was an adult I guess I felt that, like them, it was no longer appropriate. Only children cry.

With a huge lump in my throat I turned and walked towards the automatic doors leading out of the airport to the car park, trying to console myself with rationalisations about the end of our relationship. I already missed Fred and he hadn't even taken off yet. There was no doubt the romance had long gone from our relationship and I knew Fred had been unhappy about it for some time too. Although we were still friends, we knew we were probably not good for each other right now. It was doubly hard, though, because we were not only saying goodbye to each other, we were trying to say goodbye to our whole lifestyle. It was such a struggle internally and it hurt. We'd spent so much time together, more than three years, but the truth was, we hadn't been lovers for a long time—it was the heroin that continued to bind us together, not love.

We stayed in contact by phone while Fred was in New Zealand. After only a short time he seemed to have settled in well, had a job and was having a lot more success than I was staying clean. I was quite envious of him when we'd talk on the phone: I was struggling on the methadone program and, because I felt lonely without Fred, I was increasingly seeing old friends, particularly Danni and Chipper, and using with them. I don't know why, but I certainly wasn't talking in any meaningful way to Ron or the counsellors at Gresswell. I felt like I was trying hard, but the goal of being heroin free seemed increasingly unattainable at that stage. Although I thought I was committed to not using, the fact was, heroin was the best painkiller I knew. Maybe that's why I wasn't talking to Ron or the counsellors, maybe I didn't want to hear their rational explanations for my behaviour. Honesty can seem too brutal sometimes and the thought of being a failure in their eyes, even at the meagre goal of drug rehabilitation (it seemed meagre in comparison to school, calisthenics and piano), was just unacceptable to me—I didn't want to face up to it.

In only a few weeks I went from catching up with Danni and using occasionally to calling into Chipper and her girlfriend Marie's house on a daily basis. Their place just happened to be in a suburb which was on the route to Gresswell, and because they were selling to maintain their own habits, they were quite generous, often giving me a free hit. Mind you, I was only having one hit nearly every day so I didn't require a large amount. Marie was able to get someone to pee in a jar for me, which meant I wouldn't get sprung with dirty urines.

Chipper had been a close friend from the time Fred and I started using. I still enjoyed her company, and I trusted her. Only a couple of years older than me, she was quite small with dark hair and an outwardly tough manner. She'd been in the drug scene and working down at Fitzroy Street as a prostitute since she was about twelve, trying each night to get money to score so that she would be stoned enough to work. It seemed like she'd had to fend for herself all her life. She had a certain crag-giness about her, and you could tell from the many scars on her body that she had taken a lot of beatings; she'd been raped and bashed countless times while working the street. She had also been abused as a child and had been a ward of the state; she was no stranger to institutions and had been in prison a few times already. She didn't have much respect for men and had been in a relationship with Marie for a couple of years.

Chipper had trouble finding her veins, just like me, because the ones in our arms had all collapsed. She and I would often take an hour or two to have our hit. We both had to search for a vein in some other location such as our hands, feet, ankles or legs—anywhere there was a little bluish coloured bulge. The upside of this situation was that we didn't have the fresh scars on our arms where heroin addicts are known to repeatedly hit up. It was useful if you were pulled up by the police because the only place they checked for telltale signs of using was your arms. Despite everything Chipper had suffered, she had a cheekiness about her and the cutest face that you just wanted to squeeze. We'd laugh a lot and I found her easy to talk to.

Marie was a nurse and she was trying hard to keep it together for work, but it had been getting harder for her, too, as heroin took control of her life. She didn't want to lose her job. I spent a lot of time with both of them and, really, it was a big ask to expect me to give up the companionship of my trusted friends. Therein lies the difficulty of trying to break free of heroin addic-tion: it's not just the drug that you have to give up, it's also your friends. For most people the void between giving up herion and commencing a new life with new friends and interests is just too bleak and lonely. For someone accustomed to the instant grati-fication of drug use, it takes far too long.

Meanwhile, each day the staff at Gresswell seemed more interested in catching me out with dirty urine than in knowing how I was feeling, not that I would've told them anyway. I'm sure they had their suspicions because, other than picking up my methadone, I wasn't participating in the program in a committed way. My 'counselling' sessions were brief and I'd avoid them whenever possible. I often left there in tears of frustration, although not until I'd walked out of the centre. I didn't feel comfortable showing them how I was really feeling. I didn't want them to know and yet I blamed them for not understanding me. I'm sure it felt that way because I was being consistently dishonest with them. I was confused because I wanted to succeed but was failing dismally. My psychological craving for heroin was overwhelming and it had become, yet again, my best friend. It never let me down, always comforting me.

Instead of being honest with the staff, I kept using and then submitting false urines. Ironically, on the odd occasion when I could do a legitimate urine (it takes seventy-two hours for heroin to be out of your system), I was just too anxious to piss into the jar, especially with them standing in front of me watching. Every time this happened they assumed it was because I'd been using and didn't want to get caught out. Some days I'd have to hang around for two or more hours just trying to do a urine, and the more I tried, the more I just couldn't do it. Of course, they were right most of the time, but I needed their support, not resistance. At the time I didn't realise how much I wanted to blame someone else for my pending sense of failure. My feelings of guilt because of my dishonesty kept me ashamed of myself—it was a no-win situation. If I wasn't going to be honest with them, how could they help me?

Anyway, I found it all very unhelpful as it seemed they only ever focused on the drug use and urines. I don't think they ever asked me *why* I used, not that I would have known the answer then anyway. I have a firm belief, even today, that methadone—or any drug-replacement—programs can only be successful in the long term if they contain a counselling component. If you merely focus on the drug, you never reach the underlying causes of why someone is abusing it. It's like trying to treat a person who repeatedly slashes their wrists by giving them bandaids and nothing else: you'll never get to the cause that way.

At least I did get myself some paid receptionist work. Ron had been able to get me a month's locum work at his advertising agency to fill in for their receptionist, who was on annual leave. After that I managed to get some other locum jobs, which at least gave me an income. I also bought another old car on hire purchase, with Mum agreeing to go guarantor again. Initially, we hadn't told her I'd returned to Melbourne as I wasn't sure how long I'd be staying, but it seemed like I'd be there for a while, so I went to visit her to tell her I'd come back.

Also around this time I came into contact with one of the guys who'd been a roadie when I was in the band TRAMM. He was a salesman now and we started seeing each other socially. He'd never had anything to do with drugs so it was all new to him. I'd often ring him from Gresswell in tears after another upset with the staff there: 'Neville, I need to see you,' I'd sob into the phone, barely able to put two sentences together, I felt so desperate.

'I'm on the road, not too far away,' he'd say, 'Can you wait there for about half an hour? I just have to see one more client then I can drive over to see you.'

'Yeah, I can wait,' I'd reply, still crying. 'I'll be out the front near the phones.'

'Okay, just try and stay calm. I'll be there as soon as I can.'

I'd feel so relieved when I saw his car approach; I'd get in and then we'd drive to a spot under some trees. He'd cuddle me and make me feel safe and cared for, and he'd listen while I protested about how unfair it was that the Gresswell staff didn't believe me. I just couldn't admit that I was creating this conflict myself and that it wasn't the staff's fault. I saw them as the enemy and I was locked into self-pity. Why couldn't I admit I just wasn't ready to give up using heroin? Neville was very patient and loving. We'd talk for about an hour and then, when I felt okay again, he'd return to work. Once I felt better, on the days I wasn't working and with nothing else to do, I'd drive straight to Chipper's house and score and use with her and Marie.

I decided to ring a couple of my old friends from TRAMM, as a result of which I met with Pete and told him the whole story. He listened as I revealed the drama that had been my life for the last couple of years, and he seemed relieved at finally being able to understand what had happened to me and why my personality had changed. He went away and talked to his partner, Wayne, with whom he shared a flat, and later they asked me if I would like to stay with them as they had a spare bedroom. I knew they were genuine, even though I couldn't understand why they'd be so keen to try and help me.

I thought about it for a week or so, trying to weigh up my current options. Unfortunately I wasn't in a very stable state of mind, but I could still muster up some rational thoughts occasionally. It had been about eight weeks since I'd started the methadone program and Fred had gone back to New Zealand. I was still based at Ron's girlfriend's place, but was increasingly staying the night at Chipper and Marie's, particularly when I was stoned. I didn't ever want Ron and Suzanne to see me in that state, but it also spoilt the 'fun' of being stoned if you had to try and act straight. I'd pretty much decided to remain in Melbourne for a while and I was aware that it would be helpful to stay in a 'straight' environment with friends who cared about me so much. Pete and I had been close when we were singing in the band, and so it felt like a good option. I knew I'd have plenty of support from both him and Wayne, so I decided to take up their offer. David, Annie and Jan, all from the old band, also spent some time with me during the next three or fours months, helping me through the long days and nights without drugs ... well, perhaps not without drugs, but at least with a reduced heroin intake. The conflict inside me never ceased—wanting to use/wanting to stop. Although I still felt anxious and confused, I also felt quite blessed to have these beautiful people as friends, as well as Ron.

I continued going out with Neville, the ex-roadie, for a few weeks, but emotionally I was all over the place and I think I frightened him off. I needed him so much and wanted someone to love as much as I wanted to be loved, but I didn't have much love to give. I usually seemed to be in a highly anxious or negative state in relation to either the methadone program or my heroin use and most of my energy was being consumed by the conflict, leaving little time and space for loving or positive thoughts. Besides, he was still married, and although when we'd started going out he'd said his marriage was over and he was in the process of finding another place to live, he didn't seem to be progressing in that direction. I realised he was probably lying about his marriage, but in any case he didn't hang around for too long and I didn't blame him. I was disappointed and hurt, though, because he just stopped ringing and coming to see me without any explanation.

Fred had been gone a couple of months and I was still only doing locum receptionist work, so Pete offered me some permanent part-time work in the factory of a business run by his family in Box Hill, about fifteen kilometres east of the city. Because it was part-time, I'd still be able to attend Gresswell daily. Between the job and the methadone program, my time would pretty much be taken care of, so I was glad to take up Pete's offer, going to work about four days a week. I sensed that Pete felt he could keep a closer eye on me there and that if I was kept busy I'd find it easier. He was right, of course, but it still didn't stop me from going to Chipper's after work several days a week and scoring. When I got back to Pete and Wayne's flat later in the evening, I'd usually take myself to the bathroom to hit up.

I needed access to water to mix up the hit and, later, to clean out the syringe. Also, because I had such difficulty finding a vein, sometimes the substance in the syringe would coagulate with my blood, and I'd often have to remix my hit with more water. At times it became a complicated and lengthy process having to squirt it back into the spoon several times before locating a successful vein. This meant that I was often in the bathroom for the best part of an hour. It never occurred to me that they might find this suspicious, not that they would have been angry with me anyway: they would have just tried to discuss it. I was oblivious to the fact that everyone around me could see I was still using. In my own mind I thought I was trying hard, but it wasn't enough, and my shame continued to make me hide. I didn't want to let everyone down.

After staying at Pete and Wayne's for about three months, I was once again using daily. I stopped going to Gresswell for my methadone as it wasn't working and I had no commitment to the program. I obviously wasn't ready to give up smack. This meant I had to start selling in order to maintain my habit. I'd never been able to face working on the streets as a prostitute, like so many of my drug-using friends. Prostitution was a way of making money if you could bear it, but I knew that it wouldn't matter how stoned I was, it wouldn't be enough to block out the fact that there was a filthy mug lying on top of me having sex. I just couldn't bring myself to do it. The image of some stranger breathing all over me while he was lying on top of my body almost made me vomit. I always respected all my friends who worked as prostitutes because it took a lot of courage, a lot more than I had. I also knew I'd never do burglaries or steal from people as I didn't think that was okay—I wouldn't want it done to me, so I wouldn't do it to others. Selling was my only option.

I came across a couple of new contacts in the drug scene, and it was back to selling and using, selling and using . . . Eventually it became too difficult to stay at Pete and Wayne's any more, because I was out all night trying to sell enough to score for the next day. I also didn't want to drag them into the illegal world in which I was caught. It must have been obvious to them, but their friendship was unconditional. They were even sad to see me go and made it clear that I was welcome to return any time I wanted. They were so genuine and I knew how much they cared about me. I also knew how unreachable I was. I just wasn't ready to open up and tell them all that was going on for me; besides, I barely knew myself why I continued to do it.

I felt like there was a wall between me and the straight world and it was getting higher and thicker. These dear friends could see something special in me, but damned if I could. Although deep, deep down inside I still believed I was a good person, there were so many shadows and layers in the way it was difficult to have any faith in myself, particularly as my behaviour was driven by my addiction. I must have had some degree of control, though, because I still stuck by my own value system. I think the fact that what I was doing—selling and using—was illegal increased my sense of shame tenfold, but my friends didn't see me as a criminal; they just loved me as a person. Maybe that's why I kept running from them; maybe I thought that if they really knew about my drug-using behaviour, then they mightn't like me any more. If that sounds conflicting, that's exactly how it was, and that conflict lived every minute of every day inside me; the solution to it was to get stoned.

I moved into a flat with a guy who worked with my brother. He was straight and we shared the costs equally. He didn't ask questions and he was out all day and some nights while I was home during the day and out all night, every night, so it worked okay for a while.

I started up a relationship with a guy called Paul, an old friend of Chipper's who I'd met at her place. We started using and selling together, but soon enough we got busted and down to South Melbourne police station we went. He kindly took the rap for the smack, and by morning we'd both been released. I was free to go and he was granted bail. We were left in a dilemma, though, about how to pay the dealer for the heroin that we'd just lost in the bust.

We went home and made the dreaded phone call to our contact, to let him know we'd lost almost all of the previous batch of smack. He wasn't impressed; because we'd usually collect quite a few days' worth at a time on credit, the bust meant we'd lost a fair bit. In monetary terms it amounted to a few thousand dollars, an amount we'd never be able to repay. Our contact said he'd phone the dealer and organise a meeting with him. Only a couple of hours later, he rang back to tell us we had to meet the dealer the next morning. We weren't told what to expect, or even his name. It was all a bit scary, really, and we just hoped that the dealer would believe our story. At least we had Paul's charge sheet from the police to prove we weren't lying.

We turned up the next morning trying to act calm, although I was shaking in my shoes. I didn't ask Paul how he was feeling about it. A friend of ours, Adele, had recently disappeared from the streets of St Kilda and there was a rumour going around that a big-time dealer had disposed of her, so we were acutely aware of the possibilities facing us. We introduced ourselves to the dealer, who wasn't a drug user. He was short, unshaven and tough looking, with a body like a boxer or weightlifter. When he opened his mouth he sounded even tougher than he looked.

We explained what had happened and he wasn't too happy about it. He asked us how we were going to pay back the money owing to him, and I shrugged my shoulders. I had no idea, but as he was my contact, not Paul's, it was my responsibility. I was getting more and more anxious as the conversation continued— in fact, I was really scared. The only consolation was that we were in a busy, public place, a pub actually, so I felt safe for the time being. He then suggested a couple of options for wiping out our debt, both of which included illegal activity. One of them was for me to take a trip overseas, financed by him, to buy some smack.

Having been overseas before made it a bit less daunting. Certainly it seemed like the least frightening of the options offered to us, so I quickly came to an agreement with him. He certainly wasn't going to allow us to walk out of that pub without a solution to the problem. The reality was that this was probably the only chance he had of getting his money back; besides, once I agreed to make the trip, he was willing to give us more smack on credit so we could continue using and selling until I left. That at least solved the immediate problem for Paul and me, which was that we would soon be starting to hang out.

Within a couple of weeks my trip was organised and I was off to Malaysia again to score. Knowing what to expect, it seemed easier than my first trip, and I spent some time with Rahim in Kuala Lumpur again. He was thrilled to see me. I sensed that he was getting quite serious about the possibility of coming to Australia and starting a relationship with me, but I played it down as I knew my lifestyle would freak him out; and I didn't intend to stop using.

Again I went to Penang and scored from someone I met on the street. As it turned out, on my return flight to Australia I was pulled in by customs for questioning. I wasn't sure why they'd chosen me, or if they'd had any information, so I decided to act dumb. As the customs officers led me into the interview room for questioning, I felt like I was going to faint. I imagined my parents' surprise as they read the newspaper headlines the next day and found out their daughter was a heroin addict and, worse still, that I'd been caught bringing the stuff into the country. My body went numb with fear and resignation as the impact of being caught out hit home.

I was hoping like hell that maybe they were merely suspicious about the fact that my previous trip to Malaysia had been so recent. In fact, because I'd already thought it might look suspicious, I'd changed my destination from Melbourne to Sydney. I tried to answer their questions as briefly as possible and act like a normal tourist, which was pretty difficult knowing that I had a plastic bag of heroin wedged up my bum. In fact I was petrified because they kept threatening to call in a doctor to perform an internal examination on me. Even though I knew that if they followed through I'd be sunk, I offered no resistance. What was the point? My only hope was to appear as naive as possible. I think that my state of shock must have made me appear calm because after what seemed like a couple of hours of intense questioning about my 'holiday', they finally said I was free to go.

I thought I was hearing things. I couldn't believe it … and my legs turned to jelly when I tried to stand up. I didn't want to draw any further attention to myself, so I just willed my legs to walk out that door, then I wandered around Sydney airport for a while in a daze, trying to pull myself together but expecting that at any minute someone would tap me on the shoulder and pull me in for questioning again. I thought they must be watching me on a camera or something, that it was a trick, and really they were waiting for me to make a wrong move. There was no point in leaving the airport because I still had to return to Melbourne on a domestic flight. At the same time, I realised things were getting hot and my luck was running out. I wouldn't be having any more overseas holidays for a while.

When I was over the shock of nearly being busted, my fear seemed to fade away and I was able to sell enough of the smack to clear up the debt with the dealer, with enough left over to maintain my own habit for a little while. I searched the streets for Paul but couldn't find him, which made me suspicious. I started wondering if he had given the police information about me. Then I discovered that while I'd been away, he'd been sexually involved with at least two other women, and it made me feel sick because I was really keen on him ... at least I thought I was. We'd only been together a couple of months, but after my recent experience I was left with too many doubts about whether I could trust him. Anyway, I couldn't even find him, so that took care of that relationship.

After my debt was paid off I was able to continue scoring from my previous dealer, who'd decided to deal directly with me from then on rather than using an intermediary. I signed up with an employment agency for a straight job and began to get regular locum work as a typist/receptionist. With steady employment I was able to move out of the shared flat to one of my own in East St Kilda. It was a little one-bedroom place and I now had room for the furniture that I'd kept stored at my parents' place. I hadn't seen them for quite a while, not even visiting Mum much. I seemed to have become even more consumed by my heroin habit.

Around this time Fred decided to return from New Zealand, and he moved into a place just around the corner from me. Unfortunately for him, it wasn't long before he was back using again. He formed a relationship with a girl we both knew from Fitzroy Street; she was also a heroin addict and worked as a prostitute. Fred seemed to go downhill quickly. He wasn't looking after himself and often his appearance was pretty shabby, but we'd established a good friendship and we helped each other out, in terms of the smack, whenever we could. There was a longstanding mutual respect and love between us.

Over the next couple of years I became romantically involved with first one and then another non-using dealer, and my life changed in a way that I could never have imagined. This was a fairly common pattern for women users to fall into. You usually meet dealers through having to sell drugs to maintain your own habit and, soon enough, they use the drug to lure you in. It's not so very different to prostitution, except the payment for having sex with them is a couple of free 'tastes' (hits). At first things seem to go along okay, and the heroin addict feels she's better off because she's not living with another addict. Even Ron and my mother thought I was doing much better during that time in my life. The dealer I was going out with had a straight business as well, so he met both Ron and Mum; they thought he was all right and that I was less chaotic. I didn't dare tell them he was actually my dealer!

The situation soon changes once the 'romantic' period is over and the dealer feels like he owns you. Most of these guys actually hate junkies, so they either won't allow their partners to use or, alternatively, they dole out controlled amounts (under *their* control) from their own resources. Soon you find yourself begging for another hit, and further down the track you'll do just about anything to get them to give you some more smack. Of course, because they can't stand junkies, this desperate behaviour makes them disrespect you, and it usually isn't too long before they're giving you a smack in the mouth instead of a hit of smack to shut you up. Six months later, you're not only a slave to heroin but to him as well. The more you beg for drugs, the more they hate you. Then they decide you have to get clean and straighten up. After months of a relationship where begging, pleading and violence have become the norm, you don't have much self-esteem left, and you start believing the abuse and put-downs. Once caught in this vicious, isolating situation, it's impossible for most women to stop using; they just get sneakier at finding another dealer to score from and hiding the needle marks. And so the put-downs, arguments, suspicion and violence escalate.

One day during this time, a dealer–boyfriend did something to me that will remain etched into my heart forever; while the superficial wounds may have healed, the scar, although faded, will always remain. It was a pretty typical evening. I was living in his house at the time, and he'd invited his close friends around for dinner, a married couple who lived nearby. All was well until he went upstairs to receive a phone call. He often took phone calls out of hearing distance. I was happy for it to be that way as I felt the less I knew about his drug business, the better off I was. That way I could never be suspected of telling anyone anything. This time, however, when he came back downstairs after hanging up the phone, a shudder moved down my spine right through my body as I looked at his face. I knew something was seriously wrong. He entered the room, sat down and quietly asked our visitors to leave. As we were only part-way through our meal they were as surprised as me, but they knew better than to ask any questions.

Somehow or other I just knew it had to do with me and my heroin use. Had he caught me out using? Could somebody have told him? A feeling of absolute panic swept through my body as he cleared everyone out of the house. 'Don't you move,' he said to me nastily, after he'd seen everyone out the door. He picked up the phone in the kitchen and rang my brother Ron.

'Have you seen Helen?' he asked Ron. 'I was wondering if you knew where she was. She took off a couple of days ago and I haven't seen her since.' He was setting up an alibi, so I knew what that meant. He had his back to me so I couldn't see the expression on his face. When he turned around, though, I noticed he was white and seething with anger. He wouldn't look at me.

Fuck!, I thought to myself, he's found out I've been using. He'd threatened me often enough with what he'd do if he caught me. What happened next was the only time I can remember totally losing any sense of pride.

He'd hung up the phone and turned around with the most despicable look on his face. 'Get upstairs,' he spat in a gravelly voice. Without waiting for me to get up from my chair, he grabbed me roughly by the arm and pushed me ahead of him, forcing me upstairs into the spare bedroom. He locked the door behind us, shoved me onto the bed and stood over me to begin the interrogation, bending so that his face was only centimetres from mine.

'Who did you get the heroin from?' he asked, anger spitting from his mouth.

I looked down, saying nothing, trying to escape the hatred in his eyes. Someone had rung him to tell him I'd been using. I wondered who would do that to me, knowing the consequences.

Whack! The back of his hand struck the side of my face, the force of the blow wrenching my head sideways. I reeled in shock.

'Who did you buy the heroin from?' he asked again.

'I can't tell you,' I said softly.

Whack! Another blow, this time to the other side of my face, wrenching it back the opposite way. Just as well I was sitting on the bed.

'Who did you get the heroin from? Answer me, you fuckin' scumbag!' he screamed. Terrified, I scuttled across to the other side of the double bed, jumped off it and jammed myself into the small space between the bed and the wall. He hurled himself onto the bed after me.

Whack! Whack! Blows to both sides of my face. My head

started to dangle as I cringed, trying to tuck myself into a ball in the small space on the floor.

'Tell me who you bought the heroin from!' he screamed again. He'd lost it. He couldn't stop. Whack! Whack! I saw stars and collapsed on the floor while he continued to hit me. I tried to get up and clamber back across the bed again, but there was no way I could escape: the door was locked.

'I'm not telling you,' I sobbed.

He chased me around the room trying to beat a confession out of me until I was only semi-conscious, my head dangling involuntarily, blood splattered over my clothing. Both my nose and ears were bleeding and I could barely see through my eyes.

Then it stopped. I tried to watch him through my haze as he walked to the door and unlocked it. He flung it open, just about forcing it from its hinges. I dreaded to think what was coming next. I just hoped it would be quick.

Suddenly he grabbed me by the arms, pulling me up from the floor like a rag doll, and pushed me down the stairs and into the rumpus room, where he forced my limp body to turn around and look at the wall straight in front of me. Through my swollen eyes I found myself staring at his gun rack.

'Choose which gun you want me to kill you with,' he said, with a disgusting, guttural laugh.

I sobbed and sobbed, refusing to choose a gun. I had nothing to lose. At least he had stopped hitting me, and I was grateful for that. In a way I hoped the bullet would be quicker than the beating had been.

Angrily he wrenched one of the guns from the rack, marched me downstairs into the garage and forced me into the passenger seat of my car. He started the engine and drove off, his madman's voice vomiting abuse at me nonstop. My mind was as blank as the black night.

'You'll make the headline in tomorrow's newspaper,' he

taunted me. 'BODY FOUND—FATAL GUNSHOT WOUND TO THE HEAD.' He let out that horrifying guttural laugh. It was like he was psyching himself up for the execution.

Eventually he stopped in a lonely spot surrounded by bush. He got out and came around to my side of the car. He pulled me out and marched me back around to the driver's side, flinging me roughly into the driver's seat and slamming the door closed. He returned to the passenger side door, winding the window down and grabbing his shotgun before closing that door on me. Then he leaned through the passenger side window, and I felt coldness at my temple as he pushed the barrel of the gun against my skin. I couldn't look at him; I was afraid to move my head. I stared, only semi-conscious, straight ahead through the front windscreen into the blackness of the night.

'You fuckin' lying scumbag junkie,' he growled. 'You no-good piece of shit! You don't deserve to live.'

'I love you ... please don't kill me,' I pleaded to any sanity that might be left in his mind. I didn't feel angry, just profoundly sad and misunderstood.

'Just because I lied to you about using doesn't mean I don't love you. Please ... don't kill me ... please ... Please ... don't kill me ... I love you.' I begged him with every bit of will to live that I had left inside me. I didn't want to die. I tried not to sob ... I continued pleading, begging him not to kill me, the barrel of the shotgun poised against my left temple the whole time. I expected my head to explode at any second.

After what felt like an interminable amount of time, his finger slowly released its pressure on the trigger and, slowly, teasingly, I felt the metal of the barrel depart from its resting place against my temple. I was paralysed. Afraid to move my head, I continued sitting there, looking straight ahead through the front windscreen of the car. I gasped as I drew in a ragged breath, praying that he really had changed his mind.

He opened the passenger side door and slowly got back into the car. He was silent now as he forced me to drive home from the isolated patch of scrub that was intended to be my resting place. It was as though he had exhausted himself.

I had no idea how I managed to drive home and I don't remember arriving. I was barely conscious.

'You can sleep in the spare bedroom, then in the morning, pack your things and get out,' he growled, 'you lowlife fuckin' junkie.'

He was still angry and I was still petrified of him, but I was so exhausted I was almost beyond caring. I felt numb. I couldn't even feel any physical pain from the injuries he'd inflicted on me. It wasn't until I went to the bathroom that I noticed all the dried blood covering my nose and ears; my eyes, once blue, were now closed, black and swollen.

I tried to clean myself up a bit before going back to the spare bedroom. I sat on the edge of the bed, trying to gather my thoughts. A while later, after I'd heard him go to bed and thought he was asleep, I snuck into the toilet and had a hit to ease my terror and exhaustion. I didn't even think about the consequences of being caught. The instant warmth flowed through my bloodstream and I sighed ... I went to bed trying to wrap the doona around me, like it could protect me. I was grateful to be alive.

He allowed me to stay there after this incident, and I'm ashamed to say that I was even grateful for that. I also told myself that he must have loved me because he couldn't actually bring himself to pull the trigger. If he hadn't loved me he would have killed me, and somewhere inside I believed that his actions would have been justified. I believed that his love for me had saved my life. Although I was grateful for his 'compassion', I was also ter-rified of him. And while it's true to say that I did still love him, I couldn't bear to have sex with him any more, so increasingly he'd force himself inside me, sometimes in the mornings before I'd even woken up. I thought it was a peculiar way to treat someone you loved, but I sort of felt I had to accept it, even though I found it disrespectful.

Like most women in this situation, I had left my own flat to move into my partner's place, at his insistence. I'd eventually given up my job, too, again to please him. Of course, then I found myself financially dependent on him, but still couldn't stop using. Once they've taken your independence away, they withdraw the free access to heroin. You find yourself almost a prisoner in their house, with no job, no money and no smack. If there ever had been love in the relationship, by now it was an almost forgotten memory. When things got too abusive for me, I'd just pack my bags and take off, but I'd always return. Somehow they always manage to entice you back, with promises of changing their ways. Whenever I disappeared I'd go and stay with my drug-using friends, like Danni or Chipper. I was always welcome there. Danni had been through this scenario in relationships countless times. She was always good to talk to. She'd always give me a free hit for comfort, too.

The woman usually returned to the relationship a few days or a week later, after they'd agreed that she wouldn't use and he wouldn't be violent. But they'd be back to the same behaviour within hours. I always returned because I believed that these dealers, not being users, were superior to me, and that I was better off in a relationship with them rather than another addict. They always seemed more respectable than drug addicts yet, in reality, they were just thugs. But they appeared successful—the nice house, furniture, cars and, importantly, plenty of money—so to a drug addict with no self-esteem they had a lot of power, and they never stopped telling you. It made me seem more important if I lived in a big, flash house, even if he never gave me any money. He'd sometimes spend money on me for clothes, but he'd never give me any cash. Never give a junkie cash! At times this way of living seemed easier than the desperate merry-go-round of the street, trying to sell enough smack to get your own hit at the end of every day. Living with a dealer, you always hoped there was a way to scavenge or beg some smack from them. At twenty-five years old, this is what my life had become: hiding, secrets, drugs and violence.

Around this time, in early 1979, my mum was getting sicker, even though they'd given her the 'all clear' after her third operation the year before. Within months she had to give up work and needed someone with her all the time. Back she went to hospital for more tests. I happened to be the person with her that day as Dad was at work. While she was elsewhere in the hospital, a doctor called me into the office and gave me the bad news: the cancer had spread throughout her body and was out of control. There would be no more surgery. In fact in their estimation, she only had months—or maybe weeks—to live. Again, thinking it was a secret, I didn't discuss it with Mum after we got home. When Dad arrived from work I walked out to the back yard with him to tell him what the doctor had said. He was shocked and, to his credit, he treated her well after this.

Because I was still living with a dealer and not working, I called in and sat with Mum most days while Dad was at work. He and I still hardly talked, but at least he and Mum were closer than I'd seen them in the last ten years. I fitted in my scoring, selling and using around this new routine, sometimes dropping off some smack to Danni or Stella to sell for me, or picking some up from another dealer on my way to and from Mum's. This only lasted a few weeks, though, because Mum was giving up. It appeared she didn't want to be in this world any more. Unfortunately she didn't talk about how she was feeling, but I knew that once she got to the stage where she couldn't look after herself, it wouldn't be long before she'd let go. She had too much pride and would never want to be a burden to anyone.

When she found she couldn't even bathe herself, Isabel, her older sister and an ex-nurse, came and took her to her farm at Pakenham, about an hour east of Melbourne. Mum was only there a couple of weeks before Aunty Isabel decided it was time for her to go to hospital, which meant the end was near.

We all went to visit, but Mum looked so different: her body had been ravaged by the cancer and she was now bony and frail. She was slipping in and out of consciousness as I stood by the bed not knowing what to do, feeling like a stranger and not knowing how to talk to her. This person lying there was my mother and she was dying, but I'd never felt so distant from her. I was frightened to touch her. Each time I visited I felt the same and, as always, I couldn't tell what she was feeling or thinking. I didn't know if she could hear us any more—most of the time I couldn't even tell if she was conscious.

She was only there a few days. All the relatives, sensing time was running out, came and paid their last respects. I found it all confusing and overwhelmingly sad, this confrontation with death and a mother who I didn't seem to know, who was now going to disappear from life as I knew it, so I used more heroin. On her last evening alive, I visited Mum and felt just as distant as ever as I watched her almost lifeless body lying there. I didn't like the way she looked and her mouth was strangely open, but it didn't seem to bother anyone else. She died later that night. I wasn't even there; no-one was except the nurses.

A few days later I attended the funeral, sticking close to Ron. He and my father had organised it because I was too useless to help with anything like that. I was too caught up in my own shit and what I was feeling. I think I cried on Ron's shoulder, but I wasn't feeling much because I was so out of it on heroin. I needed a buffer between me and the world, between me and all these confusing feelings—between me and the sadness I felt for a mum I never really knew. After that I didn't visit my parents' house, although Ron returned to stay with Dad for a little while. For a long time after that I had no contact with Dad; there seemed little point.

Besides, just six weeks after my mum's death, my life changed in a way that I could never have prepared for.

Part II
Death

7

On my way to prison

E ven though I wasn't living there, I'd maintained the lease on my little East St Kilda flat. There were virtually no bills to pay and I was still doing locum receptionist/typist jobs, which more than covered the rent. It seemed that at least I was hanging on to a bit of security or independence or something, and the flat was just around the corner from Fred's place—we were still good friends. I visited the flat a few times a week as it was convenient to hide my drug-using paraphernalia there. It was also somewhere to base myself on the days when I did come into town.

One day while I was on a quick visit there to have a hit, I received a desperate phone call from Fred. I already knew he'd been away to Malaysia picking up some smack for a local dealer, and I was expecting him back any time.

'I need you to help me out!' he said anxiously.

'What's the matter?' I asked. 'Are you okay?' I was aware not to say too much on the phone because you never knew if they were tapped.

'No, I'm not actually,' he replied. 'I need to meet with you, like—now.' He sounded extremely nervous.

When we did meet, his story unfolded. He'd brought back

some smack from Malaysia, arriving in Melbourne only two days previously, but the dealer who'd financed the trip and who was supposed to meet him at the airport hadn't turned up. Fred didn't even have his phone number, so there was no way to contact him. As a result he was left with a large package of heroin (much more than we'd ever be able to afford) which someone else had paid for. He was staying at a local motel, afraid to take such a large amount of smack to his own flat. Fred was scared that the dealer might think he had ripped him off, so he asked me to keep the smack in a safe place until he could locate the guy. I also knew this dealer and was sure one of us would find him within days. It didn't seem like a problem to me as it could be kept at my St Kilda flat and, besides, I was sure I could sneak some for myself, just a little bit ... enough for a few hits. My current partner would never find out.

Even though Fred was frightened, I reassured him. Actually I felt excited at the thought of some free hits. In a way I hoped we wouldn't be able to find the dealer for a few days! We went back to the motel where Fred had been staying and he handed the smack over to me. I wrapped it in a cardigan, being careful not to get my fingerprints on the package, and put it behind the back seat of my car. Feeling confident that his package would now be safe, Fred was able to check out of the motel and return home. I drove straight to my flat.

As my car turned into the driveway to what had been my cosy little home, my life changed forever. All of a sudden a couple of men jumped out from the bushes and surrounded my car. All I could think of was Fred's package sitting in the back. Fuck! I've been busted, I thought to myself, realising the gravity of what was happening. I'd never expected this to happen to me again, which was probably unrealistic, but the ability to live in an illusory world is an essential component of the drug-addicted personality. If you can't remain constantly stoned, you soon come to realise that this problematic lifestyle, based on fear, shame and hiding, is bloody awful.

Almost immediately my car door was yanked open and several boofy-looking men—drug squad detectives, I was soon to discover—dragged me out and took me upstairs to my flat. They made me sit down and keep still, which was just as well because I felt like I was about to faint. All the way up the stairs they had fired a barrage of questions at me and in the flat they kept them coming, asked first by one man, then a woman, then back to the first guy, while several others started pulling my flat apart, strewing my belongings everywhere. It's what they called 'searching'. They asked me about Fred and how long I'd known him, and they even mentioned the dealer's name, which freaked me out. Obviously someone had given them a lot of information and they were pressuring me to name the dealer. No way was I going to say a word about anyone, my only admission being to my own heroin addiction.

A couple of them had remained downstairs to search my car, so I knew it was only a matter of time before they found the heroin. Of course, they soon found all my syringes and things in the bedroom wardrobe, and brought them out to where I was sitting. They placed the stuff on the table in front of me as if it were a prize. This situation was looking worse by the minute! Then the detectives from downstairs came through the front door and placed the familiar package, still with the cardigan around it, on the table beside the syringes. It hadn't taken them long to discover it in the rear of the car.

Then came another barrage of questions about who the package belonged to. At least they knew it wasn't mine—not that it made any difference, because they kept threatening me that if I didn't name the owner, I'd be charged for it. They didn't seem too fussed who took responsibility as long as someone took the rap. I knew I was in big trouble because it was a large quantity of heroin, so I was careful not to say much, just giving them my name and address. That pissed them off, of course, but I wasn't going to dob anyone in, even if it looked like I'd be going to jail for a while. I didn't even know how much dope I'd been busted with, because it wasn't mine—what an irony!

My pride momentarily discarded, I begged them to let me have a hit before they carted me off to the police station for further questioning. Just one hit would make the ordeal marginally more bearable. I knew I'd soon be hanging out badly, and that was my most immediate concern. As an addict it's difficult to look any further than your next hit, and anticipating the pain and anguish, both physical and psychological, of hanging out terrified me. But they weren't in a sympathetic mood and denied my request.

I spent a couple of hours at Russell Street police station in the city, resisting their attempts to get a statement out of me. I maintained my right to silence and answered 'no comment' to everything. I'd been allowed to make a phone call to a solicitor, whose name had been given to me by my current partner in case of such emergencies, and that had also been his advice. The relationship between me and the drug squad detectives was, needless to say, strained and tense, but one bloke seemed a bit sensitive toward me, even though he wasn't gaining any information. Unlike the others, he was respectful and kind. I thought that maybe he felt sorry for me, even perhaps a bit guilty or ashamed at charging me with possession of illicit drugs that they knew didn't belong to me. The woman detective seemed to hate me.

Eventually I was taken to the cells where I would remain until Melbourne Magistrates' Court opened the next morning. In the cell I could hang out in isolation and turn my thoughts to the possibility of getting bail the next morning, which I soon realised was a double-edged sword for me. On the one hand I wanted to get out more than anything, particularly to score and put an end to the drug withdrawals. On the other hand, if I was granted bail I was sure my current partner would be waiting ... waiting for an explanation. He'd discover that I was hanging out, which meant discovering that I'd been using, which meant I'd been lying to him about using ... I couldn't bear to think what that would mean. I wondered who'd tipped the drug squad off about the stuff in my car; someone had certainly been aware of Fred's movements.

Because I'd been locked up once before, at the South Melbourne cells, I knew what to expect. Even so, it was like an assault on my body, especially when I was already hanging out. I guess it doesn't get much worse than this. These particular cells consisted of four solid, bluestone walls, no windows, with concrete on the inside covered in graffiti, and only a small vent high up one wall to allow air to enter. There was no natural light, except a tiny bit that came through the small trap door when the police opened it to talk to you or pass food through. It felt cold, and very old. A shiver made its way down my spine as I tried to settle in. It reminded me of a castle dungeon in a fairytale.

From somewhere close by, maybe through the vent, I could hear men yelling every five minutes: 'I want a smoke!', or 'I want to see my lawyer!', or 'I want to make a phone call!' The requests were endless and they continued day and night. Most of them were ignored.

You could walk about six paces from one end of the cell to the other. I wonder how many people have paced up and back right here?, I pondered. It's common for prisoners to pace. Sometimes it's called 'the prison shuffle', because a lot of prisoners drag their feet while they walk up and down in these confined areas, a reflection of their containment and lack of purpose.

The cell was very dim and I could almost feel the desperation oozing through the walls. It seemed to mingle with the smell of heroin seeping out of my body, through the beads of sweat and goosebumps. I was a solitary figure here within these four cold, uncompromising walls, but I wasn't alone, although I'd never felt so lonely. I'd lost my right to privacy, and I had uninvited company in this cell, although it wasn't human. There was a little eye up in the right-hand corner where the ceiling met the wall, and I could never tell when it was looking at me. I was shocked when I first noticed it. I'd forgotten that I was no longer entitled to my own private space in the world.

After alternately sitting and pacing for several hours, I was busting to go to the toilet because of the diarrhoea and stomach cramps that heroin withdrawal causes. I was trying to put it off for as long as possible, but the inevitable diarrhoea and vomiting were uncontrollable.

'I want some privacy, please?' I said to the little eye directed towards me. I couldn't wait any longer, though; I had to go. I took three steps and sat on the toilet seat, hanging my head in shame and hoping that, somehow, if I couldn't see them, they wouldn't be able to see me.

How many of you in that office are watching me on your screen? Are all you coppers perving on me as I pull down my pants? Is this your entertainment? Are you enjoying my lack of privacy now that I'm a criminal, even though I've not been found guilty yet? The questions rolled round and round in my head. In my heart I anticipated that, in all probability, it really wouldn't be long before I was legally deemed a criminal.

I remained on the toilet, physically and emotionally sick. 'I need a doctor, not the police,' I told myself out loud, looking up at the camera lens in vain. It seemed really unfair. 'Do you guys really believe you're helping the world by causing people like me to suffer like this?'

I stayed sitting on the toilet for a long time; the diarrhoea was so bad it was easier just to keep sitting there, although the shame was unbearable. I wished I could have flushed myself into the sewer. I knew that was where they thought I belonged.

'You're nothing but a scumbag junkie! I should have left you in the gutter where I found you!' I had heard that so many times from my current partner; I could still hear him screaming at me in a fit of rage when I'd done something wrong. But he could yell abuse at me all he liked, because there was this little part of me that refused to accept those insults, and although that little part of me had grown smaller and smaller, it had never totally disappeared. I don't belong in the gutter and, actually, you didn't find me there, I would think to myself, usually too afraid to say it out loud. I had my little flat in St Kilda and I owned everything in it, which was a long way from living in the gutter. Sometimes I did speak back, those tiny snippets of pride keeping me alive. I realised now how precious my pride was. It helped me survive this hell of a life I seemed to have chosen.

At times there in that small stone cell I had both diarrhoea and vomiting simultaneously. The smell of hanging out lingered in the trapped air, unable to escape either. When I wasn't sitting on the toilet, I'd try to walk up and down, six paces up and six paces back, to ease the spasms that made my legs jerk involuntarily. In the end it was too hard, I just didn't have the energy. I lay down on the wooden bench and covered myself with the filthy, army-style blankets the system provided. 'Is it night-time out there in the world?' I asked the little lens. I knew what I was in for during the night, if indeed it was night-time.

I tried desperately to sleep while my body screamed for a hit, craving the warmth of heroin flowing through my veins. My muscles cramped and twitched, my legs jerked of their own accord. I let out a groan. I was hot, then cold, sweating and shivering concurrently, my body aching and my skin covered in goosebumps. I wouldn't have cared about the filthy cell if I could just have had a hit. Just one and this hell would be over, at least for a few hours, until my body began withdrawing again . . . only to be followed by that incessant craving.

I fell into a disturbed sleep, tossing and turning, groaning and sweating. Anxiety turned to terror when I felt an intruder present, watching me from above. Coming out of my nightmare in that cold stone environment, I wasn't sure if it was the judge sitting high up above me, but as I looked up toward the adjacent corner, I could see it was only the camera lens staring at me.

Every slow-motion minute was excruciating, both physically and emotionally. Morning inevitably arrived, marked not by the dawn light but by the presence of police at the trap door of the cell. I shivered as I strained to open my tired eyes. I was exhausted.

'The solicitor is here to see you. It's almost time to go to court,' a voice said from the other side of the trap door.

Time to face the real world, I thought to myself.

The big, iron cell door creaked open and a policeman led me down a passageway and into a small room. There sat a solicitor in his lovely clean shirt and suit. I immediately felt like a hopeless, dirty moron in comparison. He surprised me by telling me that he wasn't altogether certain that I'd get bail. I had thought it would be relatively automatic. I knew almost nothing about the law.

Soon we were called into the courtroom and, at the end of the short process, as the solicitor had predicted, I was denied bail, which meant I'd be taken to the remand section at Fairlea Women's Prison. I'd have to remain there until the date of my court case, or else apply to a higher court for bail. I didn't even get to say anything to anyone. I just stood up and sat down when told.

As I was escorted back to the cells by the police, my solicitor caught up with us in the passage way. 'I'll come out to the prison to see you in the next few days,' he said. 'We'll have to go to the Supreme Court for bail. It'll take at least two weeks for your application to be processed.'

'The Supreme Court?' I asked him, puzzled. I thought the Supreme Court was for really bad people.

'Yes . . . I'll explain when I see you at the prison.'

With that, the policeman and I turned a corner and I found myself back at the doorway of the rotten, smelly cell. 'Great!' I said. 'How long before I'll be taken to the prison?'

'Not sure,' he replied. 'It could be later this afternoon, or it might not be until tomorrow.'

'Great!' I repeated. 'Thanks,' I called through to him as I heard the key locking my door.

I plonked myself on the bench and resumed my hanging out. During the court process I'd managed to be distracted by my fear, but now it all seemed like an anticlimax as I wiped the sweat from my brow. I knew I must have looked like shit in that courtroom.

Prison, I said to myself, trying to absorb the turn of events in my life. Although I was a bit scared, I felt it couldn't be much worse than this. I thought of my many old friends from the streets of St Kilda who were already in Fairlea. At least I'd know a lot of the women, even if I didn't know what else to expect. I began to wonder if Fred had found out what had happened to his smack yet. If he had, he'd be shitting himself, but I couldn't really feel sorry for him at this point—after all, I was in much more trouble than him! I just hoped he knew that I wasn't going to dob him or anyone else in. I'd also need to let Ron know so that he wouldn't worry that I'd disappeared from planet earth. I wasn't concerned about my father; Ron could deal with him. 'What a fuckin' disaster!' I said out loud.

For the next few hours I tried to rest, but the muscle

spasms wouldn't allow me to lie still. I became tired of walking the three paces to the toilet to vomit or shit. The diarrhoea was unbelievable. My thoughts were jumbled as the reality of my situation kept trying to creep in through the barrier of my physical sickness. Then I heard the noise of the trap door being opened.

'The van's here to take you to prison!' a brusque voice yelled through the small opening. 'I'll be back in five minutes.'

My mouth remained dry and silent. I'd been taken for a quick cold shower earlier, but I had no change of clothes and I wasn't allowed a brush to untangle my hair. I couldn't stand the smell of myself.

I dragged myself up from the bench which had served as a bed, leaving the filthy blankets strewn on the floor around me. My head began to spin and my legs felt like jelly. I staggered as I tried to stand up straight. My body exuded beads of sweat, continuing its detoxifying process. Suddenly my legs gave way and I crumpled in a heap on the cold stone ground, the filthy blankets surrounding me. I pitied the next person who would have to use them. I wondered how many others had been in the cell before me, and how long it had been since the blankets had last been washed. I'd heard how they cleaned the cells in the men's section—they squirted a hose in there for a couple of minutes, and that was it. Junkie scum, have no doubt, that's what we were.

A few minutes later I heard the sound of keys and the heavy iron door swung open. Part of the cell was bathed in daylight, but my eyelids closed, unable to adjust.

'Time to go,' one of the police said. There were two of them. They stood near the doorway, not entering, as if they thought they might be contaminated if they stepped inside the cell. The way I felt, and no doubt looked, I couldn't say I blamed them.

'Have a rough night?' one of them said with a tinge of compassion.

'Yeah,' I replied, lacking the energy to say any more.

In silence they escorted me to the back of a large, square police van. The cabin at the front was light and full of windows. Attached at the back, completely separate from the cabin, was a big, square tin-looking box in which they put the prisoners. It bore a remarkable similarity to the cell I'd just left behind. Although it was metal instead of bluestone and concrete, it was just as dark and dirty and isolating—once on the road the police couldn't see or hear you from their position in the front cabin.

I levered myself in with my weak arms and they locked the door behind me. Feeling cold and empty, I collapsed onto one of the wooden benches that ran down each side of the graffiti-covered box as the van took off. Every time the brakes were applied, I slid up to the other end of the bench. I tried in vain to hold on but I was so weak from hanging out that, as soon as my grip loosened, I'd find myself up the other end again.

Noticing a small window just above eye level, I pulled myself up to try and have a last glance at civilisation, unsure of how long it would be before I saw it again, but the window was so heavily covered in bars and wire that I could hardly identify anything outside. 'Goodbye, cruel world,' I said to the blurred scenery passing by. I could imagine people going about their daily business. I was just like you yesterday, I thought to myself. Today the world had changed drastically. No, today *my* world had changed. I found myself beginning to understand the true meaning of freedom, the sense of loss just dawning inside me.

After about half an hour we arrived at the prison. The police in the cabin upfront tooted the horn and I could hear the sound of a roller door opening. The van lurched forward one last time, me going with it up to the other end of the bench, then it came to a halt. I nearly fell onto the floor trying to keep my balance.

A few minutes later the police opened the back door and I was allowed to climb out. Again the sunlight blinded me, and it took a while before I could open my eyes properly. When I did, I saw a woman prison officer looking me up and down, making a quick assessment, no doubt.

'Come with me,' she said pleasantly enough. She had a massive bunch of keys hanging from her belt and they jangled as she walked. I trailed along behind her through a series of doors which she first had to unlock, and then lock again behind us. The building looked very old and, because it was made of tin rather than bluestone, like the cells I'd just come from, it seemed too physically fragile to be a prison.

Eventually we came to a medium-sized room with old wooden cupboards and tin lockers lining each side. The linoleum on the floor was old but highly polished—in fact the room was so clean it looked like it had been sanitised. It made me feel even dirtier, like the filthy scum that some people believed I was. 'Scumbag!' That word seemed permanently implanted in my brain. That's probably what the officer was thinking too. I noticed another, smaller room opening off the main one; a big, open book sat on a bench just in front of it.

'What's your name?' the prison officer asked; the induction process had commenced.

'Take all your clothes off and put them over here,' she ordered, pointing to a spot on the floor.

'You're kidding?' I said for time; I needed a moment to adjust to the shock of being forced to strip naked in front of her. Another woman, not in uniform, was standing close by. I later discovered that she was a prisoner who worked in the clothing store.

The officer didn't need to reply—I could see by the look on her face that she wasn't joking. I wanted to cry but I held back the tears, my anxiety, as well as the hanging out, making my body sweat even more. I stood there not moving, paralysed by my humiliation.

'Come on, hurry up! Take all your clothes off, we haven't got all day,' she repeated impatiently. 'They'll be washed and placed in your property. You're allowed to wear your own clothes while you're on remand. Do you have any other clothing with you?'

'No,' I replied, starting to peel off my clothes piece by piece.

'We'll get you some prison clothing then,' she said. 'Do you have any identifiable marks on your body, like scars or tattoos?' she inquired next, glancing down my body like it was a lump of meat awaiting inspection. She went over to the big book on the bench and picked up a pen.

'No.'

She found some anyway. Under the heading 'Marks and scars', she wrote: 'Right arm, needle marks; left arm, needle marks; right thigh, 18 yellow bruises; left thigh, 3 yellow bruises.'

I felt really embarrassed, especially about all the bruises on my legs. That's where I'd been hitting up in order not to have noticeable needle marks on my arms like every other junkie I knew. I looked at the date at the top of the page. It was 16 June 1979; I was twenty-five years old.

The other woman left the room through a side door, and soon I could hear water running.

'After I write down all your items of clothing and jewellery, you can go and have a bath. There's a towel in the bathroom,' the officer said like she'd done this a million times before.

'Can I wear my jewellery when you've finished writing it down?' I asked her.

'No,' she replied.

'What about the sleepers for my pierced ears?'

'Not allowed.'

'But the holes in my ears will close up.'

'It can't be helped. No-one's allowed earrings. They can be ripped out of your ears if you get into a fight,' she explained calmly.

With that, she handed me a bottle of lotion. 'Put this in your hair,' she instructed. 'It's for lice.'

'Thanks,' I said to her, feeling bewildered, 'but I don't have lice.' I pushed the bottle away, wondering if her offer was a result of how filthy I must have looked.

'Doesn't matter, you have to put it through your hair. Everyone has to when they arrive here,' she said. 'Take it with you and comb it through your hair while you're having a bath. You can wash it off later.'

I walked through to the bathroom, glad to be in a room on my own for a moment. I stepped into the bath and sat down. Because I was still hanging out, my body came out in goose-bumps as soon as it came in contact with the water. My skin felt like it was crawling but, even so, the clean water felt good. It was one of those big old-fashioned baths with claw feet, and I lay back in it, allowing the water to cover most of my body. People pay a fortune for these in antique shops, I thought to myself, although I noticed that the enamel had worn off this one. I'd never imagined I'd be soaking in an antique bath inside a prison.

'What size are you?' the other woman asked, poking her head through the doorway.

'Probably size 12,' I replied.

She went away and returned soon after with underwear and a prison-issue striped dress. 'When you've finished, put these clothes on and go back to the officer in the other room. Don't take too long,' she said.

I was so sick from hanging out that, after my induction to prison, I was sent to the prison hospital for observation rather than the remand dormitory. As I walked in I noticed half a dozen beds in a row, three on each side, and it looked like I was the only resident. I really needed someone to talk to, just to relieve my anxiety and fear of the unknown. I wished that someone else was in there, too, a fellow scumbag. The hospital was sterile and isolated from the rest of the prison, and the windows had all been painted over so I couldn't even see outside. I felt like I was in a cocoon. The only break in the monotony was when I vomited, but I knew it would only last a few more days. How I longed for an end to the physical withdrawals. I had no idea how I was going to feel after my focus moved away from how sick I was feeling. Then I'd have to deal with both the legal situation I'd found myself in, as well as the feeling of emptiness that would surface now that my access to heroin had gone.

While I was in hospital the nursing sister did all the standard medical tests. She tried her best to be friendly; I think she was glad to have a patient to attend to. In fact I think she was enjoying the company and in a few days, when I'd begun to feel better, she assigned me to being the hospital 'billet', which meant cleaner, and kept me there until my bail hearing. There wasn't much cleaning to do because I was the ward's sole occupant, but at least it meant I would be paid a wage—about $1 a day. That meant that on 'canteen day', which occurred once a week, I could buy some coffee, chocolates and toiletries.

After I'd been in the hospital about seven or eight days, which all seemed to have rolled into each other, my solicitor arrived and I was escorted to the visit centre to see him.

'You're going to the Supreme Court tomorrow for your bail application,' he said.

After he'd walked away, I somehow knew this would be my last night in jail. I hadn't even made it out of the hospital, although I had managed to talk to a couple of my friends who'd snuck around to the window when they'd heard where I was. For the last few days I'd also been allowed out into the mainstream prison at lunchtime and for the after-work dinner hour before 4.30 pm lock-up.

The following morning I was awake early, ready and waiting for the van to take me to court. I wasn't feeling sick and nauseous any more, although I still didn't have much energy. I was a bit frightened about going to court again, particularly after what had happened the previous time, but I felt reasonably confident I'd be free that afternoon—after all, it was my first offence. The main thing I was looking forward to was scoring and having a hit.

It all happened pretty quickly, actually. Before I knew it, the judge was announcing that bail had been granted and I was led back to wait in the cells until the paperwork had been processed. The next couple of hours seemed to go slowly down there in those rotten cells, but then I heard that joyous sound of keys, the cell door opened and I was led to freedom.

Once I was out I discovered that the police had been on to Fred and had traced his phone calls to my flat in St Kilda, waiting there until I arrived. It seemed that Fred had told a supposed friend—a drug user–prostitute to whom he'd given a few free hits—about not being able to find his dealer. When she left the motel where Fred had been staying, she rang the police and informed on him.

As it turned out, I didn't have long to settle back into a life of freedom. Only sixteen weeks after my release on bail, I was cooking dinner one night at my then partner Frank's place when I looked out the window to see several cars full of detectives pulling up with him and three of his mates inside. As the cops began to lead them toward the house I rushed upstairs, grabbed my syringes, raced out the back and threw my bag of goodies over the fence. When I got back inside, they were already there. I hoped like hell they hadn't seen me.

The search of the house went on literally for hours. It was

a big house. Eventually, much later, a couple of detectives came into the kitchen, where we'd been forced to stay seated, and threw some plastic bags of white powder onto the table.

'Look what we found,' they said.

I couldn't believe my eyes. Frank never kept drugs anywhere near me—if I'd known it was there, I could have been having some free hits! I immediately suspected it was a set-up. There was no way there'd be any smack in that house. Anyway, that didn't seem to matter much. We were all taken to the local police station and charged with possession and conspiracy to import a prohibited substance. They hadn't even been interested in me until they discovered I was already on bail for another drug charge. My luck had certainly run out and I was really in trouble now. There was no way I would get bail while I was already on bail, and that was exactly what happened the next morning in court. Frank and his mates all got bail, and I was refused.

Off to jail again! It was 31 October 1979. As the cell door at the Frankston police station closed behind me, I shuddered. Of course, I had a habit again so I'd soon be hanging out. It was going to be another long, cold night. The Frankston cells were a bit more modern than the ones at Russell Street and the Supreme Court, and they weren't bluestone but they were just as grimy. As the diarrhoea, vomiting and sweating started, I slowly began to grasp the fact that I didn't have a hope of getting out this time. I didn't even have a trial date for my first possession charge yet. I tried to settle in for the restless night ahead, my thoughts as jumbled as ever. It seemed pretty ludicrous to me, but this time I had even less idea who owned the smack that I'd been charged with possessing. My life was getting weirder by the minute. Maybe one day I'd be charged with possessing something that did belong to me!

When the prison van arrived the following morning, all I could hope for was a break in the vomiting and diarrhoea during

the now familiar ride to the prison. After my arrival, I was processed through the reception area much as before, except now
they knew me. Once again I went to the prison hospital, but
this time I had no doubt I'd be staying long enough to make it
to the remand section of the prison. The medical sister greeted
me almost like an old friend. She seemed pleased to see me and
I think she actually did like me. I certainly wasn't troublesome,
just sick. Over the next couple of days we went through the
usual medical checks and tests again.

'When did you last menstruate?' she inquired.

'I wouldn't have a clue,' I said to her. 'When I was in here
last time, my contraceptive pill got mucked up because I couldn't
see a doctor in time to continue it. I don't think I've had a period
since then. It pissed me off because when I came in last time I'd
just gotten my period back again after about two years.' Most
women don't menstruate while addicted to heroin. It had happened to all my women friends.

The sister continued her questioning about my cycle or,
should I say, the absence of a cycle. As it turned out she decided
to do a pregnancy test along with all the other urine and blood
tests, looking for who knows what? I didn't take much notice.

A few days later, when the vomiting and diarrhoea had
ceased, I was allowed to move to the remand dormitory, which
accommodated about twenty women. I was shocked when I
arrived there. I'd been told the prison had been a venereal disease
hospital in pre-war times, which explained why the buildings
looked so old. Once I entered the remand dormitory I discovered
what was basically a big rectangular shed made of pressed tin
with beds in a line against the wall, all the way around three
sides of the rectangle. If you leaned over the side of the bed and
reached out with your arm, you could touch the one beside you.
Grey army blankets were stacked neatly at the end of each bed;
when the weather was cold, we'd pile as many of them on our

beds as we could get our hands on. Sometimes the weight on top of you felt as oppressive as the prison system itself, and you never seemed to be able to get warm anyway.

One end of the tin shed, which was semi-partitioned off, was the lounge-room area where we'd sit after lock-up at 4.30 pm, watching television or chatting and drinking tea and coffee into the evening. Bad luck if you felt like some space because there was none to be had in there, although I have to say I was glad for the company after the isolation of the police cells and the prison hospital.

One of my close friends, Stella, was also on remand, so we quickly organised for me to have the bed next to hers. I'd known Stella almost as long as I'd known Fred, Chipper and Danni. We'd been using together for years and had both sold to each other when we were onto a decent contact. It was Stella's house I'd call into on my way to see my mum, just before she died. Between Danni, Stella and I, we'd all been able to keep our habits going during that time. Stella and I trusted each other, so it was comforting to have such a good friend so close.

There were also a few single rooms down one side of the tin-shed remand building. They were mostly occupied by women who'd been refused bail on murder charges; they'd be living in the remand section for some time before their trials came up. At least they had a little privacy; even though they couldn't lock their rooms, at least there was a door to close behind them, unlike the rest of the dormitory. These women were different to us. They weren't drug users and they tended to be a bit older and more serious. A couple of them seemed incredibly depressed, rarely talking. Sometimes we'd worry that behind the privacy of their closed doors one night, one of them would decide to end it all and kill herself. I dreaded the thought of not seeing someone at morning muster, then opening their door to find them dead. I guess those women were trying to deal with massive emotional trauma, but the rest of us didn't think about it all that much; we were too concerned about ourselves.

With Stella there, I settled in quite well. She was always good for a laugh, and we didn't think too much about the seriousness of our situations, mine in particular. She was also in for drug charges, but they were relatively minor compared to mine. We were really only capable of dealing with the present and, with the assistance of heroin, were accustomed to instant gratification—although, of course, it was hard to satisfy those needs in jail. I gradually became accustomed to the daily routine. We were woken by officers unlocking the doors and calling out to us at 7 am. We'd get up and go to the communal dining room, only fifty metres from our building, for breakfast. Then it was back to the dormitories to clean up and get ready for work. Employment opportunities included working in the laundry, the sewing room, the garden or as 'billets', which meant cleaners. At 8 am we were called to 'muster' where we had to form a straight line and respond as our names were called out one by one. After that we'd go to our work posts until 11.30 am, which was lunchtime. We had to go to the dining room for lunch, then we could fill in the rest of the hour outside. At 12.30 pm another muster was held, after which we'd return to our work posts until 3.30 pm. Remand and sentenced prisoners could mix freely until we were finally locked in at 4.30 pm.

The only change to this routine happened at the weekends, when we got an extra hour in the mornings before having to attend the first muster at 9 am. Each Saturday after muster we had 'inspection', which consisted of the governor visiting every section of the prison to inspect it for cleanliness. When he walked into your area, you had to remain standing while he checked it out. If he approved of what he saw, we'd be free for the remainder of the weekend.

My work post was in the garden, or 'horticulture' as they called it. What a laugh! Unfortunately, instead of it being an interesting job, the officers managed to make it tedious. Some days they'd make us fill the wheelbarrows with pieces of broken concrete, rubbish or leaves—or anything else that was lying around—then they'd make us wheel it to another part of the jail and dump it. Later in the day, they'd make us go and collect the stuff again and dump it somewhere else. Really, they were just inventing tasks until it was time to finish for the day instead of letting us do useful things like creating a vegetable garden or something else that had some purpose. Of course, you came to know the officers who made you do these worthless jobs; if you complained, they'd provoke you until you lost your temper, then they'd charge you with verbal abuse. Some days it seemed like such a waste of life and such a bullshit existence. With them there certainly didn't seem to be much chance of rehabilitation occurring, but when there was a decent officer on duty we were able to do some useful things, and we were treated with some respect.

As often as possible I tried to get the mowing job as there was a big oval as well as plenty of grassed areas in the jail. The prison was located on five acres of land which ran almost alongside the Yarra River in Fairfield, a suburb north of Melbourne. Outside the walls was beautiful parkland, so even though the buildings were old and ugly, the land was actually very pretty, with some lovely old trees. When I was able to get the mowing job, I would put on a large pair of gumboots, start up the mower—the sound of which drowned out all of the other 'prison' sounds, like the loudspeaker—and mow to my heart's content, at least until the lunch break. Then I'd do the same during the afternoon until knock-off time at 3.30 pm. On those days, I'd daydream while I pushed the mower and, being outside, I actually enjoyed that solitary time.

After work, we'd go to the dining room for our evening meal and to collect our mail; we could remain outside until 4.30 pm, which was lock-up time. Then we had to go to our respective dormitories for muster and we didn't see the officers again until night medication time, about 8.30–9 pm.

The routine was so repetitive and unstimulating that we became like naughty children. What we really needed was access to doctors and counsellors, not the police and prison officers, but the system wasn't set up for it. The bottom line was that we had to be punished by removal from the community so that it could be protected from us. We found ourselves continuing to hide in a cloud of secrecy and, when necessary, lies, just the same as on the outside. There were so many rules in prison that you could rarely discuss anything with an officer because it might imply that you'd broken one. Of course, you'd never tell them about sneaking drugs into the jail because it was just as illegal in the jail as it was outside but if you never talked about your drug use, you'd certainly never get to the reasons why you used. My heroin use had provided me with good training for prison and in a funny sort of way I was grateful, because the few women who arrived there without previous experience as illegal drug users seemed to have much more trouble adapting than we did. What you had to grasp in there was to keep your mouth shut, mind your own business, and not tell the officers anything.

We looked forward to medication time in the evening just to relieve our boredom. We'd get our dose of prescribed drugs, usually sleepers which, of course, they gave us quite freely. Sometimes, just for something to do, we'd inject the drugs. We thought it was fun, but in reality what it did was put you to sleep as soon as it entered your bloodstream.

One night after receiving our sleeping medication, I went to the bathroom and filled the syringe with the murky, chalky mixture and hit it up. Stella was the only one who had been able to smuggle in a syringe, so we all had to wait our turn to use it. After my turn, I had to move quickly back to the lounge area where I sat on one of the chairs and closed my eyes with my head leaning against the back of the chair. I didn't wake up until hours later when the officers came to do their rounds and ordered us to bed. At the sound of their voices, I shook myself out of my self-imposed sleep and looked around me. Stella seemed pretty dopey; no doubt I did too. We dragged ourselves to our beds and returned to sleep. At least it made the night pass quickly, but I started thinking how easy it would be to wish my whole life away in there.

We tried to make fun of our situation but in darker moments, of which there were plenty, I couldn't cope with the routine, the boredom. I didn't feel like I belonged there. In fact hardly any of us did. Most of the other women I met seemed so lovely, not bad like you might imagine prisoners to be. The majority appeared to have come from deprived and abusive back-grounds, and they used illicit drugs to escape the memories. Hardly any of us had committed crimes of violence. I couldn't accept that I had to be there, yet I knew there was no way out. I didn't think much about escaping because the idea of being on the run didn't appeal. I was adamant that I wasn't going to be there for long.

One day after I'd been there a couple of weeks I heard my name called over the loudspeaker as I was walking to my work post in the morning: 'Helen Barnacle to the medical centre,' boomed over the prison grounds.

'Wonder what I'm wanted there for?' I asked Stella, who was walking alongside me. I had no desire to go back to the hospital, but I did as I was told.

'Come in and sit down,' the sister said in a motherly kind of way as she ushered me into her office. 'I need to talk to you.'

I was immediately suspicious. I knew I wasn't there to be

told they were going to put me on a free trial of prescribed heroin, and that was about the only news I'd be interested in hearing from the medical centre. I was still restless and moody from coming off the stuff, and I really just wanted to be left alone to do my own thing. But I didn't have a choice, so I sat myself on the chair opposite her.

'I just received one of your urine tests from pathology,' she said, pausing for breath. 'You're pregnant.' She stared straight at me from behind her desk. 'We'll get the doctor in this afternoon.'

'What?' I said in shock, thinking that I was hearing things. 'I can't be,' I continued in a feeble voice. My mind wouldn't work quickly enough to grasp the full extent of this news. 'I don't even have periods any more. How could I be?' I pleaded with her.

'Just because you haven't had a period for a while doesn't necessarily mean you can't conceive,' she replied. 'In fact, that's probably because you're pregnant.'

'What, for the last two years? I haven't had a period for two years ... well, at least only a couple of times. How?' I asked her.

It couldn't have happened at a worse time with my future so uncertain, although any time would probably have been terrible for me, given my lifestyle then. I bent over, holding my head in my hands, and started sobbing as the reality hit me. The sister gave me some time without intruding. I felt defeated as I breathed out a big sigh. My body was only just beginning to recover from the physical effects of heroin withdrawal. I was so weak I could barely lift my arms above my head, and I'd lost a lot of weight. My whole world had been turned upside down—getting busted, coming to prison, and now this.

I immediately began to think of the options, abortion being the most obvious one. I was aware that the sister was a pro-lifer because she had posters up all around the medical centre, so I kept those thoughts to myself. I cried tears of dismay and confusion. I felt like a little girl, yet I was about to become a mother! It was more than I could comprehend. The sister tried her best to comfort me.

Later that afternoon I was called back to the medical centre for a medical examination by the doctor. I walked in dejectedly and lay down on the bed. The doctor undid the buttons on my prison dress, half of which were missing, and started feeling around my stomach, mumbling as he touched and prodded.

'You're about five months pregnant,' he concluded as he pulled my dress back over my stomach to cover me.

'No way!' I exclaimed. My body was showing no outward signs of pregnancy. After the many years of addiction, there was little connection between my physical self and my thinking self. My body was no temple—it was merely the external receptacle within which I existed.

The doctor walked out of the room, leaving me there alone in my confused state. He didn't seem to want to know how I felt about the news. A few minutes after he'd left I did the buttons up on my dress and slowly walked outside, avoiding the sister. I didn't feel like talking. Fortunately, she was locked away in her room with the doctor. I was lost in my own jumbled thoughts. I began to grasp the fact that abortion was not going to be an option. I was twenty-five years old, still psychologically caught up in the merry-go-round of heroin addiction and facing a possible prison sentence. This is no time for a birth, I told myself. Births are supposed to be joyous celebrations, and I felt like a corpse. I knew that wasn't how it was meant to be. I had little to offer anyone just then. I couldn't even seem to help myself.

I thought about having to tell the father, Frank, and my brother. I nervously anticipated their shocked reactions. I already knew it wasn't what Frank would have wanted. I didn't have much credibility in their eyes at that point in time. I felt like a hopeless case. As I walked slowly from the prison hospital trying desperately to grasp hold of reality, it seemed like I couldn't get anything right.

Because I was on remand I was able to have a mid-week visit, something sentenced prisoners weren't allowed. I asked my brother and Frank to come in to visit me. Wednesday afternoon arrived.

'Helen Barnacle to the visit centre!' the loudspeaker shouted across the prison grounds.

My stomach clenched tight with nervous apprehension. I felt like I used to whenever I'd had to ask my father something; there was that same tightness and churning in my stomach. I was so frightened of their judgment, and their almost certain condemnation of me. I felt a failure. I believed Ron wouldn't think I was capable of caring for a baby, and I knew Frank wouldn't want to have one with me. It wasn't a very secure relationship. I felt like a child who had done something wrong, not an expectant mother! Sometimes Ron had an aloof way of dealing with emotions, and these days he was more a parent than a brother. However, the time had come to face them both and tell them the news.

I walked into the visit centre and sat on the prisoners' side of the table. No touching allowed. No privacy either. Because I was a known drug user, I wasn't allowed contact visits yet. It was something you had to earn. Not what you'd call an ideal setting to convey this sort of news!

'Hi Ron, hi Frank,' I said, trying to act calm. They looked suspicious, wondering why they'd been called into the prison mid-week.

'Sorry to ask you to come in here at such short notice, and in the middle of the week, but I've got some news I need to tell you,' I said to them meekly. 'I'm pregnant.'

I looked across at them, nervously awaiting their reactions. How I wished I could flee from the visit centre. I knew they wouldn't be impressed and, of course, they would see it as my fault—men usually do. I knew Frank wouldn't take responsibility for this 'accident'. They tried to remain composed, as though we were having a conversation about what we'd eat for lunch, but their faces said it all.

'What are you going to do about it?' Ron asked.

Get ready for the next blow, I was thinking to myself. 'Nothing I can do,' I replied. 'I'm five months pregnant.'

Silence. Ron raised his eyebrows, momentarily stuck for words. It was an unfortunate setting in which to receive such dramatic news. We all needed time to absorb it. I hadn't digested it myself yet.

We continued the visit until the regulation half an hour was up. I sensed they wanted desperately to get out of the room but were too polite to leave early, so we talked about nothing much until the officer told us to finish the visit. At that point in time Ron didn't know Frank all that well, but they got along okay. I'd omitted to tell Ron about Frank's involvement in the drug world; Ron thought he was a regular bloke who ran his own business. I didn't have the heart to tell him the truth.

I felt relieved to have the news out, but I also felt judged. I knew they thought I wasn't capable of looking after a baby. I knew they thought I couldn't even look after myself and, from external appearances, they had a point. I did seem to act like a child when I was around either of them. It was like having two fathers looking down authoritatively on me, except that I was twenty-five years old and they were only a few years older.

Although I did feel pretty hopeless, I also sensed my first protective stirrings towards my unborn child, and something inside me shifted ever so slightly; maybe it was acceptance, or maybe I'd just resigned myself to the fact that I was having a baby. I certainly didn't feel joy that I was pregnant—probably ambivalence would describe it better—yet now that an abortion was out of the question, I was pretty amazed at the fact that I had a baby growing inside me. I also knew that I could never give it up for adoption, so I was going to be a mother. I kept my feelings to myself as I didn't feel comfortable or safe enough to discuss them with Ron or Frank.

I knew Frank hadn't planned on a having a child with me; our relationship was too rocky and unstable. In fact, I was just starting to realise how abusive it was. He'd also never trusted me, because I'd always lied to him about using heroin. I did feel lucky that I was no longer addicted to smack. At least the baby wouldn't be born with a habit. It suddenly dawned on me that I'd just gone through the gruelling withdrawal process with a fetus living in my womb. It was a miracle it had survived. It must be a very strong-willed baby, I thought. Certainly it was going to need to be.

A month later, six months into the pregnancy, my body began to take on the shape of a pregnant female, although I still felt very little psychological connection with the child. It seemed like once I was aware of being pregnant, my body suddenly had permission to exhibit the fact. I wasn't overjoyed about my stomach protruding out in front of me. It felt very uncomfort-able, but I knew it had a bit more growing to do yet. All my friends in Fairlea seemed quite thrilled and were becoming very protective of me, particularly Stella. One day when there was a bit of a scuffle between two women in front of us, Stella grabbed me by the arm and gently walked me out of punch-throwing distance, shielding my stomach with her body. It was like they all wanted to look after me. It was really sweet and made me feel warm and wanted. I realised I'd never really felt that with Frank, certainly not recently anyway.

Danni, my old friend from Fitzroy Street, wrote to me just

about every week but she was unable to visit because she had a criminal record. One day she decided she wanted to see me and, next thing I knew, there she was, walking to the dining room with the admitting officer. When she saw me she ran toward me.

'Hi!' she said, giving me a big hug. 'I decided to pull in some outstanding fines [for prostitution],' she told me.

'You're joking!' I exclaimed.

'No,' she said, 'I miss you. It's not the same out there without you around.'

'You are amazing! It's so good to see you!' I said to her, overjoyed at this surprise.

'I'm only staying for a few days. I've got a couple of hundred dollars' worth of fines, so I thought I'd do the time instead. It's the only way I can get to see you!' she said with a laugh.

Although we were not accommodated in the same dormitories because I was still on remand, Stella and I spent lunchtimes and our after-work hour with Danni. We had all been so close on the outside. It made me feel very special that Danni would willingly come to jail in order to see me. I still couldn't quite believe she'd done it.

'You're in a lot of trouble,' she said to me the next day at lunchtime. 'The cops think you're a really big player in the drug scene,' she said. 'I tried to tell them you're not, but they just laughed at me.'

'Yeah, I know, but what can I do? I'm not saying anything.'

'You know you could get years. Everyone down the street is really worried about you,' she explained. While it was very thoughtful of her, she knew there was nothing I could do about it, except keep my mouth shut, which of course got me into more trouble with the police. She'd been around for years and we all knew it was just the unfortunate truth. If you dobbed people in, you'd end up dead—courtesy of the dealer—and the police never respected 'informers' anyway. However, the police also didn't seem to like people who wouldn't give them information.

'Anyway, let's not get morbid about it. Let's just enjoy your time here. It might be ages before I see you again!' I said to her, laughing, although I was really only half joking.

Danni spent a few days with Stella and me and then it was time for her to go, her fines now 'paid'. We said goodbye to her and watched her walk towards the gate, returning to freedom. We laughed about her 'visit' for weeks afterwards.

Not long after this a couple of men came into the prison to 'talk' to me. I walked into the visit centre after being summoned over the loudspeaker. Seeing them sitting there in their dark suits, there was no doubt in my mind that they were some sort of police. Sure enough, I soon found out they were federal police wanting to question me in regard to the 'conspiracy to import' charge, the subject of my second trial. They both smiled at me like we were old friends, or at least about to become friends.

How peculiar, I thought to myself as I walked towards them. I couldn't understand why they'd want to see me given that I'd already been charged.

'Hello,' I said to them pleasantly enough while I pulled up a chair. They introduced themselves and I immediately forgot their names. They started pressuring me to give information about the others who I'd been charged with, particularly my partner, Frank. They even offered me a deal—an indemnity if I'd be a witness for the prosecution. They were trying to scare me by telling me what a long sentence I'd receive if I were found guilty, but I wouldn't say anything about drugs, except to admit to my own use of heroin. I found it strange that they didn't understand that. My silence annoyed them and made them persist even more.

'You know you'll be doing years if you don't talk to us,' one of them said.

Unfortunately, I knew he was probably right! 'That's my bad luck,' I responded. 'I can't tell you anything. I've got nothing to say to you.' I wouldn't discuss any of the others involved, and I wouldn't make or sign a written statement, which made the meeting a pretty short one. I also hadn't succumbed to any of their offers of a deal. It seemed to me like a weak thing to do, dobbing someone in just to save my own skin.

I guess I just thought all along that I wouldn't ever get caught—that's every junkie's wish. It's easy to deny the truth of a situation if you are constantly stoned. I'd known all along that drug use was illegal; as a result, I was going to have to wear the consequences, even if that meant I was found guilty of something that I wasn't guilty of. A deal with the police or prosecution would mean that I could be given an indemnity in return for giving evidence against the others. No deal. I'd see them in court.

8

Temporary freedom

In January 1980, when I was seven months pregnant, the trial for my first charge, possession of heroin, came up. I knew I could go down on this one even though it wasn't my smack. The drug squad knew it wasn't Fred's or mine, but they'd charged me anyway—better to have the wrong person than an unsolved case.

It seemed the police still thought I might be the confessing type, probably because I was quiet rather than outwardly abusive towards them, but I knew I was never going to tell them anything. I didn't trust them. I didn't believe in their system, its dishonesty and its disrespect for us drug addicts. I'd seen how they'd treated some of my drug-using friends in St Kilda. Once they got them behind closed doors down at the police station, they could do anything, the heroes! Sometimes they'd handcuff drug users to a rail to prevent them using their arms, then they would start bashing them with their fists, batons or boots, trying to get information out of them.

Once when my friend Danni was trying to detox herself and was out of it on barbiturates, they raided her third-floor flat in St Kilda. They dragged her out of bed naked, across the floor to the front door, and down three flights of stairs until she had carpet burns all down her back. When she landed at the bottom they finished her off with a few kicks, then one last big one, a boot right between her legs. I've never seen bruising like it, all around her vagina and the inside of her thighs. It was a horrific, vicious attack—I'd never felt so disgusted. The fact that any human being could do that to another human being is unforgivable, but that it was done by the police is inexcusable. Fortunately, Fred and I turned up soon after and we were able to take care of her for a bit.

No, I wasn't going to tell the police anything. One thing I'd learnt in this illegal, black-market world of drugs was that the police were to be avoided, not talked to and not trusted, no matter what the cost to myself. I was loyal to my friends and I perceived the police as the enemy.

During my trial a classic example of dishonest police practices actually turned things in my favour. My lawyer exposed the two detectives as having different versions of the way they had supposedly achieved their statement from me. And the statement was a lie because I'd only given the police my name and address and 'no comment' answers to their questions. When they were called into the courtroom separately to give their evidence, it became obvious that they were lying as several details were quite different in their respective stories about my 'statement'. These facts were not lost on the jury and, after all the evidence was presented, I was found 'not guilty'.

It was a relief, and I realised I was lucky because, although the detectives and I knew that the confiscated heroin wasn't mine, technically I could have been found guilty of being in possession of it. It was found in my car, although none of my fingerprints were on it as I'd never touched it. Anyway, the drug squad were not happy with the outcome, but I reckoned it was karma for lying and making me wear a charge that I shouldn't have. I've always found it strange that drug addicts are perceived as dishonest, prisoners more so, yet my experience of the straight world is that people are often just as dishonest as any drug user I've ever met.

I couldn't be released from prison immediately because I had to apply for bail on the second lot of charges I'd incurred with Frank and the others. It was another week before I went back to court. This time bail was granted and I returned to the prison jubilant, knowing I'd be released before the day was over. It was just a matter of Frank organising my bail money, then he'd be there to pick me up.

It's funny how drugs had always been the only thing I'd ever lied about. I always felt I had to, at least to straight people. It's illegal in this country to use heroin and, unfortunately, it was my favourite drug. If I'd become addicted to prescription drugs I wouldn't be in all this trouble and I'd be getting treated by a doctor. I'd be placed on a controlled amount of drugs and the doctor would also check out how I was feeling and have some understanding of addiction, unlike the police.

Later that day I was released from the prison. As I walked out the gate and looked ahead to see Frank walking towards me, I felt elated to be free and relieved to have a reprieve from that monotonous existence. I looked forward to a drink of Coke and a tub of yogurt. It's amazing what you miss when you're in jail. I was also relieved that I'd be able to give birth outside the prison.

After I settled in at Frank's, he invited Ron for dinner one night. At that point in time Ron still had no idea that Frank and his mates had been charged with possession and importing heroin, as they had gotten bail the following day. Ron and Frank had decided it was time to talk about what I was going to do with the baby once it was born. After dinner we went upstairs to the billiard room where they sat themselves on stools in front of the large bar, which extended from one end of the room to the other. I'd sensed earlier that there was going to be a parent-to-child kind of discussion, and I'd had a hit in order to deal with it. I'd only used a couple of times since my release, so I didn't have the pressure of having to maintain a habit. I felt that the fetus would be okay as long as I wasn't addicted.

I relaxed into a beanbag in front of the open fire, the billiard table between them and me. The way they were talking, you'd reckon it was them carrying the baby. They both seemed to think it was up to them to decide what to do with it! They both came to the conclusion that, after the birth, I should put the baby up for adoption. Then they asked me what I thought.

I'd been sitting there on the beanbag only half listening, feeling angry at having not been included in the conversation. I was glad that I'd had a hit only a couple of hours before because their conversation was making me feel like a useless lump of shit, like I wasn't even intelligent enough to comprehend the situation. I knew I wasn't giving up this baby, I'd already decided, but I also understood what a neat solution it would be for them if I gave it away. That way, they wouldn't ever have to worry about it. I felt like telling Frank not to worry, I'd never ask him to pay maintenance or child support. It quietly deepened my resolve to be a mother to my unborn child. I'll show both of them, I thought to myself.

When I told them my decision they didn't put up much of an argument, probably realising it would be a waste of time. Although they thought I was pretty hopeless, they also knew I was stubborn and incredibly determined when I wanted to be.

About 5 am a few weeks later, when I was about eight and a half months pregnant, I was in bed asleep with Frank when I awoke and got out of bed to find liquid dripping all down my legs. I couldn't stop it. I thought I must have been pissing myself and I was immediately embarrassed, but I just couldn't do anything about it. I walked around the bed and straight into the bathroom, but by now I was getting a bit panicky. I'd never experienced this before so I figured it had something to do with the pregnancy, although I wasn't due to give birth just yet. I hadn't received much information during the pregnancy and hadn't attended any of the classes at the hospital, mostly due to being in prison. This had been such a confusing time for me, what with the trial, getting off heroin, and making the decision about keeping the baby. I was still so disconnected emotionally from all of it.

I tried to clean myself up a bit, then went downstairs and rang the hospital. After I explained what was happening, they told me my waters had broken.

'You'd better come in quickly,' the nurse said calmly. 'Don't panic, but don't waste any time.'

I suddenly realised I was about to give birth. Wow, I thought to myself, how amazing!

By this time Frank had also woken up and we got into the car, with me perched on about six thick towels to absorb all the water. Frank was a bit anxious and sped all the way to the Women's Hospital, a trip of about forty minutes, then dropped me at the front door.

'See ya' later,' he said, then gave me a kiss. He didn't want to stay. 'Can't stand the sight of blood,' he said. 'I'll ring the hospital later and see how you're going.'

The nurses brought a wheelchair and took me inside. I soon found myself in a room with many other women all at different stages of pre-birth. I was taken into a small room, given an enema and told to keep moving to try to bring on the contractions, which apparently should be coming more often now that my water had broken. A few hours later, it seemed I wasn't making enough progress, so they discussed putting me on a drip to induce the labour. Not long after, though, the time between contractions decreased and I was wheeled off to yet another room where I was surrounded by people in white coats.

I was feeling pretty lost and alone with all these strangers, but I figured that was how it was meant to be. I'd always felt a bit 'separate' from the rest of the world, and my experience of giving birth was no different. I didn't find it strange that I had no-one to support me through the birth, or even that there was no-one there for me afterwards. It had never occurred to me to ask anyone—my mother wouldn't have.

A nurse in white started telling me how to breathe and when to push. It was bloody hard work and it went on relentlessly. 'Push!' she'd say. And again, 'Push.'

'I need a break,' I told her, out of breath.

'Push! No break, not yet. Here, try the oxygen mask. Just a few more pushes.'

I was sweating and getting tired. I'd lost track of how long this 'pushing' routine had been going on, but it seemed like a bloody long time.

'Push!' she said again.

Then I heard someone else say, 'The head's coming out!'

'Push!' she repeated. 'Just a couple more.'

'That's what you said before,' I responded, struggling for breath. I discarded the oxygen mask; it made me feel like I was choking.

'Once more, come on, one more!' Then they all started fussing around at the end of the bed.

I heard a baby squawk and, at one minute past four on the afternoon of 18 March 1980, my baby was born. The nursing staff told me it had been an easy birth.

'I'd hate to have a hard one!' I replied, only half joking.

One of the nurses brought my baby over to me and I lay her on top of me, holding this little human bundle in my arms for the first time.

'She's a girl,' I said to the nurses. 'She's so tiny, so beautiful.' I was in awe, fascinated that I'd produced something so exquisite, although I knew Frank would be disappointed—he'd wanted a boy. I can't be all bad, I thought to myself.

Frank came into the hospital with his mates that night to visit. They were drunk and he seemed quite proud when he saw our daughter, but mainly he was joking around with his mates. Although I laughed with them, I really didn't feel much connection and, besides, I was quite exhausted from the ordeal. Anyway, they didn't stay long and I fell asleep, catching up on some much-needed rest.

I spent the next few days in hospital. The nurses taught me how to hold my baby properly and how to breast-feed. I learnt how to bathe her and change her nappies. I was like a sponge soaking up this new information. I was a mother now, and I celebrated this feeling with my newborn little daughter.

A couple of days after the birth, someone brought around some paperwork. My little baby needed a name. The deal between Frank and me had been that, if it was a boy, he would name him, but if it was a girl, the task was mine. I realised how lucky I was that my baby had turned out to be a girl. I knew inside she was going to be a friend as well as a daughter. From the moment she was born, something inside me changed. She was my gift of life. If she hadn't been born I think I would've been dead by now. In my deepest moments of despair and helplessness she has come to me. Her voice says, 'Don't do it, I need you. There is no-one else in the world I want to grow up with.'

Because my own mother had died almost a year before, she would never see her grand-daughter. She would have loved being a grandmother so, since the task of naming the new arrival was mine, I decided that my mother's name, Alice, would be nice: Ali for short. Maybe it was a tribute to her, although I did love the name anyway. I always felt that Mum's life was sad and that her sadness caused her life to end sooner than it should have. Maybe little Ali would live the full life that my mother, for whatever reason, never lived. I liked the comparison to Alice in Wonderland, too; all that fantasy and madness, much like my own life, I guess. I began to hope she wouldn't take after me too much!

Fortunately I had an aunty, Isabel, who reacquainted herself with me and helped with Ali for a while. She was my mum's sister, the same one who'd nursed Mum prior to her death. Because I'd been addicted to heroin for many years, I'd lost touch with any sense of family, except for my brother. Aunty Isabel was lovely and reminded me of the mother I never got to know. She even looked like Mum.

A week or so after leaving the hospital I went to stay a few days at Aunty Isabel's farm in Pakenham, about an hour south-east of Melbourne, taking with me a small amount of heroin. I didn't have a habit at that stage, but I was still using occasionally. The urge never seemed to escape me. I felt a touch guilty hitting up in her bathroom, but not guilty enough not to do it. There was still a hole inside me. I hadn't learned how to express my feelings and my self-worth was low. Although having Ali made me feel more worthwhile, the future now appeared even more frightening.

My next trial, on conspiracy to import and possession charges, was ever-present in my mind, and I knew you were only allowed to keep babies inside prison until they turned one. The trial seemed to be developing into a big one, particularly as there were five of us who had been charged. The police were still trying to implicate others. I hoped like hell I wasn't going back to jail.

Unfortunately, my developing relationship with Aunty Isabel didn't last long. Only three months after Ali's birth, she collapsed on the kitchen floor one morning and died almost instantly.

Although I hadn't been living with her full-time, I stayed there a lot and had found it a relief to be away from Frank. I prepared myself to go to the funeral. I felt confused and hard done by from this loss, although I must say I was more concerned about my own selfish needs than feeling compassion for my aunty and her family.

I had a hit prior to leaving for the funeral in order to cope with the sadness. I was angry at Frank as he didn't seem to understand how I was feeling and how much this loss meant to me. He didn't accompany me to the funeral, just like he hadn't been there at my mum's. He told me he didn't like funerals. Somewhere inside me I knew this relationship was doomed, it was just a matter of time. My brother and I attended the funeral together and I cried on his shoulder, tears of self-pity. I was lost. I needed my mum, I needed my aunty, and they were both gone. Maybe I just needed someone or something, but didn't know who or what.

Heroin continued to fill the gap, although I was still only having two or three hits a week. At first I struggled with breast-feeding, colic and sleepless nights, but after a few months things settled down and motherhood became a natural part of my life. I embraced it with all my heart. I clung to that little girl like my life depended on it, and she was rarely out of my sight. She meant more to me than my own life because through her I felt worthy.

It was June 1980, I was twenty-six years old, and although I had Ali there still remained a seemingly unfillable emotional hole inside me. I was living in Frank's big house, but it had become my prison. I rarely saw anyone because I wasn't hanging around the streets of St Kilda any more. In this relationship I'd promised to live a 'straight' life, so I continued to use in secret and there was only one friend that I trusted to score from.

The relationship between Frank and me was becoming more distant. I didn't see much of him as he only came home late at night to sleep, leaving early the next morning for work. Some nights I thought the only reason he came home at all was to fulfil his bail conditions—he had to report in to the local police station before midnight every day. Although it was a blessing not having him around much, it was an isolated life and there was an absence of adult company. I befriended a married couple who were neighbours, but I didn't discuss my drug use with them because it has a tendency to frighten people off. You never knew with straight people whether they would judge you or dob you in to the police. My secrecy limited any friendship that could develop and the days often seemed very long.

The house, Frank's house, was big and full of furniture. It even had a dishwasher, and a fridge that turned ice cubes into crushed ice. I'd buy Coca Cola just so that I could press the button on the ice crusher and have a Coke and ice. Grrrrrr, it would rumble as it did its thing.

Whammo! Crushed ice! Fascinating!, I'd tell myself—because there were never any other adults around to listen.

Other than caring for Ali I had no purpose, and there were only so many times a day you could get excited about pressing the 'crushed ice' button on a fridge. I felt aimless and, it seemed, eternally empty. I still had little self-esteem, I was financially dependent and I barely made any decisions in regard to my future. On some level I knew I wasn't feeling fulfilled, but I didn't seem to have the capacity to change it. There had even been a couple of periods when I'd stopped using, but each time I stopped, I wondered why happiness didn't walk through the door, and I kept waiting ... waiting for it to arrive. Instead I found myself feeling sad, confused and lonely and, not wanting to remain in that state for too long, I'd resort to the one thing that I knew would ease my discomfort. It always did, and I even felt more loving towards Ali after a hit. I'd become a passive recipient of life and all that surrounded me.

I knew that in Frank's big house I was merely a visitor waiting for the opportunity to leave. I couldn't seem to hold on to any firm belief in myself. My dependence on Ali was huge. She was the only interest I had, having long since given up my musical aspirations. I didn't even sing any more, and my piano had been left at my parents' house. Music was the one thing that could have dragged me out of my hole, but I just didn't have the motivation or energy for it. I invited my old singing friends from TRAMM—Pete, David and Jan—for dinner a couple of times, but that was the extent of my socialising during that period. It was always fun to see them, but there was so much they didn't know about my life, and I didn't tell them. If I allowed myself to think about it too much—the missed opportunities, the musical gift of the voice I was born with, the voice that now remained silent—I felt even more of a failure.

Each day I'd return to the empty house with Ali, awaiting that warm feeling that would flow through my veins as soon as my finger pressed down on the plunger of the syringe. It always worked. I didn't feel so isolated any more, the loneliness would immediately dissipate. My using was solitary, and even though I felt more compassionate after a hit, there was only Ali to benefit from it. Still, at least compassion lived somewhere in my heart. It was the only time I felt self-love. During the day was the safest time for me to use as I knew Frank wouldn't be home for hours. I was able to look as stoned as I liked without the worry of trying to hide it from him although, with Ali there, I didn't use as much as previously.

The weeks rolled on with my drug use increasing until, of course, I had a habit again. Things were also getting more tense at home, although I didn't see much of Frank as he seemed busy working. Still, a sickening apprehension lived permanently inside my stomach. I gave up on breast-feeding Ali after about ten weeks as it seemed my milk wasn't nutritious or satisfying; no doubt it was affected by my high level of stress and increasingly regular drug use. In fact once I stopped breast-feeding, there was no barrier to using more heroin. The pending trial was always somewhere in my consciousness, and when I was asleep it would emerge in the form of unpleasant dreams or nightmares. With my predominant thought being the uncertainty of the future for me and Ali, I was continually in a state of anxiety.

On the morning of 25 August 1980, I woke up, attended to Ali and did my usual cleaning up in that empty bloody house before noticing a newspaper which had been left on the bench. I sat down with a cup of coffee to read it, and quickly saw the headline on page three: 'BOYS FIND MYSTERY BODY NEAR BUSH SIDING'. I began to read the article underneath about two boys finding a man's dead body near a deserted railway siding in outer Melbourne. The body had gunshot wounds to its back and stomach.

I didn't think any more about it until the next day when, again in the newspaper, I saw a small photo of Fred on the front page. The police had identified the body as Fred's. He'd been murdered. Fred … my friend, my ex-lover. We had travelled Australia together, become heroin addicts together and now he was dead? Since Ali's birth I'd only seen him about once a week, but we'd still kept in touch and he'd often ring me.

He can't be, I thought to myself. I only saw him a couple of days ago, it has to be a mistake. 'Bullshit!' I exclaimed out loud as I forced myself to read on, my heart beating faster. I felt like it was going to burst out of my chest. It was unusual in the drug world to have lasting relationships, but ours had survived, sustained by mutual respect and caring.

'I can't believe this!' I again said out loud. The shock moved through my body like a tidal wave. Somewhere inside me I just knew his death was related to heroin, and as I read on, the article left me in no doubt that it was in fact a sleazy, drug-world murder. Fred was described as a 'low-level' member of a drug ring, with a long criminal history, and even as a 'violent' criminal with connections in Melbourne's vice area. I'd never known Fred to be violent and we'd known each other for seven or eight years. What a way to describe him now that he was dead.

Why?, I asked myself. Fred had been such a kind, unassuming person. What could he have done? But I was also aware that life in the drug world was cheap, and the newspapers talked about him having been a police informer. Everyone was dispensable, including me. I'd come so close to being dispensed with myself.

I spent the remainder of the day wandering around the house in shock. I did some cleaning just to keep busy, like that was going to help ... When Frank came home later that night I shared the terrible news with him, but he didn't care. He thought heroin addicts were scum, not human beings. 'He's just a junkie,' was his response.

What a cold-hearted prick you are, I thought as I stood there looking at him. I walked slowly upstairs knowing I'd receive no sympathy from him, the differences between us seeming cavernous. He never seemed to be there at important times when I needed support.

The following morning a loud, authoritative knock on the door interrupted my daily chores. I knew that knock.

'Police!' they called from outside. They were from the homicide squad and they'd come to take me in for questioning about Fred. They were the last people I wanted to talk to. I didn't trust them.

I gathered a few things together for Ali, who I had to organise to drop off at my father's place on the way. He'd been living in a de facto relationship with Jan (my mum's friend who we'd known since we were kids) since six months after my mother died. I needed someone to mind Ali as I didn't know how long the interview was going to take. My anxiety and fear rose to another level: having to deal with the drug squad was one thing, but the homicide squad was something else. I felt unsafe.

'Fred was worried about you,' they said to me in the car on the way, as if sensing my fear. 'He thought you might be next on the hit list. He's been talking to us,' they said as they looked at me inquiringly. I immediately felt uneasy, their demeanour seemed so sleazy and manipulative.

I don't believe a word of it, I thought to myself. Those guys gave me the creeps. 'Yeah, sure,' I responded out loud. I realised they were going to try and scare me into giving them information on Fred. They already assumed I knew something.

I felt angry and disgusted with them. Angry at being hauled to the station to talk to them about Fred. I felt that they didn't care about him—they just didn't want it to go down as another unsolved murder case. A drug-using friend of mine was, at the time, serving a life sentence for a murder that he didn't commit. In fact my friend Lou had even received a bullet in his thigh trying to stop his mate from shooting the guy who was murdered. The police knew the truth. Lou's mum had pleaded with them not to proceed with the murder charge. Their response was that if Lou wouldn't name his mate in court, then he'd wear the charge. My experience with 'the law' had made me cynical and distrusting of any sort of police. I felt anxious and scared heading into their territory, but I tried not to show any sign of it. I knew they had the power to lock me up for something I wasn't responsible for.

We arrived at homicide headquarters and two detectives led me to a small room. There were two men and me. One was being nice, the other was being ugly, which was easy for him since he had an ugly face. I couldn't remember Nice-Guy's name, but Ugly's name was Jim and he was behaving like a real smartarse, which didn't help the situation. I hated the way they talked about heroin addicts as if they were a sub-human species. I'd already decided he was never going to know what was going on in my head. Here I was at bloody homicide headquarters, when all I wanted was to be left alone to grieve over Fred's death.

After a few hours of useless questioning, my anger transformed into overwhelming sadness. Fred had died. I had only seen him a few days previously. The tears began to flow and the anguish set in. It was such a waste of a life. I knew it had something to do with drugs.

'Are you hungry? Can we get you something to eat?' they asked, trying to act compassionate. All of a sudden they'd turned into two 'nice guys'. Jim called out to someone to go and buy me some lunch. They'd already kept me there for half a day. I didn't bother telling them I wasn't hungry.

'I'm upset, you fucking idiots. My friend has just been murdered!' I shook my head in disbelief. Disbelief that Fred was no longer alive. Disbelief that the police seemed to think I was in on it. Disbelief that my life had come to this. The only thing I needed was a hit. I wanted to get out of there.

They left me in the room on my own for a while and I was lost in my thoughts. The world now seemed an even darker place with one of my closest friends murdered. Life was cheap in the drug world and I already knew how quickly it could be taken from you with a quick press of the trigger. Sooner or later you become aware that violence is a companion to drug addiction. I remembered how one night, when I used to hang around St Kilda, I was walking along Fitzroy Street when a guy, who until then had been a friend, jumped out of his car, charged over towards me and smashed my head against the fish and chip shop window. Apparently he thought I'd said something negative about him to someone else. No questions, no discussion, just 'smash'! No matter how much you minded your own business, hit up in isolation, didn't mix in 'the scene', violence always seemed to be just around the corner. It scared the hell out of me and was something I would never grow accustomed to.

Even the dealers' opinion of drug addicts (most of the big dealers weren't drug addicts) was that addicts were dying a slow death anyway, so sometimes they'd just hasten the process if they thought someone had ripped them off by not paying them their money. Most dealers carried a gun, which was often visible in their car, and when someone was killed it was meant as a lesson to others. Straight dealers disrespected drug addicts, even though they were their source of income.

I couldn't talk to Ron about all this. It felt too dangerous and I didn't want to place him at risk. I couldn't talk to anyone. I certainly wasn't going to talk to these homicide squad detectives about how I felt. There were some things I'd never talk to anyone about. It was like I was living in the shadows, and my bag of secrets was growing larger. Finally, after a whole day with them, they let me go and I didn't hear from them again.

The fact that I had a habit again brought with it a certain type of desperation. Frank and I argued often. 'You scumbag junkie,' he'd yell after me. I'd just turn my back and block it out. It didn't even go skin deep any more. I maintained my secret and snuck out most days to score. There was only one person in the world that I trusted to score from, Danni, and sometimes she was able to give me a free hit. I knew she'd keep my secret even if someone tried to bash the truth out of her, but she lived across the other side of town and some days it was difficult for me to get there.

'I can't stay and talk,' I'd say to her. 'I've just come to score.' She knew that I was facing a long prison sentence if found guilty, so she'd quickly produce the heroin that I needed so desperately.

'Be careful,' she'd say. I knew that she meant it. She had always been a good friend. Sometimes when I'd sneak out during the day I'd stay at her place a while and talk. She was one of the few contacts I had with the world outside the house. She was always kind and generous. She was also a bit wacky, which was a relief from my repressed world. She was using heaps and had a raging habit compared to my small one, so she had to sell enough to maintain her own addiction. She always talked of the day when she'd stop using.

One day when I arrived to score she surprised me: 'I'm going to detox myself,' she said. 'I've got a heap of Serepax and Valium, and I'm going to bring myself off this habit.'

'Shit!' I replied incredulously. 'Do you really think you can do it?'

'Of course. I'll be fine, I've done it before.'

'It'll be awful,' I said to her.

'Nah, she'll be sweet, mate.'

'You're such an optimist!' This was another thing I liked about her. No matter how bad things were, she seemed to be able to look on the bright side. She even emerged positive after that beating and kicking she received from the police—even after she was advised not to press charges against them. I would have been angry and bitter for a long time, but she just bounced back. I admired her spirit. In fact I felt quite attracted to her, but I was never going to tell her and I wasn't going to act on it either. It was another of my secrets. Danni was then twenty-four years old, a couple of years younger than me, and she'd been working on the streets half her life to support her habit. We'd grown to love and respect each other and I found her interesting . . . more than that, I found her intriguing.

Sometimes at night, if I hadn't been able to score during the day, I'd have to sneak out even when Frank was home, otherwise I'd suffer the consequences of hanging out and would have to try and find an explanation for my profuse perspiring and illness. I'd wait until he fell asleep in front of the open fire, then I'd get

Ali, in her bassinet, and off we'd drive, returning about two hours later. I always hoped like hell that he wouldn't wake up, but I'd prepare a pathetic excuse in case he did. He never caught me out, and the relief would flow through my body each time I returned home safely. It was worth it, though.

In fact it was getting harder and harder for me to find the money to score, but somehow I managed to maintain my habit. I had another source, a dealer who didn't know much about smack; I'd convinced him to let me sort of coordinate the cutting up and capping (measuring the heroin into caps) of his smack, which always gave me an opportunity to sneak some for my own use. One had to be innovative in discovering ways to maintain a source of supply at minimal or no cost. At twenty-six, this was my life—fear, scoring and hitting up—and the only certain thing about the future was the pending trial. I wasn't even sure if Ali and I would be able to remain together.

Ali was a major light in each day. It was her presence in my life that kept my drug use, at least to some extent, contained. Because I had become so dependent on external things for fulfilment and happiness, she became the object of that dependence. I loved her so totally, so unconditionally. I cherished the love we shared. She was with me twenty-four hours a day and even slept in my bed with me. The only break I had away from her was when my father and his de facto wife, Jan, wanted some time with her.

Having Ali took the focus away from the troublesome relationship between me and my father and, because I saw so little of him, there hadn't been any arguments. Ron had become a mediator between Dad and I, and had passed on the information about my charges—not that he'd had to, because it had been in the newspapers. My father and I never once discussed my drug use. Jan pretty much kept out of it and, having known her most of our lives, it was a little easier with her there, although because she was planning to marry Dad, I didn't perceive her as an ally like I had in the past. It was now almost ten years since I'd left home so, except for Ron, who was now brother/parent/mediator, I didn't have much of a sense of family and therefore didn't miss it.

9

The court case

M y second trial on the charge of conspiracy to import heroin and possession was set to commence in August 1980, not long after Fred's death. The police seemed to have settled on the five of us who'd originally been charged. Many others, most of whom were heroin addicts, had been threatened, but they'd done a deal with the police to give evidence in return for an indemnity. Apparently they were now on 'protection' programs. The remaining five of us were all pleading 'not guilty', but I was the only woman and the only addict on trial. I was also allowed to remain on bail, whereas the others were taken into custody.

On the morning the trial commenced, I kissed Ali goodbye after dropping her at Dad and Jan's place, and drove into the city to meet with my barrister in his office. He was an older man who I could've related to easily if I hadn't been so confused about what was going on. So many lies were being told that I was afraid to say much most of the time. Frank had organised legal representation for all of us and the young lawyer who had been involved in my previous bail application was also on the legal team as a junior solicitor. As we walked over the road to the Supreme Court, I was very uncertain of what lay ahead. As it turned out I didn't have to attend court in the early part, because it involved tape-recorded evidence and I wasn't implicated. Because of this my barrister tried to get me a separate trial, but he was unsuccessful. The definition of 'conspiracy' is 'to be knowingly concerned' so, with a past history of drug addiction and a previous de facto relationship with one of the defendants, it wasn't hard to implicate me in the case.

The five of us had to sit in a row at the rear of the court, awaiting the judge's arrival. The barristers and solicitors were all chatting with each other at the front of the court, quite a distance away. There was a male guard sitting beside the four guys and a female guard separating me from the other defendants to prevent us from talking to each other. As the judge entered the court we had to stand up and bow our heads. Once he had taken his seat behind a huge, wooden desk-like structure which was elevated above the body of the courtroom, we were allowed to sit down again. The only talking permitted was between the barristers, the judge and, subsequently, the witnesses. I tried to listen, but I was totally out of my depth. I didn't understand the legal jargon. For days on end they carried on legal arguments, none of which I comprehended. It was an alien world from which I seemed excluded, even though the five of us were the central characters in the plot.

Ali was just six months old when our trial commenced and, after the first couple of weeks, the police scared me enough to consider moving to my father's house for a while, at least for the remainder of the trial. They told me that some 'underworld' figures had the plans of Frank's house, intending to bomb it. As much as this story sounded fanciful, it still frightened me and I didn't want to take the risk of Ali being hurt. I decided to stay at Jan and Dad's as they were more than happy to baby-sit Ali for me during the day while I was in court. My dad had now retired, so they were both home all day. It was a difficult time and things were tense there. It had been many years since I'd lived at the family home and my drug addiction and resultant behaviour were unfamiliar to them.

Although I was out on bail during this time, I was very unhappy and a doctor had prescribed temazepam for anxiety and Mogadon for sleeping, but my emotions and drug use grew increasingly out of control. In hindsight, I would have been better off locked up, but more for my own safety than anyone else's. The other four on trial were returned to prison every afternoon, which made me think that on some level the police didn't consider me to be a threat to anyone. They had no interest in withdrawing my bail. I doubt they realised how much at risk my own safety and well-being was, not that they would have cared. I'd had very little to do with them. Because I'd never given a statement, I'd never really talked to any of them, but they'd certainly made plenty of assumptions about me. In fact I'd spent so little time in their company that I didn't even recognise them in court, yet each time I'd been charged or interviewed by them, they'd tell me stories they'd supposedly 'heard' about me. I thought they told more lies than I did!

Every day for three months I had to go to court. Things were looking pretty negative for us, which made me feel more and more insecure about the future. With Frank in jail it was difficult to get a chance to talk to him about the trial, so I really was out there on my own. I was still secretly using as much as I could. Heroin was the only thing that provided me with some sort of relief from the tension, and because the pressure was mounting and I had no support, the need to be 'out of it' was escalating. I didn't want to just have a hit and feel nicely stoned, I wanted to be totally out of it. I wanted to be nodding off and unconscious for as long as possible. It's very difficult to judge how much to hit up in order to be really stoned but not to overdose; as the days progressed, though, I didn't seem to care.

With Ali at Jan and Dad's all day I felt that I'd even lost responsibility for her. I'd often wake up in my room at night, hours after a hit, with the syringe still hanging out of my arm. Shit!, I'd exclaim to myself as I'd gradually open my eyes and return to consciousness, aware that I was lucky to have woken up at all. In fact I never seriously thought I would die of an overdose, I just kept thinking I was going to stay lucky.

When I left for court in the morning Ali was usually asleep, and when I returned after court, she was again sleeping. I missed her company and the responsibility of looking after her during the daytime hours when she was awake. At 4 o'clock in the afternoon after court closed, I had to go to the barrister's office across the road from the Supreme Court to discuss issues relating to the trial. Once that was over, I always had to find a way of scoring drugs.

Money was scarce as always, but I had a habit to feed and there were plenty of emotions I was running from, although I couldn't have named any of them then, except maybe fear. Some afternoons I'd have difficulty scoring, so I'd be late getting back to my father's place, and this would lead to another round of arguments. It wasn't long before, once again, our relationship turned sour. I treated him with increasing disrespect and he became increasingly angry. If it hadn't been for Ali, I'm sure he would've tossed me out there and then. In fact one day after court I'd walked into the house and immediately become embroiled in an argument with Dad about arriving home late. I packed my things, put Ali in her carry basket and was walking out the front door when Dad furiously rang Ron to mediate. It was just as well for all of us that the arrangement was only temporary. I was certainly out of control.

One weekend when I couldn't scrounge any money or find an alternative way of scoring, desperation overwhelmed me and I decided to go shoplifting. I'd heard my drug-using friends talk of how they did it, and I needed the money to score before I started hanging out. I drove to a large shopping complex and parked the car in the car park. As I was putting Ali in her pram, I looked around at all the 'normal' people doing their 'normal' shopping. For a moment I wished I could be just like them— they looked happy enough—but then I brushed the thought aside and focused on the job at hand.

I'm not normal, I told myself: I have a habit to feed and if I don't do something real soon I'm going to be hanging out. With that reminder, I walked into the shopping complex and decided I'd be least noticeable in a large department store.

I stole a few things and succeeded in getting them out to the car. With my confidence growing, I returned to the same store to get a few more things. I made two trips to the car with my stolen goods, but I didn't know about store detectives. On my third attempt, a hand grabbed hold of my arm before I could reach the outside doors of the shopping complex. Shit! I thought to myself as I looked around to see the stern face of the woman who was holding me firmly.

'Could you come with me, please?' she said politely, trying not to make a scene. I was grateful for that. She took me and Ali to an office behind the store and asked me some questions, mainly to see if I was going to admit to shoplifting.

No point denying it, I thought to myself. What a bummer, though. I'm in a bit more bother now.

I admitted to shoplifting and she rang the police. They arrived pretty quickly and escorted me out of the building to their car. It was really embarrassing. I had Ali in my arms while they lifted the pram into the police car directly out the front of the shopping centre, and of course people were watching. I guessed they felt pretty disgusted watching me with a baby in my arms, although I felt too ashamed to raise my head to see the looks on their faces.

We arrived at the local police station where again I admitted to the shoplifting offence. I'd had some smack on me when we arrived so I had to make an excuse to go to the toilet and get rid of it without them realising what I was doing. Fortunately they didn't know what I was up to, nor that I was a drug user at that stage, so I dropped it in the cistern of the toilet. Soon after, they searched my bag, finding my syringes and a spoon. I admitted to self-administration of a drug and proceeded to give them a statement. I also told them I'd gone to the shopping centre on the bus and they'd believed me, not bothering to check whether I had a car there; I'd gotten away with that part of my shoplifting.

The police were really nice to me and I thought they might even be feeling sorry for me. They asked me if I could raise bail, so I rang Ron to see whether he would come and bail me out. Fortunately Ron was at his place and when the police talked to him on the phone, he was okay about it. Before long he arrived at the police station. He had a bit of a bewildered look on his face, but he probably knew it was pointless to question or argue with me. I guess he knew my shoplifting had something to do with drug use, and he probably also knew I'd lie about it anyway. I was granted bail and Ron drove Ali and me back to my car which was still at the shopping centre.

'Is there anything else I can do for you? Are you sure you're okay?' he offered kindly as he pulled in beside my car.

'No. I'm fine,' I said, lying again. 'Thanks for your help.' And without any more discussion, he gave me a hug and drove away.

I remained standing there in the shopping centre car park staring after him, amazed at how supportive he still was. I always knew he'd stand by me, even when he was hurt, angry or frustrated, which was probably most of the time! I was left wondering how he really felt about me; I mean, he must have felt a bit helpless and hopeless ... Thinking that way felt a bit too close to the bone, though, so I turned my attention to my immediate problem—how to score, because I'd already started to hang out. With the remainder of the clothes I'd stolen still in the car, I got in and headed to a dealer's place.

The following Monday the trial was nearly aborted because of my weekend offending. I didn't care, although I was frightened of the possible consequences. They could have decided to lock me up and I knew that Frank would be furious, but I was comforted by the thought that he couldn't get to me because he was already locked up himself. Right now I was more worried about what the judge might do when he found out. Please don't lock me up, I was saying over and over in my head as I walked into the courtroom. I avoided eye contact with Frank and sat down after the judge had entered.

I've got a habit to feed. You can't send me to jail. I'll be sick, I was thinking to myself while my stomach squirmed. Of course, if they had known, that was exactly what they would have done to me. I'd been attempting to present myself as 'reformed' rather than as a current addict. I looked at the judge and knew I couldn't tell him how desperate I was. I felt too ashamed to tell my brother, and was too scared to tell Frank. I was really losing it. The only people who understood were my fellow drug users, and we were all so caught up in the merry-go-round of addiction that we couldn't offer much support to each other, except by continuing to use heroin together. Our assistance was limited to sharing any decent contacts we could find to score our drugs from.

In the courtroom I wasn't getting any closer to understanding the legal process. I didn't really understand how I'd gotten so caught up in the conspiracy charge. Because none of us on trial had given statements, the police had tried to piece together bits of evidence to argue a case. Many of the 'facts' presented by the prosecution were so wrong, I felt like they were talking about someone else. I certainly hadn't had the sort of involvement they were trying to claim I'd had, but I didn't get up and speak out. It was just not the place for it, and there was a process to be followed, so I walked away each day feeling silenced and frustrated. I hoped like hell that the barristers and everyone else knew what they were doing, because it was beyond my comprehension. I figured that all I could do was turn up each day and do as I was told.

Because of the overwhelming powerlessness I felt and my seeming inability to do anything about it, I moved further away from any lucid thought. The best way for me to cope with what was happening was to use as much smack as possible, and I eagerly awaited the lunch break each day for that opportunity. That was my priority as it was the only thing I seemed to have any control over. Given that I could spend so little time with Ali, the one positive aspect in my otherwise chaotic life, heroin was the only other thing that provided me with some solace, and perhaps the patience to sit all day while this court process unfolded.

I always carried a syringe, water, spoon and belt with me, and at lunchtime I'd head straight to the toilets. Once in the cubicle, I'd put the lid down on the toilet, rest the spoon on it, tip in the powder-like substance from its foil package, mix it with some water and apply some heat from a lit match until the heroin dissolved. Then I'd suck it up into the syringe through a small piece of cigarette filter and examine my arms, legs and hands for a suitable vein. I'd then sit on the lid of the toilet and slowly push the pick through my skin. 'Ah,' I'd sigh out loud as some blood appeared in the syringe, my signal that I'd found a vein. 'Comfort me, please?' I'd ask the drug as I slowly pushed the plunger down. I'd remain there, sitting on the toilet lid, awaiting release from my chaos.

'My reliable friend.' I'd speak to the drug as though it was a human being, while all my worries gradually faded away from my consciousness. It was so nice to feel warmth flowing into my bloodstream in contrast to the coldness of the courtroom with all its formalities; there I felt like a pawn in a game of chess, with someone else making all the moves. But now all those legal arguments became fuzzy in my head and I felt it all slipping away ... anxiety ... worry ... gone. 'There's nothing to worry about,' I'd say to myself as my eyelids became heavy and my body gave in to the drug. I'd nod off in the toilet cubicle for most of the lunch break, my head hanging limply over my knees. Often I didn't wake in time to grab a coffee, let alone any food. I never even thought about the disastrous outcome if I were to be caught hitting up in there.

Other people would go out to the local café and have sandwiches. Sometimes in the mornings, before court commenced, I'd see some of the jury members in there. I'd try not to look at them as I bought my take-away coffee, but it was such a weird situation and I couldn't help wondering what they were thinking. Of course, I wasn't allowed to communicate with them, so I tried not to make eye contact.

At lunchtime, however, I rarely made it to the café, and no-one knew I spent most of the break in the toilets. As long as I was coherent and alert enough to walk back into the courtroom an hour or so later, that was all I concerned myself with. When we returned to court after lunch I always dozed off, only waking periodically, shocked that I'd nodded off but too stoned to care. I'd noticed previously that the guard sitting beside me often fell asleep as well, so I didn't think I'd look too conspicuous.

For most of the trial I remained on bail, but as we approached the final weeks and the summing up commenced, I knew my days of 'freedom' were over. I had to be taken into custody from the commencement of the summing up.

Apparently that's how it worked and each afternoon after court finished I would return to the prison until the day the verdict was delivered. If I was found not guilty, then I'd be released, but if I was found guilty, then my free days were over. I was aware that the latter was the most likely scenario, although I refused to accept it.

On the day the summing up was to commence, I again kissed Ali goodbye in the morning and took my last anxiety-ridden trip into town to go to the barrister's office for my final discussion with him as a 'free' person. His office was in Owen Dixon chambers, which is one of those huge high-rise buildings just across the road from the Supreme Court. Inside, it was a rabbit warren of corridors, offices and lifts. I didn't know how to prepare myself emotionally for this day, so the only thing I had prepared was my drug supply. I stepped into the lift and went up a few floors where I headed straight to the toilets for my last hit as a 'free' person. There was no joy in it any more. It was merely a necessity in my life, much like a cup of coffee in the morning; it just made me feel 'normal'.

What am I going to do with the fit?, I asked myself after hitting up. It was a problem that had been on my mind for a while. I was worried the pick on the end of the syringe would be discovered by the metal detector when they searched me going into the prison. I couldn't hide it in my clothing, let alone in a body cavity, which meant I had to get rid of it, so I placed it in a paper bag as a disguise. After having my hit, I left the toilets and found a rubbish bin in one of the many corridors. I hesitated before dropping the bag into it . . . the sense of loss was immediate. I wanted to change my mind, but I knew I couldn't, it was too risky. Now, even my drug use was out of my control and that was the scariest part of this whole ordeal.

'Goodbye, old friend,' I said as my eyes followed the syringe into the darkness of the black plastic lining the big metal bin which was built into the wall. Part of me wanted to jump in and retrieve it, while the other part struggled with reality. I stood there staring down into the bin for a long time, afraid to move away, knowing that each step I took toward the court was one step closer to that enforced loss of freedom. I couldn't move. I didn't understand any of it and, more than that, I didn't believe I deserved to lose my freedom. I knew that if I was discovered using drugs in this building, no-one was going to be impressed, particularly my barrister, and they'd probably call the cops. I'd become a prisoner of my own secrecy. The shame surged through my body once again and I realised I'd been standing in the corridor in front of this bin for a long time. I truly felt like the lowlife that we drug users are often seen as.

I'd kept a small amount of heroin to sneak into the jail, as much as I could afford to buy. I had to secrete it in a body cavity, my vagina; I didn't think it'd be the back passage this time. How am I going to cope when the drugs run out?, I asked myself. But it was too hard to contemplate, and I forced myself to concentrate on the task of hiding the stash. Secrecy had become a way of life.

I walked from my barrister's office to the Supreme Court. At the end of the day, instead of being able to walk out and go home, a guard grabbed me by the arm and escorted me to the cells. Suddenly I was considered a danger to society. Even though I'd been locked up in cells quite a few times before, it still felt bloody awful and I could feel my anxiety rising. I was comforted a little by the knowledge that at some point I'd be able to have a snort of heroin (sniffing it up your nostril), but I wouldn't be removing it from its hiding place until well after I'd been installed in the prison remand section. How I wished I could have sneaked a syringe in with me. At least I managed to sneak the heroin into the prison without any complications. Of course the problem with snorting is that you have to use more heroin to get less of a buzz, and I only had a small amount which I had to try to ration out.

Once in prison I ran into my old friend Stella, who had been sentenced and was now living in a long-termer's cottage. After a couple of days she was able to lend me a syringe. I spun her a story that I was trying to organise some smack to come in and I wanted the syringe for when it arrived. It was actually true—I was trying to organise some more—but I desperately needed the syringe to try and make the remainder of my small supply last a bit longer. I hadn't told a soul that I had some heroin as it was too risky, and I didn't have enough to share anyway.

My first few days in custody were relatively okay, although I missed Ali. She was staying at Jan and Dad's until the outcome of the trial. I still had some smack and was only back at the prison to sleep at night, leaving me just a couple of hours in the evening to chat to the others in the remand section, most of whom I knew as we were almost all drug users. As the days passed, though, and my supply got lower, it became an issue of survival. I was going to be history when the smack ran out. I found myself trying not to think about it. I'll worry about that later, I'd anxiously tell myself, but after I'd been in custody for nearly a week, the dreaded day arrived and I was forced to face reality.

I awoke with a feeling of impending doom and a shiver ran down my spine. My body ached all over and I felt sweaty and disgusting. I was in the remand dormitory and it was my fifth morning in custody. I knew this feeling so well. I didn't have any smack left, so there was nothing I could do about it, and I knew it was going to get worse over the next few days. I lay there in my bed, blankly staring at the ceiling. I felt so bloody helpless … I thought this must have been the emptiest day of my life. Anxiety crawled through my body. It felt like it was scratching at my central nervous system, sending scrambled messages to my brain, irritating all my nerve endings. Somehow during the day I had to try and look normal as we were still only in the middle of the summing up. I wanted so much for the trial to be over, but on the other hand I never wanted it to conclude as I was terrified of the outcome. I had already tried every avenue I could think of to score, but it was difficult to make contact with anyone now that I was in custody with a guard watching over me all day.

I don't give a fuck about court, the trial, about anything, I silently said to myself as I heard the jingle-jangle of the officers and their keys approaching. I heard them walk into the dormitory.

'Time to get up!' they called out, then left again.

'Get fucked!' someone yelled back at them, pulling the blankets up over her head, trying to resume her sleep.

From my bed I looked around me at the green-painted pressed-tin walls of the remand dormitory. Behind those walls the possums and rats were long-term dwellers and it felt like we were already well acquainted. At night the noise was uncanny, amplified behind the tin. For those afraid of the dark, the nighttime produced haunted sounds—scratching, footsteps, running, scampering, squealing and hissing. Sometimes a woman in the dormitory would join the chaos from somewhere deep in her subconscious, lost in a world of night terrors, screaming, sweating, emerging from a nightmare only to find reality. Some nights that woman was me.

During the nights I had drug dreams. I was there, out on the streets, waiting to score, waiting for someone to arrive with the heroin. Waiting for a car to turn the corner, a familiar car, the one I was so desperately waiting on; waiting for someone to step outside, walk over to me, make the exchange—money for drugs—but every time I reached that point where they handed the drugs over, chaos ensued. Sirens squealed, police cars sped around the corners from every direction, screeching to a stop, guns pointed toward me.

'Don't move!' they always yelled at me.

As if I'm going anywhere, I'd think to myself, with all those guns pointed in my direction like I was dangerous! I was petrified, frozen to the spot. I knew they thought I was scum and I knew how easy it would be for them to pull the trigger. I imagined they were thinking, '... one less junkie to deal with'. I had to hope none of them yielded to the temptation to do away with me. I'd wake up screaming, sweating, my eyes searching the blackness for signs to bring me back to reality and then it would hit me ... the green pressed-tin walls, the rats and possums squealing, scratching. I'd collapse back into the saturated sheets.

During these nightmares I'd awake gagging, choking on my dry throat. I had a desperate need to go for a walk, but I couldn't even get a breath of fresh air because the windows didn't open. I'd get out from the saturated bed and look out, beyond the glass, beyond the bars. All I could see was wire fencing and barbed wire, and beyond the fence another dormitory contained within another square of wire fencing and barbed wire. I'd never felt so trapped. I longed for the big, empty house that I used to hate, with the ice-crusher fridge; a glass of Coke and ice. I never realised that being unable to make a choice would feel like this.

I wanted to scream but held it in because I didn't want to disturb the other women in the dormitory. At least they seemed to be sleeping tonight. No doubt the sleeping medication assisted. I longed for the comfort of heroin, wanting a hit more than anything. I wished that at least in my dreams I could get to use the smack that I was scoring, but I never did. The police always intercepted and I'd wake up, saturated in my own fearful perspiration. Tonight it's my turn, I'd silently tell myself as I began to calm down.

On that fifth morning, half an hour had passed since the officers had come to wake us, but I hadn't moved from my bed. I was supposed to go to court again. I was sweating, hanging out, tossing and turning. I leaned over and vomited into a bucket on the floor at the side of the bed. The ugliness of the surroundings didn't help. The feeling of collective emptiness contained within the tin walls was overwhelming.

I heard an officer opening the dormitory door again, the footsteps getting louder as they approached my bed. I didn't even look up from under the bed covers. 'I'm not going to court today,' I said in a feeble voice.

'Come on, Helen, you have to go,' the officer replied.

'I feel sick. I just want to stay in bed.' I turned over, pulled the blankets up and hoped he would go away.

'Look, I'm sorry, I can see you're sick, but you have to get up,' he replied. 'If you just get up to the front of the prison, they can call a doctor when you get to the court cells.'

I felt too sick and I just didn't care any more. I didn't respond.

'I'll be back in ten minutes to get you, okay?' He wasn't really asking, he was telling me. Even the thought of a shower sent goosebumps and shivers all over my body. I didn't know how I was going to drag myself out of there, but somehow I knew I had to.

Of course they made me go, so I eventually stumbled out of bed, got dressed and was escorted to the front of the prison. The officers didn't care either, they just had to make sure that I turned up at court. It was their job. I arrived at the Supreme Court cells and they called in a doctor. He gave me some tablets. I didn't even know what they were, but I figured it was better than nothing. I didn't tell him I was hanging out. He had an air of disinterest about him and I wasn't in the mood for talking anyway. The people who administer the courts eventually gave up on me for the day and adjourned due to my 'ill health'. I didn't care. Back to prison for the night; back to court the next day. On and on it went. Sleepless nights, sweating, tossing and turning, nightmares, followed by seemingly endless days, but after about five or six days the vomiting and nausea stopped and the worst of the physical withdrawal was over. Then came the lethargy: I had no motivation or desire for life, I just wanted it all to end. In a day or two I got my wish.

The last day of the summing up finally arrived along with the usual van to escort me from prison to court. I had a small ray of hope inside that was telling me I could be free after today, but my more rational self knew how unlikely that was. Halfway through the day the summing up was completed and, after a break, the jury retired to consider its verdict. They didn't take long, which was no surprise to me really, but even so the wait was nerveracking. I could sense that doorway to freedom closing as we were all called back from the cells into the courtroom for the verdict. One by one the judge named each of the five of us and our respective charges. Then he called on the foreman to respond.

To each name and charge the foreman replied, 'Guilty, your honour.'

It felt like an anticlimax to me. My most desperate moments throughout the trial had been in relation to my drug use and hanging out. It had been hard to concentrate on anything else. Throughout the proceedings many of the drug addicts who had been called as witnesses had had more involvement in these charges than me, but they had agreed to a deal with the police to give evidence in return for an indemnity, and they were allowed to remain free. They weren't even charged with conspiracy and were given protection by the police in return. I've been told some of them were also given air tickets and money. Although it struck me as being incredibly unfair, I never once regretted my decision not to become an informer. In the drug world I had to accept what came my way.

Although the verdicts of 'guilty' were returned that day, we had to wait another week before returning to do a plea for our sentencing. When you do a plea, the defendant usually gets character witnesses to speak on their behalf and the barrister might give the judge a bit of background information about you. I was feeling much clearer as I was off the smack and only starting to realise just how 'out of it' I'd been through the ordeal. I was also beginning to realise just how much trouble I was in ...

On 10 December 1980, four days before my twenty-seventh birthday, we returned to the Supreme Court for sentencing. As I was escorted into the courtroom, I glanced around and noticed Ron in the gallery. I supposed that he'd be feeling pretty nervous. My plea for sentencing didn't take long because, although I'd written out a personal history for my barrister, and Ron got up, trying to speak positively about me, I didn't think there was much to be said really. My ability to be objective about my behaviour wouldn't develop until years later. My barrister was hoping the judge might take into account my history of heroin addiction and choose a drug treatment sanction rather than prison. But the judge, in announcing my sentence, seemed to be under the impression that I'd had a good life with plenty of opportunities, and therefore had no reason to become a heroin addict.

He sentenced me to 12 years with an 8 year minimum, and gave all but one of the others even higher sentences, the longest one being 25 years with a 21 year minimum, which is the maximum sentence for this crime. So much for my hopes of a rehabilitation program or a Section 28, where drug counselling was part of the sanction. Because I'd tried to present myself as relatively together, rather than as a hopeless case, maybe the judge felt that rehabilitation wasn't appropriate and went harder

on me. I have no idea what he was thinking. I felt numb, which
wasn't unusual, and I suppose I was in shock, but I didn't show
any outward emotion like crying. I wouldn't have given the
coppers the satisfaction.

As we were led out of the courtroom a short time after our
sentencing, I looked over towards Ron, who gave me a resigned
sort of smile. I was escorted back to the cells, my barrister arriving
soon after to discuss the sentencing with me and to explain in plain
English what had just happened. He advised me not to appeal.

'Given the high sentences dished out to the others on trial,
I think you should just accept it and not take a risk with an
appeal,' he said wisely, although I thought I deserved another
opportunity. 'At least yours is on the lower end of the sentences,'
he added.

'Yeah, well ... shit, lucky me,' was about all I could say at
that point. He informed me that Frank was already talking about
appealing. I didn't have to make a decision right there and then,
so I waited a few days and thought about it. Then I got a letter
and a phone call from Frank in Pentridge; he told me they had
all decided to appeal and convinced me to go along for the ride.
He thought it would look odd if I didn't. I eventually agreed,
despite my barrister's advice to the contrary.

A few weeks later, I received news by mail that the prosecution were also appealing against my sentence. They wanted it
increased! The notice of appeal read:

GROUNDS OF APPEAL

1) That the sentence imposed was manifestly
   inadequate in all the circumstances.
2) That the learned trial Judge failed to give
   proper or sufficient weight to the aspect of
   general deterrence in the circumstances of
   the case.

3) That the learned trial Judge failed to give proper or sufficient weight to the evidence that Helen Margaret Barnacle was a principal participant in the conspiracy.

4) That the learned trial Judge gave undue weight to the fact that Helen Margaret Barnacle had previously been a drug addict.

DATED the 5th day of January 1981

'Fuckin' hell!' I said in astonishment after I'd read it aloud. Stella and a couple of my friends were peering over my shoulder.

'Shit!' said Stella. At least I was surrounded by people who understood. It came as a huge shock to me that the prosecution actually believed my sentence wasn't long enough; more specifically, that they believed I was a principal participant in the case. Still, I guess I only had myself to blame for that as I'd told them so little. Anyway, I had to accept that there was going to be another battle in court and that, either way, I was going to be in prison for some time. Even if my appeal was relatively successful, at best it would only mean a year or two off.

There was no-one I could really talk to about any of it because it involved so many secrets, most of which I'd never told Ron, and a great deal of my drug use was unrelated to this trial. Ron had only recently discovered that Frank was involved in drugs. I'd also never told him about the violence I'd experienced. I didn't want him drawn into that underworld, especially as he was still reeling from the shock of finding out about Frank's involvement. Anyway, I could only see him at visits and there was no privacy there.

Immediately after my sentencing, Ron and I did discuss Ali's and my future. We decided that she should stay with me even though, under prison regulations, it would only be for a couple of months, until her first birthday in March 1981. Ron and I agreed that any amount of time spent together was better than none and, besides, we hadn't yet worked out any other option. We were both still adjusting to the reality of my sentence and were only just beginning to think of what that was going to mean for Ali. She was still staying at Dad and Jan's place, and Ron was the one who communicated with them; after all the arguments we'd had when I lived at their house during the trial, we weren't really talking again except, when necessary, in relation to Ali. My father disagreed with our decision, thinking Ali should live with him and Jan rather than with me in prison, but I never spoke directly to him about it, preferring to leave the discussion to Ron.

I got through the first few months of my sentence relatively easily, partly because I was an expert at not facing up to reality. Also, until the appeal was dealt with, I didn't feel I had to accept my sentence. I clung onto some hope that my luck might just change. But the main reason I initially survived so well was that Ali was with me. I had no idea that having a child would mean so much to me. I didn't really think anything through, actually, but from the moment Ali was born something inside me had changed. I'd never experienced anything that came close to the love I experienced as Ali's mother. It was unconditional and it was always there. No fear, no doubts, just love. It was the only thing I was sure of.

After my sentencing the prison accommodated Ali and me in a small room attached to the hospital. It was barely adequate but sufficed for that precious little time we had remaining. However, she did have to leave the prison after her first birthday in March 1981, despite my efforts to change the ruling that children could only reside with their mothers until the age of one. I had written to government ministers, Dame Phyllis Frost and Father Brosnan, who was the chaplain at Pentridge. Although I'd received no positive response before Ali left, the fight wasn't over and these people were still trying on my behalf.

Ali went to live with my dad and Jan, who were now married and who both adored her. She was the only grandchild, my brother not having married yet or produced any offspring. Now I would only be able to see Ali at the weekends, when Dad and Jan, or Ron, brought her to the visit centre for an hour, and on Saturdays once a month, when children under the age of twelve were allowed into the prison from 9 am to 3 pm. The Saturday visits were fun as the kids were free to move around the prison grounds, even coming into our accommodation units. At that stage I'd been moved into Wing 1 of the mainstream prison, which was a dormitory housing mostly long-termers.

In May 1981, two months after Ali had left the prison, the five of us returned to the Supreme Court to hear the results of our appeals. It was the first time I'd seen Frank since our sentencing day the previous December. As I watched him walk into the courtroom, I felt like we were total strangers. So much had happened since the days long ago when we'd shared a relationship. He smiled warmly at me and I returned his smile, although he was escorted to the other end of the bench. We were not allowed to sit next to each other.

The three judges then entered the courtroom and we all stood while they seated themselves high up in front of us, seemingly above the world. They went through the normal courtroom formalities. The four men were dealt with before me and they were all unsuccessful with their appeals, which in a way prepared me for the fact that nothing was going to change for me either. Then came my turn and I was asked to stand up.

'Your sentence is to be increased to 15 years with a 12 year minimum,' one of the judges said. It was a majority verdict, with two of the three judges having decided an increase in my sentence was appropriate. I thought I was hearing things. Then he said something like, '. . . because you're a woman and the mother of a young child, that is no reason to give you any less than any of the men on trial.' My mind became blurred and I didn't hear anything else. I only remember needing to hang on to the back of the seat in front of me for fear of fainting.

What about the fact that I'm a heroin addict?, I thought. Doesn't that make me different to the others?

I was expecting my barrister to say something to defend me, but no words came from his mouth. I looked over to him and he slowly shook his head. Apparently this wasn't the time to speak. None of the other four was a drug user, but this fact seemed to be lost on everyone. There was no understanding of the burden of addiction. Anyway, it didn't seem to matter what I thought. No-one has the opportunity to express themselves in court except the legal representatives. For me to have spoken up then would have been considered disruptive and would only have validated the judicial system and community's growing disrespect for us drug addicts. We didn't have a voice. I guess they'd only say that I should have talked to the police.

After the judges handed down the increased sentence, no-one said anything and the court formalities came to a conclusion. We all had to stand again for the three judges to leave the room. To be quite honest, I didn't feel like paying them any respect at all, except the one who hadn't agreed to increase my sentence. It was all over and I found the silence disconcerting. I thought I should have been yelling at them, trying to make them understand, but no words found their way out of my open mouth. I guess what I was feeling was what they call 'shock', and I didn't have any heroin to help me deal with it either. I'd just made history ... the longest drug sentence ever given to a woman in Victoria. They obviously felt like justice had been done.

The police who were involved in the case looked really chuffed with the result. They behaved like they'd just backed a winner at the races, they were so elated. I imagined they'd go

out and celebrate, probably get drunk. They were allowed to—
alcohol is legal, unlike the drugs I was using. I wondered if they
ever thought about people like me, drug addicts, as perhaps
worthwhile human beings, not just junkie scum. I wondered if
they ever thought to look behind the mask we wore in court
and police interviews. Their reaction of glee shocked me. It felt
inappropriate that they should be cheering at such an occasion.

How can they feel so pleased that I'm going to jail for all
those years?, I wondered to myself, feeling even more disillusioned. This lack of understanding of my struggle, of not
knowing where I fitted in, was at the core of my drug addiction—it was the reason I used heroin, and right then heroin was
the only thing that could have eased my pain. This society could
offer me no alternative except prison. I sat there on the hard
wooden seat with reality slowly dawning. I realised I was looking
at serving two-thirds of the minimum, which effectively meant
eight years if I received all my remissions for good behaviour.
My minimum sentence had been increased by four years, but at
least the sentence would be backdated to the beginning of the
trial, which was a few months' concession. Ali would be eight
years old when I was due to be released.

After the judges had left the courtroom, I was still trying to
process my thoughts. As we were leaving, Frank gave me a small
wave and a feeble sort of smile. He was speechless too, and
looked a touch embarrassed, probably because he was the one
who had pushed me to appeal. I didn't know whether to feel
angry or not. It was like watching a movie, except I was in it. I
turned the corner as I was escorted back to the Supreme Court
cells, and he disappeared from my sight. I wondered if I'd ever
see him again ... I couldn't think clearly about anything as there
were too many conflicting thoughts surging through my mind.

I had never expected to receive more time, and now, safely
back in the cells, I sat down on the concrete floor and waited

until the officer had locked the door and walked away before I allowed the tears to flow ... quiet, lonely tears. The pounding of my heart was the only sound to be heard in that bluestone dungeon, except for the occasional rattle of keys. I wept noiselessly with my head between my knees, a solitary figure, nobody to witness my grief. The concrete surrounded me, the coldness enveloped me and the tears slid down my cheeks to their resting place on the floor between my feet. I was truly alone. There was nothing anyone could have done or said even if they'd been there. Eight years ... I was trying to let it sink in. I was somehow glad for this time alone in the cell before they came to return me to the prison. It gave me a chance to tuck my emotions back in again, to piece myself together before I had to face anyone.

What will I say to the women back at the prison?, I thought to myself. How will I act? In my heart I knew that they cared about me and they'd be so shocked at the ridiculous length of my sentence. They would all be looking at me, probably wondering what to say.

I ran through the upcoming scenario in my head. I didn't want to appear too sad or they would all start crying and if they let go, then I might, and I didn't know if any of us would be able to stop. I knew I couldn't cope with that right then. I just have to hold it all together, I bravely told myself. I had to believe that I could.

Eventually I was returned to the prison in the big, hollow, metal police van. Word had already gone around so the other women were prepared. Some of them gathered around me with a caring hug or a knowing glance. Words were scarce because there was no need for them—almost all the prisoners were drug addicts too. Although I felt alone and shocked, the presence of those women was comforting. They, too, were separated from their children and they, too, were criminals. They were also probably the only people in the world at that moment who had any understanding of what I was going through. They shared time with me in this new and foreign land.

Early that evening my brother rang the prison. Normally prisoners weren't allowed to receive phone calls, particularly after 4.30 pm lock-up, but the night officer came and took me to the governor's office so I could speak to him. In exceptional circumstances they sometimes break with normal procedure and the senior officer on duty that night obviously considered my sentence 'exceptional circumstances'.

'I can't believe it!' Ron exclaimed in a shocked but quiet voice. It felt awful hearing him so upset. He was crying in disbelief, unable to hide his grief. He sounded even more shattered than me. I'd sort of settled down a bit as the day had progressed. 'I'll come out and visit at the weekend,' he said. What else could he offer? The senior officer on duty looked concerned but didn't say much. I was glad because I didn't feel like discussing it with her, although I appreciated her thoughtfulness.

'Are you okay?' she asked.

'Yeah,' I replied. 'Thanks for the phone call.'

I was escorted back to Wing 1 in silence by another officer, the sense of despair in Ron's voice lingering in my head. I now had to resign myself to the future, at least the next eight years of it. I couldn't bear to think what that meant for Ali and me. It seemed like the odds were stacking up against us sharing a happy life. What would it be like being released from prison to be reunited with a child I hadn't lived with since she turned one? What would it be like for an eight-year-old to have a mother who was virtually a stranger? Although I was already starting to feel like I had to let go, there was still a tiny glimmer of hope living inside me. Without it, there seemed no point in going on.

10

Adjusting to a long prison sentence

E ven though Ali had been gone from the prison for about eight weeks, I hadn't totally given up hope that the rules couldn't be changed to allow children to live with their mums. However, after my appeal and its devastating result, I looked around the prison differently, perhaps for the first time taking in the details. I suppose it's called acceptance.

In the landscape of prisons, Fairlea, although very old, was certainly one of the better ones. At that time it was the only women's prison in Victoria, so it was responsible for women with security ratings ranging from 'minimum' through to 'maximum'. Prisoners with longer sentences were always classified as maximum security until about the halfway point, when their status might be changed to medium or minimum security, depending on their behaviour. Within Fairlea, the range of security classifications had to be accommodated within the five acres of land on which the various buildings stood.

The land was circular in shape with a wall surrounding it. When I was there initially, the wall was brick to about eye-level, with wire on the top; during the 1980s, when almost all of Fairlea was demolished and rebuilt, it was replaced with a tall concrete wall topped with razor wire, so that you could only see the tips of the biggest gum trees in the parkland surrounding the jail.

Once inside, there was a front administration block and a hall, which doubled as an activities centre as well as a visit centre. A short walk to the left was the communal kitchen and dining room where most prisoners had to eat all their meals. On the other side of the hall, the accommodation commenced with Wing 1, a rectangular tin dormitory sectioned off by a wire fence, which housed long-term prisoners. The next block was Wing 2, which consisted of two square rooms, each containing about twelve beds, with a hallway separating them. This area housed short-term sentenced prisoners. Again it was segregated by wire fencing. The next dormitory was remand, which could accommodate about eighteen women who hadn't yet been sentenced and who had either been refused bail by the court or, having been granted bail, couldn't raise the necessary money or surety. Beyond its wire fencing were Cottages 1 and 2. These were the 'luxurious' quarters for trusted long-term prisoners. The cottages were like normal houses, each accommodating six to eight women. They were self-contained, with their own laundry and kitchen facilities, and they had bedrooms running off each side of a hallway. Women in the cottages were able to cook their own meals in the evenings. Next to the cottages was the prefabricated Education Centre building, and completing the circle was the 'cell block'—the punishment cells. All prisoners and remandees mixed freely during the day, only being segregated after 4.30 pm lock-up for the night.

Although the buildings were archaic, the grounds were much better, with some lovely old trees and, in the middle, an oval and a netball/tennis court. During the years that I spent in Fairlea, most of the old buildings were demolished so that, by the time I left, Cottages 1 and 2 were the only original ones left.

Prison visits are both important and yet difficult. On this issue I was no different to any other prisoner I've ever spoken to. At least initially, they are a lifeline to the outside world, to all that was once precious, and you try to cling on to those relationships in the one-hour visit allowed each weekend with approved visitors. People with criminal convictions generally weren't allowed in to visit unless they'd been granted special permission. Having received such a long sentence, at first I would eagerly await my weekend visits, which were usually with my brother or, occasionally, my old singing friends from TRAMM. As time passed, though, and I became more ingrained in the microcosm that prison is, I also became less interested in the outside world. In my case it was an enforced disinterest. It was a bit like going shopping with no money. Why go looking at clothes that you can't buy? In the same way, why see and hear about people from a world that you can't be a part of?

The other problem with visits is that they are always followed by a strip search in front of two officers. To some degree, at least early in my sentence, I became desensitised to the strip searches, but that meant I was also forced to become good at tucking away the different parts of myself, particularly my feelings. The many techniques that you devise to survive in such a controlled yet emotionally deprived environment certainly don't contribute to the development of an integrated personality. Some of my friends, the ones who didn't deal with the humiliation and powerlessness in the way that I did, got angry and abusive at the officers, showing their frustration outwardly, but these outbursts were always followed by punishment. I tried to discover simple ways of coping. Mostly it was avoidance, steering clear of officers as much as possible so that I wasn't subjected to their pettiness.

Later on in my sentence I minimised contact with the outside world, thus reducing the amount of strip searching I was required to endure. It made it easier to create and believe in the fantasy world I'd needed to construct. Ultimately on a long sentence, the goal is to stay sane and I did what was necessary to achieve it. This process is called institutionalisation.

I remember well my first visit with Ron after being sentenced. Because I was no longer a remand prisoner, all my personal clothing had to be replaced with prison attire. During summer this consisted of a striped dress during the week and a plain-coloured dress for weekend visits. Unfortunately my weekend dress was bright orange and about as ugly as you could imagine, especially with my red hair. I was sure those weekend dresses were part of a character building exercise. See if you can feel good in this, I imagined the officer thinking as she handed over my new outfits. Our winter attire was a blue tracksuit. All prison clothing was made by prisoners who worked in the sewing room.

When I was first there Fairlea didn't have a proper visit centre, so we used the hall. Also during the late 1970s and early '80s, women were beginning to receive long sentences for drug-related crimes, which meant there was an influx of these women, increasing the prison population to about sixty. Women who came in on drug sentences weren't allowed, initially, to have contact visits; they had to prove, over time, that they could be trusted. It was supposed to prevent the smuggling in of drugs during visits. To accommodate visits in the hall, large tables were joined together lengthwise down the centre, with visitors sitting on one side and prisoners on the other. Unfortunately, because ninety per cent of us were there for drug-related crimes, the majority had to sit at the table; only the murderers could have contact visits, sitting on chairs around the edge of the hall. Ironic, really. Because there were so many of us sitting along one side of the tables, we were shoulder to shoulder and would have to talk loudly for our visitors to hear us across the expanse between us. Needless to say, there was no privacy, especially as three or four prison officers were stationed at various intervals around the hall constantly watching and no doubt listening.

I was living in Wing 1, a dormitory-style building accommodating about sixteen women. It also had pressed tin on the inside walls but, unlike the remand dormitory, the space was partitioned off into 'bedrooms', where women slept two to a room. The partitions didn't reach all the way to the ground or the ceiling, but they did provide some degree of privacy. None of the rooms had doors. The building was rectangular in shape, with a lounge room at one end and a communal bathroom at the other.

Wing 1 prisoners had to eat all their meals in the communal dining room. The only prisoners exempt from this ritual were those in Cottages 1 and 2, who were provided with a daily ration of bread, meat and vegies.

The dining room had to seat about sixty women, and Stella and I had an allocated table at the front near the food—Stella worked in the kitchen and I've never seen a woman eat like her! We staked ownership of 'our' table as we were the 'permanents'; the other two spaces had changing identities as women arrived then left again.

The food from the dining room was very basic and we mostly filled up on white bread. It was the only thing there that was plentiful, because it was made by the male prisoners at Pentridge. For breakfast, there was a choice of porridge or toast. Every Wednesday and Sunday we had roast beef and vegies for lunch, then roast beef and salad for tea. It was like bloody leather. I've never touched beef since. We were given a ration of half a piece of fruit a day. If it was an apple and you didn't eat it straight away, it would go brown. Christmas day was when we received our real treat—roast chicken and a 'Carnival Twist' icecream for dessert. Most women put on weight in prison, some becoming quite obese.

After our evening meal at 3.30 pm, we were given a jar of milk and another of sugar for the whole dormitory; there was enough for one cup of tea or coffee each.

At our work posts we earned approximately $1 per day which could be spent on our weekly 'canteen'. With this money we had to buy cigarettes (fortunately I didn't smoke), toiletries, condensed milk to substitute for the lack of fresh milk, and any chocolates or lollies for ourselves or for our children when they came in for children's visits. Even now, prisoners' wages are still only about $30 per week.

I shared a room in Wing 1 with Barb, who was quiet like me. We both just wanted to be left alone to do our time. She was also in on drug charges. She had three children, boys, who had been placed in state care as a result of her imprisonment. At night she would lie on her bed staring at the ceiling. I often wondered what she was thinking, but I wasn't intrusive enough to ask. She did this night after night. I bet she's thinking about her kids, I'd ponder to myself. She was the strong, silent type, but I could see the pain behind the mask she wore. Her boys meant everything to her and the father wasn't around. On the all-day Saturday children's visits she tried to make up for her absence from their lives, but afterwards she'd return to this room we shared, lie on the bed and just stare silently at the ceiling again.

I never wanted to ask any questions of anyone because I felt that, like myself, if you started talking you'd never stop. And if you started talking about how you felt, you'd start crying . . . and if you started crying, you'd never be able to plug up the hole again. My body felt like it was composed of tears that had frozen; if I got near any warmth I'd start melting, and then there would be nothing left. No me, just a puddle where I'd once stood.

During the early months of 1981, Barb and I spent many silent hours in that room after lock-up. It never felt uncomfortable between us, though, more like mutual respect for things that both of us knew were too painful to talk about—after all, we were both mothers.

Since Ali had gone I'd resumed my work post in the garden, so I was at least enjoying being outdoors during the day. After 4.30 pm lock-up, I'd also gotten back into the habit of playing the piano as there happened to be one in the lounge-room area of Wing 1. Unfortunately, one of the women there found it really annoying. I thought I was being considerate by playing it early, before the news and other shows came on television, but all she wanted to do once she was locked in for the rest of the day was watch TV. The problem was, both the TV and the piano shared the same room. I'd never been interested in television like the rest of the world seemed to be. Every afternoon when we were locked up after work, this particular woman would turn the telly up louder, which would make me play louder. We'd argue, neither of us willing to compromise. She was Maltese and small, but very vocal. She was in for murder, which I kept in the back of my mind! She'd continue to watch telly and I'd continue to play, louder and louder, on and on, every night in this small-minded world that I'd become a part of.

Who gives a shit?, I'd think to myself. With Ali gone, so had my sense of purpose and I needed to find other things with which to fill my time. In prison time can seem relentless rather than enjoyable; it can merely become something that you have to endure.

The monotony was starting to get to me. Sometimes at night, before our sleeping medication took effect, we'd call out to each other from our beds, our voices carrying easily around the partitions of our rooms. We'd bad-mouth the officers, one of the few opportunities we had to release frustration. There were only a couple of officers on duty at night; even if the noise got out of hand, it was unlikely they'd bother to do anything.

'Hey, what about jex-head today?' I'd yell from Barb's and my room to anyone who was listening. This was our nickname for one of the senior officers who had hair like steel wool.

'Wish we could turn her upside down and use her as a mop,' someone else would yell back. We'd all burst into laughter and think it was hilarious! Tragic, really!

'Let's request a new mop for the dormitory—a jex-head mop! See if they understand what we're talking about!' I called out.

'Who wants to write it in the request book?' someone else yelled, screaming with laughter. We imagined the governor reading the request.

'It's almost worth being charged for!' a voice called out. It was a fact that if we'd written it in the request book, we'd have been charged.

'No bloody sense of humour,' someone else said. Some nights this yelling would go on for hours until we had released all our tension and frustration and had screamed ourselves into an emotionally exhausted sleep.

Meanwhile, night after night the tension between me and the Maltese murderer was increasing; she'd turn the telly up louder, I'd play louder. She'd yell (or squeal might be closer to the truth), 'Stop playing that bloody piano!'

'Get fucked! I'll play for as long as I like!' I'd yell back.

The other women were getting pissed off with both of us, so eventually, to ease the strain, a compromise was reached. There was also a piano in the adjoining hall and each night the officers would let me out to use it for an hour. I imagined I was Liberace and played to my heart's content.

Possibly the most fortunate thing that happened to me in prison was coming into contact with the teachers from the Education Centre. Once you were sentenced, it was compulsory for every prisoner to be offered a minimum of a half-day session of education a week. Within a week of the teachers returning from their Christmas break in February 1981, just before Ali left the prison, I was escorted by an officer to the Education Centre for my initial interview. The centre was funded by the Education Department, not the Corrections Department, and therefore was quite separate from the prison, although it was located within the prison grounds. The building was one of those portable prefab ones that you often see at schools, and the officer left me at the front door as it was an unwritten rule that prison officers didn't enter this building.

Once I was through the door I was greeted by Heather, one of the teachers, who walked me around, then invited me to the kitchen area to sit down and have a chat. I was astonished at the different atmosphere in there. It was quiet and peaceful, and women prisoners were occupied in different sections of the building, studying or participating in classes. There was a large room at one end which held classes in jewellery, pottery and woodwork, all of which seemed popular. The lack of tension was remarkable in contrast to the rest of the prison.

While I helped myself to a coffee, Corliss, another friendly teacher, introduced herself. She and Heather explained how the centre worked. It was open five days a week, with some night classes too, and they offered a range of academic subjects as well as creative outlets. They asked me if there was anything I'd particularly like to study, so I told them about my piano tuition and my love of music, but said that I didn't really see how I could resume music study in prison.

'Why not?' said Heather. 'I teach guitar to a small group of women, but we could look for a piano teacher if you're interested.'

'Could you really?' I asked in amazement. 'I guess if I'm going to be here for a while I'd love to learn classical piano again. I could probably start at about fifth or sixth grade.'

'Okay, give me a little time and I'll see what I can organise,' Heather said.

Corliss asked me if there was anything else I'd like to do,

explaining that they would put up a good case to the Classification Committee which, aside from the governor, was really the governing body of the prison. The committee consisted of the governor, representatives from head office of the Corrections Department, an Education Centre representative and a welfare officer whenever there was one in the prison. Any requests for education sessions, temporary day leave, change of security rating, prisoner reviews and any number of other things had to be approved by this committee.

Unsure of myself, I told them I'd dropped out of school early, in Year 11, when I was sixteen, and that I really didn't know what I'd be capable of. 'I wouldn't even know how to go about writing an essay any more,' I said.

'What about having a go at Year 12 English? We have a teacher coming in weekly and there's already a class organised. You could join them.'

'Well, why not? I've got nothing to lose, hey?' I replied. 'I'd also love to be involved in the group that's learning guitar,' I went on excitedly. Heather played both guitar and piano and, as it turned out, was very helpful where music was concerned.

After a bit more discussion, I walked out of the centre and returned to my work post feeling quite different. As time went on I realised the environment in the Education Centre was always different to the rest of the jail. In the centre they treated me with respect and they sort of just assumed I was intelligent. Everywhere else in the jail everyone was treated like a dummy. I was really looking forward to spending more time in the centre, the teachers seemed so easygoing and genuine.

A week or two later the loudspeaker commanded me over to the Education Centre, Heather excitedly welcoming me at the door. The news was good. It looked like she'd found a piano teacher, Jean Starling, who lived locally and was willing to teach me on a voluntary basis. She was going to come in and meet me the following week. Of course, approval still had to be given by the Classification Committee, but I was so surprised at my good fortune that I was having difficulty believing what I was hearing. More difficult to believe was that the teachers had gone to all this trouble on my behalf. At least they must have thought I was worth something.

'Fancy learning classical piano in a prison!' I said to them.

'It is unusual, but why not?' Corliss replied. 'Besides, we want to listen to you practising!' We all had a bit of a laugh together, then I returned to my work post where I resumed my daydreaming on the end of the lawn mower.

Initially, the Classification Committee granted me three sessions at the Education Centre, and so I resumed my childhood study of classical music. During this early part of my sentence, as I began preparing for a 6th grade exam, I decided to study music theory as well. With Heather facilitating, I also joined a group of lovely women in another session where we learned chords on the guitar and sang along. It was such a nice group; everyone was very creative and we all shared similar interests (aside from using drugs). It was fun and, at least for short periods of time, it took my mind off Ali's absence from my life. I certainly hadn't grasped the reality of our eight-year separation—I just couldn't allow myself to think of it in those terms. So it was great to have education sessions filling three half days a week as well as my one-hour piano practice in the hall at night.

I loved the discipline of classical music; it was the antithesis of my life. Maybe it gave me some balance. Sometimes during that solitary hour in the evenings I felt totally free playing the beautiful Beethoven sonatas, Debussy's 'Claire de Lune', trying to master the Chopin *Etudes*. There were moments when my playing was truly beautiful and I wondered at the sounds I could produce. I felt like a child with all the delight that a new discovery brings. In those moments I felt strong and powerful; I wished I could have captured that feeling and allowed it to guide me through each day, but drug use had always intervened.

As I spent more time at the Education Centre, I observed how the teachers had an absolute commitment to the women prisoners, and they seemed to have developed an uncanny knack of working alongside the corrections system to achieve positive outcomes for us. They were somehow able to avoid alienating themselves from the prison officers so they could get some degree of cooperation from the prison, yet they maintained the centre as a safe place where women were treated compassionately and with respect. I grew to trust both Heather and Corliss and they became important role models.

However, low self-esteem doesn't change overnight; it was to be some years before I believed the positive reinforcement provided constantly by the teachers. I was also still struggling with my separation from Ali. The nights, particularly after 4.30 pm lock-up, were long and lonely. I hadn't heard anything from Dame Phyllis Frost or the relevant minister about the possibility of Ali returning to me, and I desperately missed being her mother. For the first time in probably nine years, though, I was experiencing an almost drug-free period, except for prescribed medication, of course; I was no longer abusing heroin or, as I'd done earlier, a mixture of alcohol and diet pills.

Around 8.30 each evening the officers would arrive at the trap door in Wing 1 to administer medication, just the same as in the remand dormitory. It was one of the rituals of prison life that women looked forward to. The other three medication administration times were in the morning before muster, at lunchtime, and after work in the afternoon. It was easy to get on prescribed medication through the doctor who visited the prison once a fortnight, or the psychiatrist who came less often (the only full-time medical staff was the nurse). All you had to do was say you couldn't sleep, or that you were anxious or depressed, and they'd prescribe tablets like Serepax, Rohypnol and Valium; sleeping medication was very popular. It's often been said that medication is used as a management tool to keep prisoners quiet, and that was certainly my experience. Most of us were on sleeping pills or some type of sedative, and so for a few hours each night we were released from the reality of our lives. We were placed into a false sleep, into another time where our drugged imaginations could take us elsewhere.

One particular night, Barb and I didn't need our prescribed medication. We'd managed to score some Serepax from one of our friends. Although it was one of the drugs prescribed in there, you could never get the quantity we'd acquired. Neither of us had been pill abusers outside, at least not with sedatives, but it was different in jail—it would provide a change from the monotony.

'Hey, Barb, how many should we take?' I asked her when we were back in our shared room ... like she'd know.

'Let's try two each for starters,' she replied. Down the hatch. We lay back on our beds waiting for them to take effect.

After a while I said to her, 'I can't feel anything yet, can you?'

'No, let's take another couple,' she suggested. I was always a pig with drugs, so down the hatch they went.

'Hey, Barb, I still can't feel anything, can you?' I said after a while.

'Do you think we should have the rest?' she asked.

Being naturally an all-or-nothing type, I replied, 'Yeah, come on, might as well. Nothing else to do, hey?' So we swallowed some more, then I lost count as well as consciousness. I don't know how many we ended up taking.

I don't know how Barb fared, but I lost three days. Stella told me later how she had to pull my face out of my food in the dining room after I'd collapsed head first into my dinner plate! Three days I couldn't account for. I didn't have a clue what had happened. My friends looked after me, must have got me to muster on time! I didn't get charged either. It was a mystery.

'They creep up on you, those pills. Don't think I'll be in a hurry to try them again,' I said to Barb days later. She nodded her head in agreement. We both decided it had been fun, but we also decided that pills weren't for us. I liked to at least remain conscious. I also liked to remember where I'd been and what I'd done and said, which was usually the case when you used heroin. This was one of the few occasions early in my sentence that I used any drugs that were outside my prescribed medication.

However, since Ali had left the prison after her first birthday in March, I started feeling different, like I had nothing left to lose. While Ali had been living with me, the threat of losing her was always hanging over my head, but without that my motivation to behave was fading. Prisons operate on a reward and punishment system and you can earn things called 'privileges', which included contact visits or, once you were eligible (you had to be halfway through a sentence of at least three years), temporary day leaves. The only punishment they could inflict on me was to send me to the cell block; because it was so early in my sentence, there were few privileges that I could be granted so there were few to lose. I guess they could have added time onto my minimum sentence for bad behaviour, but my release date was so far away that it didn't even seem a threat.

Of course, it was different in the Education Centre, but that only took up twelve hours every week and I still had to fill the other 156 hours. I began to tire of playing this stupid, unintelligent prison game. It was difficult, particularly on work posts, to be polite to the officers who were abusive or petty, or who invested their time and energy in trying to provoke you so that

you'd get angry and then charging you with things like 'disobeying an order' or 'verbal abuse'. Unfortunately, it was under
the watchful eyes of the officers that you spent most of your
time. I had a lot of reasons and plenty of time to feel sorry for
myself, and without the constant focus that Ali had required, I
was churning inside, angry and resentful at having to sit in that
hellhole for all those years separated from my daughter.

Surprisingly, I wasn't so much resentful at my long sentence
as at having my motherhood taken away from me. I felt like
spitting it all out and smashing up everything in the dormitory,
but instead I sat there at the desk in my shared room at night
writing poetry, nasty poetry, aimed at anyone I'd had an issue
with in my life. In between thinking up lines that rhymed, I
stared ahead at the blank wall, my heart twisted. It felt like a
hard, burning rock in my chest. It wasn't a very nice emotional
space to be in. I was trying to keep my feelings in; if I had an
outburst, there would be no help forthcoming. Instead I'd be
sent to the cell block for punishment. The cell block consisted
of about six antiquated bluestone cells in a row; there was
nothing in them except a concrete slab with a mattress on it for
a bed, just above ground level, and in winter they were freezing
cold.

If you were considered really unmanageable, they'd put you
in a straightjacket before throwing you in a cell. Sometimes
women who were upset or angry would hassle each other and
end up in a fight or, alternatively, take their anger out on an
officer. Sometimes it would take half a dozen officers to contain
a woman and lock her into one of the cells, although you could
also be sent there for a couple of days for simple things like
disobeying an order, back-answering an officer, or not being at
muster on time.

Even though I felt like I was going to burst and needed to
release the tension, I knew I had to hang on and 'behave' or I'd

Ali and me and our dog, Charka, taken in 1999, in our local park near the beach at Elwood, one of our favourite spots these days. PHOTO NICK CUBBIN

Me and Ron as very young children. Childhood was a happy time for me, both at school and at home. It wasn't until my early teens that things started to fall apart.

Me (left) and my best friend Libby, at about age nine. We were inseparable during primary school, and spent most of our out-of-school hours together too. We lost touch when we went to different high schools.

At my twenty-first birthday party, with Mum and Dad. They had organised a marquee in the back yard. I was living in Sydney with Fred at the time, and we came back to Melbourne that weekend just for the party.

At hairdressing school, aged sixteen. I had no intention of ever practising hairdressing but Mum didn't want me to leave school (during Year 11) unless I took an apprenticeship, so it suited me at the time.

My hairdressing friend Sue and me, in our late teens, at Phillip Island surf beach. Sue worked in the same salon where I did my apprenticeship. We became great friends, and we're still good friends today.

Above: Mum and me not long after one of her breast cancer operations. Despite three operations, after which she was always told she had the all-clear, Mum died in 1979.

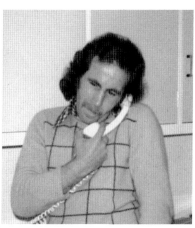

Fred in our flat in East St Kilda, before we headed for Darwin. Fred and I remained close even after our relationship broke up in the late 1970s. I was devastated when he was found murdered in 1980.

Bottom: Me in Malaysia, with groovy 'Afro' hair, taken by Rahim, the guy I scored my drugs from.

Above: Me with one-month-old Ali at Aunty Isabel's house. I couldn't believe it when I was told that I was five months pregnant during a routine health check in Fairlea, but this little girl completely changed my life.

Left: Me in my cell in Yarrabrae, with Ali in the little pine bed that Vicki had made for her. Ali was adored by most of the other inmates as well as some of the prison officers, and the psychologist's report said her social development was well above the norm.

Aunty Isabel with Ali when I stayed at her house after Ali's birth.

Me and Ron out for his birthday during my trial.

Damien and Ali outside Cottage 2, where Damien and his mum had moved to when they left Yarrabrae.

Ron with Ali when she was two months old.

Clockwise from top left: Vicki, Ali, me, Corliss and Carol in our study area at the Education Centre. Vicki, Carol and I were full-time students at this stage. The Education Centre was a haven away from the bleakness of the rest of Fairlea, and it gave so many women skills and opportunities to begin a new life outside.

be judged as 'bad mother' material and I'd lose any chance of ever having Ali return to live in the prison. I hadn't quite given up the fight to get her back in. During those early days, this was my motivation to survive each monotonous day, and I clung on to that small hope even when it appeared futile. It was hard, though, because the prison's idea of being well behaved was so peculiar, especially for adult women who'd been running their own lives for any length of time. It was like the prison officers were our parents and we were the naughty children.

Another motivating factor that helped me stay sane during this early period of my sentence came about from a chance meeting with a beautiful man called Greg, who was a musician and part of a drama group that came in to run evening workshops in the jail in 1981. As well as the drama workshops, Greg later offered music sessions at the Education Centre on a voluntary basis, and a couple of other women and I were keen to take up his offer. I was able to utilise part of one of my two music sessions for this purpose, my piano lesson only requiring half an hour, and I kept my third session for English. Because Greg also knew a lot about Buddhism, sacred geometry and alchemy, amongst other things, I became fascinated by discussions he held on these topics. Other women came and went from this group, but it became a lifeline for me. Even though I wasn't yet putting any of this new information into practice, I was intrigued. I came to trust Greg implicitly and, like Corliss, he was later to become a friend, way beyond my sentence. These two people have touched my soul in a way that very few people ever could.

The drama group started after a couple of Victorian College of the Arts students brought a play into the prison and put on a performance for the women. I didn't attend, I was too busy back in Wing 1 writing resentful poetry, but Brenda, one of my guitar-lesson friends, did and she was impressed. Never one to miss an opportunity, Brenda later approached Maud and Stella (two of the students) to ask if they would be interested in providing drama workshops for the women in prison. They were around the same age as us, in their mid twenties, and both Maud and Stella, plus Greg (who was in a relationship with Maud), were immediately, and perhaps somewhat naively, interested. Soon after this, allowing time for the formalities such as police checks and individual clearances, our first drama workshops began. They were held out of work time in the evenings after lock-up and so weren't classified as an 'education' session.

I attended these workshops with the rest of my group of friends. I found them difficult because I was so shy, but the other women didn't seem reticent at all. For a couple of hours one evening a week we were locked into the old recreation hall where we played drama games, made loud noises and ran around with abandon. Even I had to admit it was a release, although I still felt inhibited and self-conscious. I remember a couple of times when we had to pretend we were animals ... I was able, if only for a short time, to leave my self-consciousness somewhere else. I didn't realise it then but obviously the environment they created, as well as the particular women involved, made me feel safe enough to be able to do this. It was only for a few moments but I felt free, moving around with grace and abandon. There was no-one there judging me, so I was able to be unconcerned about what anyone thought or if, in fact, they were even watching me. I could be any way I wanted and could move anywhere I wanted—within the hall of course!

Greg, being a musician, often played music for us while we were playing these games. He enabled me to find a comfortable way into the drama group through our mutual interest in music, and he encouraged me to play the piano. Of course, I was chronically shy, but I began to play occasionally. Over the weeks this unruly group started to take shape and we began to talk about writing our own play, based on the material that came out of our weekly evening workshops. I knew I didn't have the confidence to get out there and perform, but I was developing a deep connection to Greg, which was gradually assisting me, ever so slowly, to discover some belief in myself as a decent human being.

As the story line for the play evolved, Greg encouraged me to start writing some music. My response was cynical and sarcastic, but Greg persisted.

'I can't write songs,' I always said to him. 'I've never written a song in my life!'

'Yes you can. Give it a go,' he'd reply, seemingly certain that I could produce the goods.

This exchange was repeated for weeks, until I finally broke through the barrier of that voice inside that had learned to tell me 'I can't'. Of course I still didn't believe that I could write the words for the songs; the idea that I might be able to write the music was enough for me to grapple with at that stage. On the other hand Val, who was also a member of the drama group, wrote beautiful poetry, and she offered me some of it as possible song lyrics. I felt quite honoured as Val's writing was extraordinary.

The next day I sat at the piano reading Val's inspiring words and allowing my body to absorb their meaning. I fiddled with some chords, a melody began to form, and I started to hum along as I played.

'This is how you do it!' I exclaimed to myself (because nobody was listening). I don't know how long I remained there, but I didn't leave the piano until the music was complete.

At the next drama workshop a week later, I walked excitedly over to Greg: 'I did it!' I said to him. 'I wrote a song!' I still couldn't believe it myself.

Greg smiled. 'Play it for me,' he said, sharing my excitement.

Anticipating that he wouldn't like it and that I was about to

be judged, I immediately began to explain that it probably wasn't
very good.

'Just play it,' he interrupted, dismissing my justifications. I
sat down in front of the piano and tentatively, quietly, sang Val's
words to my melody, which was later called 'Passing Through'.

> *PASSING THROUGH*
> *Where are you coming from, tell me your story.*
> *Maybe I've been there too.*
> *Where are you going to, have you a dream?*
> *Will it be waiting for you?*
> *I don't really need answers to all my questions,*
> *Time's drifting away on a breeze.*
> *Come lie by the fire, we'll fulfil our desire*
> *that in time will be sweet memories.*
> *Will you be taking my memory with you,*
> *or are you travelling alone?*
> *Will you be living in permanent dwelling,*
> *or are you going to roam?*
> © *Val, 1981*

When I finished, I couldn't even look at him I felt so embarrassed. I was paralysed with the fear that it might be rubbish and
he'd have to find a kind way of rejecting it. I imagined him
trying not to be patronising, but rejecting the song anyway. Then
I heard, 'It's great!' I immediately thought he was lying to make
me feel better, but I turned my head around to see his smiling
face.

'Play it again!' he said with enthusiasm.

After I sang it again I could tell Greg's reaction was genuine
and he really was impressed with my song. I was filled with
absolute wonder that I had created the music for this thing . . .
a song.

Maud called out from the other side of the hall, 'What are you doing over there? Can we all hear it?'

For a moment emotional paralysis struck again as I realised that I now had to sing in front of all of them! I was so nervous and so shy, but somehow I got through it and they all clapped and cheered. I didn't even know if I'd sung it loud enough for them to hear me, and I was sure they were exaggerating, but I felt good. I hadn't sung publicly since my days in TRAMM, about five years before.

Maud and Greg wanted me to perform it in the play.

'Well, maybe if I can hide behind the piano,' was my response.

Greg seemed content with that and we returned to my song, reworking a couple of chords until we were both satisfied. This was the commencement of my songwriting career, and I haven't stopped since. After Val was released from prison a few months later, I even wrote my own words. I developed a talent for humorous, 'tongue-in-cheek' songs and they slotted in well to the format of our plays. We only heard from Val a few times after she left. No-one ever discovered where she had gone or what had happened to her, and I only hope she's okay.

The English, music and drama sessions only occupied a small part of my week, unfortunately. The rest of the time, when I wasn't on a work post, I kept hassling for Ali to come and live with me. In my heart I didn't believe that I would be successful, but the fight was still being fought with Dame Phyllis Frost as the main player. I'd done all I could from within the prison; I'd written letters seeking support for my case to relevant people such as Walter Jona, the Minister for Community Welfare Services. In a way it helped that I'd received the longest drug sentence of any woman in Victoria: one thing that everyone seemed to agree on was that my sentence appeared ridiculous. As far as I know I was the first woman in Victoria to challenge the rule about children having to leave the prison at the age of one. Of course I had no credibility—I was just a prisoner and a heroin addict to boot!

The two main advocates on my behalf were Dame Phyllis Frost, who ran the Victorian Women's Prison Council, and Father Brosnan. He worked as the Catholic chaplain at Pentridge men's prison, and Frank had discussed with him my predicament regarding Ali. The media became interested as, if we were successful, it would be the first time a child over the age of one would be allowed to live with its mother in a Victorian prison. I seemed to become the leading case in the debate, and I began to receive a lot of requests from television and print media for interviews. The letter I received from Channel 7's news department was fairly typical of those requests:

> Ms Helen Barnacle,
> This letter is following a request by the Minister, Mr Walter Jona, for us to outline the aim of a television interview [to be] conducted with you at Fairlea.
>
> We believe the issue raised by the Minister to consider allowing your baby daughter to remain with you in the prison is a significant social development. Certainly one of community interest [...] and no doubt one of debate—for and against.
>
> We would like to hear your opinions about keeping your daughter with you [...] the advantages you see [...] the disadvantages if any [...] your attitudes to her early life being spent in the jail [...] your attitude on whether women prisoners should be able to keep their

children longer than the 12 months the Minister has permitted at this stage.

This interview will not delve into your personal life, and will not discuss the offences for which you are in the prison [...] short of a cursory explanation of your sentence in a short introduction to the interview.

I attach a list of the questions I would like to put in the interview [...] but will certainly consider your suggestions.

We at Seven National News certainly look forward to an informative interview with you.

The struggle to regain Ali gave me something to focus on and distracted me from the pain of our separation. It made me feel that I was at least doing something about it, even though I believed I had no power to change anything in the system. Because of the media attention, I received lots of mail from members of the public supporting my cause, but the Minister for Community Welfare Services and the Corrections Department didn't appear to be responding favourably. The governor of the prison was adamant that there'd be no children living there while he was in charge.

Then later, in May 1981—and totally out of the blue—the kitchen officer who we'd nicknamed 'Granny' ran up to me, gushing with excitement, when she arrived at the prison for work one morning: 'Congratulations! It's fantastic!' she said.

'What?' I replied. 'What are you on about?'

'I heard it on the radio on my way to work, about Ali being able to come back in and live here.' She adored Ali too.

I looked at her, bewildered. 'What are you talking about?' I pleaded with her. 'I've not been told anything.'

At that point the loudspeaker barked out: 'Helen Barnacle to the governor's office!'

The governor was just about frothing at the mouth. 'How dare you! Why didn't you tell me about this?' he demanded in his deep voice. He was a large man, and although I hadn't had any trouble with him, his size was intimidating.

'Tell you about what?' I replied.

'About Ali being allowed to live in the prison indefinitely,' he said. 'Your father's been on the phone wanting to know what's going on too.'

'I've not been told anything,' I said to him, 'but Granny just said she heard something on the radio coming into work this morning.'

He ranted and raved for a bit longer, not believing that I'd been told nothing, then he ordered me to go back to my work post. He should have known prisoners were always the last to be told anything. The system thrived on lack of information— it was part of the power game—but I guess it was an embarrassing position for him to be in. It appeared that someone had leaked the news to the media before he had even been notified.

Unbelievable, I thought to myself as I walked from his office. I couldn't understand how he could be so unhappy about a mother and her child being reunited, although I wasn't certain it was true myself yet. Surely there was a tiny part of him that was happy for me? If there was, he didn't show it. A smile found its way across my face as the news sank in: My little girl is coming to live with her mum! I ran over to the dining room to tell the others. Stella squealed in delight! As the day progressed I was formally told that the Minister for Community Welfare Services had changed the rule about children only residing in the women's prison until their first birthday. Obviously Dame Phyllis had done a lot of work behind the scenes. I was annoyed that I hadn't been told officially before the story broke in the media, but nothing could seriously erase the smile from my face that day.

It took a week or two to organise as Ali had been gone about ten weeks, but finally she arrived back at the prison and we were allocated a temporary place in which to reside. It was not ideal, but I didn't care as long as we were together. It was the same small room leading from the prison hospital that Ali and I had occupied previously. On the other side of it was Wing 1. It had a kitchen area with a bath, but it didn't have a toilet, so a portable toilet was installed in another small room. The space was about ten metres square in total.

Immediately after the ruling was changed, other women also became eligible to have their babies with them. Lynda, who had a similar drug sentence to mine, was due to give birth soon and Viv, who had a six month sentence, successfully applied to have her little boy stay with her, so the three of us took up residence in this small area where we remained separated from the rest of the women after 4.30 pm lock-up. We decided to put our beds around the walls at one end and the three cots at the other, separated by a cloth partition. We were used to beds in close proximity in the dormitories, and we really didn't care. Because it was so cramped, I think the prison authorities hoped that we would find it unbearable, but we weren't about to give up this opportunity of having our babies with us and we made it work, particularly Lynda and I, who were both in for such long sentences. Over the next year or so, the prison administration allowed the media into the jail to interview me on several occasions for current affairs and daytime chat shows. I think the story had such a high level of human interest, with most journalists coming from a compassionate perspective, that the prison was glad to receive some positive publicity.

As winter approached it got very cold, and sometimes the babies suffered with colds or bronchitis. Ali got bronchitis quite seriously only a couple of months after returning to the prison and had to be admitted to Fairfield Hospital, just down the road. However, we were willing to put up with the difficult conditions and we fought for small things like not having to take our babies over to the dining room in the morning for breakfast because it was so cold. Although we had a kitchen and could cook for the babies, we still had to eat in the communal dining room just the same as other prisoners. We weren't given rations to cook for ourselves like the women in the cottages.

Some prison officers made it difficult for us by doing extra searches of our accommodation, and they even checked our pockets when we were leaving the dining room. One woman officer found a single portion of butter in my pocket (that I hadn't eaten at dinner time) and confiscated it, threatening to charge me. Most prisoners took any leftover butter and jam from their meals as there was so little available. Food was always a major item that was smuggled around the prison; it was also used as an exchange commodity between prisoners, or for favours. Usually leftovers from meals weren't confiscated, but because we had the babies and therefore access to extra food, some officers saw us as having privileges that were not available to other women. They were quite open about their resistance to having children living in the prison, and some of them told me how selfish I was. One of them said he'd be seeing my daughter in there in about twenty years time.

'Ha! Ha!' I responded, not allowing him to see how hurt I felt.

I found it difficult having my mothering skills judged on a daily basis, but there were also some officers who loved having the children around. Playing with the kids revealed a warm, caring side to a few officers which we may never otherwise have seen in their strict work roles. The other women were happy for us. Viv was only in for a few months, so after she left there were just Lynda and her son, Damien, and Ali and I in the small room.

Our accommodation was at the top end of the communal recreation hall. If you imagine a capital 'T', the hall was the vertical bit, Wing 1 was the left-hand top of the 'T' and our room, plus the hospital to which we were attached, was the right-hand bit of the top. Wing 1 and our room shared a common wall. Our front door opened out onto the hall, which was old, but quite large. It had linoleum floors that had to be cleaned and polished daily, so for my new work post I became billet for the hall. It was suitable because I had to keep Ali with me at all times, and she could play in the hall while I was cleaning. It also gave me easy access to our accommodation to cook her food, bathe her, or do any of the other things required of motherhood. We enjoyed our time together.

Because the hall also doubled as the visit centre, I was quite busy preparing it and cleaning up afterwards. Sunday was visit day for the whole prison, although remand prisoners were also able to have visits on Wednesday afternoons. In between times, there were often professional visits taking place on weekdays. The good thing about being hall billet was that I didn't have an officer standing over me all day, giving out orders, so I had more freedom than on some of the other work posts; the only time officers were around was during visits, and I had to clear out while they were being conducted.

During lunch breaks we could spend time with the other women, and Carol, a young woman who'd become attached to Ali, got into the habit of coming over to play with her as soon as she'd eaten her lunch. I'd join Stella, Val, Brenda, Marg, Kathy, Vicki and the others with whom I learned guitar and drama. There were about eight of us, mostly in our early to mid twenties, who hung around together and seemed to have common interests.

I was allowed to continue my three sessions at the Education

Centre, even though Ali had returned to live with me. The teachers were fantastic, occupying Ali's time while I was involved in my classes. Sometimes when I was studying I could hear laughter coming from Ali and Corliss in another room where they'd be playing games or watching videos like *The Wizard of Oz*. Ali and Corliss became very close, so much so that by 1982 Ali would spend some weekends out of the prison at the home of Corliss and her husband Kurt, and she grew to love them both dearly.

I also continued my involvement in the drama workshops. Ali loved drama, and she'd squeal with delight playing all those fun games. She was developing some loving relationships with the other women prisoners, particularly Carol. Although a prison would seem an unlikely place for a child to develop positive relationships, it was proving to be a nurturing and caring environment for her.

As 1981 progressed, the drama workshop participants developed into a core group of women—consisting of Brenda, Carol, Marg, Val, Kathy, Sue, Vicki and me—who all attended regularly one evening a week. We began to focus our creative energy on devising the prison's first play, based on our life experiences. Maud and Stella directed the drama/acting and Greg was musical director. As well as being a creative outlet for our feelings, it also provided us with an opportunity to work as a group and develop trust. We began to learn to negotiate and to compromise which, sadly, was something that some of us in our drug-using world had only learnt through physical or verbal abuse. With our lack of communication skills, most of us believed that to get what you wanted you basically had to blast your way through, so in some sessions there were six or seven of us telling Maud and Stella how to do something, or telling them that a particular song we preferred was going to conclude the play. There were times when some of us were in tears trying to battle through, trying to force our point of view. There were times when we pushed Maud and Stella to tears with our determination to have something done our way. Although there were difficult times for all of us, these workshops contained powerful, and yet sometimes subtle, lessons.

For some of us, this was our first real opportunity to communicate positively with other human beings, particularly in the jail setting. It gave us our first sense of responsibility to a group, and most of the women in this group also became involved in developing a netball team, the 'Fairlea Foxes', so we became quite cohesive. After lock-up, a couple of times a week, the night officers would come around to collect the women whose names were on the netball list. They'd lock us into the netball court, which was enclosed by wire fencing, for about an hour before returning us to our accommodation. We tried to start as many activities as possible so that we didn't succumb to the monotony of prison life and turn into 'vegetables'. I guess that even though we were drug addicts, we were intelligent and creative beings; it's just hard to see those qualities when you're caught up on the addiction treadmill.

As the date of our performance drew closer, our drama sessions increased to almost daily, with approval from the governor. Even just the change of routine was a relief. There was an air of excitement within the group which carried over into the whole prison; the other women were happy for us too. Our boring lifestyles had been transformed into new challenges, excitement, apprehension, new achievements and new skills. Being part of all this activity, you just couldn't help feeling worthwhile, as though you had something to offer, even if it was only fleeting. It allowed us to escape briefly from the futility of the jail system, and we formed a close bond and a sense of working together to achieve something. Even some of the prison officers were surprised by our commitment to each other and the goal we were working towards. I guess they assumed we would drop out one by one, just like we had dropped out of society.

One of the women in the group, Sue, was due to be released on the day of the performance. Because prisoners are released in the morning and our performance was scheduled for that night, it looked like she would miss it. Instead, Sue asked to see the governor and requested for her release to be delayed until the evening after the performance. We laughed at the irony of it. Fancy asking to remain in prison longer than you had to, but such was her commitment to our play! The governor, although apprehensive and unable to comprehend her request, granted permission.

Our days became filled with challenges, joy and tears. We felt fulfilled. We even felt important. For the couple of weeks preceding our performance we did almost nothing else but rehearsals for our play. It was wonderful not having to fill our days on futile work posts. This was the antithesis of prison life. There were highs and lows and we endured them mostly without drugs.

The big night arrived and we were all very excited and very nervous. I had agreed to sing the songs I had written provided I could stay behind the piano, which was off to one side of the stage, with Vicki singing harmonies beside me. She didn't want to go 'on stage' either. The others were all out there, centre-stage, performing. I admired their courage.

An audience of about fifty people were treated to our show, mostly friends and family. I'd invited Ron and his girlfriend, and I could see them in the crowd. From our position at the side of the stage Vicki and I could watch the women perform and we were amazed at how talented they were. I wanted to weep and laugh at the same time. I loved those women. All of us had contributed material from our own experiences, and Maud and Stella had woven it into a story. 'Passing Through' represented our journey through drug use, prison and, for some, release. On the one-page promotional flyer for the play was an excerpt:

> *Ever tried to rip a shirt or a piece of strong*
> *material that hasn't any flaws in it?*
> *It's hard.*
>
> *Now have you tried to rip a piece of material that's*
> *damaged or has a flaw? It rips fast and easy. All it*
> *needs is a little hole, a small fault and you can rip*
> *it to pieces.*

At the end of the performance we all took a bow. We stood there in a line, proud. At that moment our hearts were full of joy and we were strong. We could feel it. The applause was loud and genuine—the show had been a success. Even the prison officers who were on duty agreed. Many more performances would follow in the coming years.

After tea and coffee, supplied by the prison, and a chat with our friends and families, it was time for everyone to leave. Until now, caught up in the excitement, we'd forgotten it was also time for Sue to leave the prison; it was her release day. We were taken aback with the starkness of this reality. Although filled with joy and pride, Sue cried as she hugged us all. You could tell that, in a way, she didn't want to go . . . she didn't want to leave those friendships behind.

'I'm gonna miss you all,' she said with tears in her eyes.

As I gave her a hug I tried not to think about the fact that I couldn't see her for another seven years or so, unless she got locked up again. It was too hard to comprehend. Ex-prisoners weren't allowed back into the prison to visit. It was rarely that they made exceptions to this rule, and 'friendship' wouldn't be considered grounds for granting special permission.

'Good luck,' I said to her, 'and don't come back,' even though in my heart I would have loved to see her again.

'I'll write to you all,' she said. 'I love you.' Then she turned away and walked towards the gate. After a few steps she hesitated and looked back at us. She had tears streaming down her cheeks and so did we. It was a confusing moment and I felt my heart wrenching, my throat tightening. Then she turned away and, without looking back, followed all the visitors out that gate to freedom. We stood there in shock, happy that she was leaving, but with conflicting thoughts about why we had to stay. We cried, then we laughed. We were not bad women! And this was to be the title of one of our next plays: 'Bad Women'.

Ali went around for months after the performance humming the melodies from the songs, occasionally singing some of the words. She was now twenty months old. The contrast was stark between the excitement of preparing the play and the emptiness of the normal prison life we returned to once it was over. On the one hand we felt lucky to have had the opportunity to be involved in something we might never have known 'outside', but on the other hand it was glaringly obvious that the prison system overall doesn't work. The wonderful opportunities provided by the drama group had come to us almost by accident, not because of any planning by the Corrections Department. In fact a lot of the officers thought that the drama group and education sessions were privileges we shouldn't have had. I'm sure some of them thought that Maud, Stella and Greg were quite mad because of all the noises and laughter emanating from the hall on the nights when we had drama workshops. It was an indictment of the system that joy and personal fulfilment were not encouraged by the officers. Some of them were even jealous of the educational opportunities offered to us.

We returned to our monotonous daily routine hoping that we could repeat our creative experience in the future.

Performances were good advertising for the Corrections Department. It made it appear to the outside world that rehabilitation was taking place, and all at no extra cost to the taxpayer.

Later in that first year of my sentence, after we'd lived in our small, segregated accommodation for some months, Lynda and I thought it would be better for us and our babies if we lived in the main prison, rather than being isolated there beside the hospital, so we talked to the governor about it. By this time we'd built close friendships with several women and wanted to be able to share more time with them, given that we were locked in for so many hours every afternoon and evening. We had discussed this possibility with many of the other women prisoners, both Lynda's friends and mine, and there were plenty who were willing to share accommodation with us and the babies. The governor asked us to come up with some suggestions in writing. He was willing to consider our request because, in actual fact, it would make it easier for the management of the prison which, because of the huge increase in women being incarcerated, was having to expand its capacity.

Within weeks Lynda and I, with our two babies, were transferred to Yarrabrae, a new maximum security building where we shared a unit with two other women. Our move coincided with the opening of Yarrabrae. I'd wanted to move there ever since they'd begun building it, thinking it would be preferable to living in the old tin buildings. The governor was willing to allow it on a trial basis and, if there were no problems, we would remain integrated with the rest of the prison population. It was nice to move into a cell that had never been lived in, that didn't already contain someone else's emotional pain.

Yarrabrae was built in the style of most modern prisons—a concrete rectangle built of grey brick. Inside it contained a four-cell unit in each corner, which meant four women to a unit, each with their own cell. Each of the units had a sturdy metal door, inset with the standard small trap door at eye level, which could be locked to contain the four occupants. The unit door would be locked at about 9 pm and individual cell doors at about 11 pm, although these times changed like the wind. Each unit was square in shape and had a large floor-to-ceiling window covered in bars on the outside. It was a nice change to be able to look out.

In the middle section of the building there was a small laundry with a washing machine and dryer. Next to the laundry was a large kitchen, then another two-cell 'punishment' unit with an office beside it. This punishment unit—Unit 5—had replaced the old bluestone cell block. The floor was tiled in concrete, a sort of beige/salmon colour. The open middle section of Yarrabrae formed a large recreation area with a television and seating for up to one hundred women. It also became the communal dining room after the old one was closed; the whole prison came there for lunch, and except for the women in Cottages 1 and 2, for dinner at 3.30 pm.

Lynda, Damien, Ali and I moved into Unit 4, which was at the top left-hand corner, right next to the laundry. Our window looked out onto an expanse of grass that extended to the rear wall of the prison. Inside the unit was a small, square central area with a table and chairs. There was also a pantry-style room containing a small fridge, kettle and toaster and some wooden shelving. This allowed us to make our own breakfast and cups of tea and coffee after lock-up. The air in this building was recycled; once you were locked in there was no fresh air. The heating was operated centrally and often didn't work. However, it was a vast improvement on the old tin dormitories and offered some privacy. It's all relative.

Each individual cell contained a bed, which had to face the door so the officers could see you when they came to check. Each cell door also had a trap door inset like the main unit door.

There was a tiny window above the bed, with bars on the outside of course, and a small bathroom with a shower, toilet and hand basin, all stainless steel. Even the mirror above the basin was stainless steel, so that people couldn't break it and use pieces of broken glass for self-mutilation, which was very common, particularly in women's prisons. We spent ten to twelve hours a night locked in our individual cells, so when those demons came to torment you in that solitary space, women sometimes relieved the pressure by slashing at their skin, particularly their wrists, with anything that was sharp and available.

At the far end of the cell was a wardrobe, made of real wood, containing our prison-issue clothing. There was also a dressing table built in beside it. Pictures were not allowed on the walls, so every cell looked identical. Individuality was not encouraged in prison; it made people harder to manage. It's all about not thinking that you are special, which was easy for most of us because we never thought we were. We were allowed a television and a radio/cassette player if we owned one, but the taping function of the cassette player had to be disabled.

Because I'd resumed my study of classical piano, I was required to do a couple of hours' practice a day. By 1982 I'd been able to get permission to have my piano brought in to the unit so, thanks to Ron, who organised to have it transported to the jail, I had it with me again. It somehow made me feel safer.

11

Finding love in prison

You would never think of prison as a place for romance or love—it's more a place for violence and abuse, or mass containment of emotional pain, but it was there that I was to find my first 'real' adult love, and it took me totally by surprise. Between the crevices a touch, a glance. It's necessary. I learnt that love could make me feel safer in that unsafe environment, even if it was only momentary and, in a way, illusory. In that sense it was like a drug, yet so much more. It was a heart connection amidst humiliation and deprivation, where any enjoyment or happiness could be swept away almost before you had time to enjoy it.

However, it was dangerous to have anything or anyone to love in prison because it became ammunition that the administration could use against you. You were never allowed to forget that everything you gained was a privilege, and the more privileges you had, the more control the system had over you. Having Ali with me gave the prison authorities enormous power. I knew how the rules worked. I knew that if I behaved badly, the first thing they'd take from me would be Ali. Under those circumstances, therefore, I conformed. However, to some extent the reason I was so willing to take part in the publicity about Ali and me was that I felt that the more the outside world knew about our case, the less likely it was that the prison would be able to use Ali as a punishment tool against me. It offered me some degree of protection. I certainly hadn't done all those interviews because I wanted to be a famous criminal. Sometimes it's frightening in jail when you realise that an officer or governor with a sick mind could do anything to you and no-one (outside) might ever know.

My love story began early in 1981, just after I'd been sentenced and was awaiting my appeal. The drama group had also just commenced. I was sitting on the grass area outside the old dining room, in front of the tennis/netball court, playing with Ali and talking to some of the other women, like we did most days during our lunch break and after work. We all looked up as the sound of the van bringing a new arrival reached us and, before too long, there she was, walking down the path towards the dining room. It was a winding little path we called the 'yellow brick road', seeming to lead nowhere, and she was trailing along behind the officer, trying to look proud or confident or something, but not knowing where to go or where to look in that unfamiliar territory. She'd been bathed and de-liced and was carrying a second set of prison-issue clothing. Her short dark hair was still wet. She was wearing the standard cream-coloured dress with thin brown stripes and buttons, most of which were missing, all down the front. On her feet were riding boots, which weren't prison issue, and her short legs were barely visible between the hem of the dress and the top of the boots. She looked funny. She looked like she felt really uncomfortable but was doing a pretty good job of disguising it. I liked that, it took courage. It was hard to feel any pride in the gear they dressed you in. I was immediately inquisitive. She looked vulnerable and intelligent at the same time.

I knew the appearance of vulnerability wouldn't last long.

You have to toughen up because often kindness is taken as weakness in prison, particularly with commodities such as cigarettes and coffee. Everyone's deprived of something, although mostly it's love. After getting sucked in by a manipulative long-termer in my first few weeks, I quickly learned not to be taken for a mug. Prison is really just a microcosm of the wider community—there's good and bad everywhere.

We watched the newcomer being escorted to the dining room to collect her evening's rations: her little piece of butter, bread and some milk to make tea or coffee.

'Do you know her?' I asked Stella, my old friend from the street, who was sitting on the grass with us.

'Yeah, her name's Vicki,' she replied.

'What's she in for?'

'She's on a similar drug charge to yours and has a big trial coming up,' Stella answered. 'She could get a long sentence too. It's not looking good for her. I know her quite well from the outside,' she went on.

'Really?' I said to her quietly, not entirely sure why I was interested. I suppose it was that, when you're in prison for a long time, the possibilities for friendship are limited. I already knew that the friendships I wanted to make were with other women serving lengthy sentences. It would have been too difficult to get close to short-termers because they would always be gone too quickly, which was great for them but would leave me feeling abandoned.

After collecting her rations, Vicki was escorted to the remand section. On the way, several of the women who knew her called out, including Stella: 'Hi, Vicki! I'll catch you later, okay?'

'How are ya?' another one yelled as she ran over and gave Vicki a hug. Quite a few of them seemed to know her. It's a small world, the drug world, but I'd never come across her before.

In the time remaining before lock-up, Vicki came over and sat with our group. I just watched and listened. Apparently her trial was to commence within weeks. They'd caught her on the run in Sydney and she wasn't very happy about it. She had been charged, along with four other men and women, on a drug conspiracy charge similar to the one I'd faced. Her girlfriend, who'd been caught a couple of months earlier, was in custody too, but her charges didn't seem to be as serious.

Vicki also had a heroin habit that she had to come off, so she was going to be sick over the coming week. It happened to most of us and there was no medical assistance provided except, if you were lucky, some tablets to settle the nausea, and some sleeping medication at night. Problem was, it usually took a couple of weeks before you could get to see a doctor, so by the time he could prescribe anything you were already over the physical withdrawals. Usually you'd be placed in the prison hospital for a few days, but if you were put in the dormitory instead, all you'd get was a bucket in which to vomit as you leant over the side of your bed. Sometimes women hassled like hell not to be placed in the hospital because it was so isolating. Often women wouldn't admit that they were addicted to heroin because, once the prison authorities became aware of it, they'd treat you differently, like automatically placing you on the 'drug table' at visits. It was difficult to pretend you weren't sick when you went through withdrawals, though, so they usually found out even if you'd lied.

I didn't see much of Vicki for a couple of days because she was too sick to go to work and was locked in the dormitory during the day. Although I didn't have much of a chance to mix with her, after a week or so, when she'd recovered, I found I was watching out for her, surprised at how much I looked forward to seeing her. Whenever we were all sitting around near the netball court or outside the dormitories, she'd come and sit with the group of friends I hung around with. Vicki was with her girlfriend most of the time, and she wasn't one of my close friends, but Vicki and I became acquainted, although I was so shy it was chronic. Homosexuality had never been an issue for me as many of my friends were lesbian or gay. I saw human beings as human, and gender, in many ways, was irrelevant to me. But without heroin to boost my confidence I had become so self-conscious I could barely deal with anyone looking at me, let alone initiate a friendship or conversation with a stranger.

If I ever raised my head to look around and found someone glancing at me, my face would turn bright red. I hated it when that happened because it prevented me from talking to people. I felt like I owed the world an apology for being alive, and I wanted to crawl into a corner somewhere so that no-one would notice I was there. But people did notice me and I felt 'raw', like a sore that wouldn't heal; each time you scratched it, it bled. I felt like such a loser back then. Meal times were especially bad, probably because I was in an enclosed space, but the dining room had a series of concrete pillars extending from floor to ceiling, so I could at least hide my face behind these when I got embarrassed.

There were times when I'd despair that I was worth nothing to anyone. This battle between my feelings of worthiness and my sense of worthlessness would go on in my mind day in, day out. I guess when I arrived at the prison I was probably at my lowest in terms of self-esteem. My world had certainly become ugly: as my heroin addiction had increased, my self-esteem had plummeted and I had allowed myself to be treated more and more abusively. Prior to coming to jail, the only role in life that made me feel good was being Ali's mother. I felt, as a 'no-good useless junkie', that I deserved whatever happened to me. Even after my close brush with death I remained grateful that my partner still wanted me. He told me to leave and I begged him to let me stay. He told me he was going to shoot me and I begged him to spare my life. I told him how much I loved him and, eventually, he released his finger from the trigger. In that moment I had never felt so grateful in all my life and I did still love him, I wasn't lying. Back then, love was a need, not a joy, in the same way that my heroin addiction was a desperate necessity.

With a bit of distance between me and my last relationship outside, I began to see more clearly how, over the previous couple of years, I had found myself making very different choices to the ones I'd made earlier. After my relationship with Fred, I seemed to have chosen men who were both controlling and abusive, which pushed me into the silence I'd observed in my own mother. By the time I reached prison years later, I was fearful, insecure and felt ugly and ashamed of myself. I'd always hated violence so much that I never would have believed I'd end up in relationships with violent and abusive men. I thought back to childhood and how successful and confident I'd been. It was so difficult to reconcile the child I'd been then with the person I was now that it felt as though I was looking at a child from a completely different family. What had happened? Where had all that confidence gone?

Since my jail sentence and, subsequently, my withdrawal from heroin, I'd been intrigued to discover a feeling that I could only identify as relief. I talked to my brother about it at visits when he expressed surprise at how well I'd adjusted to jail. I'd slowly begun to realise that I was feeling relieved because I was no longer living in the sort of fear that had been ever-present in my life prior to my imprisonment. The absence of fear was partly a result of the enforced separation from my previous partner, but also a result of no longer being addicted to heroin, always anxiously awaiting the day when I would get caught out, as I knew inevitably I would. In prison I was using only on the rare occasion when an old friend arrived with some heroin on them and was willing to share it, but that was always only one or two hits anyway. So there were few secrets, and much less fear. There was a sort of freedom in that alone. In one sense life was simpler than it had been for a long time, except for the fact that I knew Ali was going to have to leave the prison again in the future.

It was all quite baffling, but I was beginning to question what my previous perception of love had been and, now that I'd had time away from any intimate relationships, I was beginning to wonder what love had offered me in the past. What does that word mean? I'd ask myself. In my relationship with Ali, I totally understood its meaning—'love' means unconditional—but what about love with another adult? No longer looking through the needy eyes of addiction, all I could see in the last few years of my life was abuse. I'd sit in my cell at night, writing down these thoughts in my journal. It was such a revelation.

I wished I could feel better about myself, but I didn't know how. Meeting someone new and interesting was a good distraction. I'd also noticed that Ali liked Vicki too, and that Vicki paid her quite a bit of attention. In a sick sort of way I began to hope she was going to be around for a while! As the weeks passed slowly by, I noticed that I was looking out for her whenever I walked around the prison grounds. I also noticed that my heart did a flutter when she returned my glance, or sometimes when she said something to me or was playing with Ali. I was perplexed by my reaction. There had been so many changes in my life just then, I wasn't sure who or what I was any more—as if I ever had known! I wasn't drug-affected, though, so at least I was having a natural look at life. This clarity felt peculiar, making me both self-conscious and vulnerable. I wasn't used to it yet.

Finally Vicki's trial date arrived and her time was taken up going to court every day. I did my work as a billet and when I'd finished, I played with Ali. Since moving to Yarrabrae, I'd been allocated the job of 'Yarrabrae billet', which meant doing much the same as I had previously in the old hall. I had to sweep and mop floors, and clean up when meal times were finished in the central communal area, which was now our new dining room. The old one had been closed and was to be demolished. I began to accept my life in prison. I had Ali with me and I was happy not to have a drug habit any more, so things were going along well. Because I'd become involved in music, education and drama, and had made some lovely new friends, I had some degree of relief and escape from the monotony of prison routine. I couldn't understand how the women who never got involved in any of these activities stayed sane. I knew that if I didn't keep my mind busy, I'd be in serious trouble. You could almost just rot away in jail and hardly anyone would notice. However, Vicki hadn't been through the whole adjusting process yet, and when I looked at her I could see that a part of her was still clinging precariously to the hope that she might be able to walk out of there. It had only been a couple of months since I'd also held on in vain, like trying to hold on to the last rays of the setting sun. Inevitably it sank and disappeared over the horizon, then it was gone—freedom.

I looked forward to the weekends because Vicki didn't have to go to court and I could observe her more—from a distance, of course! My shyness hadn't left me yet, nor had my lack of confidence. About once a month my father and his wife Jan would come in for a one-hour weekend visit, and we'd get through it without an argument because Ali was the focus of their attention; I knew they were really only coming to see her. Later on in my sentence, after Ali had left the prison, they stopped coming to visit—in fact they moved to New South Wales to get further away. Apparently my father was ashamed of me. It didn't bother me, and I didn't blame them. There was fault on both sides where that relationship was concerned, which doesn't mean I excused my father's behaviour towards me (and

Mum) when I was younger, but my angry responses didn't help either. However, I was never going to blame him for my drug use and subsequent lifestyle. Blame doesn't help anyone—it just keeps you emotionally stuck where you are.

As Vicki's trial approached completion she realised it wasn't looking too good. I could see the change in her, the resignation setting in. She was being much more realistic than I had been during my trial, although of course she was having to experience it straight, rather than stoned. Vicki seemed to be taking the rap for most of those involved in the case. Someone usually does, I guess. At least that way some of the others had a chance at freedom. Once the summing up of her trial was completed it wasn't long before a guilty verdict was handed down, as she had expected, and her sentencing day became imminent.

Since the shock of my sentence and the precedent it had set, women on drug charges were frightened that they, too, could be sharing this space with me for a long, long time. In the late 1970s sentences had become longer, but none was as extreme as mine in 1980. Of the friends I'd already made in jail, there was Marg serving 7/5 year minimum; Carol, 6/4 year minimum; Kathy, 5/3 year minimum; Brenda, 5/3 year minimum; and Lynda, nearly as lucky as me, with 13/11 year minimum. Drug use and its consequences were effectively changing the prison system. We watched as our numbers increased and knew that this system would have to adjust to accommodate us and to deal with our many other associated problems, aside from the issue of our drug use. It's a fact that eighty per cent of women drug users in prison have experienced sexual and/or physical and emotional abuse. It's therefore not hard to understand where the sadness, anger and high rates of attempted suicide and self-mutilation come from. Most of these women have never learnt how to express their feelings, repressing the conflict in regard to their abuse. Many secretly blame themselves for having been sexually abused, thinking that they had somehow acted promiscuously, not realising that five-, six- or ten-year-olds have a right to a safe space and that, back then, their innocence shouldn't have been corrupted. It is peculiar that women who have already been punished so irrevocably at such a young age should continue to be punished for, it seems, the remainder of their lives. The long sentences I and others received labelled all of us 'serious' criminals, when all we felt like were people who had become dependent on an illegal drug. We were doubly 'bad' for being women drug addicts, and triply 'bad' if we were also mothers, which three-quarters of us were.

As Vicki's sentencing date approached, she was painfully aware that she could receive quite a few years. We tried to be supportive and help her to prepare for that day—as if you could!

'What did the sentencing judge at your trial say?' she asked me one morning as we walked into the dining room for breakfast.

'He wasn't sympathetic at all. He seemed to think I'd had a good upbringing and ample opportunities in life and therefore had no justification for becoming a heroin addict,' I replied.

Vicki was not impressed with this news. On the surface, she appeared to have had a similar upbringing to me. She'd lived only a few suburbs from me as a child, although we'd never met as children or in our drug-using days prior to prison. Some people had even assumed, I guess because we were both relatively articulate, that we'd come from privileged backgrounds, but we were both working-class girls, although Vicki appeared more confident than me, even if it was a facade. In prison none of us talked much about childhood or our emotional difficulties. I guess we weren't really that open or trusting, or maybe we just didn't think it had any relevance to our current lives. We weren't aware of so many things—that there were options open to us, that it was possible to stop using heroin. Even though we weren't currently physically addicted, we all knew that we would use again given the opportunity. It was just a matter of when. I found myself hoping that by the time I was fifty or sixty years old, I'd have my drug consumption more under control, only using on the weekends. I thought I wouldn't get into so much trouble that way! It just never occurred to us drug users that you could actually stop—I'd never witnessed anyone who'd overcome their addiction permanently.

Vicki's sentencing day inevitably arrived. At breakfast I noticed her fiddling with her toast rather than eating it. The dining room contained about fifteen sets of tables and chairs, each seating four women; Vicki's table was a couple behind Stella's and mine, and diagonally across, more in the middle of the room. Ali was over with Vicki, chatting away incessantly, and I could see Vicki was making a real effort to be interested, possibly glad of the distraction. But none of it hid her anxiety, and my heart reached out to her. It was such a torturous process, going to court, your future to be decided by someone who didn't even know you except for what they'd been told by the prosecution and defence lawyers. After breakfast we all gave Vicki a hug, then waved to her as she was escorted to the front of the prison to be taken to court.

'Bye! Good luck!' we called as we peered out from behind the bars. We hoped that it wouldn't turn out bad for her.

After that, the day passed exactly the same as any other: it was back to Yarrabrae to clean up, attend muster, work—which for me was cleaning, mopping and polishing—spend lunchtime playing with Ali, sit and chat with my friends, attend another muster, do more work, more cleaning, finish work, collect mail, eat dinner ... Then, just before our final muster and afternoon lock-up, Vicki was brought back to the prison. She looked devastated. Head hanging, eyes staring at the ground, she said nothing at first. She must have been able to feel us all watching her. She was on her own, which meant at least her girlfriend must have gotten off. She looked up and I caught her glance. In that moment, although I didn't know her very well, I wanted to hold her, to try to comfort her, but there was a gate and a wire fence separating us that made any spontaneous action impossible. Because it was almost final muster time, there was no way an officer would open the gate and let me through. My heart ached with the pain of this mutually shared experience, and my eyes moistened as the need to reach out to her overwhelmed me. But I could only put my fingers through the wire and press my face up against the fence, not knowing what to say. Well, what do you say? 'Welcome, Vicki, this is now your home'? Your body goes into shock until the rest of you has had time to catch up and absorb reality.

A group of women from remand gathered around her and gave her big hugs. She was sort of joking with them, trying to make light of it, trying to be brave behind eyelids conditioned to blink back tears. It was the facade we all wore in that hell, but in her case the veil was too thin and I could see the lonely, vulnerable woman behind it. She looked strangely beautiful. It's not often in there that you get to see beyond the mask. Surviving in such a deprived environment is not about exhibiting vulner-abilities and nurturing qualities—it's more about bravado and toughening up.

Then the words spilled out of her: 'I got nine years with a six year minimum.' It was all she could say before her lip quiv-ered and then she physically tightened up, holding on.

I heard the gasps from the other women. 'Shit!' someone said. She'd have to serve four years. One consolation, I thought to myself, the judge obviously didn't think she was quite as bad as me.

'Muster up! Muster up!' the loudspeaker interrupted my thoughts. I allowed my fingers to uncoil from their grip on the wire mesh of the fence and walked back to Yarrabrae to get counted and locked in. I spent the night thinking about Vicki, wondering how she was feeling over there in the remand section. I bet she wished she could crawl into a hole and hide. Not that there'd be a hole—in fact there wouldn't be any privacy for her at all. I hoped the women were being kind to her. She'd have to move out of there soon now that she'd been sentenced. Darkness arrived and I hoped she'd be able to sleep because sometimes in prison the nights could be very long.

'It could have been worse,' she said bravely when I saw her at breakfast the next morning. I was glad she'd spoken to me because I hadn't known what to say. Anything I could think of seemed inadequate. I decided to trust that she knew I understood.

'Look at your sentence. Guess I should feel lucky,' she said, as much to herself as to the rest of us who were gathering around her. I knew that she was just trying to adapt to the reality, trying to give herself some space and time. She'd discover none of the former and plenty of the latter.

'When she looks around the prison now she'll look at it differently. This is her home for the next four years,' I said to Stella, who was standing next to me as Vicki went to get her breakfast and sit at her designated table. It puts a different perspective on things. Until you're sentenced you can cling onto a tiny hope of freedom like it's your last hit. No-one ever accepts the reality until they absolutely have to.

But, you know, in every negative situation you can almost always find a positive and for me, now that Vicki had been sentenced, it meant she'd have to move to a different section of the prison. I immediately opened my mind to the possibility that she could move into the Yarrabrae unit where Ali and I were living. There was no doubt I'd become intrigued with her and desperately wanted to know her better, but I was so shy in public. I wasn't sure what it actually was that I was feeling towards her, but if she moved in it would offer more privacy and a chance to talk.

Lynda and I had been sharing the same accommodation for a few months now. Lynda, who was easy to get along with, was also in on drug charges. She had received a similar sentence to me—13/11 year minimum—only months after my sentence was announced. When she and her husband, who was also in jail with almost the same sentence as her, had completed their sentences, they would be deported back to England where they'd come from. Lynda had given birth to her son, Damien, since she'd been in prison, so he was younger than Ali. They'd become like brother and sister. They were so funny together. Ali was like a miniature mother, telling him off when he did something wrong, even though he was only a newborn baby.

In one of the other cells was Carol, a co-heroin user serving 6/4 year minimum who Ali and I had become friendly with. She was a gorgeous young woman in her early twenties, about seven years younger than Lynda and me, and she was learning guitar with us at the Education Centre. She was also involved in the drama group. Ali and Carol adored each other and Carol was like a little girl herself. She was so childish in some ways and her eyes were almost always full of mischief. She was loud too. The prison officers found her demanding and didn't seem to like her much. They thought she was a troublemaker, but we loved having her around. While we were all living in the unit together, we grew to care for her so much that we didn't want her to leave. Carol had a bubbly, happy energy, and with her, Ali and Damien in the unit, we found ourselves laughing and having a lot of fun, so it was a pleasant unit to be in if you didn't mind children. Conveniently, one cell remained empty, and Lynda knew Vicki from the outside, so I encouraged her to talk to Vicki about the possibility of moving in. I was too embarrassed to talk to her myself as I knew I was attracted to her, even if she didn't know it! Lynda was quite keen to oblige because she liked Vicki too. We were also all aware that if we didn't come up with an option, the prison would put someone of their choice in the spare cell, and it could be someone we didn't get along with. It was these small things that you had to try and manipulate to make life easier.

Lynda reported back that apparently Vicki had a couple of other options she was exploring, but she'd shown a bit of interest in moving in with us. Because Ali often sat with her in the big dining room at meal times, they'd struck up a fun type of relationship. Lynda and Damien sat at the same table as Vicki too, so at least she seemed to enjoy the children.

I was increasingly puzzled about my desire to become more closely acquainted with Vicki. The feelings I had towards her were so strong and I didn't seem to have any control over the urge to be near her, my heart clearly taking over from my head. Vicki was involved with the night netball activities, and sometimes I found myself going out with Ali to watch. I knew I wasn't out there purely for the fresh air. I was attracted to her! I was such an obsessive person, but I'd never acted on my feelings towards a woman before, even though I'd felt attracted to a couple of women in the past. I'd always preferred to identify as heterosexual, but maybe this was something else. I recognised that I wasn't missing men from my life at all, which in the scheme of things surprised me. I thought I would.

In the end Vicki applied to move to a cottage, the flash accommodation for trusted long-termers, but the governor denied her request. Like me, she wasn't trusted enough yet. After that fell through she decided she'd apply for our unit, because basically she was running out of desirable options. Lynda and I discussed it with the governor while he was walking around the prison one day, suggesting it would be a good idea, and within days he informed Vicki that she was to move to our unit in Yarrabrae. One of the tragedies of prison life is that you have to be manipulative to get what you want.

That day Vicki moved in and shyness overwhelmed me. It was pathetic. For a while I hid from her so much, she must have thought I was a recluse. Every afternoon when we'd come in after lock-up I'd go to my cell, too self-conscious to show my face. I was so confused about what I was feeling towards her. I couldn't even make myself sit in the unit's central area with Vicki and the others, but gradually I discovered we had a common interest in music. I knew that was my way in ... into her cell. What a place for romance!

Maybe she'd like some extra guitar lessons, I thought to myself, even though I could only play basic guitar. After a few weeks I worked up some courage, more from obsessive desperation than anything else. 'Would you like to learn some chords? I could help you,' I offered.

'Yeah, that'd be great,' she replied.

Phew! I was so excited, but it didn't really mean anything—it wasn't as though she had anything else to do. It was late 1981 and Vicki had been living in Yarrabrae for a couple of months by then. I'd still not told anyone about my attraction to her, so I had to keep my excitement to myself, but I was used to that. I didn't know how I was going to break the news to her either, but at least her guitar lessons commenced! Then I became driven by desire. It's amazing how quickly you can adjust when you have to, and there was nothing much else to focus on! I was doing fine in the scheme of things.

In the evenings after lock-up when Ali had gone to bed, I would go into her cell and croon to the accompaniment of the guitars. We'd both sit on chairs beside each other facing the bed, which served as our music stand, guitars resting on our legs. It was nice to have her that close but, of course, the reality was that she couldn't really get away! I sang the Dan Hill song, 'Sometimes When We Touch', reading from the music. I'd always finish with tears in my eyes, longing for her to reach over and cuddle me. I was too frightened to tell her how I felt towards her in case I made a fool of myself. She was genuinely interested in learning and practising guitar and I was genuinely interested in her, and her guitar for that matter. But I could tell she thought I was straight, as in heterosexual, so it was unlikely to enter her mind that I would be interested in a woman, any woman, let alone her.

I'd always looked 'straight'. At times I'd found it extremely frustrating. No-one ever thought I was a drug addict either although, at times, that'd been handy. On the street, people often used to think I was a 'plant' (undercover cop) because I looked so straight. I would try to make myself look rougher, grubbier, ruffling up my hair and looking a bit more untidy, but it never seemed to work. In Yarrabrae I found myself wishing I was a lesbian, then Vicki might have grasped the situation. It was a painfully slow process and, really, I didn't even know what I was doing or feeling, except that every time I was close to her or she looked at me, my heart started racing!

Poor Vicki had a lot of adjusting to do, but I didn't take that into account. Her girlfriend had been released from prison after the trial, so Vicki was probably still getting used to the fact that their relationship was over, or at least that she wasn't going to see her for years. I didn't even think how that must have felt, even though I'd just experienced the same 'parting' in my own relationship. Maybe it was because my own separation hadn't caused me much grief—it was the contrary for me, actually. Somehow that relationship seemed like years ago.

Vicki and I both belonged to Heather's guitar group at the Education Centre, and we all had a lot of fun in the class. There were about eight of us who came together for our music lessons, as well as the drama group one night per week with Maud, Greg and Stella (not my drug-using friend Stella) coming in from the outside world. In a sense we'd created our own little community within the larger community of the prison. We were all 'druggies' without the drugs, so we understood each other. It was a nice group of friends and we developed a real sense of caring and respect for each other. I hadn't felt this sort of friendship for a long time, particularly with women. I'd been so isolated in my last relationship before coming to prison.

While I was enjoying the change of friends and the new companionship I'd found, I had serious intentions where Vicki was concerned and no-one knew. I needed to talk to someone, so I worked up the courage to talk to Brenda one day when there was an opportunity. She was a friend who I admired and respected, and who hung out in our group. She was also a lesbian, so I felt like she would be understanding about my predicament. When I explained to her how I was feeling about Vicki, she was helpful and supportive and didn't ridicule me, which was comforting.

'Just take your time,' she said humorously, 'it's not like either of you are going anywhere!' I was relieved to have shared my secret and Brenda thought it was great as she was friends with us both. I was nervous yet excited, and had butterflies in my stomach all the time. I'd previously always stuck with what I knew but, let's face it, there was no chance of a heterosexual relationship in jail! I guess I'd always thought I was peculiar enough being a heroin addict without adding another 'abnormality' but, in my situation then, that all seemed irrelevant.

After Ali went to sleep at night I went to Vicki's cell, and we sang and played during the remaining hours until lock-up at 10 or 11 o'clock. It felt good and I began to teach her to sing some harmonies. It was simple after the complicated world I'd just left. In a way it felt like the adolescence I'd missed out on as a result of my drinking and drug use. Vicki told me stories about her experiences and it seemed like her life had become complicated, violent and ugly too. If anyone ever tells you drug use is fun, don't believe them. Well, maybe socially it's fun, but we weren't social users.

I continued to sing 'Sometimes When We Touch' in Vicki's cell nearly every night, but it seemed to be taking a long time and I still hadn't worked up the courage to disclose my feelings towards her. She'd been in prison about ten months by then so, one night before we were locked into our units, I went and visited Pauline, another friend in Yarrabrae, feeling like I needed to hurry up this drawn-out process. I knew she had been able to sneak in some Serepax.

'Pauline, can I have a couple of pills?' I asked innocently after I got her alone in her cell.

'You're not into pills,' she replied. 'How come?'

'Well ...' Should I tell her or not? 'I just need to relax a bit,' I said to her, lying, having decided not to divulge my secret.

'Yeah, sure,' she said, 'although I can only give you a couple.'

'A couple will be plenty,' I replied, pocketing them. 'Thanks,' I said as I hurried away.

Not wanting to waste any more of the night I headed straight into my bathroom for some water, and down the hatch. I waited a little while for the pills to take effect and when I felt the barriers coming down and my confidence building, I walked across to Vicki's cell door and invited myself in.

'Do you want to play our guitars?' I said to her, peering in.

She was in there, sitting at her desk doing some Education Centre homework. She had just begun studying by correspondence for a business degree. 'Yeah, sure,' she said, 'I'll just pack up my things and make us a coffee.'

'Beauty!' I said to myself with a little chuckle. 'Tonight's the night ... I can feel it!' It was a wonder I could feel anything after two Serepax! I returned to my cell, grabbed my guitar and music, then went back to Vicki's cell. After we'd been playing and singing for a while, it was time for 'Sometimes When We Touch'. I started singing, my eyes almost immediately becoming moist with the thought of her, and then, like a click of the fingers, she got it, which was good because I was getting so sick of that song. She leaned over and kissed me. We held each other and I thought I was going to stop breathing on the spot.

'It's you I've been singing about,' I whispered. 'I've wanted you to hold me for so long, but I didn't know how to say it. I was so frightened you'd reject me.'

'I thought you were singing about someone else,' she said. We laughed together, both amused and yet self-conscious. For the first time in a long while, another adult made me feel warm inside. I felt cared for and I felt passion stirring within. I didn't tell her until months later about the Serepax!

After a few weeks of spending a few hours every night together talking, getting to know each other, making love when we were brave enough to risk some uninterrupted time, it was obvious we'd fallen in love and into a relationship. Progressively our lives became more and more self-contained and, as our love grew, we came to depend on each other, although we still maintained our other friendships. Life had a simplicity to it. For the first time in many years, perhaps ever, I was in love. I didn't even know what that meant, but I was sure this was it. From our first glance there was something about her that appealed to me. She was strong where I was weak. It seemed to me that we fitted together like a jigsaw, two incomplete human beings who, when put together, just possibly formed one complete human being. It strengthened 'us', although at times it became our downfall. It was difficult to be with someone day in, day out, with no holidays and no break in the routine, but we managed it quite well. We tried to live in the moment because it was all we had, all we could rely on. The prison could change things in the blink of an eye, and they often did. They never wanted you to feel too safe, too secure.

I hoped our relationship would be long-term, just like our sentences. I was busting to tell my brother, so I planned to talk to him when he next came in to visit, which was about once a month. When that day arrived I gave Vicki a kiss and a hug as I prepared to go to the visit centre and break the news to him. I was a bit nervous because it's hard to know how people will react to anything outside the ordinary, or at least outside their own experience, but I was so excited I couldn't wait to tell him of my good fortune. Fancy meeting the love of your life in jail! I walked in and he greeted me with a smile. I hoped he'd still be smiling when he left.

'Guess what, Ron?' I said from the other side of the visit table.

'What?' he replied apprehensively, probably not knowing whether to get caught up in my excitement or not.

'I'm in love with someone. Her name is Vicki.' I waited anxiously for his reaction.

'Really?' he said.

I sensed he needed some time to absorb the information. I knew I'd done some pretty harebrained things in the past, and I knew he wouldn't necessarily see me as a very good judge of character. He probably also needed to adjust to the fact that it was a woman that I was in love with.

'She's wonderful,' I continued regardless. 'I've never met anyone like her. She's intelligent (I always felt I had to tell people we were intelligent because so often people assumed prisoners and drug addicts were dumb), and she loves music and we're both learning guitar, and we're singing together. It's hard to believe it's real. I want you to meet her one day when we can organise for us both to come to the visit, okay?' I said to him before drawing breath.

'Yeah, well that would be good,' he said, 'I'd like to meet her.' I knew he'd be wary given some of the people I'd become involved with in the past, but he was still supportive. 'I've actually wondered if this might happen given the length of time you have to be here. It's human nature to want to love someone,' he said in an understanding way. I was so happy. I took his comments as approval. Even though I knew Ron would have liked me to be 'normal', it looked like things just weren't going to work out that way.

After the visit and subsequent strip search, I raced back to our unit in Yarrabrae.

'Ron was fine about it,' I said to Vicki. 'He looked a bit stunned, but he was happy for me.'

'That's a relief,' Vicki said. I was aware that it must have felt peculiar for her having not even met Ron. It's funny, but I'd always looked for his approval; it meant a lot to me.

Life moved on day by day and we created a fantasy world with Ali. For a while it was almost as though we weren't in prison, I was so 'in love'. After the prison staff eventually realised we were in a 'lover' relationship and they got over their shock, cynicism and the usual judgment, we were left alone to some degree. As I've said before, it's all relative, although we were grateful to some officers who weren't intrusive, giving us some privacy and space. There were always some who were compassionate and who genuinely cared. Of course there were the others too, but they had to catch us out, and at least we were smart enough to have learned how to manipulate the system. I don't think it was in their book of rules, but the prison didn't approve of lesbian relationships between inmates, so it was another thing that we had to try to hide even though, eventually, everyone knew.

Late at night, after Vicki and I were locked away in our individual cells, we dreamed of one day spending the whole night together in each other's arms, because we could never have that pleasure in jail. Often we'd write letters to each other:

> To Vicki,
>
> Would you like to come out with me for the day? We'll go to a nice restaurant for lunch, then get a couple of bottles of wine, our guitars (they come wherever we go!) and head for a quiet beach. Then we'll spend all night together. Dream away . . . but, one day we just might get to do it. In the meantime we'll keep each other sane . . . love H.

Life became more 'human' for me. I felt softer, more gentle. I'd come out of my cell in the mornings and a tender hand would find its way to my shoulder, a kiss to my cheek.

'Good morning,' she'd say. 'Like a coffee?' Human touch . . . it felt good. The look in her eyes was kind and my heart melted in those simple moments. Someone cares about me, someone knows I'm here, I'd think to myself. Because the outside world was increasingly excluded from the reality of prison, I often felt so alienated in jail that I'd wonder if there was anyone at all out there on the other side of those cold, concrete walls. Does anyone remember me? I'd sometimes think to myself. After a while, though, most of us long-termers didn't even bother. It was easier. Having been inside nearly a year, I had some vague memory of how the day would have passed for me outside, but 'normal' human beings had no idea how life was, hour by hour, inside these four oppressive walls. It was so nice to have someone with whom to share an intimate relationship.

Night-time lock-up would arrive and once again Vicki and I were separated into our individual cells. Vicki wrote:

> I'm sitting here wishing you were close enough
> that I could reach out and touch you—you're
> close in my heart and mind always, but touch is
> special. When I touch you I can feel you com-
> pletely and from that feeling I know that this is
> real. I feel special with you and I know you're
> special. We can look to each other for the
> strength we need to make it through. We can
> never run on smooth waters, there will always
> be something or someone who will create a
> ripple, but it's up to us together, to ride it
> out . . .

Those mornings that Vicki handed me a letter, I'd read it and allow the words to carry me through the day. 'See you at lunchtime. I love you . . .' she'd say as the loudspeaker made its daily 8 am announcement: 'Muster up! Muster up!' I'd hang on to those words like I'd never held on to them before.

'I love you too,' I'd say to her as she left for her work post. Love seemed hugely amplified in there. Many things seemed somehow 'bigger', and yet as a human being I felt so much smaller.

Each day after eating lunch, Ali and I would go outside with Vicki and Carol. It was a short but precious time to share together with the rest of our group. We'd go to the tennis/ netball court, sit around and chat, or maybe throw some goals. With Carol living in our unit and Vicki and I in a relationship, we were like a little happy family. Lynda and Damien had recently moved out, having been promoted to the cottages. Ali usually went off to play with Carol during the lunch break. We could often hear their laughter dancing across from the swings and slide, which were also used on the Saturday kids' visits. I'd never seen Carol as happy as when she was playing with Ali. I was aware that Ali, Vicki and I were going to miss Carol enormously when she was released from prison, she was so full of enthusiasm and laughter. In prison you find yourself in this 'catch 22' situation, wishing your friends didn't have to leave, but at the same time wanting them to leave, because prison is so dehumanising.

'Muster up! Muster up!' the loudspeaker again interrupted our relaxation. Back to work posts until 3.30 pm.

Sometimes I wished that loudspeaker would choke. 'Fuck off!' I'd yell at it. However, we came to look forward to the sound of it toward the end of the day, because at least after 4.30 pm lock-up we had some privacy. We removed ourselves from the daily chaos of women abusing officers, officers abusing women, none of it achieving anything, and the boredom of jobs that are meaningless and repetitive. That's why it was so valuable to spend as much time as possible at the Education Centre, because at least there you didn't have to be around the officers, some of whom seemed to gain an inordinate amount of pleasure from provoking you or making you feel angry or worthless.

Looking back, I still remember this time with an incredible amount of warmth. It was almost like an interlude in my sentence. However, in prison you have to enjoy every skerrick of joy that comes your way because one thing is for sure—it won't last.

12

Death and a new governor

U p until early 1982 I'd been lucky that, considering I was in prison, it had been a reasonably peaceful time. Personally I'd experienced some new and positive events: Ali being returned to my care, the relationship with Vicki, the Education Centre, my return to study and the incorporation of music into my life once again. To a large degree I'd been so absorbed in my own experiences that I'd been able to ignore the daily goings-on in the prison, and I was still enjoying the relief of not living with a violent male. Of course there were the daily altercations between women prisoners or women and officers, but I didn't get involved. Also, because it was so early in my sentence, there wasn't anything much I had to ask the authorities for, except maybe more education sessions. But times like these are rare in prisons because it's difficult to contain so much emotional suffering in such a small space. Invariably, someone is grieving inwardly, inflicting physical pain on themselves by way of self-mutilation, or exploding outwardly, being physically and/or verbally abusive. Everyone is feeling some kind of loss.

On one particular day in February 1982, Vicki and I, together with some friends, were chatting with a few of the women from remand. They seemed a bit unsettled, particularly one of them, a young woman called Danni who hadn't been in long. Although she was a drug user, none of us knew her from outside. A couple of Vicki's friends from her previous life, Marie and Clelia, had only recently arrived in prison and were awaiting a bail application on drug charges. They lived in the remand dormitory with Danni and were concerned about her.

It seemed that Danni was upset because her close friend Judy, who had been caught trying to escape a couple of days earlier, had been placed in the old cell block for punishment. Let me tell you, the old cell block was not a pleasant place to be. It was a rectangular bluestone building that looked centuries old—it appeared to have had no maintenance for centuries either. In fact it was scheduled for demolition after Yarrabrae was built, but the few cells it contained were still used when Yarrabrae's two punishment cells were full. At one end there was a little shed-like building where the officer sat whenever anyone was in the cell block for punishment. If a woman was difficult to control, they'd lock her in a solitary cell in a straightjacket. It was an incredibly dehumanising experience that, if you were considering suicide, would certainly push you to your mental and emotional limits.

I remembered how, not long after I'd first come to prison, Carol had been locked up in the cell block for punishment, probably for swearing at an officer or some similarly insignificant reason, and she developed serious stomach pains. She was there for days and we could hear her yelling out for help. Sometimes we'd stand outside the wire fence surrounding the cell block and call back to her, trying to comfort or reassure her in some small way, but usually an officer would threaten us with a charge and force us to move away, so we could never hang out there for long. Unfortunately the cell block was within view of the governor's office, so you couldn't sneak around anywhere near it and be out of sight.

During what turned out to be her last evening there, Carol's stomach pains got worse and worse until she constantly yelled out for help to the duty officer, who chose to take no notice. Then, in the middle of the night, we heard an ambulance arrive, apparently to take Carol to hospital. Her appendix had already burst and she nearly died as a result. The officers had thought she was just complaining about nothing. They often have that attitude, so it's amazing that more deaths haven't occurred in custody.

On this occasion in February 1982, Danni was so upset at Judy being in the cell block that she wanted to cause some trouble so she would be sent there for punishment too. She felt that at least if she was in the cells down there she'd be able to communicate with Judy. A few of us talked to her, trying to calm her down before lock-up, but as the day's final muster approached, her anxiety was increasing. You'd think the prison would have just let her go into the cell block and talk to Judy for half an hour, but no, that would be too simple. Besides, Judy was there to be punished—no privileges for her. Trying to escape from prison is the ultimate crime! I wish you could have met Judy; she was one of the nicest people I'd ever come across. But of course, we were all considered dangerous!

Marie and Clelia kept Danni with them before returning to remand for final muster. In their early twenties, they were also drug users in on drug charges. Vicki knew them from the outside and they seemed to be nice women. If the court viewed them as it had us, they were going to be in for a long time too, so it was likely we would become good friends. Vicki and I returned to Yarrabrae and the quiet of our unit, where we spent the evening with Ali. After she went to bed, we played our guitars and sang some songs as usual.

Suddenly, at about seven o'clock, one of our friends from Unit 3 came running over to our unit door, calling out to us anxiously, 'There's smoke coming from the remand dormitory.'

She quickly turned and left again. We ran out of our unit to the communal area in the middle of Yarrabrae. Other women were also moving around, looking at each other, wondering what was going on. We looked for Mr Mercer, the Yarrabrae duty officer for the night. We discovered him in Unit 2, where you could get a clear view across to the remand dormitory.

'What's going on?' we asked as soon as we saw him looking out the window.

'I don't know,' he replied. 'The phone isn't working.'

Most of Yarrabrae's inmates had crowded into Unit 2, and from there we watched smoke billowing up into the sky above the remand area. Mr Mercer ran back to his office to try the phone again. He quickly returned, cursing in frustration at not being able to make contact with anyone outside our building. We watched the night duty officers running around outside, opening up fire hose cupboards. As two officers turned on one of the fire hoses, the water burst through its seams, rendering it ineffective. The fire hoses probably hadn't been checked for years and it looked like this one hadn't been unwound properly before they turned it on. It was all happening very quickly and, to our dismay, flames soon started leaping from the building with more and more smoke billowing up into the sky. Some of the Yarrabrae women were getting agitated. They started yelling out, but no-one outside could hear us because they were too busy trying to get the fire hoses working. Mr Mercer didn't have any keys for the outside of our building, making it impossible for any of us to get out of Yarrabrae to help. We all had to stand there watching helplessly. Some of the women started screaming at Mr Mercer to do something. It was getting scary.

'That's our friends in that dormitory! Do something!' someone screamed at him. He ran over to his office again and tried desperately to make contact with the administration block, but the line was down.

Ali, me and my friend Danni when I was out on a day leave in 1983.

Corliss, Ali and me on the steps of the Education Centre.

Ali and Carol, taken when I was out on a day leave after Carol's release.

Ali, aged five, asleep with 'Mima when she was a kitten.

David (left), me and Pete (back) singing songs at Ron's house when I was living there after my release. Good friends from my days with TRAMM, we have remained close through the ups and downs.

Ali at ten years old, with Jemima, who was rescued from an animal shelter when Ali was living with Ron while I was completing my sentence.

Me singing at one of the Wring Around Fairlea protest rallies outside the prison with Lou Bennett, of Tiddas, on guitar.

Me, Julie and Ali at my birthday dinner in 1989, not long after Julie's release. After all my years in prison, it was odd to be doing 'normal' things like sitting with friends in a restaurant.

KEEP FAIRLEA OPEN FOR WOMEN

Say NO to Women in Jika Jika
Say NO to Women in Mens Prison

WE NEED YOUR SUPPORT

Join the 24 hour vigil
Outside Fairlea Prison
For more information
Call 363 1811
Marg, Wendy or Chris

Above and opposite: Carol and Ali featured on the handbill we produced for the rally to stop women prisoners being sent to Jika Jika. THE SAVE FAIRLEA COALITION

WHY MOVING WOMEN & CHILDREN FROM FAIRLEA TO JIKA MUST BE STOPPED.

JIKA: A maximum security, sensory deprivation prison of tunnels and cages; 24 hour air conditioning; Award for Excellence in Concrete; Exercise is in a cage with 12' concrete walls; 8 men have died there; it is inside Pentridge; it is a prison in a prison; 15 hours in 2 bunk cells.

FAIRLEA: The first women's only prison in Australia. Accomodation is cottage style, trees and gardens. In these cottages, women can cook for themselves and have private time with their kids for 6 hrs on the weekend. Education & health centres at Fairlea cater to the special needs of women.

THE WOMEN & CHILDREN: 75% of women in for non violent offences, 18% for shoplifting and car theft, 86% unemployed. Of women inside for drugs, 80% are abuse survivors, 74% have kids. Of women gaoled for prostitution, 25% are under 24.

WHY JIKA IS UNACCEPTABLE: Women have been in men's prisons before. Of 6 women who have suicided, 5 have done so in men's gaols. Women have always suffered discrimination in men's gaols, they have no freedom of movement as they are in a prison in a prison, many women and child care agencies won't allow children to visit at Jika because its too frightening.

WHAT WE ARE DOING: 7000 people have signed a petition; there's a 24 hour vigil outside Fairlea-all welcome; we're lobbying; women inside are going to Equal Opportunity.

WHAT CAN YOU DO?: PETITIONS/ DONATIONS/ JOINING VIGIL ROSTER **PH: 363 1811/LETTERS OF PROTEST:** Pat McNamara, Corrections Minister, 222 Exhibition St, Melb 3000/Jan Wade, Women's Affairs, 200 Queen St, Melb.3000

TOGETHER WE CAN STOP THIS DISASTER HAPPENING

A publicity shot from my days with TRAMM. Front row from left: me, Annie, David and Jan.

Helen Barnacle

Pianist, Singer, Songwriter

Ballads and soft rock for your Piano
Lounge or Restaurant

The poster I used to advertise myself as a singer. The photo was taken at Barkly's restaurant, which no longer exists. Being able to express myself musically has always been important to me, and was one of the things that helped me survive prison.

Me and Rikki after her release in 1992. Rikki was a dear friend who helped me survive the difficult days in prison. Her death a few years later was one of the tragedies that moved me to honour the lives of my lost friends by writing about our experiences.

Me and Greg at my end of parole party in August 1995. Greg's compassion helped me through my bleakest time in Fairlea. Now a Buddhist monk, he continues to visit women in prison today.

Me and Amanda, who remains one of my very special freinds, in a boat on Myall Lakes during our camping holiday in New South Wales.

Clockwise from front left: Ali, Kurt, me and Corliss after a Somebody's Daughter performance in Ballarat during a regional tour in 1998. Corliss gave me unconditional support during very difficult times in prison, and she and Kurt are now our dearest friends.

'I'm a first aid officer, I could help over there,' he told us, but there was nothing he could do except stand there and watch with us as we listened to fire engines arriving. It was so frustrating standing there doing nothing, and a sense of panic set in.

Our anxiety and fear increased tenfold as we watched firemen running towards the remand building, aiming their fire hoses up high at the roof where the flames now formed huge orange and yellow streaks against the darkness of the night. Windows were exploding, but of course that didn't create an exit for the women trapped inside as the bars were still in place. In Yarrabrae, some of the women started screaming hysterically at the sound of crashing glass and the sight of parts of the building crashing down to the ground. Our friends were over there and we knew they couldn't get out.

I went back into the communal area to try to calm down some of the women, while Vicki remained in the unit with Mr Mercer. After a short time I returned to Unit 2. There seemed to be a lot of action around the other side, but we had no way of knowing whether the women had been dragged to safety or whether they were still trapped inside. The flames quickly engulfed the whole building, and we could barely see through the smoke. Because we could only see from one limited angle, we couldn't tell what was happening beyond the front of what had once been the remand dormitory.

'Have they got the women out?' we asked Mr Mercer frantically, but of course he only knew as much as we did, which was very little. Some of the women in the central area of Yarrabrae were screaming through the bars at the front entrance for someone to let us out, but they couldn't be heard through the chaos outside. The prison staff and firemen were totally focused on trying to get the fire under control and, we hoped, removing the women from the dormitory to safety. One thing we did know was that, if they were still stuck inside, they had no hope of surviving.

At least a couple of hours passed before the fire was brought under control. Where the old wooden remand dormitory once stood was now a smouldering black shell of a building. Eventually, some prison staff came over to Yarrabrae with news. Most of the women in remand had been rescued from the building, although some had minor burns and some had suffered from smoke inhalation. For three of them, though, assistance had arrived too late—only their charred bodies remained. We were almost speechless. 'Who?' we whispered, hardly daring to ask, not really wanting to know the answer. To our horror, it was Clelia, Marie and Danni, the three women we had been talking to before lock-up. Vicki, Carol and I just looked at each other, numbness and shock enveloping our bodies.

'How?' we asked. No-one seemed to have an explanation. The officers looked back at us blankly, obviously upset and trying to come to terms with it themselves. After a few quiet minutes they told us that some of the rescued women believed Danni had started the fire and that Clelia and Marie had tried to stop her. Danni thought that her actions might get her transferred to the cell block where she could be closer to Judy. We wandered off aimlessly after receiving the news, many of us hanging around in the central area of Yarrabrae for a while in a daze, periodically returning to Unit 2 to have a look at the remains of the burnt-out building, as if to validate that this wasn't just a terrible nightmare.

Vicki, Carol, Sue and I eventually returned to our unit in shock. Ali had slept through the whole disaster, thank goodness. The four of us sat down and made ourselves a coffee, sitting around the table in the centre, grasping for words. We tried in vain to make some sense of it, but it just didn't seem real yet.

'How silly would you have to be to start a fire in one of these buildings after lock-up?' I said to them.

'You'd have to know that the chances of anyone getting you out in time would be slim,' Vicki added.

We went through it, over and over again, but there were no answers. We talked about Danni's agitation prior to lock-up. Who would have dreamed it would come to this? We had to wait until morning before we could talk to the other women involved, although the only people who might really have known were dead.

An eerie, solemn mood spread through the jail in the days that followed, officers and women alike not knowing what to say. We were still trying to accept what had happened. It was the sort of thing that you knew could happen quite easily in a jail, but you never really expected to have to face that reality. All of us were looking for explanations, answers to our questions, but no-one had any. We all reacted differently. Some of us were angry, some were quiet, some just plain sad, and some didn't show anything. Some of us wanted to talk about it, while others didn't. Above all this, though, the relentless routine of prison was maintained as the prison authorities tried to contain our grief, frustration and anger. Wake up, breakfast, muster, work posts, lunch, muster, work posts, dinner, muster, lock up, muster, sleep. Then the same again the next day.

The only break in the routine was the arrival of a new governor, Governor Smith, who moved immediately into damage control. Our previous governor went off on sick leave. I didn't blame him. Volunteers arrived in the prison handing out free cigarettes and lollies. It made me sick how they always handed out cigarettes to keep prisoners happy, or at least quiet. I didn't even smoke, although Vicki appreciated it! A couple of days after the fire, after we'd wandered around in shock trying to comfort each other, we organised a memorial service in remembrance of the three women's lives. My friend Val had written a poem to which I composed a melody, and Vicki and I sang it at the service.

KEEP HOLDING ON

When everything seems to be slipping away,
and you don't know what's real any more,
for everything once, that you knew and believed
doesn't feel as it once did before.
Find something to keep holding on to
that can never be taken away,
that will always be there, come tomorrow
and is yours to believe in today.

Chorus

For rivers run deep, mountains are strong
No-one should ever pay twice for a wrong
Sunshine is wisdom, rainbows don't lie
and you'll always have your piece of the sky.

Do you ever feel close to surrender,
you feel lost to know where to begin,
for each time the tide starts to drift on out,
it seems that you drift back on in.
Through tragedy we must stand united,
share our feelings together as one,
Even though our resistance is shadowed,
at the end of each storm is the sun.

© Val, 1982

Sadness continued to hang like a cloud over the prison for some weeks. We didn't know what else to do except the same old thing we did every day—not that we had a choice. Sadness was a common emotion in prison, but you never got used to it. You never knew where to put it. Surely life wasn't meant to be this meaningless. I later wrote a song about the fire, but I never sang it publicly. I couldn't. I placed it in my music book with my other original material. Some things were just too sad to bring out into the open. Wasted lives. Three beautiful women, so young, so full of future plans. What a place for it to end.

Smith, the new governor, was nice to us for a couple of weeks after the fire but, before too long, we started to get a glimpse of how it was going to be in there while he was in charge. My first eighteen months in prison had been a picnic compared to what lay ahead. I had no idea how much our lives were about to change. Welcome to the unknown!

In the subsequent months a strange disquiet settled on the place and a seed of distrust was planted between the women and Smith. He had decided that, because the old cell block was now closed, he needed a 'punishment' unit for women who didn't behave. Although Unit 5 in Yarrabrae had two cells, he obviously didn't think that this was enough, so he arranged for a section in Jika Jika at Pentridge, in the men's prison, to be used for the punishment of women. Already a couple of women had been sent there because pills such as Serepax and Rohypnol had been found in their cells. On both occasions, the women had been mystified as to how the drugs had found their way into their cells. One of the new rules introduced by Smith was that whenever he walked into a room, everyone had to stand up, officers included; for us, the threat of transfer to Pentridge was ever present. It was his new tool and he used it with abandon.

Since the fire, the Corrections Department had decided that most of the old buildings at Fairlea would be demolished and the prison rebuilt. Only the newer buildings, such as Yarrabrae and the cottages, were to remain, accommodating up to about thirty women. On 15 April 1982 we were told that at least half of the women, approximately thirty, would be moving to Pentridge men's prison where a new section, called B Annexe, was opening up while the rebuilding took place. In fact it wasn't a 'new' section at all, just part of the old B Division which they'd separated to house the women. We'd been managing at Fairlea by doubling up women in cells to accommodate those who had previously lived in 'remand'.

Everything seemed normal the evening prior to the move until tea time, when two 'troublemakers' were removed to the old cell block. This didn't really upset anyone as the two women concerned weren't very popular. A few hours later, Governor Smith appeared in Yarrabrae and ordered everyone to their cells. It was only 9 pm and cell lock-up time was normally 11.15 pm. He said 'not to worry' and assured us that nothing was wrong, but nevertheless we were locked away for seemingly no reason. A couple of women dared to complain and were immediately removed to the cell block. No-one knew what the hell was going on. I was luckier than most. Having Ali with me, I wasn't able to be locked in my cell, only in the unit, as I had to be able to get to the fridge to make up bottles for her during the night.

Night passed and morning arrived, but no officers came to wake us or unlock the doors at the usual time.

'What's happening?' Vicki asked me as I opened the trap door of her cell.

The others started calling out to each other through their trap doors. We soon found out. Officers came and took us one by one to the Classification Committee. The first ten on the list, including Carol from our unit, were sent to their cells to pack their belongings for immediate transferral to Pentridge before the rest of us were let out of our cells. They continued transferring women in groups of ten—the smaller numbers making the women more manageable, because hardly anyone wanted to be removed—until they reached thirty. Then later, as the governor would report it, 'the move to Pentridge was completed without a hitch'.

But now Vicki and I had to explain to Ali where Carol had disappeared to so suddenly. It was only a little more than a week later when we heard from Carol.

Dear Helen, Ali & Vicki,

Helen, I received your letter this evening. It was just what I needed after a torturous day—a little ray of sunshine to take with me to my cell. Days here are full of twists and are never straightforward and bloody torturous mentally.

Everything is still rather disorganised here, with men building around, on top and under us—noisy, damn it near drives you crazy—oh, for the sweet silence of Yarrabrae ... god, I never thought I would be saying anything in favour of that building ... see, must be losing it—next I will be telling you what a wonderful person your boss is!!! That's enough of that sarcasm.

It was so good to see Corliss the other day. I was feeling so cut off from you all and she walked in and brought it all back to me and left a bond that I haven't let go of, reminding me of you all and that you are indeed real and still living in this world with me!!

Our living conditions are not the best, tiny one-out cells, but really I can overcome that by not really being here, imagining I am at home in my bedroom. The only thing I can't stand is the absolute isolation. We tap on the walls to each other at night, then go to the trap and call out to reassure each other that we are okay. We go out to our exercise yard during the day, no trees, no grass, only gravel and high, high blue-stone walls, but I suppose it could be worse—they could block out the sky!

Is little Ali missing me? You tell her I'll see her real soon. I miss her so much; those big brown eyes and her little voice so peaceful and calm. There's certainly nothing like her voice here. Now Vicki, I hope you haven't let anyone take over my part of our education area? Hmm?? I also hope you haven't given my position on the netball team to anyone too spectacular ... believe me, I'm in terrible physical condition, my muscles have all turned to fat!!

Well this paper is coming to an end. I have so many memories to keep with me, so how could I ever forget you. I love you all—Helen, Vicki and my darling Ali. XXX

However, as with everything in prison, you just have to try to get on with it and do your time, so Ali, Vicki and I did just that, although we kept writing to Carol in Pentridge.

One day we planted a garden with Ali, right outside the large window of our unit, so that we could watch the seeds burst through the ground and grow into flowers. It helped to remind us that nature was still functioning somewhere. We found some jasmine and planted it so it could wind itself around the bars on the window and we could smell the beautiful fragrance. We imagined it would grow so thick that the officers couldn't see in any more, but then of course we also wouldn't be able to see out. It was hard to win in there. The horizon of concrete and razor wire never changed, so we tried in our small way to create a view that contained some green, at least in the cavity between our unit and the perimeter. We tried not to look too far ahead because there was nothing to see except that cold stone wall.

Also outside our unit window was a small grassed area. Sometimes, just before lock-up, we'd let the hose run on the grass until the water formed a puddle, then after we were locked in we'd sit in the unit and watch through the window as the birds bathed themselves in the water. We pretended that one of the many willy wagtails was called Harry and that he was our pet willy wagtail who visited us every afternoon. Ali loved waiting for Harry to arrive. 'Ooh! Look!' she'd squeal with delight as she watched the birds playing. 'Hi, Harry! I love you, Harry!' she'd call out at the top of her voice. When Carol was there with us she used to squeal just as loud as Ali. 'Yes, Ali, Harry's come to see you again!'

These moments were precious for Ali, Vicki and I. It used to be a precious time for us with Carol, too, until she was transferred to Pentridge, but we were sure she'd be returning as soon as possible. We couldn't bear to think of it any other way. Because she had full-time education, the teachers at the Education Centre could also put forward an argument that she needed to be returned to Fairlea, which might increase her chances, but you could never be sure.

With Carol's departure, I was only too aware that I would lose all of them in the coming years. Carol was due to be released first, then Ali would have to leave the prison, and then Vicki a year later. I tried not to think about it and just enjoy the time we had.

The best days were when we had sessions in the Education Centre. There we'd participate in meaningful activities and, unlike in the rest of the prison, we were treated with respect.

Vicki and Carol were the only two women to be granted full-time education. Later on, in 1983, I applied and eventually was also successful. Days spent in the Education Centre were certainly more stimulating than working in the jail. We developed close and intense relationships with the teachers, mainly Heather and Corliss. Ali continued to spend occasional weekends with Corliss and her husband Kurt.

After a couple of months our wish came true and Carol was returned to Fairlea. Best of all, she returned to live in our unit. Ali was ecstatic. As individual women were released from Fairlea after completing their sentence, space was created for women from Pentridge to be returned, although B Annexe was now utilised as a reception prison for women on remand and those with the highest security ratings. Carol was very wary of Smith, and Vicki and I had noticed that he didn't seem to like her. Whenever we talked to him about her, he grimaced at the mention of her name and always referred to her in a derogatory way. We couldn't figure out why Carol had been one of the ones moved to Pentridge in the first place, given that she was a long-termer with full-time education and was in the last third of her sentence. Of course we'd never know the answer. Anyway, we were glad to have her back in our little 'family'.

Vicki and I continued our relationship, still writing notes to each other after we'd been locked into our cells for the night. There's something about forced separations that makes you want to be with someone even more. As Vicki wrote in late September 1982, 'Here I am sitting on my bed on my own again. I hate that locked door that separates us. I need you right now. I need you to hold me. I need you to be tender and warm and gentle with me ...' She'd leave her letters on my bed in the morning and I'd find them after muster when she'd gone to the Education Centre. I loved reading those caring words and I couldn't believe how lucky I was to have found love in an environment such as that. I'd only used heroin once or twice during the previous two years, so life was pretty simple. We'd spend our spare time with Ali, who was in my care twenty-four hours a day, because that was the rule. Prison officers weren't even allowed to pick her up in case they dropped her. The Corrections Department was worried I could sue them if she was injured.

Because there were now only about thirty women in the jail until the new buildings were completed, it was relatively quiet. But overall there was a feeling of confusion and, for some, desperation, which still hadn't settled since the fire. No-one said much, though. With the arrival of Governor Smith, I personally felt suspicious, never knowing what was going to happen next, and not knowing what to expect. I didn't feel depressed, more like a restless, uncomfortable feeling. At least Governor Curll, who had gone on sick leave, was upfront. I didn't agree with him a lot of the time, and he was always opposed to having children living in the prison, but at least you knew where you stood. I didn't trust Smith. He made me feel queasy inside, although Vicki thought he might be all right as she had been able to get him to agree to allow us to resume netball, and to continue some of our night-time music and drama activities.

Every few months Vicki and I, together with anyone else who was around and who was musical, would put on a performance for the women, assisted by Heather, the teacher from Education. We'd sing a variety of songs, accompanying ourselves on piano and guitars. Vicki and I worked on harmonies, with our voices expressing the love in our hearts, which contrasted so much with the regimented environment surrounding us. We'd get very nervous as we prepared for our little public performances, and I think sometimes the other women were bored, but they had limited choices for entertainment and they were always supportive. There was really only the drama group or us. It was a big step for me to perform again, although I was sitting at the piano, but with Vicki by my side I felt like I could do anything. It also gave us a goal to work towards, however small. In comparison to a large percentage of the women, Vicki and I seemed highly motivated and were always thinking up new ideas for night activities like netball and aerobics. Actually, we both felt that if we didn't keep ourselves busy we'd go mad with boredom. It was also about minimising the amount of time we'd have to spend locked inside after 4.30 pm—the more night activities, the more opportunity to be outside under the stars.

However, amidst the bliss of being in love and sharing my time with Ali, there were the usual interruptions. Any prisoner could tell you about them. Since Smith's arrival we appeared to be subjected to an ever increasing number of cell searches and strip searches. He also seemed to enjoy surprising everyone, prisoners and officers alike, by ordering the Pentridge 'dog squad' (officers with dogs trained to detect drugs) into Fairlea to search the whole prison in the middle of the night. We'd be woken from our sleep and herded to a central area. Usually they were looking for drugs, but also other forms of contraband. Prior to Smith's arrival this had only ever occurred during the day. He also started moving prisoners around within the prison as well as sending them to Pentridge, often for being 'under suspicion' or other similarly unsubstantiated reasons. Women would be removed from a cottage back to Yarrabrae, which was the maximum security building and much less comfortable, without ever finding out the reason.

After I'd done my usual morning work one day in October 1982, I was at the Education Centre for one of my sessions. At 10.15 am someone noticed the dog squad going into Yarrabrae. We watched them conduct their search from the windows of the Education Centre. When we tried to enter Yarrabrae to retrieve our guitars at lunch time, we were surprised when the officers refused to allow us into our cells. The lunch break passed and we returned to Education. We noticed the dogs and their handlers eventually leaving our units at approximately 2 pm. Why had they had taken so long to search our small cells?

At 3.15 pm I went directly to our unit. As I walked in I was amazed to be confronted by a total mess in the pantry. I went on to my cell and checked my cupboards and drawers. They had obviously been searched, but were left reasonably neat. I then went to Vicki's cell and couldn't believe what I saw. Her books, private letters and papers, and things from her desk were scattered all over the floor. Her cupboards were open and everything in them was dishevelled, with clothing half hanging out. What a disgusting mess! They had even opened a packet of her cigarettes and smoked two of them, then butted them out on her floor.

Needless to say, when Vicki saw the state of her room she was so angry that I had to keep following her around to make sure she didn't explode or do something that could result in her being charged or transferred. There were so many 'privileges' they could take from you. All they needed was an outburst of anger and she could lose her full-time education, her future chances of temporary day leaves or, worse still, they could just tell her to pack her things and off to Pentridge she'd go. It was an antiquated bluestone prison and because the women were always a minority there, they didn't have access to much in the way of facilities or programs. Even more important than that, women sent to Pentridge felt isolated from their friends at Fairlea. I had to remind myself of this constantly whenever I felt angry after officers had degraded or humiliated me, or brought to my attention, once again, that I was merely a prisoner. I had to control my feelings and calm down, suppressing all the aggression and frustration. After being there for almost two years, I'd become quite good at it.

In Vicki's case, when she asked a senior officer if she could lodge a complaint about the state of her room, or if she had any rights at all in the matter, he smugly replied, 'Well, that's one of the hazards of being a prisoner, isn't it?' They found no contraband in any of the rooms, but a comment from one of the senior staff implied that they believed there was some contraband in Vicki's room—the dogs just couldn't find it! Anyway, life continued on and in the end it was just another day interrupted by the usual pettiness that is constant in every prison that I've ever had knowledge of.

On the odd occasion we were successful in gaining some small concession, most probably because Vicki was incredibly persistent when she was arguing for something. It was amazing how little we had in comparison to male prisoners in Victoria, so most of the time whatever it was that we gained was only something that the men already had. Around this time Vicki and I successfully argued for the introduction of a quarterly 'spend', like the one the men had at Pentridge. It was really just what 'normal' people do every week—go to the supermarket and buy what they need—although we couldn't purchase any fresh fruit or vegetables, and were limited to what appeared on a list. There were things like decent coffee, yogurt, cheese, dry biscuits, soft drink and other grocery items on the 'big spend' list, although you could only have a 'big spend' if you were lucky enough to have money. We were allowed to spend up to $30 maximum. Vicki was studying accounting at the time, so she offered to organise the whole thing, with me as her assistant of course! It was no extra paperwork for the prison, so they allowed it to go ahead. Of course, they had to do the shopping, but we did all the administration. It meant that, at least every three months, we had an opportunity to order things that weren't available from our normal weekly 'canteen', which only stocked things like cigarettes, toiletries and terrible coffee, along with a few varieties of biscuits, lollies and chocolates. For the 'big spend', we'd compiled a list of everyone's order, then the officers would buy the stuff for us. It was quite a big task gathering all the items together for each prisoner, but we enjoyed it. When we'd finished we'd return to our cells for a decent cup of coffee—Nescafe Blend 43. It even smelt like coffee. The rubbish we received from our canteen every week tasted like the sweepings off the floor. I think it was packed specially for prisons as it didn't have a label, just clear cellophane packaging. It really was disgusting. The first thing we did when we were in our unit was to unseal the Blend 43 jar and take a great big 'whiff'. Our treat later in the evening would be Salada biscuits with cheese. For a moment we felt as if we were living like queens!

Another small positive in the prison at that time was that in early 1983 our netball team had been granted permission by the Corrections Department to participate in a local netball competition. This was the first time this had been allowed and we were so excited. We called ourselves the Fairlea Foxes and, actually, we were okay. Carol, Vicki and I had already been training as it was an excuse to go out for night activities, but now we were really keen. It was something to work towards. Vicki was nominated coach and I was voted captain, although it had taken some time for Lynda and I to convince the governor to allow the two of us, as mothers, out for sporting activities. Two or three evenings a week we persuaded the officers to let us out to train, which was great for Ali too. I felt a bit guilty that she was always locked inside from 4.30 pm. It was something we really came to look forward to, although it often depended on which officers were on duty in the evenings. There were always some who seemed to gain pleasure from spoiling any sense of enjoyment we might have created.

I facilitated the aerobics part of the training and the sessions were quite gruelling. Some of the women whined and complained at being pushed to train, but actually they enjoyed it as it broke the monotony and we were all getting fitter. Vicki facilitated the skills training component and decided to learn how to be an umpire. An added benefit of training was that we were able to release a lot of frustration and pent-up energy on that court. At first, a different team from the local competition came into the prison to compete against us each Thursday night, but soon it was such a success that we were allowed to go out one evening per week to play at the local venue. Two officers would come around to collect us after lock-up on Thursdays, and the whole team was taken in the prison bus. This competition provided us with the incentive to train and we became quite obsessed with the game. We were very enthusiastic and very determined.

Ali, who was nearly three years old by then, became our mascot, and one of the women who worked in the sewing room made a netball skirt and bib for her to wear to the games. She barracked and clapped her little hands with glee every time we scored a goal. 'Come on the Foxes!' she'd yell from the side of the court in her little netball outfit. 'Go, Mum! Go, Vicki! Go, Carol!' she'd call out. I think she enjoyed the games even more than we did, and she loved the bus ride to the courts. Winning became incredibly important to us—at times too important, but that's what happens when you have very little in your life to focus on. Everything becomes amplified. Instead of strip searching the whole team when we got back to the prison after the games, they'd randomly select two or three of us for this treatment, but by now I'd been inside for over two years and had come to expect this as a normal part of life. Sometimes, though, our netball excursion would be cancelled at the last minute. That goes with the territory too—you can never guarantee anything in prison. One night, about an hour or so before we were due to go out to play a game, a prison officer came to my cell.

'Head Office have just rung and cancelled your "leave" to go to netball tonight,' he said.

'What do you mean? Why?' I asked him, baffled.

'You're not allowed to go unless Ali is with you.' Ali was away from the prison, staying at my father's house for a few days.

'But what difference does that make?' I asked him, still puzzled.

'I don't know, I've just been told to come and tell you.'

Vicki and Carol were sitting in the unit with me, and they shook their heads as the officer walked out.

'They're fuckin' arseholes!' said Carol in frustration.

'What's the story?' I looked at Vicki, hoping she might have some explanation.

'I bet they think you're a security risk without Ali,' she said. 'They must think that you might try and escape because it'd be easier to run.'

'They are such fuckin' idiots,' I replied, 'but I bet you're right. As if I'd run without Ali ... the dickheads!' Now I was getting angry. We talked about it and then Vicki and Carol sent word to the other women in the netball team. When the officers came to collect them all, they had a discussion and decided that, if I couldn't go, they wouldn't go. Those women stuck by me through thick and thin.

13

The uncertainties of prison life

In November 1982 Carol was due for release after more than three years in jail. She was excited and positive and we felt happy for her, but sad for ourselves. The only advantage to us was that, once she was outside, she was going to try and organise to smuggle some smack into the prison for us through a friend of hers. Although we were no longer physically addicted, the psychological craving for the drug still remained. It wasn't a priority any more because we were relatively happy—having a hit had become more of a dream. When we were able to obtain illicit drugs they were usually given to us free of charge by friends (drug users/sellers) who had done time in prison themselves and wanted to do us a favour. They understood drug addiction and the monotony of life in jail, so they acted from a sense of compassion born of mutual understanding. Of course, the only way they could afford to do this was if they themselves were dealing in order to maintain their own habits. Occasionally we were able to organise payment, but it was always only a very small amount.

I knew it was going to be a long time before I'd see Carol again as she wasn't allowed back into the prison to visit, but we'd arranged for my brother to take Ali to Carol's place occasionally so that they could maintain their special relationship. I was hoping that, once I was eventually eligible for day leaves, I'd be able to see Carol sometimes.

The end of November, Carol's release date, inevitably arrived and we walked to the front gate with Marg and some other friends to say goodbye. Carol carried Ali all the way to the fence separating prisoners from the front administration office.

'When will I see you, Carol?' Ali asked.

'I'll see you in about two weeks, after I settle in and organise for Ron to bring you to my house,' she replied.

'How many sleeps?' asked Ali.

'Not many, but I'll write you a letter before then, okay?' Carol reassured her.

'All right,' replied Ali

'Who's my little darling?' Carol asked Ali. She always called Ali her 'little darling' and Ali just loved it. Those women made her feel so special.

'Me!' said Ali, then waved as the officer arrived to escort Carol through the gate to the front of the jail.

'Bye, bye, Carol. I love you, Carol!' Ali yelled after her.

Carol was nervous but also overjoyed to finally be getting out. She hadn't done her time easy—her mouth always got her into trouble. She would demand that officers treat her with respect, and she'd always let them know how she felt. They didn't like that, so they labelled her a 'management problem'. But release day is the moment all prisoners live for—often it is the only thing that gives you a sense of purpose through your sentence. I guess it is a blend of happy and sad that confronts you as you walk out the gate. For Carol, saying 'goodbye' to her friends of the last three years wasn't easy, especially after the bond she'd developed with Ali, but at least the two of them would still be able to see each other, because Ali wasn't a prisoner. I had no way of understanding exactly what Carol might have been going through but I did notice that, although she had a big smile across her face, the tears were streaming down her cheeks. Vicki, Marg and I and some other friends smiled back, but we also had tears in our eyes as Carol turned and walked through that gate and out of our daily lives.

After the goodbyes we returned to our unit and tried to busy ourselves with some cleaning up, but the place felt empty and silent, and our hearts were heavy. We made a cup of coffee and waited for the inevitable call to muster. The unit was the same as always, but the empty cell where Carol had once lived made it feel so different.

'There'll probably be someone else in there by this afternoon,' Vicki remarked. At the Education Centre, too, Carol's empty desk stared back at us, reminding us of all the time and space, laughter and tears we'd shared. It didn't feel right without her bubbly energy around. I took a deep breath and tried to concentrate on my studies while the silence hung in the air. Vicki and I both knew we'd adjust—it would just take some time.

A few days after her release Carol wrote:

> Helen, I'm really missing you, not the place at all, missing being with you and Vicki so much. I'm finding it so hard to find people who understand me. Public transport has been my sanity . . . I jump on trains, introduce myself to total strangers and start telling them where I've been, what for and the strange feelings I'm experiencing being free again, but now feeling locked away from people I love—my real friends, you, Vicki and little Ali—Marg too, I worry about her. I've got a damn phone here beside me. I don't know who to ring. I want to ring you, Vicki and Ali. I want to be close to you all.

Don't get me wrong—it's so, so wonderful, fantastic, unreal just to have my whole self back again, FREEDOM, to do as I please, to talk when I want to, to wake up, to walk, to cry, to laugh, to yell, to scream and my god to feel ... all when I want to. It's like the world is mine, to mould, to shape ... I'm creating!!

Tomorrow I'm going for two interviews for jobs. I've got my lies together. I've been in Tassie for five years, studying and waitressing part-time. They'll buy it, Ha!

I'm a mess since I left Fairlea, I've managed to get six hours sleep. Somehow I don't think I'll get any tonight, hmm ... I'm going wild, everything is happening so fast, well who wouldn't after time in that place. Hmm ... it must all slow down sooner or later—I hope it's not too much longer, my body wants to stop for a while, but my mind wants to see and feel so much!! Helen, I'm still frustrated, my bed has been empty ... I've had no real inclining to be close to anyone ...

This card is something special ... for some reason you remind me of a swan ... I love you Helen. xxxx

A few weeks before Christmas, Carol and Danni surprised us with their thoughtfulness. 'Helen Barnacle to the front gate!' I heard the loudspeaker yell across the prison grounds.

'Wonder what that could be?' I asked Vicki. It was unusual to be called to the front gate as it was the entrance to the prison. Immediately suspicious, Vicki decided to come with me and Ali to see what they wanted.

When we arrived there Mitch, a really nice officer who worked permanently at the front gate, greeted us with a smile. He spotted Ali and said, 'Hi, Ali! It's actually you we wanted to see, not your mum.' He told us to come into the office and there on the floor was a mixture of boxes all wrapped in Christmas paper. There were a couple of really large ones.

'They're Christmas presents, and they're all for you!' Mitch exclaimed. Ali jumped for joy up and down on the spot.

'You're so lucky,' I said to her. 'Who dropped them off, Mitch?' I asked him, having no idea who they could be from.

'Danni dropped these ones off,' he said, pointing in the direction of some very large boxes. 'Can you guess who dropped these others off?' he asked Ali.

Ali joined in the game, loving the attention. 'Umm … Poppy?' Mitch shook his head negatively. 'Uncle Ron?' 'No.' 'Umm … Corliss?' 'No.' Suddenly, with a look of glee in her eyes, she squealed, 'I know! It's Carol, 'cause I'm Carol's little darling!'

Ali was ecstatic. Vicki and I stood there looking at each other, amazed at the kindness of this simple act. We were lucky it was Mitch on duty at the gate as he had a soft spot for Carol as well as the kids. Normally, we'd never have been able to take anything that had been delivered, particularly by ex-prisoners, without it being searched.

When we got back to the unit, we watched Ali open one of the presents, telling her to keep the rest until Christmas Day. Vicki and I couldn't believe Danni and Carol's generosity. People tend to think drug addicts are pretty hopeless human beings, and maybe sometimes we were, but this was such a beautiful thing to do that my heart filled with joy. Our two friends certainly hadn't forgotten us. Danni, whose life was so chaotic she could never even make it to any sort of appointment on time, had spent all these hours and money organising to bring

Ali's gifts to the prison. You never forget those moments.

After she'd written a couple more letters to Ali, we didn't hear from Carol again for many months, although we thought about her often. She'd managed to get a friend of hers to sneak us in some smack a few times, and we'd certainly appreciated her efforts, but losing contact with friends you made inside seemed to be the norm. Most often it was because people had become caught up again in the cycle of scoring and using. Using always carried with it guilt, shame and a sense of failure, particularly after feeling so positive about life prior to release from jail.

'I'm never going to get a habit again,' seemed to be a standard statement from people leaving, and they always said it like they really meant it. It became a joke for Vicki and me, and we learned to become cynical about it. Because we had never been released from prison, we had no understanding of what it was like for Carol out there in the big world after a few years inside. We had nothing in our own experiences to compare it with. It was frustrating to lose contact with our friends from prison—sometimes it felt like after they were on the other side of that gate they just didn't care. Everyone seemed to end up with a habit again soon after they were out. After they'd returned to using, it wasn't long before they were caught up in the merry-go-round of addiction and, predictably, we didn't hear from them again. Usually, the next contact was when they got busted and returned to jail or, sadly too often, when we heard about their death through an overdose.

Only three or four months after her last letter we heard that Carol had formed a relationship with a non-using dealer who was feeding her limited supplies of heroin. He was the one placing the limitations on her using, of course. We'd also heard that he was pretty violent, and I assumed that it was her addiction that kept her there with him.

Also just before Christmas in 1982, Vicki became eligible for temporary day leave, having been in jail for almost two years. Once you were halfway through your sentence, you could apply to spend time with your family outside the prison every three months. Fortunately the judge had backdated Vicki's sentence to the time she had first been taken into custody, which was February 1981. Vicki went out on her first four-hour day leave one Saturday afternoon in early December. Ali and I were waiting for her when she returned through the gate. It sounds ridiculous, but we'd missed her. It was almost time for lock-up so we didn't have much time to talk about her day, but that night she wrote:

> *Why weren't you with me?*
> *Why can't you be with me, to share with me this*
> *special day?*
> *Did you feel lonely while I was away? I felt so*
> *alone, so far   away.*
> *Hold me, please hold me, I need your warm*
> *embrace,*
> *to dance with and dream by your side.*
> *How long this night drags on, while I wait for the*
> *dawn*
> *to again feel your warmth by my side.*
> *Time passes, so slowly and years seem out of reach,*
> *How long 'til our journey begins?*

While it was important to have day leaves, they also created adjustment problems. Vicki had trouble fitting back into prison life even after having spent just a few hours outside. It all seemed so ridiculous, because hardly any of us were in for violent crimes. In some ways it made life inside more difficult because you'd question things more. It was like having one foot in, one foot out. Vicki was restless for a few weeks and found it hard to accept the futility of the repetitive daily routine. I tried to help, but having been locked up for a couple of years already, I had no way of really understanding. I was hell-bent on accepting this life inside—I had to.

Unfortunately for our relationship, I found out months later that Vicki had spent time with her ex-girlfriend while she was out on temporary day leave. It wouldn't have been a problem in itself, but when she'd returned to the prison, she'd lied to me. It helped explain some of her restlessness, though. I had difficulty dealing with the fact that she'd lied to me. Feeling disillusioned, I distanced myself from her for a while, but it was a difficult stance to maintain while living in such a confined space. After a few awkward weeks we continued our relationship, not only because we loved each other but because we were now so dependent on each other. However, in the back of my mind, the seed of mistrust had been planted.

It was now fast approaching Christmas 1982, my third Christmas inside, and it was particularly at this time of year that we all just wanted to be out of it . . . stoned. We had some home brew maturing for the occasion. There were a couple of bottles of 'white', made from yellow plums from the old fruit trees, and there was a 'red' on its way, derived from red plums! The only problem was, they always brought the dog squad in right before Christmas to do a search, and because the alcohol was so bulky, it was difficult to hide. Invariably they would discover our brews, but it was still worth a try—it was a bit of fun and it relieved our boredom! Once when I was still living in the old remand dormitory with Stella, we had hidden our home brew up in the roof. One afternoon it exploded, leaking through the ceiling and dripping all over the floor—we must have put too much yeast in! The officers weren't impressed, but no-one ever owned up to it, so it was hard to punish anyone unless they punished the whole dormitory.

We always tried to organise some drugs to come in for

Christmas too. It was easier to block it all out and just get through it as best we could. At least once the new year arrived, I knew I was another year into my sentence.

'Vicki to the governor's office,' the loudspeaker boomed one afternoon after work, an unusual time of day to be called. There had been another ramp (a search) by the dog squad the day before, but we hadn't had any drugs in our cells. We had a new friend, Tammy, who'd recently moved into Carol's old cell in our unit. She was a few years younger than us, with long, straight, blonde hair and, like Carol, she adored Ali and quickly became another playmate. Tammy had managed to get some smack in the previous weekend, but that was all long gone. Between the three of us, we only ever had enough to last a couple of days.

'Better go and get it over and done with,' I said to Vicki. You always think you've done something wrong when you're called to the governor's office.

She left to walk up to the front of the jail. Ali and I spent some time back in our Yarrabrae unit and then went outside again. Vicki had been gone for quite a while and some of the women had noticed that the prison van was waiting up at the front. We started to get suspicious.

Suddenly one of the women came running towards us calling out, 'I just saw two officers put Vicki in the van handcuffed!' Tammy, Ali and I jumped up and ran to the gate which separated us from the front administration block of the prison. We were just in time to see the back of the van going out under the roller door gate. I clung to the wire mesh fence with my fingers, unable to believe what I was seeing.

'Where are they taking her?' I asked anyone who was listening. After a while an officer walked toward us.

'Vicki is being taken to Jika Jika,' he said through the wire fence.

'What?' I exclaimed in disbelief.

'I want to see Smith!' I demanded. 'What's going on? What's she done wrong?' I was pleading for an answer. He promised to try to get me some time with the governor.

Not long after he disappeared towards the administration block, the loudspeaker screamed across the prison grounds: 'Muster up! Muster up!' I looked at Tammy, dazed and shocked.

'What's going on?' I pleaded with her. The same officer returned and headed towards us. 'Go to muster and Governor Smith will see you after lock-up,' he said.

'What's going on?' I repeated to him.

'I really don't know,' he replied. Somehow I thought he was telling the truth.

After muster and lock-up Smith arrived at the unit, where Vicki's door remained firmly locked. It felt bleak without her there. 'Your friend's gone on a holiday to Jika Jika,' he said.

'What for?' I asked. 'What's she done wrong?'

'Some tinfoils were found in her room when the dog squad came through yesterday,' he said. 'They contained some drugs.'

'Bullshit! There was nothing in her cell. Where do they reckon they found the foils?' I asked, quickly trying to cast my mind back to remember if there could possibly have been any drugs left in her cell. But I came up blank. I knew there had been none.

'They were found in some pages in a library book,' he replied. I immediately remembered leaving the books that I'd borrowed from the Education Centre library on the bookshelf of Vicki's desk the previous afternoon. I often left some of my education stuff in her cell because she had a desk and, with Ali's bed in my cell, I didn't have much space.

'Bullshit! If they were found in library books, they were probably the ones I borrowed yesterday. They're not even hers! When will she be able to come back?' I asked.

'When I'm ready,' he replied.

'You know she's not responsible,' I said to him.

'We'll see about that in governor's court,' he said. I couldn't believe it.

'Where's Vicki?' Ali asked me after Smith had left the unit.

'She's been taken to another prison,' I tried to explain to her.

'Why?' she asked.

'I don't really know. They think she's done something wrong,' I replied.

'I want Vicki! Where's Vicki?' Ali kept repeating, then she started sobbing.

'I want Vicki!' she called after Smith, running toward the unit door and banging on the stainless steel with her little fists. But, of course, it was locked. I was in shock, Ali was crying, the others didn't know what to say. We stared at each other in disbelief. I went into my cell. I just wanted to be alone. I couldn't understand how there could have been drugs in those library books. It didn't make sense.

Tammy took Ali to her cell and tried to distract her with a game. I started to write a letter to Vicki. What could I say? How must she feel? She knew she was innocent. I looked out from the bed in my cell. Usually when my door was open I could see right inside Vicki's cell as it was directly opposite mine, but tonight all I could see was the locked door. It was difficult to believe she wasn't there. It had all happened so quickly, I didn't know what to do with myself. Ali kept running between our cell and Tammy's, asking questions. I couldn't answer any of them. How was I supposed to explain this to her? All I could feel in my heart was anguish.

When I saw Smith in the prison grounds the next day, I pleaded with him to tell me what was happening to Vicki.

'She'll probably be charged with possession,' he replied.

'Possession of what?' I asked him.

'Heroin, although it depends on the results of the drug analysis,' he said.

'You're joking! She hadn't even opened those books. They were mine. So what happens now?'

'The investigators will decide whether she'll be dealt with by the police in an outside court, or charged internally and dealt with by governor's court. If it's dealt with internally, they'll hear the charge over at Jika Jika.'

'Great!' I said. 'So when will she be able to come back?'

'I don't know. We'll have to see what happens,' he replied.

'You know she's not guilty. She's been set up,' I told him.

'It doesn't look that way, but don't worry, she'll be back,' he said as he turned around and walked away.

The other women who'd been transferred to Pentridge had gone to B Annexe, the part that had been sectioned off to accommodate women prisoners after the fire at Fairlea. It was where Carol had been sent, and it remained a women's section until they rebuilt the rest of Fairlea, which took a couple of years. But Vicki had been sent to Jika Jika, which was the harshest punishment section of Pentridge, designed and built for Victoria's most dangerous male criminals. It was an electronic, concrete jail with cages for exercise yards. Five men were to die in a fire there in 1987, while protesting about its inhumane environment. Vicki was in a single cell and could only spend one or two hours a day mixing with the three or four other women who were also being punished for varying reasons.

A few days later I again saw Smith when I was outside with Ali.

'What's happening with Vicki?' I asked him, trying not to sound as desperate as I felt. 'When is she coming back?'

He repeated his earlier spiel—'Don't worry, she'll be

back'—like I didn't have any reason to be anxious. It felt like a game to me.

'But when?' I persisted. I sensed he was getting pissed off with me.

'When I'm ready,' he replied.

Ali started crying, 'I want Vicki! Where's Vicki? I want Vicki!' her plaintive little voice repeating that same question. He turned his back and walked away.

I had to wait until I received a letter from Vicki before I had any idea what she was feeling. It seemed like an eternity waiting for that letter to arrive, although in reality it was only a week:

> Fuck I'm missing you. I feel so empty, empty and angry that we again must go through another test. I couldn't write last night. I didn't have any letters. I suppose it was better because I really wasn't very together. I'm not now, but I'm at least thinking better. No wonder the women here go on medication, there is nothing here but concrete and an impersonal existence. Muster here is your cell door opening and your cell checked then closed again. I've again requested to see the Governor, so hopefully today we'll know more about what's going on. We're permitted to spend the day in our cell or the day room with a couple of hours outside in a closed-in cage. Now I know what a bird feels like ... When I contact a solicitor I'll try and organise a case visit with you. We're going to have to fight this all the way. I mean nobody believes me! It's not mine! I've really got to get my head together, but this place is designed for

> mind and soul destroying and I've only been
> here such a short time ... I'm sorry I won't be
> with you and Ali this Christmas or to see in the
> new year. The bottom of the last page is
> splashed with tears, now I feel, well, not so
> tight. I suppose numb explains it the best. Never
> forget the good moments and always think of
> the depth of us ... Love, Vicki.

Vicki was only allowed to send one letter per week on two double-sided pages. She tried to write a bit each day in small writing, so that when I received her letter it contained about five days worth of news. It wasn't getting any easier for her and the uncertainty was a kind of psychological torture. Meanwhile, back at Fairlea, Smith continued to be elusive.

Ron and his girlfriend came in for a visit just prior to Christmas, but I was so upset I could barely maintain my end of the conversation. He tried to be compassionate, but I knew he didn't really understand what I was going through. How could he?

Prisoners were not allowed to have visits on Christmas Day, which was why Ron had turned up the weekend before. Because it's such an emotional time of year, and because some people would receive visits while others wouldn't, the Corrections Department seemed to think it was better for no-one to have visitors as it would only add to the frustration and loneliness so prevalent in there at that time of year. In a way I think they were probably right. Everyone there hated Christmas time. The desperation and sheer intensity of our helplessness was exacerbated by the joy that Christmas was supposedly bringing to people on the outside, even if that was just an illusion. To us it felt like a wave of universal grief drowning us, particularly for Ali and me that year, with Vicki not there.

On Christmas Day Vicki wrote to us again. It also happened

to be her birthday. She'd just turned twenty-nine, the same age as me. It had been my birthday fifteen days earlier. Every afternoon when they handed out the mail, I'd desperately hope my name would be called and that it would be a letter from Jika. I tried not to get my hopes up, but it was hard. Despair alone is different to despair that's shared. Since our relationship had commenced, Vicki had been there for me when I'd lost all faith, and I had been there for her when she'd been devastated by yet another unfair decision. In prison there always seemed to be so much to lose and yet, really, we had so little. What is left when you've been stripped to the bare bones? It's a similar sort of feeling to the one experienced by victims of domestic violence after the bashing, when the manic emotion has calmed down and it all goes quiet. He looks at you, the bruised face, your terror thinly veiled behind wide eyes. The madness subsides . . . for the moment. Just being able to gasp for fresh air felt like something to hold onto in that kind of world.

In jail all the strip searches, the lack of trust and the daily lack of private, safe spaces made you feel like a victim, particularly since Smith had arrived. The trick, as I saw it, was to try to get through a day avoiding that feeling, just as in a violent domestic situation you'd try to get through a day without being bashed.

Love . . . it helped me so much in there. When I'd look into Vicki's eyes and tell her that I loved her, I'd never meant it so deeply. I'd often say to Ali, 'I love you more than anything in the whole wide, wide, wide, wide world,' and she'd repeat those same words back to me. We meant it. This was our world. This was all we had . . . each other. The three of us. We'd created our own world and we made it work for us. We had found love in there and we clung to it.

'No-one can take this away from us,' we'd often say to each other.

Bullshit!, I thought to myself now that Vicki had gone. But

in fact this separation taught us a great deal. I realised how important it was to show those you loved how much they meant to
you, because you never knew when they would be taken away.
I missed Vicki more than I could bear. The uncertainty of the
situation and the difficulty of trying to find an explanation for
Ali made it all the more painful.

Christmas came and went and somehow we managed to get
through it. Tammy was able to organise for some smack to be
smuggled in through a friend, so at least we were able to blot
out some of our turmoil. I tried to comfort Ali, but there was
no way she, or I for that matter, could really understand. I organised for her to spend Christmas Day at my dad and Jan's place
because I thought it would be better for her to experience
Christmas in the real world, with a Christmas tree and all that
stuff. I didn't know if it was the right decision—it certainly made
my day even more lonely—but I didn't want to be too selfish.
It was hard to feel sure that you were making the right decisions
in situations such as these.

When Ali returned a couple of days later, we still made the
puddle on the grass outside our unit window before afternoon
lock-up. We waited for our pet willy-wagtail, Harry, to come
for a bath, and we talked to him through the closed window.
We pretended that he could hear us. I told Ali to give Harry a
message for Vicki at Jika Jika. She called out to Harry through
the window: 'Harry, tell Vicki I love her and that I miss her,
please? Tell her I want her to come home and sing songs like
we used to, with her guitar.' Ali gave Harry messages to take to
Vicki every afternoon, and in some small way it helped her to
deal with the loss. I think we both came to believe that Harry
really did fly off to Jika Jika every afternoon. Sometimes you just
had to believe.

Five weeks after Vicki had been transferred from Fairlea I
was called as a witness for her governor's court hearing, to

explain how the library books got into her cell. It was to be held at Jika Jika, so I was taken in the prison bus to the 'concrete hell'. For this occasion I'd been granted permission to leave Ali in Tammy's care, and had signed a piece of paper stating that I was allowing Tammy full responsibility for Ali until I returned a couple of hours later.

I was shocked when I arrived at Jika Jika. Everything—and I mean everything—was operated electronically. I walked through one door with the officer and Smith and we had to wait until it locked behind us before they'd unlock the door in front of us. It took forever to get through the maze of electronic doors, but eventually we found ourselves in a little concrete room and there she was. I rushed over to Vicki and gave her a big hug. It felt like I hadn't seen her for years, although in reality it was only weeks. I wanted to cherish this moment forever. Her body felt so warm and inviting, I didn't want to let go of her, but of course we were being watched by the BIG guys—the governor of Jika Jika and Smith, the governor of Fairlea.

Smith announced he was going to hear the case. Vicki and I looked at each other in amazement. Usually these cases were heard by the governor of the jail in which you were being held. I felt very uneasy, and I knew this irregularity would only increase Vicki's anxiety. We'd not been able to discuss any of this in letters as they were all censored—any information derived from them could be used as evidence against you.

As the case proceeded, Vicki gave her evidence and I was impressed at how well she spoke. Then I gave my evidence. For a few minutes there was silence as Smith shuffled some papers around on the desk. Then he looked up with that smile on his face.

'After consideration of the evidence, I find you not guilty,' he finally said, allowing a grin to spread across his face from ear to ear. It was over, just like that!

Vicki breathed a deep sigh of relief but contained her glee. I smiled at her. Inside my heart was bursting with joy, although I tried to keep from showing too much emotion. I was scared that if I let them see how happy I felt, they might change their decision. Then, before I knew it, I was quickly escorted out of the concrete room and returned on the bus with Smith to Fairlea. He was quite chatty all the way back, unlike the way he'd been on the trip over there.

'I told you not to worry,' he said, like he knew right from the outset that he was going to find her 'not guilty'. I wondered what his game was. He had recently given permission for a couple of things that we'd lobbied for, like the quarterly spend and the netball competition, and Vicki had always been the spokesperson in these discussions. Maybe he wanted to let her know that she didn't really have any power. What could I say to him in the van? Nothing. I tried to numb myself in his presence. He made my skin crawl, but I'd never let him know it.

Of course it was not quite over. Vicki had been classified to Jika Jika, so now she had to await the next classification meeting to apply for a return to Fairlea. It all depended on the respective governors as to whether she'd come back. Of course, really, it only depended on whether Smith would have her back. Towards the middle of January 1983, after her hearing in governor's court, Vicki wrote:

> I think we are both patiently awaiting Monday's decision, only another couple of days. By the time you get this letter, you'll know what's going on. We may even be having coffee while you're trying to read the small print!! I hope so. I was told something interesting today; they only give you good news here! I wasn't found not guilty, it was that the charges weren't

sustained. They couldn't prove my guilt. In other words I'm guilty, but this time I was lucky. However, the main problem at the moment is getting back, so we can have a very long talk. That's the only thing on my mind at the moment and I'm generating as much positive energy as I can. I'm looking forward to talking to you real soon. Goodnight honey. Miss you, love you ... Vicki.

Of course by now I was busting for Vicki to return and my impatience began to show. Every time I saw Smith I asked that same question, 'When is Vicki coming back?'

'When I'm ready,' was his standard reply.

Finally, one day the following week, the prison van drove in and there was Vicki, beaming from ear to ear. I was elated. I was too scared to even think about how I'd cope in the future, once Ali and Vicki had left the prison for good.

Ali and I waited impatiently for Vicki to be processed through administration. As she walked through the gate afterwards, I felt like my heart was going to burst. 'Don't ever leave me again,' I whispered in her ear as I held her tight. The tears welled in our eyes and relief surged through each of our bodies as we clung to each other, not wanting to release our hold in case they came and took one of us away again. The lack of security, the constant 'not knowing', could make love very painful in that environment.

Vicki sobbed tears of frustration as she held me. Only now was it safe to say what she felt, out here in the open. There was no speaker in the wall or intercom to invade our privacy.

Ali was so excited. 'Vicki! I love you, Vicki! Can we sing songs and play with Fozzie bear?' she squealed with glee. Vicki picked her up and gave her the biggest cuddle. Our little family was reunited. I pushed my fear about the impermanence of our relationship to the back of my mind, allowing a warm glow to enter my heart as I watched the love exchanged between Vicki and my little girl. My heart felt full and warm again, but our joy was soon interrupted by an officer.

'Vicki, put your things away in your cell and get to your work post. You're back in Unit 4 and you're to go to the garden officer,' he instructed in his English accent. A large percentage of prison officers were English or Scottish. For once Vicki didn't respond cynically. She was just so happy to be back there, 'home' as she always called it, that she was willing to do anything they said! I didn't think that sort of humility would last long, though.

We were even more happy about the fact that we'd been able to wangle it so that Vicki returned to her old cell opposite mine. While she'd been away at Jika, another woman, Julie, had been moved in with her baby, Bianca. While that had been nice and Ali had enjoyed doting on Bianca, we had been worried about whether we could get it vacated for Vicki's return. Little things became so important in there, and you had to battle for every bloody one of them.

We returned to our posts and eagerly awaited 3.30 pm, the end of our working day, so that Ali could play with Vicki and later, after Ali had gone to sleep, Vicki and I could spend some precious time together before night-time lock up. We desperately wanted to talk to each other about all the things that had happened over the previous six weeks, things that we hadn't been able to discuss in letters for fear of repercussions. More secrets . . . sometimes I felt like I'd lived my life in the secret service!

It took us a couple of days to get to the bottom of it all. A gnawing fear was growing in the pits of our stomachs as we began to realise that this governor had absolute power over all of us. We were so concerned that we smuggled a letter out of the prison to the relevant Community Services Minister. Jan, my old friend from TRAMM, hid it and managed to sneak it out for us one day after she, Peter and David had come in to visit me, although it was all in vain—no action was ever taken by the Minister as a result.

Increasingly during Smith's reign, the dog squad would arrive in the middle of the night while we were in bed asleep. Suddenly all the lights would go on and we'd find ourselves staring into the faces of about six officers. They used a mixture of Fairlea staff and the dog squad so that the whole prison could be raided simultaneously. 'Come on! Get up and out of bed! Don't touch anything, just move outside!' they'd yell really loud. We weren't allowed to get dressed or go to the toilet. They were looking for contraband, particularly illegal drugs and/or syringes thought to be hidden in our units or cottages.

Still in our nighties and half-asleep, we'd be escorted to the visit centre, which was now a new prefab building at the front of the prison. Once there, we'd be taken one by one into another room and strip searched by two female officers. Then they would hand us a jar in which we'd have to urinate, right there in front of them. We were not allowed to go near the toilet until we'd pissed in the jar. Bad luck if you were busting to go to the toilet—you'd have to wait. There were times when some women, unable to wait, had pissed themselves in that room. Then, if they weren't able to piss in the jar within three hours, they were automatically found 'guilty' of a dirty urine and charged. The same went for anyone who might have gone to the toilet just before the raid, and therefore didn't have any urine to piss out.

One of the punishments for a dirty urine was loss of contact visits. Some nights the whole jail was locked in the visit centre for hours. It took a long time to search the prison, and it also took a long time to strip search and urine-test every prisoner. On these occasions you just had to hope and pray you didn't have your period, because that made pissing into the jar in front of the officers more degrading still. Even the officers who got called in to work on these particular nights were strip searched by the 'dog squad' before entering and leaving the prison.

As it was now the beginning of 1983, I had to start contemplating the not-too-distant future, given that Ali was going to have to leave the prison in the next year or so. The exact date hadn't been decided yet. To a large degree it was dependent on a psychological assessment which would take place around the middle of the year. I wanted to try and keep Ali with me until her fourth birthday, in March 1984.

I also decided to talk to the teachers at the Education Centre about my own future plans. While I loved studying music, the only two job options it offered me were performing or teaching. I wasn't able to complete the performing exams, for obvious reasons, and I wasn't interested in teaching music. I had decided I would never be dependent on a male again, and as a single parent I wanted some sort of qualification in order for Ali and me to survive. I was certainly never going to return to hairdressing!

During the previous two years, my confidence in my study skills had increased enormously, and I was again beginning to believe I was an intelligent human being after all, even though I still identified myself as a drug addict—implication being 'dumb'. Fortunately, school had always been something that I'd enjoyed, unlike most of the other women prisoners, whose school experiences had mostly been negative. As a child, I'd never wanted to go home from school. I'd had excellent results in every subject I'd attempted while in prison, and because I'd done so well at Year 12 English, I felt competent to attempt subjects at the standard university study would require. I'd also always been interested in human behaviour—and what an environment in which to study it! So, after discussing it with the teachers, we decided we'd request permission from the Classification Committee for me to study full-time, and I applied for mature-age entrance to a Bachelor of Arts degree, majoring in psychology, at Gippsland Institute (now part of Monash University). Gippsland offered off-campus courses, and although attendance at some weekend schools was required, we thought we'd worry about that when the time came.

When my application for full-time study at the Education Centre was considered at the next Classification Committee meeting, Smith put up a strong argument against it. The teachers persisted, however, and eventually he approved the application on the condition that I could only go to the Centre after completing my work-post cleaning duties. Of course, this was an impossible situation for me, and he knew it. There was no way I could complete a full-time job and participate in full-time education, as well as fulfilling my mothering duties, particularly as there was no such thing as day-care for Ali. Anyway, I said 'Thank you' and left the meeting. At least permission had been granted!

Vicki was the only woman in the jail receiving full-time education after Carol's release. When Vicki and Carol had been granted full-time study they hadn't been required to attend a work post at all. They just went to the Centre each morning and afternoon.

I returned to the Education Centre after work that day to discuss the issue with the teachers again. Vicki joined us. She could see how pissed off I was, but she wasn't concerned at all. 'I'll help you clean Yarrabrae in the mornings,' she suggested, 'then when we've finished we'll both come to Education.'

'Yeah, sure,' I replied cynically, not believing anyone would do that for me.

'No, seriously. Between the two of us we can get it done.'

And that's exactly what happened. Vicki and I would furiously clean and mop Yarrabrae every morning, and pretty soon Tammy, who also had a job as a billet, was wangling an hour away from her post to help us. In the afternoons we'd have a bit more cleaning to do but, with a little help from my friends, I too was now participating in full-time education.

14

Ali leaves the prison

During 1983 I continually questioned myself about whether I was being selfish having Ali continue to live with me in jail. There were plenty of officers who had voiced that opinion. Some journalists had also been critical, suggesting that I was imposing my sentence and punishment on my daughter. I had tried to ignore these comments and instead focus my energy on developing a relationship with Ali that was full of love, one that would survive the years of separation ahead. It was the only way I could see any hope for our future together. After that, I just had to have faith that our love would carry us through. She wouldn't be in my care for at least four years although, at least initially, to ease her transition from the prison she would be allowed to return for weekend stays for the first few months of our separation. After that, I wasn't sure how much contact we'd have. There were the once a month all-day Saturday kids' visits and the weekly one-hour ordinary visits in the visit centre. I wasn't confident she'd cope with normal visits, having to be contained within the visit centre.

How do you make a decision about when it's best to let go of your child? Is there a mother out there who could give me any advice? I doubt it. Having Ali had taught me about unconditional love, and she gave me a reason to continue living. Being her mother made me feel like a worthwhile human being. It was about the only role in my life since I'd been fourteen or fifteen that I felt good about. Being a heroin addict wasn't something that I could feel proud of. All I could see were empty years ahead without her laughter, without her beautiful little face to look at each night before I went to sleep and to wake up to every morning. The truth is, I didn't believe there would ever be a 'good' or 'right' time for her to leave my care but, as she was growing older, the razor wire wall, the 4.30 pm lock-up, the musters every few hours, the strip searches—the powerlessness of my position in that regime—were all becoming more and more obvious to her. I couldn't be sure what effect it would have on her in the future.

Of course, it wasn't only up to me to decide, but I hoped the decision would be reached through agreement between me, the Corrections Department and the child psychiatrist. Originally it was anticipated that Ali would leave the prison and my full-time care around March 1983, when she turned three years old. When Dr Tonge, the child psychiatrist supervising her welfare, assessed her, however, he recommended that she remain with me as there were no signs that she was suffering any negative consequences as a result of residing within a prison. On the contrary, he was impressed with her progress and in his written report in the middle of the year he stated that she was well advanced for her age:

> All aspects of Alice's development are progressing normally and in some areas of development, particularly social and intellectual, she is advanced for her age.
>
> Alice should increasingly attend pre-school and other community activities which allow her

the opportunity to meet other children and have a full range of normal community based experiences.

Alice should continue in the care of her mother with whom she has a necessary emotional attachment for the remainder of this year. Alice should spend an increasing amount of time towards the end of this year and early in 1984 with both her grandparents and Mr Ron Barnacle. This will act to prepare Alice for leaving her mother's full-time care in February 1984 at the beginning of a new pre-school year.

It was with a sigh of relief that I received this news. It seemed we had a reprieve. While it was difficult to keep anticipating Ali's leaving, I was overjoyed. I felt my body physically loosen as the tension released its hold on me ... at least for a bit longer. One of the conditions of Ali's being able to remain in the prison was that she attend a pre-school program. Unfortunately, I wasn't permitted to go with her, so Corliss, who had long since become a friend as well as being a teacher at the Education Centre, took Ali along for her first couple of sessions. Later, she wrote a letter to me, through Ali's eyes, about the first day at kindergarten so that, in some small way, I could be a part of that important day in her life:

Dear Mum,

Well, my first day at kindergarten—what can I say—it's all a bit overwhelming! Right now it's two o'clock and the things I've seen already ... 'tis truly amazing.

There are six tables in all, set up with

different things to do. Things like—play dough, pasting & cutting, colouring, jigsaws, peg-boards and one in a kitchen just my size. And there are lots & lots of different kids—all differ-ent sizes and shapes. Most of them are three—like me—but some are four years old. Fifteen in all, with me.

I was pretty shy most of the time and didn't really want Corliss to be more than about one foot away! But she started to talk and play with some of the other kids and mum—I think I was a bit jealous! I did put a jigsaw of a helicopter (like Damien's) together and at the same time a little girl named Tara worked on a puzzle of a ship and Corliss had to help her a bit.

Then Corliss and I sat at another table and all of a sudden a little girl with short, fair hair started buzzing around making afternoon tea for us.

She put the kettle on the stove and set the table and everything. Then a couple more kids came and joined in. Then they got a bit silly and noisy—by then it was time for a group sit down and a talk and sing-along! Corliss wanted me to join in—but I didn't want to. Then we had milk and fruit and I was very brave and sat at a table with four other kids and I think Corliss hid in the kitchen!! When we finished—I went outside to play with Mrs Royal (Mrs John's helper) and the other kids! I was all right until Corliss reappeared and then for some reason I thought I had to be with her!

And then we saw our taxi and it was HOME
TIME—WHEW!

Love, Ali xxx

Ali settled into her new routine easily, attending kindergarten three half-days a week. Three different volunteers from the
community organised to pick her up and return her to the prison
on each of the days. The volunteers were allowed into the prison
to meet me before taking up their role of transporting Ali, and
Ali developed an easy relationship with these three people. She
also really enjoyed the stimulation and social contact the kindergarten provided. Because she had interacted so much with adults
in her first three years, she had no trouble with the puzzles,
jigsaws and other challenges that kindergarten presented. She'd
been doing them for years. But it was the social interaction in
the normal world that was imperative for Ali. At the same time
it made me realise that I couldn't hang on to her for too much
longer. Her need to develop 'normally' in the community was
becoming obvious, and it was the one thing I couldn't provide.
It was also becoming frustrating that she couldn't wander off to
play with Damien, a condition of her living in the prison being
that she had to be within my sight twenty-four hours a day.

Although it was wonderful to hear about Ali's activities
outside the prison, at the same time it contributed to my sense
of failure as a human being, particularly as a mother—after all,
the only reason Ali and I ever had to be separated was because
of me, my drug use and related criminal activity. I was so willing
to take the blame for our pending separation, yet so unwilling
to see that I could change anything in relation to my drug use.
I felt so good as a 'mother', yet so bad as a 'drug addict', these
two differing identities always in conflict. It seemed to me that
nobody in the community ever thought that a drug addict could

be a good mother. I'm sure that even my own family agreed. Yet the mere thought of life without heroin was incomprehensible to me.

The day that Ali started kindergarten, Corliss also wrote me another letter which she left on my desk at the Education Centre. She was obviously thinking ahead as well, but it is only now that I can feel the full impact of her words. I wasn't able to comprehend others' feelings much back then—I was too consumed and overwhelmed by my own.

> I often find it hard to say what I feel, but I hope you know how special Ali is to me—as are both you and Vicki. I don't think you really know just how honoured I felt today to be the one who took Ali to her first day of kindergarten. I know that you desperately wanted to be with her on this very special day, but because you couldn't, I really did feel privileged to be allowed to go with her!
>
> Although I really try to understand, I know I can't begin to fully comprehend how you feel right now—the frustration and anxieties that you must continually cope with in your situation. The worries and fears that you have, especially regarding Ali's future and your own.
>
> But what I do know and what I think that you sometimes don't recognise, is the incredible strength that you possess and just how much of that courage and endurance that you have passed on to Ali.
>
> You mustn't stop fighting for what you want for Ali and for yourself—but always remember, regardless of what actually happens,

particularly from now until the end of the year, that inner strength will see both you and Ali through—you both will survive and more importantly, succeed in spite of everyone else. And no matter what the 'system' does or fails to do, the relationship between you and Ali can never be taken away from either of you. You have what few mothers ever achieve and you've already accomplished that in spite of the system around you so I know you can continue building.

I really hope that you can make the very most of the coming months with Ali so that when the inevitable separation does occur, both you and Ali will have loving thoughts to maintain your emotional bond even though you will be physically apart. From now until then is what will be uppermost in her mind as it will be nice for her to have really pleasant memories. I know you always try so hard to make it good for her—but it does have to be good for you too so I guess what you can't change around you has to be forgotten or ignored as much as possible so it isn't allowed to interfere with this precious time.

Well, enough from me, I just felt I wanted to try to express what I was feeling somehow. It's a helpless feeling to watch others around you when they're hurting. Hope this has helped a little.

Love, Corliss

I did sense the tone of my life changing and as I read this letter now the tears well in my eyes. My friend Corliss ... it must have been so hard. There was so much I just couldn't allow myself to feel then; so much I couldn't see, even when I was being told; so much I couldn't accept, particularly praise directed towards me. If only I could have believed in the inner strength that Corliss talked so easily about, that must have been obvious to her but that I couldn't embrace.

Corliss and her husband, Kurt, took photos every time Ali was with them outside the prison. There were so many little ways they tried to include me in Ali's life outside. Corliss and Ali made little photo storybooks of their adventures, and Ali would bring them back into the prison with her when she returned, excitedly relaying her 'outings', so unaware of what lay ahead.

She would sit giggling on the floor beside me as she turned the pages, explaining the story behind each photo. I would become increasingly pensive, watching her expressive little face, focused on the future when we would no longer share these moments. I just couldn't imagine what it was going to be like without her. These times with Corliss and Kurt were precious, and today the bond between the four of us has grown, especially with Kurt, who we have grown to know and love and who I was unable to meet until years after meeting Corliss.

But back in the day-to-day world of the prison, nothing much changed, only the people who came to reside in our unit. Most of them had shorter sentences than both Vicki and me, so there was constant movement. Tammy shared the unit for quite a while. Like Carol, she had a wicked laugh and had formed a special bond with Ali. Tammy had grown up in the Carlton Housing Commission high-rise flats with several of her step-sisters. She'd had many step-fathers throughout her childhood, some of whom sexually abused her. She was also a beautiful young woman caught up in the drug world, but when she played with Ali, the sweet, innocent child in her emerged, so unlike the abused child that in reality she was, that in reality the drugs helped her to hide from. So much like Carol and yet so unique. She was also in close contact with a dealer who was married to one of her step-sisters. Through him we were able to score a bit of smack which, as 1983 progressed, I seemed to need more and more. Even though I had Vicki, I was about to lose Ali.

As time passed, the impending doom of Ali leaving the prison cast an increasingly darker shadow over me; while trying to imagine the absence of her laughter, a blackness took up permanent residence in my body. It was elusive and I could never quite locate it, but it was always there waiting to catch me out. I tried to outmanoeuvre it with heroin, because now the game was about survival, and I knew no other way.

Tammy's contact was a big-time dealer who was more of an amphetamine user than a heroin addict, so occasionally he was able to give us stuff for nothing. Other times we managed to scrounge some money together. Two of Tammy's step-sisters were also in jail on drug charges and one of them was married to him, so he was accustomed to smuggling smack in to her and it wasn't hard to put in some extra. Around that time, too, another woman, Cheryl, moved into our unit. She had a relationship with a non-using dealer who could supply us with some gear so, with heroin becoming relatively easy to access at that point, of course our drug use increased. Don't get me wrong, it wasn't large amounts, but we found ourselves sometimes hitting up three or four days a week. Then we'd have to wait until another supply could be smuggled in somehow. It took a lot of time, effort and energy just to think up ingenious ways to sneak it in.

Initially it came into the prison hidden in flowers, usually purple irises. The officers must have been suspicious with so many purple irises arriving, but the scam didn't get busted until the day one of the foil packages fell out of the bunch up at the front gate. Whoops! Because of us—Tammy, Cheryl, Vicki and me—no-one in the prison was allowed to receive fresh flowers any more. We never admitted to knowing anything about it and, luckily, there wasn't enough evidence to charge us. Some of the women, the non-drug users, weren't too happy about it, but for us it was just a slight hitch. Heroin made us feel 'normal' and we needed to keep using it. It distracted us from reality and it also took up head space organising it.

We never told the teachers or the drama people what we were up to. It was our secret. To an observer like Corliss, I probably looked increasingly detached, but the more time passed, the less I cared about what I looked like. I couldn't see myself any more, and I certainly couldn't see myself separate from Ali. There was no Helen Barnacle, only Helen and Ali Barnacle. 'Helen and Ali Barnacle' . . . how easily the words roll off the tongue. They are meant to be together, not apart.

The mood had changed for Carol too. In late May 1983, after many months of not hearing from her, we received a very welcome letter:

> Helen, Vicki and my dear, dear Ali,
>
> I've totally abused you all BUT I've remembered you with all the tenderness which is possible for one to feel for another, no time has obliterated, no distance altered—it is the same as what we held when we were all together!!
>
> I want to say sorry, god I want so much for you to understand why, why I cut off from you all. My god it's so hard to try to find the words to write down my explanation. It was what I

had to do. I had to cut off from you—I felt torn between two worlds, between two realities. It was destroying me.

God it's bloody hard out here—well it is for me. I'm finding out I'm not as strong as I thought I was—I have so many failings, so many weaknesses and above all no drive, no determination. You know I buried myself back in heroin—from November until April. Left my job, a job given to me, entrusted to me!! I wonder when I will stop hurting myself and others in the process—I'm so destructive.

I have so many regrets in the five months I have been my own person—all in all, I've just screwed people around, including you three. I made promises I never kept—I totally abused my friendship with you. I now bare myself to you—for you to understand. I've done to you and to others what has been done to me; what I've so despised!!

No, I haven't forgotten what it is like in there—maybe I've been living the aftermath of their mental torture. They'll never understand the scars that place leaves on us!!

I've sat down and written to you so many times ... the times weren't right—the letters were superficial and for that reason I didn't send them!! Vicki, Helen, I have so much to ask you—my god all that is important is, how you are feeling; how that place is making you feel.

This letter is so dis-jointed ... I just want you to know I'm back and that I am here to stay!! My life is beginning out here once more.

I start a new job on Monday and I've moved in with a lady and her child.

 Ali, Helen and Vicki—stay close. I love you all so dearly, please forgive me as I was and receive the me I am NOW!!

Yours, Carol xxxxxxx

Carol managed to stay in touch for a while after this letter, but then the demons came again and dragged her away to that land of failure where you can't face the people who love you most. We did love her dearly, but we were so naive, so ill-equipped to be able to offer her any support. How could we? We didn't know how to live out there in the straight world ourselves! After all, that was why we were in prison in the first place. Besides, we weren't allowed contact anyway, so it was an impossible situation.

Despite my increasing heroin use, as 1983 progressed I tried hard to prepare Ali for her leaving the prison and my care in early 1984. On the one hand I was able to be incredibly mature organising for her needs to be met yet, on the other, I was like a child myself, unable to meet my own needs in any positive or healthy way. It was an emotional minefield. I loved my little girl so much, yet I had to let go of her. Sometimes I found myself watching her in a daze, daydreaming, the thoughts moving in a circular fashion around the inside of my skull, a seemingly empty cavity being filled with unanswerable questions: What's it going to be like handing her over at the gate? How am I going to do that? Am I going to cry? Is it going to feel like a razor slicing through my heart? Am I going to pretend it's not so bad? What's it going to be like in here for four years without her? What's it going to be like for her out there without me? Then came the inevitable emotional shutdown, like a curtain dropping at the end of a performance. Sometimes it just got too hard to think. I'd shake my head as if to slough off the unwanted thoughts and the unwanted headache. My head would hurt from thinking ... I needed some distance. I could feel it all moving in too close and there was only one thing I knew of that would fix it.

Although I had the assistance of the child psychiatrist, which I found helpful in terms of practical things like when to start telling Ali about her leaving, and deciding who she was going to live with, I never talked to him about how I was coping. Although I hadn't told the psychiatrist a thing about my own background, after interviewing Dad, Jan, Ron, Ali and me, he concluded that Ron was the best option for Ali. Soon afterwards, Ron decided he would take her.

I wasn't talking to anyone about how I felt. People were watching me, though, I could feel it. The whole jail knew Ali was going soon and, whether it was true or not, I imagined they were all waiting for some sign from me, for some reaction, for the tears to flow, a physical collapse, or an emotional breakdown or something. I was trying hard not to show anything, but probably was. It was hard to 'act' normal, but at the same time I didn't want to walk around like I was falling apart.

Corliss, my friend and teacher at the Education Centre, was watching ... watching me come to the Centre stoned. I guess she must have been feeling very disappointed in me, seeing me constantly in that state—so detached, so unreachable. I'd go straight to my desk, avoiding her if I could. I tried not to look into her eyes when she talked to me, knowing that mine were a dead giveaway with their pinpoint pupils constricted by heroin, leaving no doubt as to how stoned I was. I'd sit at my desk, staring downward at my books, reading but absorbing nothing, or I'd look up and stare directly at the bookshelves in front of me, still seeing nothing, everything out of focus to my tear-filled eyes. I was looking, but I just couldn't see.

I knew Corliss must have been feeling frustrated, and I did feel a bit guilty or ashamed or something, but I didn't seem to be able to do anything about it. I'd never felt so isolated and lonely, even though I was surrounded by people there in the Education Centre. Corliss wasn't saying much. I figured she'd given up. One day she left a note on my desk, because she obviously no longer knew what to say to a person who was destroying herself but lying about it. Although I read it, the words remained somewhere outside my consciousness. I couldn't let them in because it felt like, if I did, I'd disintegrate. I was only just hanging on and I couldn't stray from the course I'd taken. I didn't want to face reality because it would mean changing, and I didn't feel capable of that. I didn't want to listen or talk about the many ways I could deal with my pending separation from Ali, because the words turned into razors slashing at my heart. I didn't feel like I even had the energy to try.

So I remained dishonest about my drug use. I told myself I was protecting people like Ron and Corliss by being 'strong', that old family theme playing out: 'Don't let anyone see how you're feeling.' Really, though, I just didn't want to be confronted and told that I shouldn't be using. I knew Corliss was avoiding me by staying away from me at the Education Centre. Because she was very attached to Ali too, who knows what turmoil was going on inside her? I didn't have any emotional energy to deal with her distress and I didn't want a confrontation over the fact that Vicki and I were using heroin again. I wasn't ready for that kind of honesty. I was too frightened of what would be left.

Christmas 1983 came and went, and I felt like I was waiting for a death sentence. In my mind I knew it wasn't that bad, that one day Ali and I would be together again, but waiting for her departure date to arrive felt like the end of life to me, and I couldn't find a way to change that feeling, only a way to block it out a bit. My heart ached so badly in what felt like an empty cavity behind my left breast, I couldn't even sit in one position for long. It had become impossible to live inside my body because everything hurt. The date kept getting closer, like a huge black thundercloud looming overhead, waiting to explode and encapsulate me in its darkness. How I wished I could stop time. I'd have stayed in there forever if I could just have stopped the date of Ali's departure from ever arriving.

Vicki tried to be supportive, but I was becoming more and more detached from her too. I guess she was going through her own shit but I wouldn't know, I didn't ask her. I was locked up with my own pain, and I couldn't see much ahead of me—and, anyway, I was too frightened to look.

During January Vicki and I started to pack Ali's things, gradually sending them out to my brother's place. With each packing session, I released a little bit more of my motherly role. I tried to act calm but as I let go of each possession, each little toy or piece of clothing, a terror gripped my heart. Ali didn't understand. 'Why can't Teddy stay with you, Mum?' she'd ask. 'When will I see you?' The questions were endless and constant. In my mind I'd try to imagine someone else dressing her, someone else brushing her hair, someone else bathing her, putting her to bed, reading stories, playing 'Fozzie bear' and 'Kermit' with her. No more dancing around the piano while I played and sang songs with Ali and Vicki. None of that any more ... Ali had been surrounded by music. Vicki had compiled a personal music book for her so that I could play all her favourites while she danced and sang. It was a green plastic folder with a typed label, 'Ali's Song Book', on the front. Her life was about to change so drastically but, as I watched her playing, I knew it was impossible for me to explain clearly the implications of what was about to happen.

For me, Ali's last few weeks and days passed in a blur, partly induced by heroin, until the end of January 1984 arrived. Death sentence time. I was like a corpse going through the daily routine of the prison. Life seemed so futile. Externally, I didn't let anybody see my pain, but internally it was like someone had sucked out my insides, leaving just a terrible ache I couldn't get rid of. Heroin helped a bit, but only momentarily. I'd have to have had a hit every three minutes to maintain that warm feeling inside that came so quickly after the needle was inserted. A couple of times a day wasn't enough to maintain my stability.

The dreaded day arrived. When I forced myself to pack up the little pine bed that had, until now, given my cell a bit of character, I knew this was it. Vicki silently helped me pack Ali's last few belongings. Now it was just the excruciating wait for Ron to arrive, struggling all the time to pretend to Ali that everything was okay. I tried to walk around the jail like it was any other day, but inside all I could think of was the hour, the minute, the second that would take Ali away. You can't turn the clock back. I could feel eyes watching me, and there were so many of them. Given that three-quarters of us in there were mothers, I guess they had some idea about what was going on inside me. I imagined they were watching for the telltale signs of a breakdown, but they couldn't get near the pain either. I was trying so hard to feel nothing.

I closed my eyes for a moment as I stood there trying to shut out reality. Tell me how to feel nothing?, I pleaded with myself. As I opened my eyes again, the sunlight burnt into them and the loudspeaker announced my destiny: 'Helen Barnacle to the front gate.' The sound pierced my ears and my heart. I held Ali in my arms very tightly and I walked, but I didn't see anything. I tried to press her head into my shoulder so that she couldn't see my face. I might have been walking on the moon, I felt so disconnected from the reality around me. I consciously placed one foot in front of the other and forced myself forward.

Don't cry, I kept repeating to myself. Don't let her see you cry. Don't upset her. I can't let her see me cry, I implored myself over and over like a mantra, all the way to the gate. These useless words pounded round and round in my head as I tried to act like nothing unusual was going on. The officer was standing at the gate when I reached it. He looked at me as he unlocked it, but I kept looking straight ahead.

My brother was standing there, smiling. 'Hi!' he said, trying to sound cheerful. 'How are you?' I didn't give him any indication of the turmoil I was suffering. I'd had years of practice. 'Okay,' I replied. I couldn't think of anything else to say. I passed Ali through the gate to Ron and we exchanged a few more awkward words. It was all very formal, really, with the officer watching over us, never standing more than a metre away. It was like I was handing over some property, a piece of clothing or something, except it wasn't property this time—it was my child.

'Bye. I love you. Only six sleeps before we see you again,' I said to Ali as I let go of her, along with my motherhood. I accidentally made a gasping sound as I tried to suck in some air, but no-one seemed to notice.

'We'll be in to see you next weekend,' Ron said, trying to keep it light. 'Say goodbye to Mum.'

'Bye-bye, Mum,' Ali said. 'See you in six sleeps. I love you.' And with her little hand waving over Ron's shoulder, they turned and moved away.

It's done. It's over. I've handed my child over and I didn't even cry, I said to myself as I turned my head away from the officer at the gate, tears welling in my eyes. I drew in a deep breath, as if it would give me enough courage to walk back along that same path we'd just come down. Am I supposed to feel proud?, I asked myself. I didn't cry! Yippee! I must be so strong. The cynicism rocketed through my thoughts. I was also aware, though, that Ron wouldn't have appreciated a flow of emotion either, because it was easier that way. He always said, 'I haven't got time for a breakdown,' and it always made me so sad to hear it. That same old family theme: 'Don't say anything, don't feel anything, just get on with it.' It's funny how you can be a standing, talking, walking human being on the outside and yet, inside, your heart can be broken and no-one would know. A shiver passed down my spine.

I turned around and walked back to Yarrabrae and into my unit. Vicki was waiting there, sitting on the bed in my cell. Thank goodness she was there. She looked up questioningly as I walked in.

'Let's do it,' I said to her.

We'd prepared ourselves for this moment and I had plenty of time for a breakdown. We each went silently to the bathroom, one after the other. I went in first and she kept a watch from the cell. I mixed the powdery substance with water in a spoon, lit a match underneath, heating it so that it dissolved to form a liquid, and then sucked it up into the syringe. I hoped and prayed I'd be able to find a vein easily this time—I couldn't afford any delay, not today. After a few unsuccessful jabs into my collapsed veins, I found one in my leg. I sat on the toilet seat and watched with relief as the blood forced its way back into the syringe, a signal to slowly push the plunger down, releasing the liquid until there was nothing left. The substance moved quickly through my veins to my heart, easing the pain as reality blurred. I got up and left the bathroom to take over 'watch' duty so that Vicki could have her hit. She was much quicker than me as her veins were better.

After about half an hour, when the initial stoned feeling had worn off and reality seeped in again, I looked up from where I was sitting on the bed, back slouched against the wall, to see Vicki lying longways on the bed. The cell looked empty without the little pine bed she had built for Ali, and I knew with certainty how hard, cold and long the nights were going to be from now on. I was grateful to at least still have Vicki beside me to share the pain. Almost all Ali's toys were gone. I'd only kept a few little ones for my own comfort, to remind me that I was still a mother. If the cell looked empty, it felt even emptier. The stainless steel door glared back at me, like a mirror. Nothing looked clear in that stainless steel; everything was just shadows, smudges of colour, a movement. Sometimes fingerprints would interrupt its blurry smoothness, but not today. It was spotlessly clean. It was always there just beyond the end of my bed and it was always cold to touch. It was the last image I went to sleep with and the first I woke up to. I hated that cold, sturdy, shiny, silver-coloured door where I could always see my hazy reflection, even when I didn't want to.

Vicki and I tried to bring ourselves back to reality. We were aware that the officers would be checking on us soon if we didn't show our faces somewhere around the jail.

'Do you think we should go outside now?' Vicki asked me tentatively, reaching her hand across to hold mine.

'Have to do it some time, hey?' I replied quietly as we stood up and tried to act straight. I'd lost all sense of time since Ali had left, but when we walked outside I noticed that people were still watching me. I didn't say much. The heroin kept my head floating just above water for a while.

15

Learning to be
a childless mother

As the days passed without Ali, I tried to struggle on and
concentrate on my studies. I also wrote songs, sad songs. I
didn't know whether it was helping me deal with my grief, but
the words just poured out from somewhere deep inside, presenting themselves on the paper in front of me as if they had a
will of their own:

> I find it so hard my child, to face all these years
> apart,
> And I'm wondering what lies ahead, do you know
> what I mean?
> You're such a young, sweet child, you don't know
> of the pain ahead,
> And how can I tell you, when it's so hard to bear?
>
> I want you to understand, but you're too young to
> know
> of the heartache when we must part, it hurts me so.
> Will you still remember, all these years of our past?
> Will you need me just as much? Will you
> understand?

I'd release the first few words, trying to force the melody out, but then my throat would choke, tighter and tighter, that ever-present lump swelling until I couldn't release a sound. It was so easy to write the words and music, yet so hard to voice them. My eyes would fill with tears, but I couldn't let them flow either. I'd close my eyes tight, screaming inside: 'Someone out there ... someone help me!' I'd sit there on the piano stool all choked up and slowly open my tear-filled eyes, only to stare at the words I couldn't release ...

I couldn't move. I knew that in a little while this moment would pass. I just had to sit there and stare at the piano for a while, my eyes fogged up, my throat choking, my heart beating ... boom, boom, the words I couldn't say out loud beating in time ... until the emotional paralysis released its grip on my physical body and allowed me to move again. It happened often and I began to grow accustomed to the feeling. After a while I'd walk away from the piano. I guess it was what you'd call despair.

For a while Ali was allowed to visit the prison every second weekend, staying overnight. Apart from the normal one-hour visits at the weekends, children under the age of twelve were usually only allowed to visit one Saturday a month, from 9 am to 3 pm, but the child psychiatrist had recommended that Ali have extra visits in order to ease her distress about our separation. She would come to the prison on Saturday morning and leave Sunday afternoon. While it was always something to look forward to, once the time approached for her to leave each alternate Sunday afternoon, the smile would disappear from her beautiful little face to be replaced by a sad, grumpy and sullen look. She'd start clinging to me.

'It's only thirteen sleeps until we see you again,' I'd say to her, attempting to make the wait seem shorter than it was. Vicki would tell jokes, trying to distract her from her impending departure.

'Where does the king keep his army?' she'd ask Ali who, in spite of herself, would allow a little smile to crease her face.

'I know—up his sleevy!' she'd respond with exuberance. She'd soon revert to sulking again, though.

This went on for at least the last few hours of each weekend visit so it was difficult, under the circumstances, to make the most of our limited time together. She knew as well as we did that, all too soon, the visit had to end. The three of us quickly came to hate those goodbyes, anticipating the emptiness that would be left after Ali had gone. Vicki and I tried to have some heroin handy for those times, but it wasn't always possible.

The child psychiatrist had also recommended that the prison grant me a four-hour day leave, once a month for about six months, to assist with Ali's transition from the prison and my full-time care. This was a privilege as day leave was usually only allowed once every two months, and only for prisoners who were at least halfway through their sentence. I wouldn't reach that landmark until August 1984, my release date being August 1988 as my sentence had been backdated to the commencement of our trial.

On one of these leaves Ron introduced me to a friend of his, Elizabeth, who was some years older than me. I think he was probably trying to encourage me to meet 'normal' people in the hope that I'd develop friendships with them rather than with drug users. Elizabeth had expressed interest in meeting me and being involved in Ali's and my life. She was also willing to come to the prison for visits which, since Fairlea had been rebuilt, were now held in a new visit centre and were 'contact' ones unless you'd done something to lose that privilege, in which case you had to have visits in a 'non-contact' room. The one advantage of non-contact visits was that you didn't have to be strip searched afterwards, but the disadvantage was that you had to talk to your visitors through a screen. So far I'd managed to maintain my contact visits, which were a great improvement on the previous 'drug table' ones.

Elizabeth gradually developed a relationship with both of us and would take Ali to her own home occasionally. She was married to a doctor, and they had three children, the youngest a teenager. We became friends in that limited sort of way that's possible while in prison, and I found it interesting to talk with someone from the outside 'straight' world. Also, it was a condition of gaining day leaves that some approved person be responsible for you, and I think Ron needed a back-up for this role because sometimes he was too busy at work to do it himself. He was now a very successful advertising executive working for a large advertising agency.

On my first four-hour day leave I attended Ali's new kindergarten with her and met her teacher, who Ali immediately liked. I had a prison officer supervising me, so we had to explain her presence to the teacher; fortunately, the officer wasn't wearing prison uniform and was also one of the ones I got along with. The day passed quite smoothly, considering the circumstances, and Ron, Ali and I agreed that it had been fun.

The second leave went relatively smoothly, however a month later, on my third four-hour day leave to Ron's house, the strain of Ali's and my separation erupted. This time I didn't have to have an officer with me, and Carol and Marg, who had both been released, came to Ron's to share the afternoon with us and Corliss. I was excited at being able to catch up with them, but the day turned out to have disastrous consequences.

During the afternoon we decided to walk to the park near Ron's house to let Ali play on the swings and slides. Julie, who'd briefly lived with us in Yarrabrae after Vicki had been sent to Jika Jika, was also there with her baby, Bianca. It was like a little reunion, and Ali was excited to see all these people who'd been so special in her life.

As we all walked back from the park, I was carrying Ali and talking casually to Marg, Corliss and Carol. Suddenly Ali started crying for no apparent reason, the volume escalating until she was screaming in the street. Then she started hitting me on the head and arms with her little hands thrusting around her, struggling wildly. She was physically hurting me, so it was difficult to keep holding her. I was so shocked that tears came to my eyes and I didn't know what to do except keep trying to hold her tight. Poor Marg was walking beside me, unable to contain her own tears. She also tried to console Ali, but with no success. She was out of control. Even Corliss, who's usually great in difficult situations, was stunned.

After ten or fifteen minutes Ali wore herself out. With her voice croaky from screaming, we resumed the short walk to Ron's house in silence. Although I wasn't crying outwardly, by the time we reached Ron's I was quite shaky and had to sit down to steady myself. Ron didn't seem very sympathetic. Of course he hadn't seen the tantrum himself and probably thought we were all overreacting. He'd most likely just have told Ali to stop crying, anyway. I'd noticed he always told her to 'be a good girl and not cry' on day leaves or visits. The repression of emotion in our family was so similar to the holding on I had to do in prison, but I didn't want Ali to be brought up like that. Goodness only knows what was going on inside her little head. I had no doubt that confusion and frustration about our enforced separation was the cause of her outburst, and I guess that she'd decided to let me know that day.

After a while things settled down again and we all tried to enjoy the rest of the afternoon with Corliss and Ron taking photos, and Bianca, Ali and Marg's daughter, Niki, all playing together. Then, inevitably, I had to return to the prison. Taking into account the travelling time to and from the prison, I'd only had three hours at Ron's. On the return drive, Ron, Ali and I were pretty quiet and I couldn't help wondering to myself if it was worth all the trauma—maybe it would be better to just see Ali inside the prison. Heroin was the only thing I knew that could take the edge off the pain a little.

About a week later, the loudspeaker summoned me to Governor Smith's office. I wonder what he could want?, I thought to myself as I walked towards the front of the prison. I was soon to find out.

'What have you got to say about these?' Smith asked as he pushed the day-leave photos across his desk towards me. Obviously Ron must have dropped them off but, instead of being given to me, they'd gone to Smith.

Innocent of what was to come, I flicked through the first few, enjoying the memory of that afternoon among family and friends. 'They're from my day leave at Ron's last week,' I said to him smiling, thinking—but not daring to say out loud—Fuck, I would've thought it's pretty obvious what they are.

'Who told you that you could mix with ex-prisoners on your day leave?' he said.

'What do you mean?' I asked.

'You could be charged by the police with an offence.'

'You're joking,' I said, but I had a sinking feeling. 'They're the only friends I've got. I've been in here for the last three and a half years, where do you think I'm going to meet new friends?'

He continued on, obviously enjoying his attempt at making me look irresponsible. 'It's meant to be a family leave with your daughter, not a party with a bunch of ex-prisoners. I don't believe you didn't know it was an offence to mix with ex-prisoners,' he said. 'Your future day-leave program has been cancelled. I'll be speaking to Corliss Searcey about this incident too.'

'I didn't know it was an offence. You can see by the photos I'm at my brother's house with him supervising. I thought that was where I was supposed to be.'

'Not partying with a bunch of ex-prisoners and a teacher from the Education Centre,' he said. 'Anyway, I don't believe you didn't know it was an offence and ignorance is no excuse,' he said smugly. He was really enjoying himself.

Maybe there was a piece of paper somewhere stating that you're not supposed to mix with ex-prisoners while on day leave, but I wasn't aware of it and nor, for that matter, was Ron, or else he wouldn't have helped me organise the leave. I would have thought that Corrections would have made him aware of this rule given that he was my 'supervisor'.

'It wasn't a party,' I replied, remembering how upsetting the leave had been.

He ignored me. 'You'll be hearing from the Classification Committee about the cancellation of your day-leave program,' he said. 'That'll be all.'

I stormed out of his office. 'You fuckin' prick!' I said to myself angrily as I headed for the Education Centre. I felt like exploding.

When I walked in and saw the look on Corliss's face, I realised she'd already been informed about it. In the coming weeks Smith tried to have her sacked from her teaching job over this incident and it was a dreadful time for her. Eventually she won the battle against Smith, with the Education Department sticking by her, but it cost her a great deal emotionally. Apparently teachers weren't supposed to have contact with prisoners once they'd been released from jail, but both she and Heather were so committed to the women that they'd occasionally meet with ex-prisoners to help them out long after their sentences had been completed, even if it was just to provide an ear when the women needed someone to talk to. In the weeks that followed, I noticed that Corliss avoided me whenever I went to the Education Centre. When our eyes did meet, she looked like she was going to burst into tears. She wasn't saying much to me and somehow I felt responsible for getting her into this awkward situation, although I knew she would never have blamed me. I think that she just felt so hurt by Smith and the stupid prison system that every time she saw me her feelings of devastation increased. It was so unfair and we were both so powerless.

There were no winners because even Smith hadn't gained what he'd set out to achieve, which was to have Corliss sacked, but the biggest loser was Ali. In order to keep her job, Corliss had had to agree to Smith's condition that she not see Ali outside the prison while she was employed as a teacher. This effectively meant she couldn't see Ali at all now that Ali only came in to the prison at the weekend when, of course, Corliss wasn't working. Smith told her that if she was found having contact with Ali, she would be charged with 'trafficking information between Ali and a prisoner [me]'. It was all too much for her. She'd won the battle, but lost the war. She decided to leave her job at the end of 1984.

The upshot of this was that now Ali didn't have me coming to see her in her home once a month, nor was she able to see Corliss at all for the rest of the year. My hatred for Smith grew until I felt it burning inside me daily. It was eating me up.

Later in 1984, six months after Ali had left the prison to live with Ron, her visits were reduced to the standard six hours one Saturday a month. These visits were valuable because the children were allowed into the jail and could play in our units or anywhere else, unlike the one-hour weekly visits which were restricted to the visit centre. I wanted Ali to come on these one-hour visits too, so that I could see her more often, but because of the time restrictions they turned into a disaster.

'It's time to go, sweetheart,' I said to her after our first visit.

'No, I don't want to go,' she cried. 'I want to stay with you!' The officers had to pry her from my body, she was holding on so tight. It was like she was never going to let go.

'I'm sorry, sweetie, but you can't. You have to go home to Ron's and I'll see you in a couple of weeks.' I tried to reason with her, but by then she was screaming, and everyone in the visit centre was looking at us. The tears welled in my eyes, but this was no time to cry. I felt so tight inside I thought I would explode.

'Mummy!' she cried, 'I want my mummy!' Deep sobs wracked her little body. She was distressed and I was devastated. The officers continued to try and pull her off me, dragging at her from behind. There was no nice way to do this and she hung on to my clothes until her little fingers turned white, until she just couldn't hold on any more, and her grip released from my clothing, the material falling limp against my body.

Her little arms outstretched, I could hear her pleading, 'Mummy! Mummy! I want my mummy!' all the way to the front gate of the prison. It felt like my head was going to burst, then 'bang!', silence, as the front gate closed behind her. I felt like I was dying inside. I couldn't hear her screaming any more. Even the officer was distressed and, as I looked at him with desperation, I saw tears in his eyes too. Neither of us could speak.

I closed my eyes, let my head drop and, shaking, walked back to my cell, my heart broken.

Someone help me ... I pleaded silently as I struggled to breathe. I lay on the bed staring silently at the ceiling. Deep sobs rose to the surface, making my chest heave, but the tears wouldn't flow. My throat swelled again until I felt that familiar choking feeling. I couldn't speak. I couldn't cry. I closed my eyes and clenched my fists until they turned white, forcing the emotions down, down, deep into my body. I don't know how long I remained there.

Vicki and the women I shared the unit with knew not to interrupt.

Our second try at having visits in the visit centre was as

heartbreaking as the first, so I decided to give up. It was just too devastating. This meant that I would now only see Ali once a month inside the prison. The all-day Saturday visits were fun while she was there, but I still couldn't deal with the inevitable 'goodbyes'. Heroin continued to be my only means of escape from the pain of reality.

Once Ali had left the prison I didn't see my father and Jan any more. In fact they had decided to move interstate to New South Wales, and Ali was to go there during holiday periods to give Ron a break. Not long before, my father and I had had a couple of arguments about issues in relation to Ali. On one occasion when she'd been at his place for a few days and had caught a cold, he refused to return her to the prison, stating that the doctor had said she'd be better off in his care until she'd recovered. I'd had to get Ron to force him to return her, which eventually he did, handing her over to me in front of the prison officers without a word. Dad had never made a secret of the fact that he thought I should never have kept Ali in prison, but his opinion was of little consequence to me. Once again our relationship became silent or, more accurately, non-existent.

For me 1984 was a year of obtaining as much heroin as possible in order to stay sane and avoid facing up to the fact that I couldn't be Ali's mother for another four years. We spent much of our time organising to sneak heroin into the prison and the rest of our time using it. I was thirty years old and still hadn't found another way to cope with my feelings, particularly in relation to my separation from Ali. When I look back, it seems absurd that there was no counselling or therapy of any description offered to help me deal with the separation. That year was the most desperate in all my years of using, even though the amount I was consuming was considerably less than I'd used on the outside. The emotional hole inside me was huge, and I knew that in the months ahead it was going to get even bigger as I anticipated Vicki's pending release and Corliss's departure at the end of the year.

Things seemed to be falling apart on just about every level. Except for the relentless routine, nothing in prison was stable, not even my relationship with Vicki. Whereas once it had been filled with trust and love, now it was an empty representation of its former self, surviving predominantly because of our dependence on each other. Overnight leaves had gradually become part of Vicki's day-leave program, including overnight education leaves to Gippsland Institute at Churchill, approximately 150 kilometres south-east of Melbourne. Unfortunately, I'd discovered that she had spent some of those overnight leaves with her ex-girlfriend. When I found out I was devastated, but Vicki promised it wouldn't happen again, so I tried hard to put it behind us and move on. Although I still loved her desperately and believed she loved me, I felt tormented because I couldn't understand her unfaithfulness. There was so much I didn't understand then. We were so in love, I just hadn't contemplated any possibility that she might deceive me. I had thought the three of us would spend our lives together. Until then, I'd only experienced monogamous relationships. I wasn't really aware of any other way of relating intimately, nor was I interested.

Vicki, on the other hand, had no idea how shattering this was for me. Her life experience had been so different to mine. Her previous relationships hadn't been monogamous or committed. She had been sexually abused by an older man (a neighbour) when she was a child, as a result of which she hadn't developed an appropriate sense of boundaries in her adult life. Relationships were like a drug to her (in this we were both the same) and, with her lack of self-esteem, if someone who she found attractive showed affection or desired a sexual relationship, it made her feel wanted and therefore it was okay to engage sexually with them. While, years later, I was to come to understand why she'd behaved the way she did, back then all I could feel was hurt. And so I had competing emotions fighting inside me, love versus hate. I think it was only after she witnessed my devastation that she realised just how deeply I had loved her.

Vicki was willing to take responsibility for her actions and to move forward with our relationship but I recognised that, unfortunately, it was probably too late. Looking back now, I wished I'd had more insight at the time, but I didn't, so a part of my heart closed to her. I couldn't recapture the magic or the respect. The fantasy had disappeared and, with it, the tenderness. My heart felt hard and cold. I had to shut myself away where I couldn't be hurt any more. You know, some days I thought I was going to die from the hurt I felt in my heart and the anger I felt in my stomach.

Vicki didn't give up, trying relentlessly to pry me open. 'Can we talk?' she'd say. I'd be lying on the bed in the bedroom of the new cottage that we'd been moved to. In fact I hadn't wanted to move into this cottage with Vicki, but the governor had forced us. I told him I didn't want to move, that I wanted to stay in Yarrabrae, so instead of asking me, he ordered me. He thought I should have been grateful for the offer because it was seen as a privilege. The three new cottages were part of a trial, although the downside was that they only had two bedrooms to accommodate four women. They were situated near the front of the prison and didn't even have bars on the windows, so being placed there was an indication of trust from the prison's point of view. If I hadn't complied, Smith said he'd charge me and then I'd lose some more of my privileges. What a joke—although, knowing him, he'd probably happily take away my once-monthly visits with Ali.

One of the reasons I hadn't wanted to move was because it meant sharing a room with Vicki, and I felt like I needed space from her. The other reason was that, ironically, the officers checked on you more in the cottages than they did in Yarrabrae. Because we didn't get locked into our cell/bedrooms at night, the officers would enter the cottages every hour during the night, shining a torch into your bedroom to check that you were there. So in fact there was less privacy than in Yarrabrae where, at least after 11 pm, the officers wouldn't check on you again until 7 o'clock the next morning.

Anyway, I was in the room I now had to share with Vicki, reading a book, and I wouldn't even reply to her questions. My disrespect towards her was both obvious and painful for her. She'd try again, with slightly more aggression and thinly veiled annoyance: 'You have to talk to me!'

I'd think to myself, I can't blame her for being annoyed. I wouldn't bother with me either. I give her nothing any more, no love, no respect, no happiness, no intimacy. Why should she persevere with this so-called relationship?

But I'd continue to ignore her. It was almost like I expected her to hear my thoughts, which of course she couldn't. She'd stand in the doorway a bit longer, staring at this person who she loved but who wouldn't allow her in any more. I'd built a wall around me for protection, and it was growing thicker and stronger, much like the concrete prison wall outside. My heart was too full of pain for any love to enter.

I felt like I was being an arsehole, but I didn't know what to say to Vicki any more. As she'd turn and walk out of the room with a huge sigh, tears would brim in my eyes, but I didn't dare release them. My throat would constrict so that I could barely breathe. I loved her yet I hated her. It was hell in that room, it was hell in my head, it was hell in my heart—and there was no release. I knew I was hurting her but probably, in some ways, I wanted to hurt her like she'd hurt me. I also felt there was no point in trying to get close to her again when she was about to be released from prison. Why open up your heart only to have it hurt by the inevitable leaving?, I rationally asked myself. I only hoped that one day, in the distant future or maybe in her next life, she'd forgive me for the way I behaved then. I'd talk to that pure part of me, hoping that it was listening, hoping that it was still inside me somewhere: Please forgive me for being an arsehole to Vicki—I still love her, but I can't show it. I didn't say any of this out loud. All that Vicki could see was a cold, heartless person turned to stone.

That was what each day of my life had become. That was how I coped in there. Vicki turned her attentions to another woman in the prison, which of course only exacerbated our relationship problems. The only light relief in this awful situation came from putting our heads together with the other women in our cottage, and the one next door, to try and devise new and innovative ways to sneak our drugs into the jail. Smith hadn't realised it, but he'd inadvertently done us a favour moving us to this new cottage—it ran almost alongside the front wall of the prison. One evening after lock-up and before night medication time when the officers did their rounds, we were expecting a 'drop' to come over the wall, hidden in a tennis ball or something similarly small. We'd organised it with the cottage next door and we were all excited in anticipation of a forthcoming hit.

At the appointed time we heard a sort of crash–bang sound coming from the part of the wall where we knew our drugs were going to be thrown over. Three of us ran to the back bedroom of our cottage so that we could look out the window. Every minute or so we heard the same crashing sound. Finally, after three or four minutes, we saw a large green garbage bag flying over the top of the wall, illuminated by one of the spot-lights that surrounded the outside of the prison. It had to be our 'drop', so Vicki and I lowered Jan, who lived in the cottage with us, out the rear window. It wasn't much of a distance to the ground, just a small jump. She ran over the grass to collect the garbage bag and returned, passing it through to us. When we tried to hoist her in again, we had trouble lifting her as she was a heavy girl—we all burst into uncontrollable laughter. We were laughing so much that we didn't have the strength to lift her up and in through the window. But then Gloria, who was keeping watch for us at the front of our cottage, called out a warning that the officers were on their way with night medication. Suddenly we pulled ourselves together and hoisted Jan inside before they caught us.

After the officers had gone, we dragged the bag from its hiding place and opened it. Then we cracked up laughing all over again. Whoever had dropped off the drugs had decided to give us a surprise—there were a couple of roast chickens and some stubbies of beer as well as our precious, tiny package of heroin. Unfortunately, most of the stubbies had broken, spraying beer all over everything, but we didn't care because we were only interested in the drugs anyway. Later on, one of us snuck out the rear window again and went over to the cottage next door to give them their share. We also gave them the chickens and beer because some of them weren't drug users and we knew they'd appreciate it. With that done we had a hit and another laugh, and chatted for the rest of the night.

Who knows, it was probably those silly incidents that helped me survive. At least they took my mind away from more morbid thoughts. I was also able to be warmer towards Vicki immediately after a hit. The only time we were close now was when we were stoned.

16

Seeing through the
eyes of death

F ebruary 1985 arrived: time for Vicki to leave the prison, her
sentence completed. I was little more than halfway through
mine. Emotionally I had tried to abandon her, although my desperation and neediness seemed to increase with each person that
left. I eased this anxiety with heroin.

Although it should have been a joyous occasion for Vicki,
she was filled with torment. Of course she wanted to get outside
and experience freedom, but she was worried about how I was
going to cope, with her, Corliss and Ali gone. Although I didn't
say anything to her, I could understand her concern—I had no
idea how I was going to deal with the bleakness myself.

At morning muster the other women gave Vicki a last hug
and said their goodbyes before being hustled by the officers to
their work posts. I tried so hard to look happy, but it wasn't
what I was feeling inside. Vicki and I returned to our unit for a
last embrace ... a last kiss and another goodbye.

'This is it, I guess,' I said to her, resigned to our fate. Deep
down I didn't believe our already tormented relationship could
withstand the difficulties that more than three years of forced
separation would bring.

'I love you so much,' she said, looking into my troubled

eyes. 'I'm going to miss you, but we can get through this. I'm going to be waiting out there for you with Ali. Don't give up . . . please don't give up on "us"?'

'I'm glad that at least you'll be with Ali,' I said to her, ignoring her question. 'You have to get some smack in to me as soon as you can, okay? Please don't forget,' I pleaded with her. Then that fucking loudspeaker interrupted.

'Vicki to the front gate!' it demanded. 'Vicki to the front gate immediately!' The sound entered both our bodies like an electric shock. We stood there holding on to each other one last time. We didn't know how long it would be before we saw each other again. We were trying to gain special permission for Vicki to come and visit me, but it was difficult because ex-prisoners weren't allowed to return to the jail as visitors.

'I don't want to go,' Vicki said, holding me. 'I don't want to leave you in this shithole.'

'You have to go, there's nothing we can do about it.'

'Hold me?' she said with a helpless look in her eyes.

I reached out and held her in my arms. 'Fuck, I hate this,' she said in my ear.

The tears welled in my eyes although I hadn't been able to cry since Ali had left. It was like a blockage. I didn't know it then, but it wouldn't be until four years after my release that I'd feel safe enough to let my tears flow.

'Come on, let's go before they call you again.' The truth was, I needed to get this over and done with. The longer it took, the more difficult it was getting. I just wanted the torment to stop.

I switched off, just as I'd done with Ali, as once again I walked towards the front gate of the prison where the officer was waiting to let Vicki through. She gave me a last kiss and said goodbye. A last, quick hug, a wave and she was gone . . . to the other side of the gate, that other world from which I was to be excluded for another three and a half years.

Vicki had promised to organise regular deliveries of heroin and I was counting on that as my lifeline. I wasn't even thinking about the difficulty of maintaining my supply long-term—I just needed it now. I trusted that she'd come through as she was the only hope I really had. Other sources had dried up. We'd spent weeks devising ways to get some into the prison. We'd decided that secreting small amounts in cassette tapes was one option. It was relatively simple to unscrew the tape, place the drugs in a small, flat packet of foil inside, then screw it back together again. Because I was musical, it wouldn't seem too odd that Vicki kept dropping off music cassettes to me.

We'd persuaded Ron to let Vicki live at his place and look after Ali, as he currently only had a friend filling in as her 'nanny'. He'd had a great deal of trouble in the past year finding a suitable hired nanny/housekeeper, and Vicki seemed like the perfect solution because she had such a close relationship with Ali and me. We believed it would help fill the gap my absence left in Ali's life. Ali was overjoyed at the idea of having Vicki so close. Deep down I had some concerns as I no longer had much faith in Vicki's and my relationship, but I knew that it would be great for Ali. I also hoped that this connection might help our relationship survive, despite the mounting difficulties and the long separation we were about to endure.

Although I had tried so hard to detach myself emotionally from Vicki before she left the prison, I found that I hadn't really been that successful—the absence of both Ali and Vicki was devastating. I phoned them once a week and wrote almost every day, and Vicki was just as regular in writing to me and dropping off Ali's paintings, photos, books for my studies and, of course, the cassettes which, so far, had all gone through the system without detection. Of course, Ron knew nothing of our continued heroin use.

As well as trying to gain approval for Vicki to have contact visits in the prison, we also needed to gain approval for her to be at Ron's house as I'd been successful in my application to resume day leaves to see Ali there every couple of months and we wanted to share those special times with Vicki. As it stood, Vicki would have to remove herself from the house whenever I was there. Luckily, approval was given—this was a real win for Vicki and me, and gave me some hope for the future of our relationship. As my first day-leave visit approached, Ali, Vicki and I were excited as we had coerced Ron into letting us get a kitten for Ali. He wasn't enthusiastic, but Vicki and I believed it would give her some comfort, and we'd planned for the three of us to go to Lort Smith's lost animal home to choose one. While it was sad to see so many lost and dumped animals at the home, Ali was delighted with a little black and white tabby kitten that she decided to call Jemima. She was a sweet little pussycat and Ali played with her affectionately.

I wasn't able to get to know 'Mima as she grew from a kitten into a cat, but Ali often sent me photos of her. As for Vicki and I, we completed that day leave with a hit, which enhanced our feelings of love and closeness in a surreal world. We didn't talk about our difficulties, we just tried to enjoy our limited time together, grateful to be able to share any time at all. Vicki had also organised some heroin for me to take back to the prison, which made me love her even more. It would help me readjust to the separation from them both—there was still nothing else in my life to fill the gaping, emotional hole left by their absence. In one of her many letters, this one coming only a few weeks after her release, Vicki wrote:

> My dearest Helen,
>
> I sat down Saturday night to write to you but ended up lying on my bed for a couple of hours

crying. My turn to lose it, and this weekend I have constantly and continuously. I love you so much and God, I miss you. It's like being half a person. I feel so empty. I'm sure you're feeling similar emotions and I'm lucky to some extent that I have many things that I can occupy myself with; the only thing I want I can't have.

This weekend I've felt really lost, perhaps it's been because Ali was not with me as much. Saturday seems to be a success. You'll tell me about it tomorrow (Monday) when you ring. I hang out for your calls and I wish I could talk to you more.

Corliss was in the car when I picked up Ali after her day with you, and we went back there for a coffee for about an hour. I was really surprised at how Ali reacted. She was really quite happy and excited about seeing you and had obviously had a good day. I thought when it was time for her to leave we may have had a problem. I was glad you brought her to the gate of the prison, I think that helped. Ali didn't go into specifics about her day but said she had a good time and wanted to go to netball on Thursday night. Corliss said she'd come too.

Ali is coping extremely well. She loves you very, very much and is so brave, one can only admire her, you too for that matter. For me, I think seeing you handing Ali over at the gate, being so close and not being able to be close, really hit home just how deeply I miss you. Since leaving there Ali has kept me busy and I haven't, with a few exceptions, really allowed myself to let my feelings go. I know I miss you more than any words could begin to express, but I keep swallowing that lump in my throat whenever it comes. I don't feel any better for losing it, but I know how much I love and need you, that no matter how long we must endure this separation, I'll be here waiting for you.

Let me tell you about Sunday. I took Ali and Amber [Ron's girlfriend's daughter] to the Botanical Gardens. We'd brought some bread from home and walked over to the side of the lake. I spotted a table not very far from where we were and decided to sit and rest. Ali got a bit hassled because there were more seagulls than ducks and they were faster than the ducks and seemed to be getting most of the bread. Ali came marching up to me air-raiding about the birds, but unfortunately there wasn't much you could do about it (no window to tap on like in Yarrabrae—ha! ha!). Ali and Amber decided to sit with me and feed the sparrows instead and Ali told Amber all about our bird that comes to visit; she was talking about Harry. We don't see any willy-wagtails in Brighton at Ron's house, which Ali made a comment about, and after some quick thinking I said that Harry lives at Fairfield and still visits Mum and maybe next time when Ali comes in to spend the day in the prison, he might surprise her and come over especially to see her. I hope he does, she was really a little disappointed about not seeing any of Harry's relatives.

Anyway, after the Botanical Gardens I had

to go over to Preston so I thought I'd drop some things off for you. The little albums you'll be able to fill with photos of Ali and our little occasions/excursions that we go on. There's a week of Ali's drawings from which you'll have to decide which are to go in the scrapbook. I also picked up a Debussy tape for you; I know how much you like him and I hope this one is okay.

Well my love, I'll write a big letter tomorrow night and I'll see you Thursday at netball and hopefully by next Saturday we'll have approval from the governor for me to visit you.

I love you,
always,
Vicki
xxxx

I loved receiving these letters from Vicki, full of news about herself and Ali, but it was also very painful not being part of their lives. I was also becoming more and more desperate for those music cassette tapes which she dropped off every few days. I hassled her like hell for more and more heroin, and my anxiety waiting for it to arrive was increasing because I was so dependent on the drug for any sense of well-being. I'd certainly developed a habit by then, so if I ran out I knew I'd be in deep shit. Vicki's whole life seemed to revolve around caring for Ali, obtaining enough heroin for her own use and organising to send some in to me. She was doing a good job at keeping up with it all, but I knew it was going to get harder to obtain the amounts of heroin we each needed to keep going. It meant, of course, that she was forced to return to selling the stuff to keep up our supply. It was unfortunate that we knew of no other way to cope, and I could tell, as the weeks passed and I was allowed contact visits with Vicki, that she wasn't coping at all out there in the 'real' world.

Our visits didn't take place with the other prisoners as they were a special concession, so there would just be Vicki, me and an ever-present officer in the visit centre for an hour. Each time Vicki came, it was like talking to someone who just wasn't there. After she'd walked into the room and sat down at the table beside me, I'd lean over to hug her and whisper in her ear, 'Do you miss me?'

'You know I do, I can't tell you how much. I wish you'd believe me,' she'd respond. Then her head would drop as she sort of half nodded off. She had big dark bags under her eyes, and was always tired because she was having problems sleeping.

I'd sit back in my chair and look at her, feeling disappointed that she didn't seem as elated to see me as I was to see her. I felt like she didn't really want to be there, or she didn't really care, neither of which was true. I needed so much from her emotionally, but she wasn't able to give anything during those small snippets of time we were allowed to share. I was also concerned that the officer might notice.

'Aren't you excited to see me?' I'd say to her slumped head, unable to see her eyes.

'Of course I am,' she'd reply, shaking herself awake.

'Why don't you act like it then?' I'd retort, getting angry.

I wanted her to be emotionally available and she was just so out of it, she was like a rag doll. She just kept saying 'I love you' over and over until I was sick of hearing it because it felt like it was meaningless. Living outside, I knew she had access to much more heroin than me, and she was obviously using heaps. Although I could understand why, it was very frustrating not being able to make an emotional connection with her. It was like there was a wall between us and the closeness that I craved was not forthcoming.

Before she'd leave the visit I would always check the arrangements for my next supply of heroin, which seemed to have taken precedence over our love for each other. I was physically addicted again, so it was imperative that I receive enough to avoid hanging out. I put pressure on Vicki because I dreaded the thought of being sick. Poor thing, I was not only emotionally dependent on her, but now also physically. She must have been under pressure from a lot of places, and goodness only knows how she was managing to pay for the drugs. I didn't dare ask. Neither of us could see the futility of it all. This was what we called love, and I had never loved anyone so desperately.

We went on like this for a couple of months until Vicki arrived at the jail one day in mid April to drop off some things for me—including, of course, the usual cassette tape. Surprisingly, the officer offered her a visit with me. She was delighted and I got a shock when I heard my name called over the loudspeaker: 'Helen Barnacle to the visit centre.'

As I approached the building I could see through the windows that Vicki was sitting in there waiting. I was overjoyed and rushed inside to greet her: 'Hi! How come you're allowed in to see me?'

'I was at the gate dropping some things off for you and Smith told the officers at the gate that I could have a visit,' she said, still sounding amazed.

'Unreal!' I responded. 'Did you drop off some smack?' I asked her in a whisper so that the officer couldn't hear me.

'Yeah. I left some things at the gate for you,' she said.

'Thanks,' I said, relieved that I wouldn't be hanging out. It was also something to look forward to after she'd gone.

About half an hour later, the officer came over to tell us our time was up.

'Yeah, okay,' I replied irritably, 'just let us say goodbye?'

I gave Vicki a kiss and we stood up and held each other for

a moment, then she walked out of the centre and made her way to the gate. As I went to leave, the officer stopped me.

'Sorry, but you can't go any further,' she said.

'What do you mean?' I asked, experiencing my first wave of anxiety. This officer was well-known to me and she'd always been nice to me before.

'You're not allowed to return to the cottage. Just wait here, the governor wants to see you,' she said. This time her tone was official rather than friendly.

I tried not to look outwardly worried, but my gut started churning as I sensed that it had something to do with the stuff that Vicki had just dropped off. Shit!, I thought to myself: What am I going to do if they've found it? Even worse, Vicki would be busted and charged and she was still on parole …

I was left sitting there, waiting, watched by the officer. It seemed like a long, long time, and the more it went on, the more certain I became that we'd been busted. Foremost in my mind was the fact that soon I'd be hanging out. Even though I was starting to feel shattered inside, I couldn't show it. I didn't want the officer to suspect that anything was wrong, just in case my fears turned out to be unfounded. Inside, though, I knew it would take a miracle. First Ali, then Vicki, now my drugs gone. For me there was nothing left. Ali and Vicki were all I lived for. They were my self-esteem; the reason I had any belief in myself at all was only vicariously through them. With no drug to desensitise myself from the pain of losing them both, I would lose my way completely.

Finally the silence was broken when an officer entered, saying: 'The governor wants to see you.' She escorted me to his office and I tried desperately to hide my fear as I walked in. Smith was furious, I could see it in his eyes. He was all red and puffed up and looked like he was going to burst. I guess he felt cheated—he'd granted us the 'special' visits and probably took our subversive drug activity personally.

'You won't be seeing your friend again!' he almost spat at me. 'She's on her way to the police station!'

'What can you tell me about this?' he went on, pointing to the opened cassette tape. He was nearly frothing at the mouth.

'Nothing,' I said quietly. I actually felt like I was going to faint. It was all I could do to remain standing. At that moment, as the consequences started washing over me, I hated him more than ever.

'What do you mean, nothing?' he screamed at me. He went on yelling abuse at me for what seemed an eternity but was probably only ten or fifteen minutes. I stared back at him, saying nothing. He seemed to think it was a competition, the idiot. Although I found him intimidating, I didn't give a shit at that point in time, which only served to infuriate him more.

'Get her out of my fuckin' office!' he yelled at his officers, totally losing control with them as well as me. 'I said get her out of my fuckin' sight!' he repeated as he beat his fist on the desk.

He's going to break his hand in a minute, I thought to myself—as long as he keeps hitting the desk and not me!

The officers looked anxiously at each other, totally intimidated by him, but they quickly did as they were told. I realised that they were more frightened of him than I was. If he thought I gave a damn about his opinion, he was wrong. I had no respect for him, neither did any of the other women.

But this time it was different for me. I'd never in my life felt like this before. My spirit had broken. I didn't care any more. The smugness evaporated as I openly acknowledged I'd been conquered and my head hung limply. The shame I was beginning to feel, not on account of this arsehole but in the eyes of my brother when he heard the news, surged through my body, shame that was so all-encompassing I felt like I'd never be able to lift my head again. I imagined Ron being told about it. I imagined him shaking his head in disbelief. He'd be wondering how many more times he'd have to experience the same grief and disappointment. I didn't know how to answer that question.

The officers escorted me into Unit 5, the punishment cell. Words couldn't hurt me any more. You could have bashed the hell out of me right then and I wouldn't have felt a thing. I was somewhere between life and death ... in limbo. No-one could reach me because I'd lost the capacity to feel. A decision had to be made about where I wanted to be—here, living, or there ... dead? But not today. Alone with only my reflection in the familiar stainless steel door, I wished it could speak to me. I lay on the bed and stared at the ceiling.

It was eerie to feel the officer's eyes watching me through the trap door. She asked me not to do anything stupid. What she meant was, don't try to kill yourself. It was a real option for me now. I wanted to die and she knew it. My cynicism made me think that she probably just didn't want me to do it on her shift! Funny, I'd never really liked her; she'd always been one of the arsehole officers, but that day I could actually see that she possessed some compassion. Her concern surprised me. She'd so often charged me with petty offences—she was the one who'd nearly charged me for taking a portion of butter from the dining room back to my dormitory—but now she was acting like she cared what I did to myself. The irony was, I didn't. I just wanted to die. I wanted to experience lifelessness. It had to be easier than this.

Soon I'll be hanging out, I thought to myself. The sterile cell, the concrete and stainless steel kept staring back at me. My skin felt like it was crawling. It felt like something was eating me up. I was sure my reflection was smaller. There were fingerprints smudging the steel door, blurring my reflection. The shock of Vicki being busted was still reverberating through my body. The implications were enormous, not just for me in prison, but for her, Ali and Ron out there in the real world.

After he'd received the bad news, Ron rang the prison. I wasn't allowed to take the call, but the officer told me that he was shattered. I could have had the conversation with myself, anyway. I knew the content: How I could lie to him? When would I ever stop using and getting into trouble? I had a daughter who should be put first now ...

'Vicki has to go,' he said days later when I was allowed to receive a phone call from him.

'I know,' I replied. This was the second time she'd been caught out using while living at Ron's. We had talked him round after the first time, but this was just too much for him to deal with. I knew Vicki wasn't about to stop using—in fact what had happened would have increased her desperation and her using was probably escalating as she tried to block reality. Ali would be devastated. She loved Vicki and it was a strong link with me. Now another important person was to vacate her life. I felt irresponsible, worthless, and I knew in Ron's eyes I was hopeless. I still didn't understand the assumption that if you were a heroin addict you must be useless, but Ron shared that belief with the rest of the straight world, and I didn't think they could all be wrong.

I totally understood his perspective but, other than increasing my shame, his disappointment in me didn't achieve anything because I was hanging in limbo and the truth was, I didn't care. Only people who have been 'beyond caring' would understand. It's when that light at the end of the tunnel doesn't even flicker any more. I couldn't see August 1988. I couldn't even picture Ali or Vicki in my mind. They had become featureless shadows whose faces had faded from my memory. I made the decision to die. The only thing that concerned me now was working out how to do it.

After hanging out in Unit 5 for a couple of days, I heard a voice through the small rear window of the cell. I dragged myself up from the bed, knelt on it, and looked out. It was Rikki, one of my old friends from down the street who had returned for a stint in jail.

'How are you doin'?' she whispered. She had snuck around to the back of the unit where there was a small window to talk to me.

I told her that I had some pills hidden somewhere else in the jail and I asked her to get them for me as they'd help me while I was hanging out. I didn't really think she'd be able to find them and it would be even more difficult for her to pass them through to me. The next day, though, she was there again. She had worked out a way to get them to me via one of the prisoners working in the kitchen who would be bringing my meal to me. There were surveillance cameras at the back of Yarrabrae, but she didn't even consider the risk of being caught talking to me—she just knew I was suffering and was willing to do anything to help.

As soon as I got the pills I counted them. There were only about twenty-five and I knew that wasn't enough to kill me—how I wished there were more. I couldn't bear the thought of overdosing and then having to wake up and face reality all over again, so I just used them to help me get through the hanging out.

About a week later Ron came in for a twenty-minute non-contact visit, because I'd lost my contact visit privileges. In a way I was glad that I wasn't allowed contact and that the visit was limited to twenty minutes—at least it minimised the time that I had to listen to his anger and despair. He barely said hello before his feelings of frustration erupted: 'How could you do this? I can't believe it! Do you know what this means for Ali?' His questions were relentless. He knew I couldn't answer them, but I guess he hoped for some sort of rational explanation. I said nothing.

He continued the onslaught, desperately needing answers: 'What can you be thinking of? When are you going to stop lying? When will you ever stop using? When will you put Ali's needs first?' I sat there, my head hanging. I didn't dare ask when I could see Ali again. I knew he would be within his rights to refuse to bring her in. I didn't tell him how I was feeling. I didn't tell him I wanted to die. I knew he wouldn't understand, and would only see it as self-pity. Although I knew where he was coming from, it didn't help. It just added a few more points to my scale of worthlessness and, as I walked back to my cell, the darkness consumed me. A few days later, at the end of April 1985, he wrote me a letter:

Dear Helen,

Well I'm sure your meeting with me on Saturday did little to improve your frame of mind over the weekend, but in retrospect I don't think I could have conveyed my feelings and attitude any more accurately than I did.

However, given that we can reach some agreement about the future, I will support you although I see little hope and am at a loss as to know what to do.

I don't want you to think that I believe I am perfect or that I have a 'holier than thou' attitude. This is the first time, despite many similar instances in the past, that I have taken this approach and I feel justified in doing so. Not surprisingly, I am not the only one angry about being 'taken' but Elizabeth in particular will also support you and is planning to see you on Sunday, if the jail will allow.

Needless to say Friday's episode has brought you to the point of no return. From here you either go up or down. If it's up you will have my support.

I think at some time in the near future we will need to discuss your intentions for the future. I should tell you now I have no interest in self-pity or the past. What I want to know is how you will address the future, so please give that a great deal of thought before we next speak.

I know you want to make it work and that's the only reason I persist.

Love, Ron.

I felt black, everything around me felt black and I couldn't see any possible way out. I'd become my own shadow. It would have been easier to die. At the time I felt that probably would have been better for everyone, even Ali. I felt worthless as a mother, as a sister, as a human being. I was aware that, if I wasn't around, Ron would take care of Ali and she'd be given a stable life, even if an unemotional one. I felt like I was useless to her the way I was, because I just kept getting into trouble. I couldn't imagine a life where I didn't use heroin. I'd never witnessed an addict become drug free. I didn't believe it was possible. Personally, I didn't feel that being a heroin addict implied that I was useless or unintelligent—I'd passed exams with 'honours' when I was stoned—but the rest of society made me feel useless as a drug addict. The sheer weight of their numbers was oppressive, and my lack of self-esteem wouldn't allow me to challenge the opinions of the majority.

How can I learn to control my drug use?, I wanted to ask

Ron. But I didn't dare. I knew I couldn't. The need to use was too strong, too overwhelming. How can I stop? Someone tell me?, I pleaded silently to myself, not sharing my thoughts with him.

I also knew I wouldn't be seeing Vicki again. She wouldn't be allowed into the prison. Deep down I knew that the relationship was over, but I couldn't face that reality yet. I knew she wouldn't cope with the lack of contact. I didn't even know if she'd survive at all. A couple of weeks later, toward the middle of May, she wrote:

> My dear Helen,
>
> Hi darlin', how's my favourite lady? I hear things are still very difficult. It will only get better and know that Ali and I are out here waiting for you, that's the important thing. I know you and Ali are the only reason I keep going.
>
> I'm not in the same position as you. I can get enough [heroin] to end it, but the future, our future is too important. Unfortunately it's another test. The only thing I do know is everything that has gone wrong for us is associated with the dope. The only good thing to ever come out of dope is that we were able to meet, everything else has been disastrous. So, time to get it together where that is concerned. I'm seeing a psych on Friday. He's part of a new 'drug and alcohol forensic unit' set up by the corrections dept. I'm not quite sure exactly what it's all about, but it's a start.
>
> If you do anything silly, I'll . . . I love you

Helen. I can't, I don't want to go on without you. You are everything to me and we need you—Ali and I—so, I know it's difficult, I know that, but we do have a future and time will go reasonably fast, okay?!

The high of the day today was talking to Ali. I spoke to her on the phone at about 5.30 and she's great. She was very excited talking to me, we sang songs and spoke about things and she was just great. You should be very proud of yourself my love, you've created a beautiful little lady, and she can't wait for us to be together, well, as long as it's you, her, and then me!!!

I've tried to ring Corliss the last couple of nights. I'm not quite sure what I'm going to say, or what I want to say, but I think I need to say something.

I'm going to try and get some sleep. I'll finish for now and write again later. I know I keep saying it, should I say 'writing it', but I want you to put what's happened behind you and let's get today and tomorrow together. We can do that together, okay … I love you, always, Vicki xxx

As the letter went on, Vicki's writing became increasingly unclear and I could tell she was stoned. In my emotional state, and with my body physically hanging out, it was more than I could bear.

Sitting in the stark, empty punishment cell hour after hour (you don't get let out for work in the punishment cell), I knew my choices were limited. I had to kill myself or change—the only two alternatives. Hours turned into days, days into weeks. I no longer knew if anyone was watching me. I wasn't capable

of caring about anything inside or outside of me. During the
long, lonely nights in my cell I imagined different ways to kill
myself. I saw myself dead with my wrists slashed; hanging lifeless
from the shower in the concrete and stainless steel bathroom;
lying on the bed overdosed, looking like I'd just gone to sleep—
the last one would have been my preference. There were plenty
of options, and thinking them through gave me a sense of
purpose. Sometimes I'd just get angry and desperately want to
smash everything in the cell, but it was almost bare. Other times
I just wanted to go to sleep and never wake up. We weren't
supposed to have emotions in there; it wasn't a place where you
were encouraged to experience yourself as an emotional being.
There was no time out to deal with separation from your daughter or separation from your lover, or both. There was no time
out to contemplate the possibility of life without drugs, and there
was also no understanding of how traumatic that might be. We
were seen as sneaks and liars, not as troubled human beings.
Externally we wore the 'prisoner' label like a brand mark on our
persona; internally we wore it always … a scar that remained a
wound in our hearts. But they didn't see that, they only saw the
body earmarked 'criminal'.

After a couple of weeks, I was moved out of the punishment
cell and into another Yarrabrae unit cell. I wasn't trusted to live
in the cottages any more. I moved my possessions in, but I didn't
care where I was. I wondered where my heart had gone. Was it
packed away for safekeeping? I felt like a walking machine. How
I wished I could pack up the pain I was feeling, but I couldn't,
so my heart must have been operating in there somewhere.

I kept writing desperate letters to Vicki and she'd write back
in a similar vein. I'd carry her letters with me during the day. I
knew I had to be punished for the crimes I'd committed, but it
still didn't make any sense. That was just how the 'system'
worked. I knew that trying to sneak heroin into the prison for

my own use, in order to try and stay sane and ease my feelings of abandonment, was a criminal offence. As usual, I was punished for my drug use, not given medical treatment or offered counselling. They didn't understand that when I used heroin I wasn't trying to beat the system, or pull one over on them with my lies about getting it into the prison. I wasn't trying to beat anyone at anything. I was just trying to find enough of a reason to want to stay alive. For most of my life I'd felt like I just didn't fit in anywhere. I didn't think like the rest of society. Maybe that was my biggest crime.

I was feeling so low that there was nothing Smith or the jail could take away from me that would upset me. I'd already lost everything that meant anything to me, and the loss of contact visits had no impact on me whatsoever. Smith couldn't seem to grasp that. He didn't seem to understand that for once he had no power over me. That thought gave me some relief, some comfort. I wasn't even seeing Ali. I'd make a card and write to her every second or third day, but I knew I couldn't tolerate seeing her and having to say goodbye. I'd never believed that I was a bad mother to her, but even Ron now seemed to have that opinion. It would never make sense to me. I missed her.

Smith persisted in trying to upset me by taking away my education sessions. 'You're to be transferred to the sewing room. It will be your new work post until further notice.'

'Okay,' I responded quietly. I hated sewing and the sewing room was the worst work post that I could have imagined in the prison. On another day in another time this news would have upset me, but right then I couldn't give a shit. I turned and walked outside.

A week later I was called up again and informed I'd lost my day leaves. As if I hadn't already known. He also told me I'd probably not get another one for the remainder of my sentence.

'Okay,' I replied quietly and walked out yet again. I couldn't face the outside world anyway. I didn't even want to leave my cell, let alone the prison.

After a couple of months I sensed that he was starting to realise that none of this was having any impact on me. I was in a state of chronic depression, so nothing had much meaning. I didn't think he understood emotions like sadness. I didn't have any solitary contact with him for some time after that. The game was over—at least for a while—and that was some kind of relief.

I'd come to dread the mornings because I didn't want to wake up, I didn't want to get out of bed, I didn't want to have a shower and I didn't want to leave my cell and have to face people. I felt a sort of aching numbness. How can I describe it? It never left me, except when I went to sleep, and then I'd be transferred into another kind of horror story. I kept having drug-related dreams, bad dreams where I would wake in a sweat, screaming and full of a vicious fear I'd never known before. I must have been yelling in my sleep a lot because my friend Rikki, who lived in the adjacent unit, would often call out to me during the night.

'Barny,' she'd yell, 'are you okay? What are you doing? Barny! Talk to me—can you hear me?' It was as though she'd put herself on night duty since I'd gotten busted and become so severely depressed. After lock-up every night she'd have conversations with me through the walls and across to her cell in her unit and I'd yell back to her. Sometimes after lock-up she'd also write me letters: 'Hang on, Barny, you've got to hang on,' she'd plead with me. She'd been to this black pit herself and she knew I knew. When I had the energy, I'd reply to her letters. One way or another we managed to slip them under the doors, attached to a piece of cotton in a pulley type of system. It kept me distracted from my own self-pity for a while and so was helpful. She also made me laugh sometimes, even in my despair.

I didn't have much contact with Rikki during the day because she worked in the garden and I was locked in the sewing room but, whenever she could, she spent time with me, took me under her wing and looked after me. Even after I was moved from the 'punishment' cell to a normal Yarrabrae cell she was worried that I was going to do something stupid, like try to kill myself. It did ease my sense of isolation and, even though I had nothing to give her in return, she maintained her vigil.

One tiny piece of luck in this bleakest of times was that the sewing-room job I thought I'd hate turned out to be just what I needed. It was a mindless job and I could sit on my own in front of the machine all day, listening to the noise it made. I didn't have to talk to anyone. I didn't know any of the women in the sewing room very well, but as the days passed we began to communicate a little. The smarty-pants part of me longed to tell Smith how satisfactory my new job was, but I refrained. I didn't have the energy to say anything to Smith and I was too frightened anyway. If I never saw him again it'd be too soon. At least my reaction was a sign of 'life' in me, momentarily replacing my preoccupation with death.

I'd deferred my studies. I didn't know when I'd take them up again, and at that point I didn't care. I had no future plans. I made some new friends while working in the sewing room and they all understood what I was going through. They were so kind to me. Kerry and her sister Karen became good work companions. One morning when Kerry and I were walking through the gate of Yarrabrae, sadness overwhelmed me ... sometimes it would catch me like that, and I never knew when it was going to happen. Sensing my struggle, Kerry turned toward me, wrapped her arms around me and just held me there for a while. My whole body was heaving with dry, tearless sobs. I felt safe in her arms. I didn't have to say anything—she had children herself. We were blocking the doorway and the other women had to manoeuvre themselves around us to get out, but no-one complained. They were glad for me to be receiving some comfort in that forlorn world. 'Thanks,' I said to Kerry as we moved on to work.

During this period I was receiving letters from Vicki almost daily and was writing back just as regularly but, on 12 June 1985, I received what turned out to be my last letter from her for many months. For some reason she just stopped writing to me and she didn't even try to contact Ron about seeing Ali. After a few weeks had passed with no letters, I was at the Education Centre one day when a Salvation Army worker told me she'd seen Vicki in court with another woman and her baby. She described the other woman's appearance, and I was pretty sure that it was Vicki's ex-girlfriend. There had been no letter, no explanation, no contact—I guess our relationship had just ceased.

I felt the familiar knife stab of pain in my heart, but I didn't let the worker know what a bomb she'd dropped on me. After she left I turned to Lynda, who knew Vicki and her ex-girlfriend well.

'You know who Vicki's with, don't you?' she said softly, understanding how hurt I must have felt.

'Yeah, it's who I think it is, isn't it?' I asked her, hoping she'd find another explanation.

'I'd say almost certainly it is,' she replied.

'Fuck! How could she?' I said, as much to myself as to her.

'I don't know,' she answered. 'I really don't know.'

I couldn't say any more, the lump in my throat had grown too big. I was in the Education Centre and there were too many people around, so I made up an excuse to leave and went back to Yarrabrae and my cell for a while. I sat on the edge of my bed shaking my head in disbelief.

I knew I just had to accept that she had gone from my life. No wonder she hadn't written to me. What I really had to grasp was how difficult it was for me to let go of it. I didn't know how, and I needed her so much ... yet I also knew that 'we' couldn't survive this. There were still three years for me to serve—three years without physical contact. It had only been three months since she'd left the prison. I was shattered. All my hopes and dreams of the three of us together in the future seemed to have been caught up in the outgoing tide, and as I looked behind I saw them wash away and disappear. It left a burning feeling in my heart. It seemed so unfair.

About three months after the bust I was once again called to the governor's office.

'There's a psychiatrist here to see you,' he said when I entered his office. I looked at him incredulously. Three months before I had asked for help and it had finally arrived. It was all I could do not to laugh in his face.

'A bit late, thanks,' I replied.

'Do you want to see him or not?' he asked, losing patience with me.

'Yes, I'll see him,' I said.

It turned out that Frank, who was still in jail in Pentridge, had heard that I wasn't doing well and had organised for the psychiatrist from over there to come and see me.

'That's kind of him,' I said to the psychiatrist, 'but I was in crisis three months ago, so it's all a bit late. I believe I can manage on my own now, but thanks anyway.' We talked for a few minutes longer and he left. That was the only help offered to me during this time. It surprises me now to think I got out alive.

During his two years at Fairlea, Smith instilled a great deal of fear. Eventually, enough women and a couple of officers got brave enough to report a number of the incidents involving him. Smith was eventually charged and had to face a court case, so he was suspended from duties. He was eventually found 'not guilty', but he never returned to Fairlea or any prison service for that matter. His departure happened pretty quickly in the latter part of 1985, and he was replaced by a temporary governor for a few months. The new governor was okay—anyone would have been an improvement. Our permanent governor didn't arrive until 1986.

However, things were moving on for me. I'd like to say that I'd become 'strong' all of a sudden, but that's not the truth. It wasn't my choice, it was something that had been forced on me, but at least I wasn't using any more. Although I was devastated about Vicki and the separation from Ali, I gradually began to talk. Ever so slowly the pain of waking up in the mornings began to ease. It was a tentative process and if I'd been able to score some heroin I would have been into it in a flash, but now that my sources had dried up I couldn't get any. As more time passed without using to kill the emotional pain, my desire for heroin actually waned. It was a peculiar space to be in, not having an incessant psychological craving for heroin, but I knew I couldn't go any lower than I'd just been and survive.

For the first time since I'd begun using heroin, I began to connect my drug use to my torment and I started to feel that if I could just go on long enough without a hit, I might discover a way of finding some sort of peace inside. My thinking was changing. I was starting to feel like having a hit would be choosing to die. I now made a connection between using and misery and I knew I wouldn't survive next time round. I never wanted to go into that black pit again; it had freaked me out knowing how close I'd been to choosing suicide. I wasn't feeling much, but at least I was learning to exist. I realised now that I wasn't going to end it, this thing they call 'life'. I'd decided to find a way to move on, the major problem being that I still couldn't bear to see Ali. I just didn't know if I could ever say goodbye again.

Part III
Birth

17

Confronting the demons

I kept moving through the days, searching for a purpose. I'd get up in the morning, go to my work post, collect mail in the afternoon and eat dinner before being locked in my unit and, later, my cell for the night. Then I'd do it all again the next day. It was an empty life if you were looking for fulfilment outside yourself. I didn't even have my piano in the jail any more. After Vicki and I had been busted, Smith threatened to put the piano outside in the weather if I didn't organise for it to be picked up. Ron, once again, came to the rescue and retrieved it before Smith could act on his threat.

There were no highs or lows for me any more; I couldn't have handled any fluctuation, anyway. I was just trying to exist. I wasn't sure why yet, apart from Ali. I'd still not heard any word from Vicki and, knowing her as well as I did, I believed her guilt, shame and sense of failure would keep it that way. It was a relief, really, as I didn't want the emotional turmoil that any contact with her would bring. I needed a bit more time before facing that.

By mid 1985 Ron was at least speaking to me again. He hadn't been able to see me face-to-face since our last non-contact visit a couple of months previously. He was still feeling frustrated and angry, but we'd been communicating through letters and I hoped that he was feeling encouraged by my changed attitude. Of course it was too early for him to have any confidence or belief in what I'd been saying in my letters to him. It was now my turn to be patient.

I asked him to take over all decision-making in relation to Ali. Even though he was already doing that, it was my first verbal acknowledgment of my incapability. 'I'm not able to make rational decisions about anything yet, least of all my daughter. I just don't trust myself,' I said. This was the first time I'd been able to be realistic and honest, instead of my words being motivated by feelings of shame and guilt. For the first time, I didn't worry about how worthless those words might make me appear. I was able to be open about how helpless I felt, without any self-pity. Ron couldn't have known it then, but this was a significant change in thinking for me. Within this relinquishing of responsibility was an acceptance of hope that one day I would feel worthy enough to live, to stand alongside other human beings. Once I could do that, I knew I could again be Ali's mother— not 'need' to be her mother, but just 'be'. I had to find myself first though.

'Yes. That's okay. Whatever makes it better for you,' Ron replied. As if by way of justification, I repeated to him on the phone: 'I just don't feel capable. I feel so worthless. I know I don't deserve such a beautiful daughter.' The guilt had kicked in again.

'You take whatever time it takes to sort yourself out. Ali's being taken care of. You don't have to worry about her, only about getting your life together.'

This gave me some breathing space. I knew I couldn't go on the way I had been, although I still didn't know how to make things different, or what it would feel like. I desperately wanted to be happy. I guess that's every drug addict's goal—eternal happiness.

Ron still wasn't visiting me—aside from being angry about the trouble I'd caused, I don't think he could cope with the twenty-minute non-contact visits—but he followed up our conversation with a long letter. Maybe he'd sensed a shift in my attitude.

Well, I hope things have improved a little for you despite all the restrictions [the only privilege I had left was one fortnightly non-contact visit]. You will be relieved to know that Ali is well and seems to be having a good time this week at Dad's place.

On the subject of our particular problem I still haven't finished expressing my views, however, the purpose of presenting them is not as criticism, but as an objective view for you to consider and, I hope, learn from.

It is not my intention now or when I saw you [the non-contact visit] to make you even more depressed. What you saw was a confused brother desperate to make a contribution that will change your life for the better. Believe me, I do understand how tough it must be, but I have been trying to make you focus on the positives in your life [the number of which I have spent many years trying to increase] and not on the negatives that lead you to your various dependencies. I guess what hurt most about your current reaction to my 'hard line' was that it is the first time I have done that in all the time I've supported you. *Just twenty minutes in how many years of understanding?*

That out of the way I want to give you

some thoughts to consider. My major concern and the root of all these problems, is your need for dependence, not just drugs, but Ali and Vicki. We've discussed before the need to be basically happy with yourself, then children and relationships become a bonus. If you have that inner strength when other things go bad you can go on. You cannot compensate for that lack of self-esteem by filling or trying to fill your life with relationships be they romantic or otherwise.

I suppose the thing that concerns me most right now is Ali's long-term future. You will remember when you asked me in Frank's billiard room at his house when you were pregnant, if you should keep the baby. I said 'no' because your own life was not in order and there was the chance of jail with the court case pending. However, you went ahead and I have supported you all the way despite my prognosis being correct. What long-term effect all this will have on Ali I'm not quite sure. My point is that you have a genuine interest in Ali and you say she gives you so much and that you live for her and the day you both are together again, and that you can make up for all that has happened—that is an admirable goal and one that I hope you can fulfil. However drugs and despite what you may feel, Vicki, have been put before the well-being of this child. I am hopeful that you will focus your attention on her future and how you will secure it rather than your own relationships, be they heterosexual or otherwise.

I hope you don't think this sounds too hard. If Ali means as much as you say (and I believe you), no sacrifice will be too great to ensure her happiness.

What you really have to address is that drugs never fix problems, never overcome depression, they just put them/it off. They never make the future perfect, they don't make you stronger, they make you weaker to face an imperfect future. No-one has a perfect life, but with determination and optimism, you can achieve worthwhile things and have happiness and contentment most of the time. Until you know this is true for you there is no hope.

In your last letter when you said they had taken your piano and education sessions away, but you said you'll practise the guitar and concentrate on music, is a practical example of overcoming obstacles and setting out to achieve a goal.

Probably the last thing is that it occurs to me you may not know what 'the problem' is. In your first letter you start a paragraph by saying, 'I'll try to explain my problem to you. I feel you just don't understand the situation', but you don't explain anything, you go on to talk about other things. You do later talk about your separation from Ali and Vicki, but they are manifestations of your 'problem' not the actual problem which is inside you. That's the one that must be addressed before you can rise above the ups and downs of life.

Looking back over this letter I hope I

haven't confused or criticised. If I have I apol-
ogise. I hope, on the contrary, it provides some
insight, maybe. I can't help much while you're
there but don't lose hope, I haven't.

Please feel free to write but don't feel com-
pelled. If you feel like writing just to make
contact, terrific, but if you only want to write
when you've got something positive to say that's
okay too!

Love,
Ron

I found myself reading this letter over and over in my cell
alone, night after night. For perhaps the first time, I didn't take
it as criticism. I was so desperate to make a change to my life
that the word 'dependence' rang a bell. Until now I had always
thought my dependence on heroin was the problem. I'd always
thought it had some magical power over me, something that was
out of my control, that I could never grab hold of. That was
what it had always felt like, since I'd become addicted anyway.
I always thought that I had some genetic, incessant craving that
other people didn't have. That way of thinking meant I wasn't
to blame but, on the other hand, it also made me feel like I
couldn't do anything about it either. With this proposition of
having a 'dependent' type of personality, I could do something.

In August 1985, a couple of months after I received this
letter from Ron, Narcotics Anonymous meetings commenced at
Fairlea. Held one night a week in the communal area in Yarrabrae, they were run by half a dozen people from outside the
prison. Narcotics Anonymous (NA) is a twelve-step program,
much the same as Alcoholics Anonymous (AA) except that it
targets drug users. Its philosophy is based on the theory that drug

addiction is a disease and therefore NA is an abstinence program, the goal being to abstain from using any drugs, alcohol or other mind-altering substances, as NA calls them. Its membership is made up of people who are trying to overcome drug addiction and it holds meetings all over Australia every day and night of the week. During the meetings, which are chaired by a nominated person, the twelve steps of the program are discussed in detail and people from the audience stand up and tell their personal stories. The 'anonymous' part derives from the fact that you only ever call yourself by your first name. It's an international program, developed initially as AA in the United States.

The people coming into the prison to run the meetings were either ex-drug users or people still trying to become drug free. Like the drama group, it wasn't a program instigated by the Corrections Department as a useful tool for drug-addicted prisoners. Instead, NA had approached the prison as it already held meetings in some of the men's prisons, and AA had also previously held meetings in Fairlea. How the population had changed since then! Our temporary governor, who had come from Pentridge, was happy to allow the meetings.

I decided to give it a go as I needed any help I could get. I attended the first meeting suspicious of them all. I checked their eyes to see if they were 'pinned'—it would have been a dead giveaway that they were using smack—but they weren't. In fact they looked quite healthy. I didn't feel confident enough to speak at the first meeting, but I listened and watched intently.

A week passed and I attended the next meeting, still suspicious. I didn't believe for one minute that they were free of the bind of drug addiction. Again I was too self-conscious to speak, but I kept watching and listening. I wondered why they were doing this, giving up their own time to come and talk to us. I wouldn't have thought we were a very interesting bunch!

After another couple of weeks I realised that I was looking

forward to the Tuesday night NA meetings. The thing that I discovered about these people was that they were real. They were different from the endless Christian groups that came into the prison pushing the 'God' thing in your face. The Christians always seemed to target me—I must have had a face that said 'come and save me'! Maybe I did have that lost, forlorn look. The NA people weren't like that. Instead they talked about everyday difficulties and how the world wasn't so sweet all the time. I liked that—there was an honesty about it because I knew how difficult life could be.

After the group had been going for about a month, the NA people from outside the prison decided it was time for someone inside to take control of the meetings, and they were looking for a chairperson. I immediately put my head down, trying to look insignificant—in fact trying to disappear, knowing that there were only about half a dozen prisoners to choose from. Then I heard one of my friends say my name out loud.

'Shit! Shut up!' I muttered, physically shrivelling in my seat. 'They don't know how self-conscious I am.' I'd barely spoken more than my name so far, although after the meetings were finished I felt comfortable enough to talk casually with our visitors during the five or ten minutes before the officers arrived to escort them out of the prison.

I could feel my face turning bright red as I looked down, fiddling under my chair, trying to hide. Thoughts were racing madly through my head, but I recognised that this was an opportunity, a sort of test that was being placed in front of me. I could run and hide as I'd been doing for years, or I could stand up and take a leadership role. The next moment I did something I hadn't been able to do since I was very young. I looked up, my face still red with embarrassment, and I agreed to take on the position of chairperson. After all, it made sense when I thought about it—I was going to be there for a while! As I kept talking I could feel the flush gradually disappear from my face and I felt ... not comfortable, but at least pleased with myself. In some ways I was fairly well respected by the other prisoners particularly because, when Vicki and I were in there together, we'd been able to get a few things started, like netball and the 'big spend'. But back then I'd had Vicki by my side, and this time I was alone. I also think a lot of the other women respected me purely because I was surviving such a long sentence.

After that night I made myself talk at each meeting. Every time I began to speak I felt myself going bright red with embarrassment, but I just sat with it and allowed it to come and go and, wouldn't you know, after several months I found myself able to speak in front of the group without getting so embarrassed. It was such a major step for me and I felt proud of myself. I came to know and understand these wonderful people who gave up their own time to come into the prison each Tuesday evening, and I started to work through the steps of the program. These meetings were so genuine, honest and open, I found them inspiring. They provided my first insight into the possibility of becoming an ex-heroin addict. I'd never met or heard of anyone who had done that successfully. These people had all struggled to overcome their addiction and were leading fulfilling lives. It opened doorways to a freedom I'd not imagined possible.

Also in August 1985 I received a letter from Pete, one of my old singing friends from TRAMM. It arrived after I'd written to him and his partner, Wayne, telling them of the trouble I'd caused.

> Oh! My darling girl,
>
> What you put yourself through! How on earth do you cope with it all? You obviously have a lot of inner strength that you don't acknowledge. It's

not Ali or Vicki or anyone else, or anything for that matter, it's 'you'. Don't forget that please! Just look back at all the things that you've been through, all the traumas that you've faced. Sure, a lot of them were brought about by the negative side of your personality, but you have far more positives that allow you to survive and come through them all. Work on the positives and the negatives will disappear by themselves. You may think that by going through this second cycle that you haven't learnt anything. If you do you're very wrong, just think how long it took you the first time to get things in the right perspective. Even though you've put yourself back into the same negative situations you're coping with things, this time much faster, and in a much more positive way. Give yourself time, I know you can do it, I've never lost faith in you.

I think you forget that there is a totally different world out here, one that's full of huge 'POSITIVE' charges, people, places, things, they may seem to be far away to you at times, but I can assure you, they are still here and are just waiting to welcome you with open arms. You are obviously able to think in a positive way when you write to me, because you know that I (as in we), David, Wayne, Annie, Jan, all revolve around that world. You can too, you can leave all that behind you as though it was a dream, just as you may think at times we are all a dream. We're not, we are the reality, not what's in there, and not so far from now, you're going to kiss that all goodbye.

Start to prepare yourself. You know what your goals should be, no-one has to tell you that, none of us think you are a loser. You're only a loser if you get to the end and have gained nothing, and I'm here to tell you my petal, you've got a f... ing long time until then. We've got to sit on the front porch in our wheelchairs and sing old TRAMM songs before we get to the end, and I ain't ready for that just yet.

Try to extend yourself away from the environs of the prison and the people that are directly involved with it. Wayne and I have just spent two weeks on the most beautiful tropical island in the pacific called the Isle of Pines. It's a million miles from everywhere, but it's there for us, for you, for anyone. The people are just so beautiful, so warm and loving—it's far better than a thousand 'deals' and the positive feelings last such a long time.

Barny, hang on my friend, you'll make it, there's heaps of love and friendship out here for you, it'll be worth waiting for. You've got so much to give—god, you'll be so f... ing educated we won't be able to talk to you.

The rest of the gang—well, Annie's doing really well and is really happy. David is now working for Myers, he's in women's frocks, would you believe? We all knew that it was only a matter of time (he's really in display, but he just tells people he's in women's frocks to get a laugh, did it work?). He still sings Friday and Saturday nights though. And you know David, it's all getting a bit too much for the old girl! Janelle is still overseas, but should be back soon.

Enough of the waffle. Sorry if I've done the big lecture, but you know me, 'Poppa Pete' everyone calls me. Let me know when I can see you. I'll give you a big hug and everything will be all right. As I said before, we all have faith in you. We know you can do it.

See ya soon pal,
lots of love
Pete and Wayne

Although, by my own choice, I hadn't seen much of my old friends in TRAMM while in jail, we'd always maintained contact through letters. At least I didn't have to be strip searched after receiving letters.

Around this time I also started talking occasionally to the new full-time social worker at the prison. His name was Peter and I felt comfortable with him. In all my years there he was the only social worker with whom I could discuss things like how I felt about myself—that I felt like such a loser, a failure. The others were only ever concerned about things to do with me and Ali. I trusted Peter, although at the time I was unaware that our 'discussions' were probably what most people would call 'counselling'. Having never experienced a counselling relationship with a professional before, I had no idea what it might consist of. Peter enabled me to see how negatively I thought about myself and he'd interrupt me when I automatically put myself down. I'd walk from his office feeling refreshed. It sounds so simple but, although I'd known for a long time that my self-esteem was low, I'd never been conscious of the things I habitually did to keep it there. This new awareness had a profound effect on me.

Peter didn't focus on my drug taking either, unlike the Gres-swell staff during my one rehabilitation effort, and I found my occasional time with him constructive as he challenged my old beliefs. The problem was that he only stayed about a year, which was pretty much the norm for prison social work staff. The social worker's position disappeared and reappeared with monotonous regularity during my years in jail, and we prisoners always wrote to the relevant Minister every time the position was vacated and left unfilled. Prison administrations always seemed to think the position was dispensable, but for those inside it was imperative, even if only to organise things like kids' visits. After Peter left, the position disappeared yet again, but what he provided for me in the twelve months he was there proved invaluable. It's funny how, if you let them, people turn up in your life just when you need them. I didn't yet know how to fix my difficulties, but at least I was beginning to understand what it was that needed fixing. I was finally on a different path.

I still wasn't seeing Ali. She was allowed into the prison once a month on the all-day Saturday visits, but I felt too vulnerable to let her come. I couldn't deal with the goodbyes yet. I didn't know when or how I was ever going to deal with any more goodbyes, actually. All I knew was that I just had to get through each day. That was all I could manage. It sounds selfish, it felt selfish, but that's how it was.

Occasionally I rang Ali, but I even found that extremely difficult emotionally, especially after I'd hung up the phone. The one means of contact I was able to handle was writing to her. Every second or third day I'd send her a card, using cardboard and bits and pieces from the Education Centre's art supply. I'd paste coloured paper and glitter on them or do drawings which were a bit silly—I was hopeless at drawing. I never ceased this form of contact the whole time we were separated. At least she knew I still existed. Because of my job in the sewing room and with the help of a couple of friends, I also began to make clothes for her. I even started knitting jumpers and clothes for her teddy back in my cell at night. It helped me feel closer to her.

A couple of months after the bust, Greg resumed our weekly 'music lesson' at the Education Centre. The regulations allowed every prisoner one session of education per week, so they hadn't been able to take that from me. By September 1985, during the lonely night-time hours in my cell, I'd made a decision that I was bursting to tell Greg.

The next day as he settled himself in his seat I blurted it out: 'I'm not going to have any contact with Vicki.' His face just dropped. I'd done nothing but rave on and on about Vicki for weeks, months, ever since she'd been busted bringing in the heroin for me. In a way my decision was irrelevant as she'd long since stopped contact with me, but emotionally it was important for me to find the courage to break the tie that had bound me to her for so many years. Maud and Greg had taken Vicki into their own home when she first left Ron's house, but after Vicki met up with her ex-girlfriend again the two of them moved on together. I'd heard they were both using heroin. It still hurt and she consumed my thoughts day and night, but psychologically I had to find a way to break free of my dependence on her.

I could see the surprise turn to relief on Greg's face.

'I'm going to let go of it,' I said to him. 'I know I can't start afresh while I'm still clinging on to that relationship.'

He looked totally stunned. I don't think he ever thought I'd get to that point. It was the same juncture Fred and I had reached in our drug-addicted relationship. We needed each other for the wrong reasons, and we knew we couldn't stop using together. As painful as it was, and as much as Greg also loved Vicki, we both knew that she was a lost soul out there at that time. I was a lost soul too, but at least I was straight. There was no telling when or if Vicki would ever make the kind of changes I was struggling so hard to bring about.

From that moment on, my sessions with Greg were filled with talk about Buddhist philosophy. I found our discussions incredibly helpful in assisting me to see alternative, more positive ways of thinking. They opened my mind to all sorts of possibilities, and Greg brought me in books to read about Buddhist ideas. One in particular that made a huge impression on me, *The Last Barrier*, was written by Reshad Field, who is a sufi.

'You're devouring those books,' Greg said to me jokingly one day. I just couldn't get enough. My mind and body were soaking up all this new information and, because I'd deferred my studies, I had plenty of time to read. Greg also taught me to meditate and I set aside time to do it in my cell, both morning and night. Later he organised for someone to come in and teach a few of us Tai Chi. I attended these classes, which were held once a week after work in the afternoon, and found them particularly useful. I practised Tai Chi every morning before my meditation. At least at those times my mind was focused on something other than Ali or Vicki. I started to realise there were many more aspects to life, and to my own personality, than I'd ever imagined. I felt a twinge of enthusiasm and enormous determination. I started to realise that even if someone put me at the foot of a mountain with no equipment, I'd find a way of making it to the top.

Ever so gradually I began utilising the knowledge I'd gleaned from Greg's teachings, putting it into practice instead of just letting it in intellectually. I didn't feel so abandoned. I didn't know it yet, but I wasn't a victim any more.

In September 1985, while I was experiencing this personal revolution, another woman who was musical was sent to Fairlea on a short sentence. There were some officers who had come to know me quite well over the five years I'd been inside, and who had a great deal of compassion for me, maybe even respect. A couple of them encouraged me to introduce myself to the new arrival, knowing I hadn't played any music since Vicki's departure, my voice silenced by my pain. I hadn't been very interested, particularly in meeting someone who was only in jail for a few weeks until, approaching Yarrabrae one day after finishing work in the sewing room, I heard this fabulous voice booming through the bars in the gate. I walked in and looked around to see where the beautiful sound was coming from. My eyes came to rest on a young woman playing guitar, a small crowd of women prisoners gathered around her.

'Helen,' some of them yelled when they saw me, 'come and meet Nina. You two should do some singing together.' I walked over, shy but happy to meet someone who was also musical.

'Sing a song for Nina so that she can hear you,' they said.

'Yeah, please sing something?' asked Nina, handing me her guitar.

'No, I couldn't. Haven't played any music for a while,' I replied, retreating from her guitar like it was going to bite me. 'You sing something else—it sounded great as I was coming into Yarrabrae.'

'Okay,' she replied, happy to continue singing. She was very confident and had a fabulous voice, so I felt quite excited to meet her.

'Why don't we do some music together some time?' she asked me when she'd finished another song.

'Oh, I don't know,' I replied. 'Don't know if I could just now.'

'Oh, come on,' she urged me. 'Come over to my unit tomorrow afternoon and we can have a jam.' She was so enthusiastic I couldn't bring myself to say no.

'Okay,' I finally replied, 'I guess I'm not doing anything else, hey? I'll bring my music books with me and see what happens.

See you then.' Secretly I was a bit excited, but I also felt apprehensive because I hadn't been able to do any singing since Vicki's departure—the pain was too close to the surface and I had felt too raw.

'Come on, Helen,' Nina called out to me when she saw me across the other side of the netball court the following afternoon after work. She was such a bundle of energy, which was nice to be around after my depressed state. I couldn't help but get caught up in her enthusiasm.

'Okay, I'm coming, I'll just get my books,' I called out.

As we sat around the piano in Yarrabrae, Nina with her guitar, we found a few songs that we both knew and, after a tentative start, I couldn't help but loosen up a bit. Although I still didn't have my piano, the one that used to be in Wing 1 was now located in the communal area of Yarrabrae. I was hoping that some time in the future, when we got a permanent governor, I could put in a request for my piano to be returned to the prison. Nina and I sang some more then broke into harmonies, both of us smiling. It sounded good and when we'd finished the song we both burst into laughter.

'Wow!' Nina said with glee. She was having a ball and I hadn't enjoyed myself like that in a long, long time. It was reassuring to know that I could play and sing with someone other than Vicki. It was a big step for me.

After a week or so, Nina and I were spending all our spare time together, playing and singing, and I'd come to life again. I could feel joy in my heart. Because our spare time only consisted of an hour after work before lock-up, Greg persuaded prison management to allow Nina to spend some of her out of work time at the Education Centre. He said we were working on a project to record some songs. We did, of course, but Greg's main motivation was to try to give us more opportunity to explore music together. (Good on you, Greg!) Education staff were totally supportive and must have been happy to see me smile again.

Nina and I shared several hours together a couple of evenings a week with Greg, which also gave us some privacy, and I felt energised again. We challenged each other musically, so it was exciting and fun! Nina was a particularly talented guitarist/singer/songwriter and, in that illusory world, we soon became attracted to each other, something we both acknowledged after the first week. But what could we do in the six weeks she was going to be in Fairlea? Becoming involved would only cause more emotional upheaval and, besides, she already had a girlfriend. We accepted this, so nothing happened between us sexually, but we wrote some beautiful songs and sang them to each other. It was an important interaction for me, because it allowed my heart to open again and made me realise I could find love with someone other than Vicki. It was nice to feel warm inside, even if it was only for a short time. I didn't kid myself that I'd be seeing her again after her release, or that anything could eventuate between us. She was talking about future possibilities, but I wouldn't open my heart to that—I knew better.

We organised a couple of 'concerts' for the women and enjoyed this musical time together. The women enjoyed it too. A couple of times leading up to our performances we even managed to gain permission to remain at the Education Centre several evenings to rehearse. The officers locked us in there together until it was time for them to come and retrieve us ... how romantic! At night, when we had to be separated, we wrote each other amorous letters:

> Fuckin' hell ... why is life so complicated? Why is love so complicated? It's now 9 pm and I'm sitting in my room. I've been playing the guitar all night and trying to complete the song I

commenced last night. It's about you. I don't know what this is that I feel for you Nina, but I know I can't get you out of my mind. I also know that it shouldn't be. I was so determined not to allow myself to feel anything for you, but what is happening? And I mean to say, it's such a ridiculous situation ... I've known you just over a week and will probably know you for another four weeks, then you'll be gone and besides that, you're already taken anyway! That's what I call an impossible situation!

Oh well ... at least you've made me feel again. I had turned into a lump of stone until you came along. I at least am now aware that it is still possible for me to feel. Vicki left me feeling empty and cold. I was like a walking corpse here for quite a while.

I love doing our music together. I wish we could do it all day and all night. I feel so happy and fulfilled at the moment. I only feel sad when it gets to 4 o'clock in the afternoons and I have to leave you. Still, I can wish all I like ... what can't be, just can't be.

Maybe I'll sing the new song for you tomorrow. I'll get so embarrassed ... Still, it's what I feel—I guess it doesn't hurt if you know.

Goodnight,
Helen xx

Nina had stirred up some passion inside me which was nice to feel, but soon she was gone. I missed her, especially the opportunity she provided for me to play and sing with someone.

But that was the problem with getting close to anyone in there—I'd lost count of how many I'd had to say goodbye to. I started to realise I didn't want to find love in jail again. It was too hard.

A few months after Nina was released Greg encouraged Annie, another new prisoner, to come to the Education Centre to share my one music session. Annie was also a classically trained musician and could play cello and piano. We became close, both musically and personally. Annie was also a heroin addict, and we talked about drug use. She was interested in the fact that I'd stopped using and eventually she decided to attend the NA meetings. She was at the beginning of the road in terms of rehabilitation, though, and as soon as I felt the pull of dependence, I distanced myself. It was very difficult because everyone was so needy in there and we received virtually no support from the system.

About the same time Tammy, who had shared the Yarrabrae unit with Vicki and me just before Ali left the prison, came back in on another charge, about twelve months after her release. She was living in one of the cottages with two of her step-sisters. Sometimes she'd visit me in the afternoons before lock-up, and she couldn't believe how different I was. We'd spend a lot of time talking about how I'd changed my thinking, and how I no longer craved a hit of smack. She was hungry for information and I was happy to talk about drugs as much as she wanted, because I was as fascinated as her by how much I'd changed—after all, she'd lived with us when my using was at its most desperate. Most of our time then was taken up in devising ways to sneak heroin into the prison, the only real break from that being our netball activities.

Tammy became interested in attending the NA group on Tuesday evenings. Initially she convinced her step-sisters, who were also addicts, to come too, but they were pretty disruptive and soon dropped out. They just weren't ready to make the change. Tammy continued, however, and for the first time she'd talk to me about being able to say 'no' when all the others in her cottage had some heroin. She felt proud of herself. I guess, through watching the change in me, she felt she could also take control of her drug addiction.

I received a few letters from Nina after her release, but it wasn't long before contact ceased and I never heard from her again. I heard via the grapevine, though, that she had returned to the streets, prostitution and heroin use.

I can only describe the rest of 1985 as a 'slog', but I survived. Christmas approached, my seventh in jail. It was a time of wanting to go to sleep to forget. I'd spent the previous six Christmases getting stoned. It was going to be different this year. I felt so different. I still just wanted to get it over with, but I didn't want to be stoned. I was astonished as I acknowledged this. I wasn't very happy, but as long as people left me alone and let me be, I was okay.

That Christmas Day started badly because I couldn't manage to contact Ron and Ali when I rang at 8 am. They weren't at Ron's place or at Astrid's (Ron's girlfriend), so I didn't know where they were. That was the only chance I would have to talk to Ali on the phone for about four weeks as she was going to New South Wales to my dad's place for the holidays. He and I weren't talking, so I wasn't allowed to ring there. I didn't know what time she and Ron had left to drive there. Damn it—I'd missed her.

I returned to the unit, cleaned up and did my exercises as per usual, then Jenny (another Yarrabrae prisoner) came over rather agitated, so I sat with her for a while and talked. She had played on the netball team and also attended the NA group, so we knew each other quite intimately given that we talked so much about our feelings at the meetings. Instead of taking her anger out on others like Rikki had, Jenny internalised it and repeatedly self-injured. The officers had come to know her well over the years of her coming in and out of Fairlea, so they were quite prepared when she started showing signs of unrest, like verbally abusing them. Sometimes they'd search her for razors or other sharp instruments before locking her into a bare cell in an effort to prevent her self-mutilating. This was a major problem among women prisoners and I had lost count of how many times during my sentence different women had slashed at their skin, usually their wrists, with razors, not in an effort to suicide, just to relieve their torment for a moment. It may sound insensitive, but I had grown accustomed to it—it was a normal part of life in there.

After chatting to Jenny for a while it was muster time, and time to go to Yarrabrae for our compulsory Christmas lunch! It was nice, really—it was the only time we were served roast chicken—even though I didn't want to be there. I returned to the peace and quiet of my cell and read a book for most of the afternoon. I was still reading at about 10 pm when Mr Marshall, the officer on night duty, came to the unit asking me to accompany him to Jenny's cell. She had 'slashed up' once again. I followed him over there and was shocked to find blood splattered over the walls of her cell bathroom, a deep pool of red at Jenny's feet, her exposed arms and the upper part of her legs covered in razor slashes. As I walked in she looked up at me, still crying. Her anger had turned to sadness, the crisis over.

'I feel better now,' she said with relief. Her anguish and torment had been released once more. The officer and I stayed talking with her for a couple of hours. I was so glad that he had called me over. Mr Marshall had worked at Fairlea pretty much the whole time I'd been there and I think he sort of respected me. He knew I'd become like a mentor to Jenny, although it was unusual for officers to ask prisoners for help. After a while a medical staff member arrived to dress her wounds. She was okay, so I was returned to my cell where I went to bed. And that was the end of Christmas Day 1985.

I was relieved it was over. I guess Jenny was too. It was my first Christmas in prison since Vicki had left so, all things considered, it hadn't been too bad. In fact I thought I'd done rather well, although I'd been thinking of her on and off all day. One thing I was very pleased about was that not once all day had I wanted to block out my feelings with drugs. I thought about how, almost every other Christmas in there, we'd tried so desperately to sneak in some smack, or at the very least had a home brew going. For at least the past two or three years, we'd succeeded in being 'out of it' for a few days at Christmas time. I discovered that I no longer wanted to do that. I didn't want to waste any more of my life in that state.

Oh well, goodbye Christmas 1985. Only two more to go.

18

A new attitude,
a new life

January 1986 came—two years since Ali had gone—and I prepared for my return to study. I had to reapply to the Classification Committee for education sessions, but I felt that things were beginning to go my way for a change. I was trying hard and, with Greg's help, I was finding a way to believe in myself. There was no turning back now. The only place I could turn to was death, and I didn't want that. I've never wanted anything so much in all my life, either before or since—just a sense of peace and contentment. I knew that if I could discover it in this environment, I'd have no trouble outside. Nothing was going to get in my way, and for the first time in many years I awoke with energy and enthusiasm, without drugs. Somewhere deep inside a new feeling resided, a sort of confidence, and it began to dawn on me that drugs were no longer an issue in my life. Of course the prison authorities weren't aware of the huge change happening inside me, but I trusted that things would work out.

I didn't even have to deal with Smith any more. With the new year came our new governor, Mr Herron, who turned out to be one of the most compassionate men I'd ever come across in the prison system. He was so nice that I couldn't understand how he remained working for Corrections, but I was eternally

398

grateful that he'd come to Fairlea. I remember his first day as our new governor. It was lunchtime and about fifty of us were hanging around in Yarrabrae chatting. When Mr Herron entered the building we automatically interrupted our conversations and dutifully stood up. He looked shocked, then slightly embarrassed, obviously unused to prisoners being so diligently trained to stand at the mere presence of a governor.

He waved his arm, signalling for us to sit down. 'You don't have to stand up,' he said, 'just continue on with whatever you were doing.'

It was our turn to be shocked. I was thinking it might be some nasty trick, but his presence was so relaxed that I felt the permanent, tight knot which had grown inside my stomach under Smith's rule physically loosen. But could we trust him? After Smith, nothing would have surprised me. Mr Herron had kind eyes and we came to learn that his expectations about our behaviour were realistic. What a relief.

Only weeks after his arrival, some of the women escaped during the night. When I found out about it the next morning the anxiety automatically built inside me. Under Smith this would have meant that we'd all be punished and lose any privileges we might have gained, like netball for instance. As we moved through the following day, though, nothing happened to the rest of us. We just went off to work as normal. Later in the day I saw Mr Herron in the grounds. He was smiling! I was incredulous.

'How come you're smiling?' I asked him, half-joking, half-serious. 'Four women have just escaped!'

His reply, along the lines of, 'Well, you have to expect that sort of thing when you lock people up', indicated that it was more of a problem for me than him. As I walked away from his smiling face, too shocked to continue the conversation, I almost felt like I was going to faint. I was unable to grasp how calm he was. Finally, a smile found its way across my own face—I felt like celebrating. Welcome to Fairlea, Mr Herron! Many years later my respect for that man remains. His positive, humane and realistic attitude was refreshing. He made my last couple of years in jail almost enjoyable! Well, perhaps not quite ...

By 1986 quite a bit of rebuilding had already taken place at Fairlea, but also the number of women in jail in Victoria had almost doubled since I'd first arrived—the population was now consistently between ninety and a hundred. B Annexe in Pentridge remained a reception prison as well as accommodating women who were classified as 'management problems'. About thirty women were kept in B Annexe and about sixty in Fairlea. As well as Yarrabrae, Fairlea now had about nine four-bedroom cottages, plus the old Cottages 1 and 2. The three old cottages near the front wall of the prison, one of which Vicki and I had lived in, had been removed by Smith. They were considered unsuccessful partly because two women had to share a bedroom, but also because their proximity to the front wall became a problem. A new administration block, visit centre and medical centre were also added, all the old buildings being demolished to make way for them.

Like the new cottages, the new visit centre was a portable building. It consisted of two rooms, one for contact visits and the other—mostly used for drug users who'd been caught—for non-contact visits. The contact room had windows down the length of one side and on the adjacent side were two small rooms, one a professional visit room where inmates saw lawyers, police or the welfare/social worker (when there was one), the other a small toilet block. The building was rectangular in shape and had about fifteen small, square tables in it, one prisoner and her visitors per table. Prison officers sat in one corner, occasionally walking around the tables during visits. Running down the middle of the smaller, non-contact visit room was a wall made of glass from waist level up and wood on the bottom half. The room was divided into four cubicles, each one containing a bench. You could see your visitors through the glass and you could hear each other through a gauze-covered opening where the glass met the wooden bottom half of the cubicle. Although there was no privacy because you had to talk loudly to be heard, some women still chose non-contact visits, even when they weren't on punishment, to avoid the strip search afterwards. This was a new style of visit centre, designed mainly to overcome the problem of drug exchanges during visits. It had replaced the old 'drug table' non-contact visits where prisoners and visitors were merely separated by the table. I didn't use the visit centre that often, preferring to only occasionally have a visit with Ron or Elizabeth.

I applied for and was granted full-time education again. I took on an extra subject deciding that, if I found it too much, I would drop it during first semester. Without the burden of scoring and trying to sneak drugs into the prison, I knew I was going to have a lot more time and energy on my hands, and I felt capable of keeping up with the added workload. I wanted to keep busy. I wanted the time until my release, when I could be reunited with Ali, to pass quickly, but I also knew this was an important stage in my own personal growth.

I'd just turned thirty-two—my seventh birthday in there. The previous two and a half years had been the longest, most painful period in my life, but I was feeling positive now, like a huge load had been lifted. I was physically fit and healthy, and my need to use drugs, along with the debilitating craving, had left my body. I couldn't even begin to describe the sense of freedom that gave me. It was beyond external things like the prison walls and being mustered and locked in—being released from those things would provide another kind of freedom. Being drug-free was a freedom inside myself, and I became so involved in my own evolution that those external things almost disappeared from my consciousness for a time. After all, I was well and truly institutionalised by now.

During early 1986, not long after Mr Herron's arrival, I was asked to move into one of the new cottages. The idea with the new self-contained accommodation was that we do our own washing and cooking, learning some life skills. This time I was quite keen, particularly as I wouldn't have to share a room, so Cottage 6 became my new home. It was nice to be somewhere in the prison that hadn't been lived in before. There was no previous emotional pain associated with the bedroom, which *was* a bedroom rather than the cell I'd grown so accustomed to. Along with the Education Centre, it became my haven for the remainder of my sentence. At 4.30 pm we were locked into the cottage as we had been in Yarrabrae, but we weren't locked into our individual bedrooms, instead remaining free to move around within the cottage during the night. The only downside was that, because of the freedom we had within the cottage, the officers came to check us on the hour, every hour, during the night— but, hey, that's prison for you!

I wanted to cleanse my room with rose-water before I moved my things in. I'd read that rose-water cleans out negative energies, but I didn't have access to anything like that, so I cleansed the walls anyway with water and disinfectant and performed my own ritual, setting up the room as my special space. There'd be no drug using in this room. With that gone from my life, so did the need to tell lies. It felt like an honest, clear room and through my meditation I filled the space with the energy of love and compassion. The chaos had left my body and it felt good there. The fear of using had disappeared from my life and, except for my separation from Ali, my heart felt free.

One thing I knew for certain now: Ali and I would share a very happy life together if I never used heroin again. So simple, and yet it had taken me all these years to finally admit it. I still had moments of weakness and loneliness, a day here and there when I longed to have somebody hold me in their arms and love me. Just the comfort and warmth of somebody close, somebody to love in that very special way. Vicki had once been that person for me. She still consumed my thoughts, but at least the hurt and anger were fading and being replaced by something else. I had loved her so much when we were first together, but all that had changed. With a bit of distance I could see how much our love had enabled us to survive in there, particularly the agonising two years when Smith had been governor. With all the difficulties we'd gone through, I still hoped that eventually our love would endure. I did still love her, but in a different way. I felt in control and, although I sometimes wanted her close to me, I didn't *have* to have her. There was no doubt there was unfinished business where our relationship was concerned. Perhaps in the near future we'd have a chance to resolve it, as she still had her court case outstanding and most probably would have to return to jail.

At the mid-year exams I achieved better results than ever, even with my added workload. I was very pleased with myself. I started to believe that I could achieve anything I wanted if I stayed focused and worked hard—not that I'd ever had any trouble with schoolwork or study, but it was different now. I was starting to believe that I was an intelligent human being. People had always told me that, particularly Ron, but I never accepted it. There's a certain responsibility that goes with being successful or intelligent. I'd never felt like taking that on before. The knowledge that I'd have to maintain success if I achieved it always seemed too much of a burden. But now I was enjoying my success, and I felt proud.

I was glad that Ron could now feel proud too, although I realised he must have been waiting for the inevitable collapse. I actually knew inside that it wasn't going to happen again—I knew I'd finished with heroin. Although I was aware that Ron wouldn't be able to share my confidence, he gave no hint that he doubted me. He became totally supportive again:

> Dear Helen,
>
> It's great to get your letters now, there is so much determination yet at the same time a willingness to face up to the problems and identify the real issues.
>
> I agree that you must put yourself first until you are entirely convinced that you have it all together—then you will be able to do the best thing for Ali *and* yourself long term.
>
> I can't tell you how happy I am that you have developed so much and continue to do so. To hear you so happy today was an added bonus. You must remember however that your life can't revolve around making other people happy—it must be for you. The only way you can repay me is to be happy and successful at whatever you do in the future.
>
> At least we have everything in order at home. Elva [the new nanny/housekeeper] is great, Ali is developing well and I have adapted to the situation well looking back over the last 18 months.
>
> Well it's just a short note so I'll finish now.
>
> Love
> Ron

I continued in my role as chairperson of Fairlea Narcotics Anonymous, and a few of the inmates who attended regularly, like Jenny and me, decided to increase the number of meetings to twice a week. We asked permission to use the Education Centre for a second meeting each Saturday morning. We knew the outside people from NA wouldn't be allowed into the prison for this meeting, not twice a week, but that didn't bother us— we just felt the need for a second meeting each week where we could talk honestly about how we were feeling, particularly in relation to drugs. Of course, as with anything I did, I took on my role with total commitment and I was quite obsessive about it.

Around this time I also approached Mr Herron to see if I could get my piano back into the prison. Living in the cottage I thought it would be easy to move it into the lounge-room area. I'd already checked with the women I shared the space with and they were enthusiastic. I didn't think I'd be moving anywhere else in the prison before my release because I no longer did anything that I needed to be punished for—that is, use drugs. Mr Herron responded favourably and once again poor Ron had to hire a trailer to transport it to the jail. I promised him it would be the last time.

I also became obsessive about my daily exercise. I'd decided fitness was important to me as it made me feel better, more alive and alert, and it was one of the few things I could do for myself in there. I cared about myself now. Each new cottage had an exercise bike and, after getting myself up at 5.15 am every day, I'd ride twenty kilometres, rain, hail or shine—it didn't matter on an exercise bike. It would take me until 6 am. After that, I'd have a shower, practise Tai Chi for half an hour, then meditate for another half-hour. By the time I'd finished and was ready for breakfast, the officers had been around and woken everyone. I'd decided that I was never going to allow the officers to wake me up again. It was one small way in which I could take control of my life.

As well as riding the bike, I played tennis for an hour at lunchtimes and had netball training several nights a week. The tennis court was the same court as the one used for netball; it had always been there, but I'd never used it for tennis before. For a while I played with Stella, who had completed two sentences while I had been in jail, but after she left I played with the new 'activities officer'. I was aware of my obsessive personality, but it didn't bother me because I was now using it in a positive way. I was totally self-obsessed, but I felt like I had to be to overcome my difficulties. I was determined to find a way of living that provided me with a sense of peace inside.

My dear friend Greg had taught me an exercise to do when I was meditating to help me feel closer to Ali. I'd close my eyes and focus on my breathing, then I'd concentrate my energy on the heart area, filling it with love. I'd imagine Ali at home or in bed or wherever, and I'd send that love in my heart to her, enclosing her in it. It really felt like I was actually doing it, and I'd imagine she could feel herself being enveloped in my love. It helped me feel like I was protecting her in some way and also made me feel close to her. I believed that somewhere out there in the atmosphere our hearts met and joined together, and as her mother it allowed me an avenue through which to love her. This was a very important exercise in enabling me to cope with the time ahead, and to deal with her physical absence from my life.

Although I still had problems dealing with goodbyes, early in 1986 Ali had resumed the all-day Saturday visits, and we'd play and laugh together. We ran around, talked about her life outside, and would sometimes visit other women, such as Rikki, who she still remembered and who, like Stella, had returned to serve another sentence. Those days were filled with joy, but of course they always finished too quickly and I wasn't much better at coping when she had to leave. She adjusted to it better than me. I'd walk down to that rotten front gate with her and smile as I waved goodbye. Then I'd make the familiar walk back to the cottage, the ache in my heart still unbearable, but I didn't feel broken any more, and I didn't use heroin to deal with (or not deal with) what I was feeling.

The women with whom I shared the cottage knew not to speak to me at those times. Each time Ali left I'd walk straight into my room and lie on the bed, playing loud music through headphones. I'd lie there wishing I could ease the pain, but I didn't even contemplate heroin as an alternative any more. I'd allow the pain to reside in my body and gradually, over a couple of hours, it would ease. By evening I was usually able to make my way into the lounge room where I'd be comforted by the presence of the other women. I never wanted to say much, and certainly not about Ali, but as I sat there listening and occasionally joining in, the ache in my heart and body would dissipate and I'd feel more relaxed as the night progressed. By the next morning I was okay again—I'd wake early to jump on the exercise bike and embark on my ride.

For a while my old friend Rikki lived in the cottage next door. I didn't hang around with her much any more, even though we'd known each other since I was seventeen. She was in a different head space to me and I was at Education most of the time anyway. She was in a relationship with Jodi, who lived in the cottage with her, but neither of them was finished with heroin. Although we still respected and loved each other dearly, it was difficult to be close when we no longer had much in common. Even at weekends when there were no teachers at the Education Centre, I'd been granted permission to spend time there. This was one of the privileges that long-termers could sometimes wangle, because staff got to know you so well and could assess your 'risk' status.

Weekends tended to be times when drugs were used most

in the jail, and I found it easier to be in a space by myself. It was also a very peaceful place as I was the only one there. The officers would let me into the Centre in the morning, locking me in as they left. I would spend the whole day there, emerging only for the lunchtime muster and 4.30 pm lock-up. I'd study, and write and play music on the piano, singing along. I'd been in prison so long by then that I was sort of trusted. It probably helped that Mr Herron was governor and was willing to give me a go. The longer I'd been in prison, the more I seemed to keep to myself, particularly now that I wasn't interested in drug use.

With up to eighty per cent of the prison population having experienced sexual and/or physical abuse during their childhood, there was always an inordinate amount of repressed anger sitting just below the surface of most of the women. There were several ways it would be expressed. One was self-mutilation, or 'slashing up' as the officers had come to call it. They would make jokes about it, saying that women who slashed up were 'attention seekers'. Because we had buzzers in our cells in case of emergencies after we were locked in, some women would slash their wrists during the night and then 'buzz up' for the officers. Like I said earlier, they hadn't wanted to die, they just wanted to relieve the torment a little.

Another pathological behaviour that developed for a lot of women once they were in jail without their drugs was anorexia and/or bulimia. Throughout the eighties, the incidence of eating disorders had increased dramatically. When I first went to jail, no-one had heard of them; by the time I left, many women were suffering from them. A lot of women became emaciated while in prison, while others put on extreme amounts of weight.

The other expression of inner rage was verbal and physical violence. Incidents of physical violence occurred at least a couple of times a week. Miraculously, I was never involved, although earlier in my sentence I'd certainly mouthed off a bit, but only when I thought an officer was being unfair, which was often! Over the years I learned to ignore it. Some women fought the prison system all the way, becoming angrier and angrier. Too often they turned their anger on each other.

As I was sitting in my cottage one afternoon I heard loud banging and screaming from next door. I recognised Rikki's voice yelling abuse at someone, so I ran outside to find a small crowd of women gathered near her cottage. They were keeping their distance because Rikki was pretty worked up and a lot of them were intimidated by her. A couple of officers, also keeping their distance, were doing their best to pacify her before the situation got any worse. Rikki was directing her rage towards the cottage, and as I looked in I could see Jodi screaming back in response. Suddenly Rikki grabbed a chair and hurled it at the cottage, breaking a window. Jodi stood at the sliding glass front door brandishing a knife, threatening Rikki. My heart skipped a beat. I knew this would incite Rikki to up the ante. It looked like turning very nasty.

An officer ran over to me. 'Can you talk to Rikki?' she pleaded.

'I'll see what I can do, but I don't think she'll even hear me,' I replied. 'I'm definitely not getting too close while there's a knife, and chairs are being thrown around!'

Another officer was trying to calm Rikki down, with no success at all. She was in a towering rage and there seemed to be no turning back.

'Fuck off!' she warned them. 'Fuck off out of here! Don't come near me, you scum in that uniform!' she threatened. If they knew what was good for them, they'd back off for a bit. I stood a few metres away and watched Jodi begin to move backwards, into their cottage.

Rikki paused to grab another chair, so I took a chance and called out to her, 'Hey, Rikki!'

'Go away! Leave me alone!' she yelled back.

'Rikki! Put the chair down. Come over here!' I tried again. 'Don't throw the chair! Come here and talk to me! Come on!' She threw the chair, but fortunately not hard enough to break any more windows.

Nothing happened for a short time. It seemed like Jodi was taking the chance to back right off. Maybe she'd realised it had gone too far already. She retreated further into the cottage. I couldn't see the knife in her hand any more and there were a couple of other women inside the cottage with her.

'Come out here, you weak bastard!' Rikki shouted. 'Come out here with that knife in your hand and show me how you can use it!' she said threateningly. 'Come on, come out here and use it! Show me what a hero you are!'

This stand-off went on for perhaps another ten minutes. The officers were panicky, but at least they'd backed off. They knew if they moved any closer, Rikki's anger would escalate.

I tried again. 'Rikki, come here! Come on, it's Barny,' I called out to her.

I was about to give up when all of a sudden her body released its tension and you could see her physically crumple. She hesitated, then walked over towards me.

'Come in here,' I said as I walked her into my cottage out of everyone's view. She broke down, sobbing uncontrollably, the storm over.

'Barny, hold me.' After a few minutes she collapsed into a chair, still shaking and crying. I knelt on the floor and wrapped my arms around her while she rested her head on my shoulder, her body heaving as she gasped for breath between sobs. She stayed there crying for a long time, but gradually her body became still. She lifted her head and looked at me through her beautiful, sad eyes. She looked so innocent, yet so tormented.

The officers came in to see what was happening. 'She's okay.

Just leave us alone for a while,' I said to them. Fortunately they were a couple of the compassionate ones, so they left.

Rikki had so much anger inside I wondered if she'd ever be free of it. It controlled her life. She had been sexually and physically abused as a child and she still carried the hurt, grown now into a big, ugly monster which kept erupting inside her. She used violence, verbal abuse and self-destruction to overcome that monster. From the age of about thirteen she'd also used heroin to win these battles, and it usually kept her calm for a while. She was only a year older than me and I'd known her for about sixteen years, so at least she trusted me and felt safe.

That afternoon she stayed with me in the cottage until lock-up. She was still upset later that night so Chris, one of the few officers who allowed us to use her first name, stayed with Rikki, sitting on the end of her bed and talking to her for hours. Rikki was too frightened to be on her own and Chris was about the only officer she'd talk to. Thank goodness Fairlea had a couple of officers who were compassionate and who understood. Thank goodness Smith was gone too. Usually you'd be taken straight to 'lock-up', the management unit, after an incident like this, and often you'd be put into a straightjacket as well. It was an unusual reprieve, no doubt because Chris was in charge that day.

The evening before Rikki exploded, Julie, a young woman living in Yarrabrae, had almost killed herself. After lock-up in her cell she had cut her throat and arm so badly, it was only by luck that she was found in time to be saved. I didn't know Julie from the outside—she was in the next generation of heroin users, younger than Rikki and me—but since meeting her in jail I'd grown to care for her. She was a very sweet girl. There was so much violence in there sometimes, it seemed to come in waves. I tried to stay clear of it, but the anguish women felt inside oozed out all over the place in all sorts of ways. Sometimes, like with Julie and Jenny, they'd turn it inwards on themselves; other times, like with Rikki, it would be expressed in external rage. I had a real aversion to violence, yet in there I was forced to witness so much pain, so much senseless anger wrongly directed.

Not long after this incident, Rikki was released and returned to the outside world. Given that she'd received no counselling or viable alternatives since coming to prison, it was more than likely that she'd continue using heroin. Until such time as she stumbled across some assistance to help her get her life back together, I couldn't see it changing for her. I just hoped like hell she didn't overdose along the way. She was such a beautiful person, although most people only saw the hardened exterior that she presented to the world, and it was easier to be a monster in a world where innocent children weren't always protected. I was one of the lucky few who had witnessed her gentle soul.

Not long after Rikki's release she met and formed a relationship with a woman who had three children. She worked in parlours to support her family, but she wasn't a heroin addict. Rikki seemed to settle for a while, her heroin use under control. Because she was stable she wrote quite often. I was pleased she seemed to be handling life better and I found her letters touching:

Dearest Barny,

Hi once again sweet lady, as always you're in my heart. I hope you are well, happy and coping okay in there. You seem to be picking up the pieces and putting them back together in a different puzzle, good on ya' old girl!

I have to go to court again soon, maybe next week, and my solicitor is going to ask for a heavy fine and an attendance centre order. I've got buckley's and none I suppose, but worth a try. I hate prison and what it stands for so much,

the fucking depressing, hellhole it is. It's dead
set the pits! It makes me so cold and empty and
so much full of hate and I don't like being like
that. Or feeling like it either as it takes so long
to get out of my system. But anyway, I'll get by
being the little fighter that I am. They can't
keep us good women down, hey?

Anyway, over the page I've done a special
picture for you with a few words with a lot of
meaning. Unfortunately it's not one of my orig-
inals, being the talented person that I am! Ha!
When I read it today it strongly made me think
of you and myself also, so I wanted to share it
with you. I want you to pin it up somewhere
in your room and look and read it every
morning when you get up, okay, and understand what its meaning is.

Say 'hello' to Ali for me when you see her
again. Keep smiling my dear friend and I'll
always be here or there for you if you ever need
me, and always remember, you're always in my
heart and thoughts, so good night and sweet
dreams.

I miss you,
all my love
Rikki xxxxxx

Around the middle of 1986, I was surprised to hear the loudspeaker request my presence at the visit centre. I wasn't expecting
anyone and I'd been keeping out of the limelight and out of
trouble. I got up from my desk at the Education Centre thinking
they'd made a mistake, but then I heard it again: 'Helen Barnacle

to the visit centre!' I was vaguely aware that a Classification Committee meeting was taking place there that day because I'd already heard them call a number of women, but I hadn't made any requests for changes to my status, such as my security rating or temporary day leaves—I was still feeling too vulnerable, too fragile, for that. I was really just trying to reconstruct myself as a human being and find out how to live life as a non-drug user. I hadn't given any thought to anything beyond getting through each day.

Marg, one of the teachers, checked to see if I'd heard the announcement and walked to the door with me.

'What could they want?' I asked her. I had to admit I was a bit nervous. I just wanted to complete my sentence without drawing any attention to myself. I was sick of making the headlines, first with our trial, then about Ali being able to live in prison with me.

'Don't know,' Marg replied. 'Go and see and you can come back here and talk about it if you want.' That's what I liked about the Education Centre staff: they did far more than simply teach, and they were always there if you needed someone to talk to. They also understood how intimidating we prisoners found the system.

When I arrived at the visit centre, the officer let me into the little foyer section. 'Take a seat,' she said, pointing to a chair. I was expected to wait while they discussed 'me' in the room. I'd always hated the way they discussed you in your absence. You'd think it'd make you feel important, all those people talking about you, but it didn't—it made you face up to the fact that they had total control over your life.

After about five minutes, I was led into the main area of the visit centre where the Classification Committee—comprising people from the Corrections Department head office, senior prison staff, Education Centre staff and welfare personnel—sat in a semicircle behind a row of tables joined together. They were positioned down the far end of the room, and there was always something between yourself and them, always some obstacle to negotiate. It was also a bit of a walk, so they were able to watch you for a while before you made it to the seat placed in the middle of the half circle, slightly in front of them. It always made me feel like I was about to be interrogated. It was as though they thought that, if they didn't keep that necessary distance from you, they might catch something—like being a criminal was some sort of infectious disease.

This time I was pleased to see Mr Herron among them, with his usual calm smile. He opened up the discussion: 'We've noted that it's some time since you applied to go out on temporary day leave and we're wondering if you had any plans to apply?'

Well, I'll be ..., I thought to myself. Surely they're not asking me to apply!

'No, I don't have any plans for requesting day leave at the moment,' I responded. I wasn't nervous because for once I wasn't asking for something they could say no to. In any case, I still didn't feel up to day leaves, after all the trauma of the past year or two.

The main person from head office was next to have his say. After a few minutes of reminding me of my past behaviour, like I'd forgotten or something, he said: 'We're a bit concerned that you haven't requested any temporary leave as you're heading into the last third of your sentence and it's important for you to experience time outside the prison. More particularly, it's important for you to spend time with your daughter in her home environment.'

I was speechless, especially since Smith had told me not to bother applying as I'd never receive another temporary leave for the rest of my sentence. I knew they were talking good sense, but it was a bit beyond me at that stage. 'I'll have a think about it,' I replied, too astounded to say any more.

'Okay, you can go now,' Mr Herron said. I got up and walked towards the door feeling relieved to get out of there. It's a peculiar place, prison. I shook my head as I walked all the way back to the Education Centre. I just couldn't grasp the fact that they were asking me to consider applying for day leave.

During the weeks that followed, I discussed it with the Education Centre staff and began to open my mind to the possibility of grappling with time out of the prison. It wasn't an easy thing to do, having a few hours of upervised freedom then returning to the inside of the concrete walls again. I'd found it more comfortable to remain inside. It was simpler. It didn't fuck your head up as much.

With encouragement from the teachers, I decided to apply for a family leave which, if all went well, I'd then follow up with an education leave. I was apprehensive but it felt okay. I knew, too, that at some point I had to prepare to live outside these walls. I was due to be released in 1988. I'd done six years, only two to go.

19

Learning to live

In August 1986 I got news that Vicki had appeared in court on the charges relating to bringing the heroin in to me the previous year. She had breached her parole as a consequence, and the magistrate gave her a twelve-month sentence. While I was curious about where she was at, after eighteen months of no contact I really preferred to keep it that way. My vulnerability to her hadn't yet been challenged, although I was rock solid about not using drugs again—the desire had disappeared from my life and I was still in awe of this fact. I'd never thought I'd be able to shake off that seemingly incurable craving. After sentencing Vicki was sent to B Annexe at Pentridge, the reception prison for women. I breathed a sigh of relief knowing that I didn't have to deal with seeing her just yet. I still felt sad about her, about our lost relationship—the love of my life—but I was also hurt and angry. I wondered if she could ever begin to understand what I'd been through in the past eighteen months, let alone Ali. I wasn't about to make judgments where Ali was concerned, though, as I hadn't been able to put her needs before my own either. It made me realise how much had changed in eighteen months.

In September 1986 I was successful in gaining a weekend

leave to attend Gippsland Institute with Maud, the drama group facilitator, as my supervisor/driver. Maud drove on to Bairnsdale to visit her parents for the weekend while I stayed in the on-campus student accommodation. Having just heard that Vicki was in Pentridge, I was feeling confused and anxious that weekend, and my stomach was in knots. I felt that I couldn't become intimately involved with her again, and yet somewhere deep down inside a part of me was saying that I might want to. I knew that with the very real possibility of seeing her face-to-face, all that unfinished business between us from eighteen months ago would now have to be dealt with. It would be the most difficult issue I'd had to encounter since I'd stopped using. By late Saturday afternoon, after an awful computer class, I was heading straight for that old lonely, empty and depressed feeling that had been so familiar over the past few years.

This time, instead of staying in that cold student room all night feeling miserable and confused (I think they must have turned the heating off because our residential took place in a university break), I put on the big coat Greg had lent me and went out for a walk around the hills of Churchill in the freezing cold and rain. After about fifteen minutes I began to warm up, so on I went, walking and walking, thinking and thinking ... and thinking. After an hour or so my mind became clearer and I started to feel better, more positive. I realised that what I had to do with Vicki was the same as I'd done with heroin the previous year. I had to let go. Once I had let go of heroin I was no longer afraid of it, nor was it a threat to me any more. I no longer had to have a relationship with Vicki—or anyone else. Sounded good in theory, but what I'd failed to take into account was that relationships are matters of the heart.

A couple of hours later, I went back to my room feeling much better. I slept more peacefully and woke up Sunday morning feeling as though a big cloud had been lifted from my mind. I often seemed to have these sorts of conversations with myself, because being straight was still so new to me. It was a slow process, thinking everything through, but I'd get there in the end. At least I returned from the education leave feeling lighter, less burdened by Vicki's possible reappearance in my life. I began to wonder how long it would be before she made contact. Only days after my return from weekend school, I went to collect my mail one afternoon and my heart jumped to my throat as I recognised her familiar handwriting on an envelope. I found myself feeling angry all over again.

'You shithead! Fuck you! Why did you have to come back to jail?' I said to myself. The reality of any contact with Vicki brought all the hurt from our unresolved relationship to the surface. Would I ever be able to forgive her? I didn't want my sense of peace shattered, so I waited until I was in my room later that night before reading the letter. I shook with nerves when I opened it, but slowly I made my body relax. It was different from the arrogant letter I'd last received from her eighteen months previously. The point of this one was to ask how I'd feel if she requested a transfer from Pentridge to Fairlea. She didn't want to stay over there, but equally, if it was going to upset me too much, she wouldn't come to Fairlea. I decided to do nothing about it until I'd had the chance to discuss it with Greg when he came into the Education Centre the following week.

'What do you think I should do?' I said after he'd read it.

'How do you feel about her coming here?' he asked.

'I'm apprehensive, I know it would be difficult, but I wouldn't stop her,' I replied. 'Pentridge is a disgusting place to be.'

'Well, if you really think you'd be okay having her around then I think you should just write a very brief, neutral response. I can help you if you like,' he offered.

On 4 October 1986 I sent Vicki my response to her letter,

making it short and unemotional. I'd spent quite a bit of time getting the words right. It wasn't easy because I didn't want to slip into discussing the past—that needed to be done face to face.

Vicki received the letter a few days later and within weeks she had been approved for transfer to Fairlea. Not long before lock-up one afternoon, I was wandering around when one of my friends came running towards me. 'Vicki's up the front. She's just arrived from Pentridge,' she said.

I was glad to have had advance warning because it gave me a bit of time to prepare myself before seeing her. As I looked out my cottage window a short time later, I saw her and an officer walking past the Education Centre towards Yarrabrae. The sight of her made my heart beat faster. I didn't know if I was nervous, excited or just plain scared. She stopped to talk briefly to a couple of women she knew, but had to keep moving to keep up with the officer. She didn't look much different although she'd lost weight, probably from drug use. I felt quite anxious until I realised I wouldn't have to face her that afternoon as it was almost lock-up time—even I could be grateful for lock-up sometimes!

After muster the next morning I walked over to her, my stomach churning but my face giving nothing away. 'Do you want to meet after work this afternoon and have a talk?' I was nervous but also feeling in control ... sort of.

'Yeah, that'd be good,' she replied quietly. The look on her face was as blank as mine. It was all about bravado in there, and we were both experts.

'I'll come to Yarrabrae this afternoon,' I said to her. With that I walked off to my work post. Although I was shaky inside, I felt different to how I used to. Deep down I felt balanced, like nothing could really throw me off, and it gave me confidence. I used to allow other people to take a lead in situations when I felt unable to speak up, but since my involvement in the NA meetings and my developing confidence about speaking in groups and in public, things had changed. I just kept pushing myself through every challenge that presented itself.

When Vicki and I met in her cell that afternoon, it was obvious that we still felt a great deal of love for each other. I'd like to say I remained rational and a bit detached, but my heart took over immediately I was alone with her. I just wanted to rush over and hold her in my arms, but I didn't allow myself that pleasure, at least not yet.

'How are you?' I said to her, feeling awkward.

'Better than when you last saw me,' she said. I looked into her eyes and I sort of felt relieved. I still loved her, but I wasn't lost like I used to be. She reached her arms out to me and I moved closer and we held each other. It had been a hard eighteen months.

We sat on her bed and talked for the hour remaining before lock-up. Instead of concentrating on how I'd suffered after she stopped contacting me, I listened to her explaining what she'd been through. Hers was a story equally as painful and miserable as mine, and perhaps for the first time since she'd abandoned me, I felt some empathy towards her instead of just my own hurt and anger. Over the next week or two we talked on every occasion that we could get time out of the prison routine, and gradually we became comfortable with each other again.

I tried to pace myself, not allowing my emotions to take over completely, but I wasn't entirely successful. We did make love in those first weeks and it was as beautiful as ever, but I didn't get carried away and create a fantasy around it. As time passed I realised it wasn't what it had once been, that I didn't need or have to have this relationship any more. I was a complete human being on my own now and I didn't need Vicki or anyone to speak for me or fill any gaps. I realised that in some ways I was still the same, yet so different.

Over the next few months Vicki and I talked about our relationship, the future and her release, which again was due a year before mine. We decided, against her wishes, to remain friends, not lovers. Vicki had only stopped using since coming back to prison, and although she'd begun attending NA meetings she still had a long way to go, whereas I'd been without drugs for eighteen months and felt strong and committed to not using again. After living in Yarrabrae for about six months, Vicki moved into my cottage and we continued our friendship. I could sense her wanting more, but it wasn't going to happen.

I decided to apply for regular education leaves to Gippsland Institute where I'd been studying for my Bachelor of Arts (Social Sciences) by correspondence. After a few weeks the Classification Committee approved my proposed leave program, which meant I'd be going to Gippsland for one weekend every two months. On each of these weekends, I would leave the prison on Friday night and not return until Sunday night. Maud, the director of the Fairlea drama group, was to be my 'escort' on the first leave of my new program. How exciting—forty-eight hours outside the prison! Previously I'd found leaves from the prison quite difficult emotionally, but now it felt different. Firstly, the focus wasn't on Ali, it was an academic one, which was much easier. Also, it was 1986 and I could 'see' the end of my sentence, although it was still two years away. During the first two-thirds of my sentence I'd felt like I couldn't afford to contemplate the outside world because it made it harder to remain in the sterile environment of prison, but by now I could almost 'smell' freedom.

Another benefit, albeit a sneaky one, was that Maud, Ron and I had decided to involve Ali in these 'education leaves' as much as possible. Because the Institute had day-care facilities, I intended to take Ali with me, leaving her in day-care during the day and spending the evenings together. Ali was beside herself with excitement as we planned for the first weekend. We also did something else that was against the 'rules'. Instead of driving up to the Institute on Friday night, as per my application, Ali and I had dinner with Ron at Maud and Greg's house. We headed off for the Institute early on Saturday morning, but of course the unexpected always happens. On the way we had to stop off at a garage to get petrol. As Maud was filling the car I turned my head to look out of the window, and who do you think I saw? Mr Herron, the governor of the prison, walking past the petrol station with his dog. I just about shat myself. I was supposed to be in Churchill already! I started shaking with fear. After a few minutes I dared to look out again, but he'd disappeared.

When Maud got back in the car I told her anxiously, 'I just saw Mr Herron.'

'You're joking!' she replied.

'What if he reports me to the police?' I asked.

'You know, I don't think he'd do it. I think if he was worried, he would have come over and spoken to you,' she said. She seemed calm but I could tell she was worried too. As it turned out, he lived in the same suburb as Maud.

I wasn't even sure if he'd seen me and there was nothing we could do about it anyway, so we headed off for Churchill where I was supposed to have been. As luck would have it, after about an hour and a half of driving we suddenly heard a police siren behind us. I looked out the back window and, sure enough, they wanted us to pull over. I just about shat myself again. I felt like I was a criminal on the run. There hadn't been much sense of freedom about this temporary leave so far. I was already imagining the worst:

Name, please? Ah, Helen Barnacle. A puzzled look would appear on his face. Just a moment, he'd say, returning to his car to check my name on the computer. Drug dealer, huh? Fifteen years, huh? What do you think you're doing being driven around the countryside?

'I was speeding,' Maud said, interrupting my anxious reverie. 'Don't worry, I'll talk to him. You just sit there quietly.'

Sure enough, that was all it was, but by then I just wanted to get to the Institute and settle down. It was too nerve-wracking out there in the real world, and I kept automatically feeling like I was doing something wrong. Well, I was I suppose . . . I should have been in Churchill.

An hour later Maud dropped Ali and me at the Institute, leaving us with a big basket full of goodies that she'd prepared especially for us. After taking Ali to the child-care centre I returned to my room with the basket and excitedly looked through it. It had been so long since I'd had food like this all to myself, and real coffee! I opened the packet of freshly ground beans and sat there on the bed sniffing. I was ecstatic! What a high! There was also cheese, fresh bread, almonds and little containers from the delicatessen that my eyes feasted upon.

'Thanks, Maud,' I said out loud. 'What a nice thing to do.' She must have known how much I'd appreciate it.

After the scary start on Saturday morning, it turned out to be one of the best weekends of my life. Ali and I had the most fabulous time which, considering Churchill only consisted of a few shops, was amazing. Even the weather was awful, but we didn't care and Maud had lent me a warm, waterproof coat. On Saturday night Ali and I walked from the Institute to the shops in the rain. Actually we didn't walk, we skipped, holding hands and singing all the way. I felt so free. I wasn't sure what Ali was feeling but she was beaming with that wonderful happiness that children show so easily. If anyone had seen us they probably would have thought we were mad, but it was a very special time for us and we were going to drain every drop of pleasure we could out of it.

At the shops we bought fish and chips for dinner, sitting on one of the benches outside to eat. I'd never known such small pleasures could be such fun. When I was using I could never seem to enjoy simple things like this. There was always something missing, and the only thing I could find to fill the hole was a hit of heroin.

After we'd finished eating we skipped and sang our way around Churchill until we were ready to return to our beds at the Institute. Ali fell asleep almost immediately. I didn't let my mind dwell on the fact that we would have to be separated again the following evening, I just allowed happiness to sweep over me. I was so grateful to be free of the need for drugs to enhance my feelings. At that moment there was no joy greater than sharing two days and two nights with my little girl, who was now six years old. I felt so close to her as I looked across at her asleep. I hadn't been able to do that since she'd left the prison, and my heart filled with love.

'I *am* her mother. My beautiful Ali,' I said out loud. 'I love you so much.' I walked over to the bed and kissed her rosy cheek, listening to her breathing as she slept. I gently brushed her face with my hand—it was so soft. I ran my fingers through her long golden hair and she stirred a little. My thoughts drifted back to 1985 when I'd been locked into despair, and I was so grateful now that I hadn't killed myself. There was so much to live for.

Maud, Greg and Ali returned me to the prison at 8 pm, and not a minute before. Our goodbyes didn't actually feel as traumatic as they'd done in the past, maybe because of the extended period of time Ali and I had spent together. I felt so lucky to have such caring, understanding friends as Maud and Greg.

Mr Herron said nothing about having spotted me, so I assumed he either hadn't seen me or had decided I wasn't doing anything wrong and was going to keep it to himself. To this day

I don't know which of those was true but I figured that, because I was doing the right thing, I deserved for things to go my way.

The most difficult thing for me about these weekend schools was meeting other students and never knowing what to say after the initial introduction. Once we knew each other's name, the next question was always, 'Where are you from?' Here we go, I'd think to myself, not wanting to identify as a prisoner. For one weekend I just wanted to be a 'normal' person.

'I live in Fairfield,' I'd reply. It was the truth if not the whole truth. And then the inevitable questions would arise about what we did for a living, most of us being mature-age students. Fortunately, most of my time was taken up in lectures or tutorials anyway, so it didn't bother me greatly. I got along well with the different lecturers, who all knew my secret. A couple of the psychology lecturers had previously come into the prison to meet me and assist as much as they could, so I'd already made a connection with them. Because I was such an enthusiastic student, I imagine I was a pleasure to teach. I felt confident participating in class discussions because I was well informed, having had plenty of time to do any background reading, and I no longer had much fear about speaking in public.

The Institute, being relatively small, had a friendly atmosphere. I enjoyed the challenging interactions in the classes, but overall I preferred the solitude of studying by correspondence— not that I'd ever attended any other university with which I could make a comparison. Really, the only difficult part of the weekend schools was when the conversation became personal. In the end the only way I could deal with it was to avoid conversations with the other students. It was unfortunate but, because I spent all my out-of-school time with Ali, I didn't feel so lonely not interacting with the 'normals'. My education leave program continued in this way for the remainder of the year without any real hitches or trauma.

By the middle of 1987, Vicki was preparing for her release in July. She'd managed to remain drug-free and was committed to staying that way outside, but she was still volatile. Being outwardly angry, she'd always had more trouble than me in dealing with the officers. I was pretty quiet and didn't get sucked into their pettiness as much. One day during work hours she came storming into Yarrabrae, furious. I was in there completing my cleaning job before going to the Education Centre.

'I've just been charged by that fuckin' Mr Jones!'

Mr Jones had been at Fairlea for years, and he'd always been a pain in the arse. Once when Ali and Damien were playing outside Yarrabrae, he ordered me to stop them frolicking under the sprinkler on a hot summer's day. I had a stand-up argument with him, which resulted in Ali running to our unit crying. She thought that if I argued with the officers they'd make me stay in prison longer. This time, it was Vicki's turn to have an argument with him.

'What did he charge you for?' I asked her.

'I swore at him. I hope it doesn't affect my release date.'

'He's such a moron,' I said to her. 'You know he'll try and bait you, especially knowing that you're getting out soon. When he has a go at you, why don't you just try to keep quiet instead of always having a go back?' Mr Jones was such a game player, but the thing I'd always hated most about him was that he was just plain unfair. It was almost as though he got his kicks out of hassling people over nothing, then charging them when they reacted.

'Yeah, well that'll be hard, but I'll give it a go. I'd hate to give him the pleasure of extending my time in here, the prick!'

Vicki, whose work post was the garden, often had Mr Jones as officer for the day and, only a couple of days after this incident, he started hassling her again. Instead of retaliating, this time Vicki just stood there quietly, not allowing herself to get drawn in by him. She thought she was safe because she wasn't arguing back or swearing at him.

'If you're not careful, I'll charge you with dumb insolence!' he yelled, his face growing redder with anger.

'For fuck's sake,' Vicki mumbled as she turned away from him, trying to bite her tongue before she let him have a mouthful again. She came looking for me to tell me what had just happened, and to cool off.

'Well, so much for your advice,' she said. 'I just kept my mouth shut while Jones was having a go at me, and now he says he'll charge me with dumb insolence!'

'Bloody hell, you can't win, can you?' I said to her, bursting into laughter. 'What can I say?' She saw the funny side of it and started laughing too. Every time we looked at each other we laughed more and more until the tears streamed down our faces. We were both just about hysterical at the stupidity of it all.

I had confused feelings about Vicki's release. Although I would miss having her to laugh with over the mindless, futile happenings in the jail, in a way I was relieved she was going. I knew she still wanted us to be lovers, but I didn't feel like it was the right time for anything more than friendship. I'd decided I wasn't having a relationship with anyone for a long time. One of the reasons for this was that the only people I was likely to meet in there were probably going to be drug users, and I wasn't about to become involved in a dependent type of partnership. The tragedy is that institutions are set up in such a way that issues like these are almost never worked through, so people leave prison no better—and sometimes worse—than when they arrived. It was nothing short of a miracle that I'd come so far, and I realised I had people like Ron, Maud, Corliss and Greg to thank for it. Although I knew I'd done a lot of hard work myself, it's virtually impossible for anyone to overcome these obstacles on their own. Every human being needs love, nurturing and support, and prisons don't offer such things, although in some small way the women contained within them could sometimes fill the gap.

The imminent departure of Vicki and Lino, another woman we were close to, motivated Greg, Maud and a few others, including myself, to form a committee to set up a halfway house. Along with about eighty-five per cent of the prison population, neither Vicki nor Lino had any accommodation or support waiting for them outside, so 'Daleth House' was trialled as a model for women leaving prison. While we knew we could never expect to fulfil all their needs, we figured it was worth a try.

My involvement in setting up the house was limited, of course, but the committee held its meetings in the prison so that I could have some input. Even though I was yet to be released from prison and so didn't know first-hand what was in store, I'd seen so many other women return to prison soon after leaving that I was able to make observations about what they'd experienced. Daleth House, which operated out of a leased house in Elsternwick, about nine kilometres south of Melbourne, turned out to be worthwhile for both Vicki and Lino, as well as the other women who stayed there. It enabled them to get on their feet and settle into 'normal' life in the outside and 'straight' world. Although it ran into difficulties later, eventually closing due to lack of funds and other problems, it assisted several women who, to this day, are living meaningful lives.

When Vicki's release day arrived, I didn't feel the desperation I had when she'd left the first time. I knew I was distancing myself from my feelings, trying to avoid being hurt, but that was how I'd resolved to complete my sentence without going insane, and it was working for me.

'Vicki to the front gate!' the loudspeaker screamed out over the prison grounds. There were some things that never changed in there.

'This is it,' I said to Vicki.

'Yeah,' she replied. 'I'm nervous, but it's okay. You know it's okay, don't you? You know I'll keep in touch?'

'Yeah, I know you will this time,' I replied, my lip quivering despite myself.

'Don't give up on "us",' she said.

I knew what she meant, but I didn't really want to think about it as it hurt too much. I knew there was no way we could even consider a lover relationship until I was also free and could meet her as an equal—and that was still too far off for me to contemplate. I nodded my head by way of response, unable to say anything. I didn't want her to hang on to the hope that we would be together again, but at the same time I wanted so much for her to make it out there. It was almost like I needed someone to do well—meaning, not use drugs—so that I could know it was possible. I still hadn't seen any drug user make it after leaving prison, which was astounding, really, when you think about it.

Vicki and I walked to the front gate together. She was carrying her meagre belongings in the standard-issue green garbage bag. Everyone left like that, as though they were garbage being thrown out, the refuse of society ... When we reached the door to the visit centre we wrapped our arms around each other for what was going to be our last physical contact for a while.

'Bye,' I said to her, the lump in my throat preventing me from saying any more.

Once she was on the other side of the gate she took a long look at me through the wire mesh fence separating us. 'Ring me?' she said, needing my reassurance. I nodded my head in reply. She turned and gave me a last wave, then hesitated before disappearing from sight.

I turned and walked back to my cottage, tears in my eyes. I

walked into my room and sat on the bed. I was okay but, damn it, I felt so sad.

I'm so sick of saying goodbye to people, I thought, feeling sorry for myself. I'm so sick of the lump in my throat. I don't know how many goodbyes I have left in me, I kept thinking as I tried to 'will' the sadness to leave me. I looked out my door to Vicki's empty room opposite mine, remembering everything we'd been through in the past six years: meeting her, looking at her through the wire mesh in 1981 when she returned to prison after her sentencing, understanding the shock she was feeling, falling in love with her ... so beautiful. Then being betrayed by her ... but ultimately supporting, loving and nurturing each other in this emotionally and physically deprived environment. I sat there for a while until I put myself back together again and then made my way to the Education Centre.

I bounced back much more quickly these days, and it was a great comfort to realise that I wasn't going to fall apart. I had no desire to use heroin and, after the initial sense of loss wore off, I was happy to be on my own again—well, not really on my own, because I still had other friends in there. One of them was Julie, a special young woman with whom I'd formed a friendship over the previous few months. I'd become like a surrogate mother to her. About ten years younger than me, she was funny, beautiful and abused, and she'd been using heroin for many years already. With no permanent address and a very transient and often violent lifestyle, she was similar to a lot of young women coming into the jail at that time—I guess they were what the community calls 'street kids'. Julie had never held down a straight job and mostly thieved to get money to pay for her drugs. Just as my contemporaries had done in the late seventies and early eighties, these young women were changing the prison population once again. Like us, they were all addicted to drugs of some sort, but they were coming to jail younger and were more physically violent.

Julie and I often spent some time together in the afternoons after work. She was fascinated by how I'd managed to get off heroin and, like Tammy, even more fascinated by how I was managing to stay off it. Because she'd been in and out of jail for a couple of years by then, she'd seen what I was like before the dramatic change in my attitude. When Ali came in for the all-day Saturday kids' visits, Julie played with her and I couldn't help but notice how like Carol and Tammy she was, yet also unique. She also later became involved in the Fairlea drama group. I saw her curiosity as a positive sign and was careful not to preach to her. There's nothing worse than an ex-drug user telling you how good life is without drugs. I guess it's like an ex-smoker trying to sell their story to someone who's just lit up a cigarette. Besides, although I felt terrific now, it had been such a bloody long, hard, lonely road, I understood why most people didn't complete the journey. I considered myself lucky to have reached the point I was at.

Julie had been adopted as a baby and hadn't been able to find her birth mother yet, so she was interested in my relationship with Ali. I guess she also sensed my loneliness as a 'mother'—in fact she started calling me 'mum'. Ali adored her and, even now, has a photo of Julie in a frame in her bedroom. It's difficult to explain how at times in your life you make special connections with people and this was the case with Julie, Ali and I. It was very sweet and I think we filled a gap for each other for a while. Like everyone else, though, she was only there for a short time before being released. She did manage to write to me occasionally and was to return yet again before my own release.

Not long after both Vicki and Julie had left, Greg disappeared for a while, apparently on a soul-searching trek to the desert. It was the first time since I'd come to jail that he hadn't been involved in my life, and I was a bit thrown by it. I felt abandoned.

'What am I going to do?' I asked Peter, the social worker. 'I can't believe Greg's gone! How am I going to cope?'

'What do you mean when you say "what are you going to do"?' he replied.

'Well, how am I going to be without Greg around?'

'You're going to be fine,' he said, looking somewhat puzzled. 'Why wouldn't you be? You're a strong woman.'

'You reckon?' I asked him, needing some reassurance on that issue.

'Yes. Look at what you've achieved, what you've been through and overcome,' he said.

I let that thought run around my head a few times and I had to agree. 'Me—a strong woman,' I repeated to myself. I liked that image.

'Yep, I guess I am strong, aren't I?' I asked, not really needing a reply. 'So you think I'll be okay without my weekly sessions with Greg?'

'I'm positive,' he said.

'Shit! You're right, you know, I can deal with anything,' I said to him. I *was* strong—I could feel it.

Two months after the first education leave on my new program, I prepared to go out on another one, this time with Corliss as my 'escort'. Ali was going to come with me again, and we were both excited, anticipating another weekend of fun together in a 'free' environment, no-one watching us. When Corliss arrived at the prison to pick me up, I could see Ali trying to be inconspicuous in the car, as though she was a fugitive! We still hadn't told the prison that she was accompanying me to Churchill. I wasn't prepared to risk telling them as it was meant to be purely an education leave, not a family one. Prisons aren't known for flexibility. As we left the prison behind, Ali sat up in the back and leaned over to give me a big hug.

'It's so good to be here,' I said to them both.

'Look what Corliss has for us,' Ali said. Sure enough, there on the back seat was a basket of goodies to eat. I was so glad my friends realised how nice it was to have such wonderful food—or maybe it was just being able to have a choice of food. I guess because both Maud and Corliss had worked inside, they understood how much we missed these small things.

The weekend was as happy as the previous one had been, and Ali and I treasured this extra time together. Of course, it was good for my studies too, but that wasn't really the priority even though it was an 'education' leave. It was weird returning to the prison. I failed to understand how it could be considered safe for me to be out for the weekend, while for the rest of the next two years the community had to be protected from me. Tax-payers were forking out about $50 000 a year to keep me in this situation, which was really beginning to seem very silly. Anyway, it didn't matter—it was a fact and my sentence wasn't completed yet.

When I returned to the prison I did a supervised, voluntary urine, which was something I'd requested to do after every temporary leave as I thought it was the only way anyone would ever believe I was drug-free. I think it might have been the first time a prisoner had requested to do urines!

About a week later, I was surprised to hear the loudspeaker summon me to the medical centre. When I got there I was let in by Chris, one of the really nice nurses, who said she wanted to have a talk with me. I followed her into an office and sat down. Chris sat opposite holding a piece of paper.

'Have a look at this,' she said, passing it to me. It was a printout of my last urine analysis.

'It says my urine has "traces of cannabis",' I said to her incredulously.

'I know,' she replied.

'You don't believe it, do you?' I asked her.

'No I don't,' she said. I was relieved she hadn't immediately mistrusted me. 'How do you think it could have happened?' she asked. 'Were you in a room where people were smoking cannabis at the weekend when you were at Churchill?'

'No, not that I'm aware of,' I replied. 'I don't socialise with anyone when I'm at the Institute. I really just spend my out-of-class time either going for a walk or in my room. I can't believe this! I've never liked smoking dope!' Fortunately, she knew that to be true. I'd never been interested in cannabis, only heroin.

'Does the governor know?' I asked Chris, frightened at what his reaction might be. I mean, why would he ever believe me?

'No, I haven't told him yet,' she said. 'It doesn't make sense and I want to see if I can get to the bottom of it. At the weekend while you were out we did urines on three other women prisoners. They were all sent off to pathology together with yours, and they've all come back positive to cannabis. It's just too much of a coincidence.'

It helped enormously that Chris hadn't automatically assumed I was guilty; in fact she seemed almost as desperate as me to find an explanation. I had none—I was completely baffled.

When Chris talked to the hospital technicians, she discovered that they'd done all the tests together, at the end of their workday, and they'd tested mine last. It appeared that they hadn't cleaned the apparatus properly before testing my urine, and that was why it had shown traces of cannabis. It didn't make me feel much more comfortable, but the fact that Chris believed me was important.

I immediately started thinking about the possible consequences: What if they cancel my temporary leave program again? What will Ron think? He'll never believe me! No-one will believe I'm innocent this time! I'll lose my contact visits again. Ali's not going to cope with this! Ron will just give up on me! The thoughts raced through my head, and already I could hear

the authorities speaking in judgment: You've only got yourself
to blame! I didn't have a leg to stand on.

Eventually, however, because of Chris's determination and
her unflinching faith in me, the prison authorities believed her
story and I wasn't punished. It was a challenging situation and I
thanked my lucky stars that I'd had Chris there to argue for me.
I would have been history otherwise, even though I'd never been
associated with cannabis.

Not long after this incident, I was called to the visit centre
to see a Community Corrections worker. These workers were
still part of the overall Corrections Department, but they weren't
prison officers; instead they worked in the community with
parolees and people given community based sanctions rather than
prison sentences. Under a new pre-release program, long-term
prisoners could have their sentence reduced by a maximum of
eight months if they served that time doing eight hours voluntary
community work per week and attended a Community Corrections Centre as directed by their appointed worker. Attendance
was usually for one hour and the time could be used to discuss
any difficulties that had arisen since their release. For drug users,
supervised urines were also required twice a week. The program
had, at least partially, been introduced to ease the overcrowding
in Victorian prisons. Since illicit drug use had become popular
with young people, prisons were now full of drug users on drug-
related sentences and the numbers were escalating. Even those of
us on trafficking, selling or, in my case, importing charges were
almost all just users who sold to drug-using friends. In my entire
time in prison I'd only ever come across about three women
who were non-using dealers, in it only for the money. The
police rarely seemed to catch the big-time dealers, and locking
up the small fry had absolutely no impact on the availability of
illicit drugs on the streets.

When I arrived at the centre, the Corrections worker told

me that she had come to assess me for early release. Although I'd been aware of the new pre-release program and guessed that technically I was probably eligible for it, I'd been too frightened to open my mind to the thought that it might really apply to me. Now, if after assessing me the worker recommended I go on the program and her subsequent recommendation was approved, it would mean that I'd be getting out later that year or early 1988! I'd never allowed myself to consider this possibility, finding it easier to plan for 8/8/88, which had always been my earliest estimated release date. I couldn't have stood the disappointment if my hopes had been dashed. The Corrections worker sounded very positive, though, so as I walked back to the Education Centre I allowed my mind to entertain the possibility of being free by the end of the year. I'd always believed I was no risk to anyone but myself—maybe now even the system believed it. It felt weird but exciting to imagine being with Ali again. To think it might be this year was almost beyond me, so I put it to the back of my mind.

By the end of August I had received the unbelievable news that I was to be released on 24 November 1987, two weeks before I turned thirty-four. I was in the Education Centre when the good news came, and I ran to the teachers, hugging them with excitement. Marg, one of the teachers I was close to, came into the kitchen with me to share my elation. It was so hard to believe that this would all soon be over, that I'd be living a life very different to this. I was allowed to ring Ron to tell him, and he was shocked but overjoyed. Of course it was too early to tell Ali, but at least Ron and I could begin to prepare for this exciting time.

In the subsequent weeks we decided that I'd live at Ron's house, which would mean minimal disruption for Ali. This arrangement would suit me too, as I still had another year of study to complete my degree. I'd already decided I wanted to

embark on postgraduate studies which would enable me to eventually become a psychologist, so I had a few years of study ahead
of me yet.

After the initial excitement, life settled down again and I
really just focused on my course, which I enjoyed. I had one
more weekend study leave at Gippsland Institute, as well as
family leave with Ron and Ali one weekend in both September
and October. These had become overnight leaves so I could
become accustomed to spending the night with Ali in her home.

Vicki was still living at Daleth House, doing well and not
using. She was excited when I rang to tell her my good news.
In my heart I didn't think we were going to get back together,
too much had changed, but with only months before my release
it suddenly presented itself as a real option. It was difficult
keeping it from Ali, but the child psychiatrist had recommended
not telling her until six to eight weeks prior to my release. In
the meantime I felt warm inside waiting for the moment when
I could see the joy on her face.

20

Closing the prison gate

Now that I was off drugs and lucky enough to have suitable accommodation organised, I approached my release date without fear, unlike most other women leaving prison. Freedom actually came to me when the claws of drug addiction released their hold, around the time I started living in Cottage 6. I still couldn't believe how long it had taken to reach that point. I'd never felt so at ease inside, and physically I was fit and healthy, apart from having contracted the hepatitis C virus through sharing syringes in jail. I felt a quiet confidence, acquired from knowing and believing I could achieve whatever I wanted. I knew I was naive in terms of living in the 'straight' world, but imprisonment was the only obstacle preventing me from taking up my most important role—being Ali's mother. I couldn't look much beyond that.

I felt that my day to day life probably wasn't going to change much outside the prison, except that I'd be waking up with Ali, taking her to and from school, and at night I'd be kissing her and tucking her into bed, with her little pussycat 'Mima curled up beside her. I imagined her lying in bed at night while I listened to her steady breathing as she slept. I'd just sit there and look at her beautiful little face, like I used to do before she left the prison. It had always filled me with wonder that I had given birth to such a beautiful little 'being' ... it made my heart feel warm just thinking about it.

I knew I'd be doing everything in a much nicer place, and without the close supervision and head counting that was relentless in prison, but I'd been inside so long I found it hard to imagine what else would be different. I knew there would be physical things that had changed outside, like ATMs. I'd never used one of them because they hadn't been invented when I went in to prison—but they were all just incidental. The important thing was that I'd be with Ali and I had a home to go to. Ron and I had negotiated that I'd do the cooking and cleaning in return for rent, which would enable me to live on the single parent pension and Austudy. I'd continue my studies by correspondence, allowing me the time I needed to re-establish my relationship with Ali.

On 23 November 1987 it felt like everyone in the jail was happy for me. I was so grateful that it would be the last time I'd be locked in, particularly at the ridiculous hour of 4.30 pm. Needless to say, I didn't sleep much that night. I was awake and on the bike at 5.15 am the morning of my release. Nothing was going to upset my routine! It was the best bike ride to nowhere I'd ever had, and I enjoyed every minute of it and every ounce of perspiration it produced. I had my shower, then did my Tai Chi and meditation. By this time the others were waking and the officers had been around to open our doors. I packed my last few things into a green garbage bag and prepared for my last 'muster' at 8 am.

Rikki was back in prison, so I knew I could expect some surprises before I'd be let out the front gate. As usual, we went to muster like a herd of sheep, standing in a line along the asphalt near the netball court outside the Education Centre. It was one of the few places you could fit a straight line of about eighty women. I'd never enjoyed a muster so much as I savoured every last moment of ever having to do it. I could even allow myself to look up and down the line, acknowledging how stupid we all looked. It was bizarre!

After the head count Rikki stepped out of the line to make an announcement: 'Of course you all know that Barny, the old bag, is leaving today and us women would like to make a presentation. Barny, we've got you something that we know you'll use every day, and that way we can make sure you never forget us!' she said, while everyone laughed. 'We're gonna miss you, but we wish you all the luck in the world, 'cause you deserve it more than anyone,' she finished. They all whistled and clapped, and already I felt my heart heave at the thought of leaving these women who had helped me to crawl up from my knees when my legs weren't strong enough to hold me.

They'd all contributed to buying me a 'going away' present. As it was too big to wrap, I could see what it was immediately— an exercise bike to take home with me! I felt so special as I thought about how difficult it would have been for them to organise it, let alone to raise the money ... these women who had nothing. After the presentation of the bike, during which I noticed that even the officers were smiling, the fun began. I was thankful because at that point I felt like collapsing and crying. What stopped me was something soft crashing and breaking on my head, followed by a gooey substance running over my face. Someone had snuck up behind me and smashed an egg all through my hair, which was a signal for everyone else to join in. I saw flour, sugar, more eggs and who knows what else coming my way. I started ducking to try and miss it, but soon gave up and just stood there, a target for anyone who cared to throw something at me. I'd never laughed so much. With some foreboding, I saw Rikki and a few others heading straight towards me. They picked me up by the arms and legs and carried me to the swimming pool. Knowing what was in store, I squealed all the way.

'One ... two ... three!' Rikki called out as my body swayed from side to side. Then I was airborne and 'splash'! I was in the pool, clothes and all ... prison issue, of course, not my real clothes, so I didn't care! I knew it was useless to resist and why spoil their fun? I was just about convulsing with laughter and I didn't care what they did to me this morning!

'What's it like in there, Barny?' Rikki yelled from the side of the pool, laughing with glee. Everyone else joined in.

'I'm glad it's nearly summer!' I yelled back at them.

'Decide to go for a morning swim, hey?' Kerry yelled. There was a whole crowd of them laughing their heads off. Practically the whole jail was watching, including the officers, and everyone was smiling or laughing. It was a rare moment of shared delight in the prison. When someone who had done a long sentence was released, there was usually a real sense of joy for them, unless it was someone who was really disliked, in which case everyone was just glad to be rid of them.

After the kitchen rations had run out, I climbed from the swimming pool and walked across to my cottage for another shower. I felt happy and light inside, but while I was under the shower I started thinking about Rikki and all the other women, some of whom I'd grown to love dearly. There was no option but to leave them behind, and it made my heart feel heavy and sad. It seemed so pointless to lock them up as they were mostly only harmful to themselves, but that's the way it is. What I felt for them was the sort of love you can only experience when you've suffered and survived with someone, which was why it was proving so hard to let go of the relationship with Vicki. When I came out of the bathroom I saw that Rikki had brought my new exercise bike into the cottage for me. Tears filled my eyes. I was so happy and sad all at once. I put on another set of prison-issue clothes and sat in the cottage having a last coffee (if you could call it that) with a few of my friends until an officer appeared at the door. My time had come.

Rikki got up. 'Come on, Barny. I'll carry the bike to the gate for you,' she said, breaking the awkward, emotionally charged silence.

'Thanks,' I replied. I stood up and walked to each of the women in the cottage to give them a hug. They all had tears in their eyes. They all unselfishly shared my happiness even though we'd all miss each other. Even Tammy was there, but this time I was leaving her behind. It might be the last time I'd ever see those who were still caught up in drug use, because I wouldn't be mixing in the old crowd after my release. None of us said it, but we knew that was the reality, and they respected my choice not to use any more. I had so many emotions going on inside me I was in turmoil, but amidst the confusion there was joy in anticipation of this afternoon when I'd be going to Ali's school to pick her up for the first time. I couldn't wait to see her face. Somehow or other I would have to put all this behind me; all these women with our shared experiences over the many years; all the friendships; all this pain.

I was escorted to the gate, Rikki by my side. She passed the bike through and we held each other for one last hug.

'I love you, Barny,' she said from deep in her heart. 'Take care of yourself. I'll be thinking of you.'

'Thanks, I love you too,' I said, looking into her eyes as we slowly let go of each other. I released her hand and passed through the gate, which the officer locked behind me. As I walked towards the front office on the other side of the wire mesh I took one last look back. Rikki was still standing there.

'See ya, Barny! Say hi to Ali for me and I'll see you both soon,' she called out. She only had another couple of months to serve, so I might well be seeing her again depending on whether she was using or not.

'See ya, love you all!' I turned and called to a few of my friends who'd gathered with Rikki behind the wire mesh.

'Fuck it!' I said quietly to myself as I closed my eyes for a moment, wishing it could be different. Then I turned away and walked through the door into the front office and out of sight of all of those beautiful women.

The prison officers and senior staff all wished me well as I walked through administration into the clothing store area to take off my prison-issue clothes for the last time. It was not the same clothing store that I'd first encountered in 1979, the old buildings having been demolished after the 1982 fire, so it didn't bring back memories of that shocking time. This was the last time I'd be undressing with an officer watching me. I savoured my last humiliating moment inside although, as a condition of my pre-release program, I'd have to keep doing supervised urines (pissing in a jar in front of a nurse) until Community Corrections directed me not to. I imagined it would continue for a few years yet. After completing the pre-release program I would still have seven years of parole to do.

I put on some tracksuit pants and a T-shirt. I didn't have anything much to wear but I'd be going shopping with Ron's friend Elizabeth in the afternoon to buy some clothes. I had no idea about what was in fashion, but I'd never really been one to make a fashion statement anyway. My money had always been required for drugs up until now.

My moment arrived. Soon I would be on the other side of the huge concrete wall that had been my horizon for so many years, the wall that, on so many occasions, I'd wished I could see through, or over. I approached the officer at the front gate of the prison. He smiled and wished me good luck as he put his key into the lock that had kept me separated from the world for so long. He swung the gate open and I walked through it to freedom, clutching my green garbage bag.

After such a long time inside, it seemed there should have been a huge celebration awaiting me, with a band playing, balloons flying, people waiting to congratulate me on surviving, and a huge banner saying HELEN BARNACLE IS FREE. But there was no such thing. People being released from prison wasn't considered a cause for celebration, or even something to be noted— let alone be proud of—by the community. I was luckier than most, though: Elizabeth was there for me, waiting to drive me away in her car. She walked towards me and gave me a big hug ... As I said, I was luckier than most. I knew I had people who cared for me, who thought I was important or special enough for them to take the time to pick me up and help me out on my first day of freedom. It's not a typical story.

I didn't feel any great gush of emotion as I surfaced on freedom's side of the gate, but I guess the exciting part of the day was yet to come. I couldn't wait to go to Ali's school and pick her up—that was when I'd know I was free. Anything that went before that was really just filling in time. Our first stop was social security, now called Centrelink, where I produced my prison release papers. I was entitled to one week's unemployment benefit, but I couldn't cash the cheque until I'd opened a bank account. Our next compulsory task was to report to the Community Corrections office in Caulfield, near my new address, and meet my parole officer. I spent about an hour there chatting to him, and I felt reasonably comfortable. Some weeks later I got a new parole officer, a lovely woman named Pauline. It was a relief knowing that this part of my parole was going to be positive.

Elizabeth then took me to a shopping complex near her place. I had little money as I'd only walked out with $60 after nearly eight years (amazing, hey?), but Ron had lent me a couple of hundred dollars to get some clothes and I let Elizabeth guide me about what to buy. It was a big shopping centre and I was in a daze as we found a place to have something to eat and a coffee. I loved the smell of those coffee beans in the air and tried to imagine being able to have 'real' coffee any time I chose—it was a bit difficult to comprehend even such simple things yet. I had a bowl of fresh fruit salad, not just because I love fresh fruit, but because there were too many things to choose from, so I stuck to something simple; besides, in prison we'd only had apples, oranges and bananas, whereas here there were apricots, pineapple, kiwi fruit, plums ... a range of fruit I hadn't been able to enjoy for years.

Elizabeth drove me from the shopping complex to Ron's house, then left to go home to prepare dinner for her own family—she had a husband and children herself. Elva, who'd been caring for Ali during my absence, was still living at Ron's as we hadn't yet decided when it would be best for her to leave. We wanted to give Ali time to adjust. Although she was a lovely, non-intrusive woman, secretly I just wanted Elva to go. It was difficult to deal with the fact that she'd shared so much time with Ali over the past few years when I couldn't, and I found myself thinking defiantly, This is *my* daughter! I did respect the job she'd done, though, and I knew I had to be careful to treat her kindly, not get annoyed that she was there.

I strolled around the house that was now my home, and already I wanted to start making the space mine. I saw things I wanted to move and change and I wanted some time to myself. Take a breath and be patient, I kept telling myself, immediately grateful for the meditation skills I'd developed. Once Elva had left, I'd be moving into the bedroom she'd occupied next to Ali for over two years. I didn't feel like I could take much of a look in there that day because it was still her space. It was strange walking around a normal house that I could lock and unlock when I chose. It was hard to believe that this was now my 'home', surrounded by trees and a garden. There weren't even bars on the windows. I noticed how quiet it was too, not to be surrounded by eighty other women and assorted officers and that bloody loudspeaker. I kept expecting to be called for muster! I was sure that later in the afternoon I'd automatically line up at the front door, ready to be accounted for and locked in for the evening.

As the day wore on I was getting more and more excited about going to pick Ali up at school at 3.30 pm. In prison that would have marked the end of our workday and we'd be heading to Yarrabrae to collect our mail and have our evening meal. A happy distraction during the afternoon was the arrival of my piano; that poor piano had been moved so many times, it was like an old friend that kept moving with me into each new situation. I giggled to myself at the thought of doing time with my piano … it seemed funny now.

To fill in the rest of the time before Ali finished school, I decided to walk to the closest bank to open an account. I lined up in the queue feeling slightly anxious as I knew I'd have to explain my circumstances.

'What identification do you have?' the teller asked when I was finally served.

I handed over my birth certificate, Medicare card and prison release papers. I figured I might as well get it over and done with so, before she'd had a chance to read the papers, I told her, 'I've been released from prison today and I need to have a bank account to deposit my social security payment.' I'd already been through this same routine at Centrelink earlier in the day. It was embarrassing to have to keep explaining it. People were polite, but you could tell they were shocked. I just wanted to leave it all behind.

The teller asked me to wait while she went to talk to someone else, maybe a supervisor or manager. Feeling conspicuous,

I checked around the bank to see if anyone in the queue was listening or watching, but they appeared oblivious to my situation.

'You'll need someone to verify this information,' the teller said when she returned. 'Is there someone you know who could do that?' I was pissed off, but I knew not to get impatient or I'd just confirm everyone's worst beliefs about people who'd been in jail.

'Yes, I think I can,' I replied, gathering up my identification papers. I felt extremely embarrassed as I walked back to Ron's to ask Elva if she'd come down to the bank with me to confirm my identity. She was happy to do it and the teller was nice to me, so eventually I succeeded in opening a bank account. Just the same, it seemed a bit bizarre that social security wouldn't pay me without a bank account, and the bank wouldn't allow me to open an account unless I had someone to verify who I was. I felt like everywhere I went I had to disclose that I was a prisoner, and prisoners were not to be believed. But I wasn't a prisoner—I was free! The experience couldn't spoil my day, but it pissed me off somewhat.

At last it was time to pick up Ali. As I walked there with Elva, I wondered what Ali had been thinking about all day at school, knowing I'd be there when she came out. I watched all the kids running around at the finish of their day and all the parents, mostly mums, waiting to pick them up. So this is what normal people do, I thought to myself as I looked around me, happy to be one of them. I acknowledged it was something I'd never felt in the straight world before. I looked at their faces, at what they took for granted, and knew they could never understand what I'd been through and what I was feeling. It was so special to be here to collect my little girl—how many times I had dreamed of this moment. Then I spotted her. She was looking for me as she knew today was the day. Her eyes met mine and she came running over, pumping with excitement.

'Mum!' she called as she ran towards me.

'Ali!' I called back. She wrapped her little arms around me and we held each other for a long moment. No-one else could know what this meant to us. It had been a long four years waiting for this day, and my heart felt like it was going to burst. I just wanted to hold on to her forever and I had to keep telling myself that this time I didn't have to leave ... I didn't have to return to the prison. For the first time in years it felt safe to let go of her, knowing that now we could hold each other any time we liked. This time when I let go of her there was no pain. I was never leaving again. Holding hands, we started walking the short distance home, Ali skipping alongside me. This was freedom!

Later in the day Ron arrived home and by then I felt like I just wanted to get on with life. It didn't feel like I'd been absent for all those years. Elva cooked dinner for us and afterwards we talked about the best time for her to leave. I was fine with Ali, so we all decided that she'd go in a couple of days, returning to her home in the country. I was overjoyed because it meant that I could move into my bedroom and set up life the way I wanted it. Now that I was home, Ali had started to get smart with Elva and I could see it was going to get worse. It was awful, but understandable from Ali's eight-year-old point of view.

Because of my late November release date, my studies had finished for the year, which meant I could spend December and January exclusively with Ali. During my early weeks of freedom I really only went to the shops, Ali's school, and the Community Corrections Centre for my compulsory appointments and voluntary work. For the community work component of my pre-release program I was working half a day in an opportunity shop, and half a day for an elderly man who lived locally and who needed some 'home-help'. I enjoyed both of these jobs and, in some ways, they helped me integrate into the community.

Two weeks after my release I turned thirty-four. Ron, Ali and I were invited to Elizabeth's house for a birthday dinner. Elizabeth's family lived in a huge house with a swimming pool, so Ali had a swim in the pool. I wasn't accustomed to going out in the evenings yet—particularly for a swishy dinner! I'd probably only been somewhere special for dinner about four times in the last eight years, and that was only when I was on temporary leave. I wasn't on prison rations any more! I was feeling pretty shy and overawed by the extravagance, but we enjoyed ourselves and, being December, it was a lovely warm night. They all had a drink to celebrate, but I was sticking to my Narcotics Anonymous program and so didn't have any mind-altering substances. I didn't miss alcohol because I hadn't had any for years, and I didn't feel any need for it; besides, I was too scared that if I tried it, it might make me want to have a hit. I'd heard so many stories in NA about ex-users doing that, and I wasn't prepared to take any risks. I had enough to adjust to as it was, and I was taking it slowly.

After a few months my contact with Elizabeth gradually waned. Her lifestyle was so different to mine, I felt out of place. Her family was wealthy, wore expensive clothes, had flash dinner parties with spiffy silverware, all of which I found daunting. Because I was unable to articulate my discomfort, our friendship gradually dissolved in the subsequent months, although I remained grateful for her involvement in my life and for being willing to befriend me in the first place. We'd had many enjoyable conversations and I felt like she had also benefited from the experience. I felt a touch guilty at avoiding contact when she'd been so generous, but I needed to feel comfortable in my new life. It didn't affect Ron's friendship with Elizabeth and her family, though. Because he had been so successful in his advertising career and earned a substantial salary, he had grown accustomed to a wealthy lifestyle. I wasn't sure that I'd ever feel comfortable in that sort of life; it wasn't something that I desired or needed. I just hoped that when I'd finished studying, I'd be able to provide well for Ali and myself.

During the first few months after my release I saw Vicki once or twice a week and, emotionally, things were at a standstill between us. I think Ron still felt pretty wary of my contact with her, which was understandable, so there was no big get-together when I was released. Initially, during the first few weeks, we tried to reignite a lover relationship, but we weren't successful. Sometimes I think we were just trying to recapture something from the past that was very beautiful but that was also over. We both needed to move forward, to establish a love and respect for each other as friends, but we found it difficult to forge a new relationship. For my part, spending time with Ali was paramount and I didn't have enough emotional energy left to share anything intense with anyone else. I'd changed so much since Vicki and I had met, and my needs were different now. We needed time apart to develop as individuals in this strange and new 'straight' world. For that reason, after the first twelve months we didn't see much of each other for several years.

Meanwhile, I couldn't believe I was enjoying being 'normal'. I even found it exciting. I kept up my exercise and meditation practice, so my sense of peace continued. I didn't think it would matter where you put me now—I felt so inwardly strong, I knew I could deal with it. But it was also weird because I felt so naive ... like a little girl in many ways, so unworldly, but it was a feeling that I was enjoying. It was a sort of innocence, like I'd just come into the world, and I was finding joy in this simple life. As I passed people in the street on my way to the shops, I was surprised to notice how little they smiled. I wondered why they could be unhappy. Sometimes they would return my smile and I hoped they had as much joy from life as I was experiencing. I even got excited about going to the supermarket and when I rang Jo, the Education Centre principal, someone I liked and respected, to tell her about my supermarket shopping, she laughed.

'Hey, Jo,' I said to her on the phone excitedly, 'I've just spent two hours at the supermarket!'

'What?' she asked, trying to comprehend. 'What were you doing in the supermarket for two hours?'

'I don't know ... the time just passed and then I realised how long I'd been there. I just can't stop looking at all that food on the shelves and when I go to select something, there's about six different brands and varieties of the one thing, and it takes me so long to make a decision.' I could hear her laughing on the other end of the phone. 'I've never seen so much food,' I exclaimed. 'I want to try it all!'

'It's hard to imagine finding supermarket shopping exciting,' she said. 'It's something I do as quickly as I can on the way home.' But I knew she was sharing my joy.

Eventually I honed the shopping time down to something more like the rest of the world, but I still felt like a little child looking at all that food. I didn't mind because I liked the feeling of newness and excitement, and I didn't necessarily want it to go away. I was aware that I seemed to be enjoying life more than most people I observed, and I wanted to hang on to that happiness. I didn't want to take anything for granted.

Of course I had my pensive and sad moments, but I accepted now that you can't only have happiness, the eternal aim of the drug addict. I was willing to allow the melancholy times, and some days after I'd walked Ali to school I'd return home feeling sad for all the lost time without her. I'd sit at the piano waiting ... to sing, or to write a new song about what I was feeling ... or whatever. An intense, deep grief would wash over me. I'd feel the lump in my throat and the tears would well in my eyes, but I still couldn't cry; I think I was still too scared. If

I cried for all that lost time, I still wasn't sure I'd be able to stop. Anyway, the tears wouldn't flow and I couldn't even sing any of the songs I'd written about Ali while we were separated; it felt too raw ... maybe one day. I'd sit staring at the piano until the sadness passed, then I'd turn my mind to my studies or clean the house. Sometimes I'd talk to 'Mima, our cat. It was so comforting having an animal around. She seemed to know when I was sad and would meow and sit on my lap for a cuddle. I think 'Mima knew more about my feelings than anyone.

It was at these times, when I was alone in the house after Ron had gone to work and Ali to school, that I felt grateful for my meditation and the Buddhist idea of journeying on the 'middle road', which was like finding the balance between yin and yan, positive and negative, light and dark energy. They helped restore balance when I felt a bit off-centre. They had become as important as my daily exercise and I couldn't imagine what my life would have been like if I didn't have them. I joined a local gym and maintained my fitness level, which in turn helped me feel alert and healthy. I also joined a couple of netball teams and played in a local competition two nights a week. It still felt a bit weird being able to go out at night because in prison we were always locked in so early. I still found myself going to bed at 9.30 pm, but it actually fitted in with my lifestyle as I went to the gym at 6.30 am almost every morning.

I didn't have much of a social life yet, although I spent a lot of time at Maud and Greg's. Usually Ali and I would go there on Friday nights and sometimes they'd come to Ron's for dinner. I found Maud easy to talk to and she became a special friend. Greg had returned from his Buddhist retreat and although we didn't talk as much as we used to when I was inside, there was still a good feeling between us. I knew that if I ever did want to have a serious conversation, he'd be there.

Corliss and Kurt had sold their Melbourne house and moved

to Castlemaine, about one and a half hour's drive inland, where they'd started an antique business. Ali and I went up there to spend weekends with them quite regularly, and our bonds with both of them continued to grow. I was lucky to have both Corliss and Maud to talk to as they understood what I'd experienced, having worked in the prison themselves. When we went to Castlemaine, Corliss and I often stayed up past midnight, long after Kurt and Ali had gone to bed; there was always so much to talk about, to catch up on, particularly as I couldn't see her as often as I would have liked. These talks, particularly with Corliss and Maud, were very important in my gaining an understanding of the 'real' world.

After about six months I decided it was time to look around for a cheap car. I'd already been able to save some money and Ron was willing to lend me the balance. Ron had a mate who was selling an old Datsun 120Y for about $1500, so I decided to buy it. I had to pay off about $1000 and after about three months I had it fully paid for. I was efficient at managing the small amount of money we had to live on.

After her release Vicki had found work in a yogurt company, starting on the factory floor and subsequently working her way up to a position in human resources and administration. She was able to offer me some casual work one day a week. Most of the time I rode my bike, which I'd bought second-hand for $150 not long after getting out of prison. It was quite a ride, but I was fit and enjoyed it, especially when I was actually going somewhere, which wasn't the case with the exercise bike! I'd earn $50 for my one day and it helped me pay off the car and get a few extras in our meagre life, like a few clothes and a night at the movies. Vicki and I were still having difficulty communicating effectively, so this minimal amount of contact was sufficient for the time being.

I continued to do well in my studies and completed my

degree a year after my release, in 1988. I was one of only five people from that year who were awarded their degree with distinction. That was a confidence booster, although I didn't attend the ceremony as it didn't seem important. I'd decided to apply for postgraduate degrees at a couple of universities, limiting my choice to those that were close to home so that I could be near Ali. A couple of months after applying I received acceptances from both universities, and ultimately chose the one that was nearest to Ron's house. It was also my first preference because it was a small campus and I was worried that I'd get lost on a big one! During 1989 I was going to study full-time to complete my postgraduate diploma in applied psychology. At the end of that year, when I turned thirty-six, I'd need to get a job and work for two years under supervision. This was the alternative option to staying at uni and completing a Master's degree. Then I'd be a psychologist. I had no doubt I'd get there.

Ali and I didn't seem to have any major problems settling back into life with each other, just the usual frustrations experienced by most parents and children. It all seemed rather easy, probably because I now believed in myself.

21

Starting a social life and a career

At the end of 1988, a year after my release and just prior to commencing my postgraduate studies, I was invited to a party by Jan, my good friend from TRAMM. She was having a barbecue to celebrate her birthday one Saturday afternoon in mid November. This was the first 'party' I'd be going to since my release and, because my old friends from TRAMM would be there, I was looking forward to it. Of course, I checked first to make sure that Ron would be home to take care of Ali—it was the first time I'd gone out socially without her.

It was wonderful to see Jan and David again, as well as Tony, an ex-lover of David's who'd also remained a good friend. A hairdresser by trade, Tony had once gained permission to come into the prison to perm my hair at the Education Centre ... when I think back now, I don't know how we wangled some of the things we did! Tony and I sat in the back yard nattering as the afternoon progressed. He was drinking beer and, suddenly realising I didn't have a drink, asked me if I'd like one.

Shit, I thought to myself. I would like a beer. Nothing like a cold one on a hot afternoon, but what about this abstinence thing? NA had maintained that any mind-altering substance was dangerous when you were trying to stay off drugs, but I really didn't anticipate that one beer would reignite my old craving for heroin. I just wasn't frightened any more. I relaxed, trying to put NA consciousness to the back of my mind, and thought, what the heck?

I talked to Tony about my old fears and the NA beliefs, and he was careful not to influence me either way. In truth, though, heroin wasn't an issue in my life any more, and alcohol never had been. Alcohol had never induced the psychological and physical craving that I had experienced with heroin, nor had it fulfilled my emotional needs—it was merely a way to be 'out of it'. It had been three years now since I'd had any mind-altering substance in my body and I was feeling as pure as the day I was born ... well, almost! I decided to have a stubby of beer over the course of the afternoon, and I sort of waited for it to set me off. Of course nothing happened, because the need for me to be 'out of it' had gone. I wasn't drinking to get drunk and I'd worked hard on my emotional shit. After what I'd been through there was little in life that I feared, although that's not to say that, for some people, the abstinence program may be something they'd need to practise for the rest of their lives—everyone's different.

Tony stuck with me for the afternoon and I felt safe having my first drink in this environment. Psychologically, it was a momentous occasion. But this wasn't the only momentous thing that happened. That afternoon my dormant passion was also stirred as I watched a friend of Jan's at the party. She was about the same age as me and I found her very attractive, although I didn't want to be too obvious about it.

'Tony, do you think we could go over there where that woman is?' I asked him.

'I know what you're up to, Barny,' he replied. 'Come on then,' he said, always one for an adventure.

We joined the crowd closest to where she was sitting, and

I discovered her name was Sarah. I hadn't felt this kind of passion for such a long time, although my shyness stopped me from being too forthright. I have to say, though, she wasn't actually showing any obvious signs of interest in me.

'How can I get her to notice me?' I asked Tony. My social skills had never been great and all those years of heroin use and jail certainly didn't help. Heroin is a very isolating drug.

'Just be patient and sit here with me,' he replied.

'Huh! Patience has never been one of my strengths!' I exclaimed.

The afternoon passed and, to my disappointment, nothing happened between Sarah and me. Just as we were all leaving, Jan suggested that we meet at a nightclub later in the evening, after she'd finished a singing job she had on. A few people expressed some interest in this idea and I started to consider it, wondering whether Ron was going to be home that evening. Jan let me use her phone to call him.

'Would you be able to mind Ali if I went out to a club later tonight?' I asked him.

'Yeah, no worries, I'm not going anywhere.' My luck was in. Ron was almost always out on Saturday nights.

'Unreal! Thanks,' I said to him. 'I'll be home shortly. We're not going until later.'

I returned to the back yard where half a dozen people were making arrangements to meet later. Sarah wanted to go but she was concerned about going on her own. I took the opportunity to approach her: 'Where do you live?' I asked. 'Maybe I could pick you up.'

'I'm staying the weekend at a friend's in South Yarra,' she replied.

'I live just down the road and have to pass there on my way. I could pick you up if you like and we could go together.' I couldn't even believe the words were coming out of my mouth.

'Okay, that'd be great,' she replied. 'What time?'

'How about 10 o'clock?'

She wrote the address on a piece of paper. 'See you later then.'

Yippee!, I thought to myself. I was so excited, I felt like a child. I looked across to see Tony smiling at me.

'Good on ya, Barny!' he said once Sarah had gone. He was so happy for me. It was a very exciting day.

Once I got home I realised I didn't have anything suitable to wear to a nightclub—I still didn't even own a pair of jeans. In the end I found some tights and a loose top. They were going to have to do. I felt like a teenager getting ready to go to a party, especially as I was usually in bed before 10 pm, just like in prison!

I wanted to share my excitement with Ron but we hadn't discussed relationships since my release and I felt that, deep down, he'd like me to meet a man and probably get married, then everyone could relax! Unfortunately, it was not likely to happen because while I liked men as friends, I just didn't seem to be attracted to them as lovers any more. I didn't exclude them as a possibility, but my experience with women had been much more fulfilling.

The truth is, I was actually a bit wary of talking to Ron about relationships, especially lesbian ones. I suspected that he didn't really approve, even though he'd accepted my relationship with Vicki. I'd heard from a friend of his that he'd once said he would take Ali from me if I had another lesbian relationship. While I couldn't believe that was true, it had caused me some anxiety and I'd been glad that, until now anyway, it hadn't been necessary to discuss it with him since my release. In the end I decided not to share my enthusiasm with him that night.

Finally it was time to drive to Sarah's place to pick her up. When she opened the door she looked great, and I immediately resolved to do something about my own embarrassing wardrobe!

Aside from a couple of work type outfits that I'd bought shopping with Elizabeth the day of my release, since then I'd only acquired cheap tights and tracksuit pants and tops for casual wear. You can't really wear a tracksuit to a nightclub! We drove to the club, chatting about superficial things, and walked in together. Once inside we saw some of the others, but they were already up dancing so we ordered some drinks and then stood awkwardly beside each other, watching everyone on the dance floor. I had no idea what she was thinking and I was too shy to make a move in case I made a fool of myself.

By about 3 am the situation didn't seem to have changed and my legs were getting sore from standing there so long. I'd just about decided she'd had enough too when, suddenly, I felt an arm reach around me and come to rest on my other shoulder. I tried not to gasp, but it was hard. I took a deep breath and held my body tight to stop it shaking with excitement. Apart from the short interlude with Vicki, it had been five years since anyone had held me like this. I looked sideways at her and, sensing that she was willing, leaned forward to kiss her. Romantic, hey? You bet! It's now or never, I said to myself as I took the plunge. Now that I knew she was interested, I was enthralled—it felt so good to be held in her arms and my insides were churning with unspent passion.

After a short time we decided to leave the nightclub and drive to her place. In the car I decided I might as well tell her the truth about my 'past' before we progressed any further—that way she could make a judgment about whether she wanted to see me again. I gave her a summarised version of my heroin addiction and jail sentence, and when I'd finished there was silence. I was beginning to think that it had all been too much for her, but when she spoke again she was okay about it, just a bit shocked. After a bit more cuddling and kissing, she took my phone number and we organised to call each other the following week. As I drove away I couldn't believe that a 'straight' person seemed to be attracted to me!

The next morning I told Ali I'd met someone I was romantically interested in. While she was curious, I don't think she understood how it might affect her, and she didn't share my excitement. My next task was to tell Ron. I was worried but, not being one to put things off, I went straight into the lounge room where he was watching the Sunday Sports program on television.

'Ron,' I said to him, trying to get his attention, 'I met someone last night at the nightclub and I'm going to see her again. She's really nice.' I waited apprehensively, wondering if he'd approve or disapprove.

'Where is she from?' he asked, not terribly interested. Okay so far, I was thinking, although it felt like I was talking to a parent and I resolved to change the way we communicated. I didn't feel like I had to seek approval from anyone any more.

'She lives in Shoreham, but was staying in town for the weekend. She has a daughter a bit younger than Ali and works as a book-keeper,' I replied. 'I'm hoping she'll ring me this week. She said she would.'

Ron didn't sound thrilled, but he was accepting. I continued talking to him about my fears in regard to his attitude towards my involvement in lesbian relationships, and he reassured me that it wasn't a problem for him—although I was sure he just wanted me to be 'normal'! It was important to me that the relationship between Ron and me was open and honest. Even though I didn't need his approval, I didn't want conflict getting in the way, particularly while living in his home. I started to feel relieved that he seemed all right about it, because I wasn't going to conduct my relationships in secret. I wasn't even sure what I wanted for the future—it was too early yet—but there were two things that

I knew I didn't want: I didn't want to move out, and I didn't want a major conflict with Ron.

Sarah and I took time getting to know each other and, after some months, we developed an intense relationship. I guess anything with me was going to be intense, it's just the way I am. Our two daughters seemed to enjoy each other's company too. Ron met both Sarah and her daughter and was terrific with them. I think he really liked them.

The relationship with Sarah continued through 1989, during which I studied full-time. After completing my postgraduate studies at the end of the year, I got some casual work at youth refuges and resurrected my singing career, getting a couple of weekly gigs playing the piano and singing in a pub and a small restaurant. I enjoyed performing and hoped it might become a permanent job. Although I dreamed of singing full-time, I still planned on becoming a psychologist, knowing that it would provide a more secure career and income to sustain Ali and me.

For my birthday in December 1989, Sarah, the girls, Ron, Maud and Greg took me to a restaurant. As a surprise, Maud and Greg brought along Julie, the friend who'd jokingly called me 'mum' in jail. She had recently been released from prison again, and it was wonderful to see her. Ali adored Julie, remembering how she'd played with her when she'd come in to the prison for the all-day Saturday visits. Ali sat on Julie's knee for most of the night, enjoying her company and the attention she was receiving. It was great to see Julie in the 'outside' world and apparently not using. She certainly had clear eyes and a big smile. She'd only been out of prison a couple of weeks. Just before her release she'd been involved in a Fairlea drama group play with Maud and Greg. Ali and I had been allowed into the prison for the public session, and we thought her performance was fantastic.

The night at the restaurant was lovely and I felt very special, very loved and that I belonged ... that I had a valuable place in this world. It might not sound remarkable to most people, but that's what had always been missing from my life. I really felt that now I had a contribution to make.

I didn't see Julie again after that birthday celebration but, not long after, I heard that she'd returned to using and was back in jail. It made me feel sad. It also made me feel lonely in a way, because of all the friends I'd made in prison, there were very few with whom I could maintain a friendship now. I still kept up occasional contact with Vicki and Marg, but otherwise I didn't see anyone from my using days. People like Danni, Sue and Rikki very rarely contacted me any more, and Chipper had died of an overdose. I think they respected my transition to the straight world and didn't want to impose their chaotic, drug-using lives on me. It actually made me respect them even more. Although I didn't want anything to do with the ugly world of illegal drugs, I still missed their company and the understanding that had flowed between us. I always used to think we'd all grow old together, still friends, still using.

At the beginning of 1990, Sarah, the girls and I decided to move into a house in Middle Park, a lovely suburb next to St Kilda, along Port Phillip Bay in Victoria. It was only a fifteen-minute drive to Ron's house, and five minutes to Maud and Greg's. I was looking for counselling work, but in the meantime I maintained my singing gigs. The money was quite good but the work was irregular. The music industry doesn't offer much financial security and I was a single parent now.

One day while walking outside the local library in Albert Park, a neighbouring suburb, I heard someone call out my name. I didn't immediately recognise the young woman walking towards me. Noticing that I was puzzled, she identified herself: 'I'm Lyndel ... Carol's sister.' Of course! I held out my arms and we gave each other a hug.

'Wow, it's good to see you. What a pleasant surprise!' I was apprehensive about asking after Carol because I'd heard she wasn't doing too well and was in a relationship with a really violent dealer. In fact I'd accidentally run into Carol outside the prison when I was visiting someone a few months earlier. She had a broken arm and told me her boyfriend had done it when he found out she was using. It sounded so similar to the relationships I'd had before going to prison. It was the only contact I'd had with her since my release.

'How is Carol? I haven't seen her for such a long time ...' I trailed off.

'Don't you know?' Lyndel asked me.

'Know what?' I said to her, uneasiness spreading through my body.

'She died a couple of months ago ... an overdose.' Lyndel closed her eyes, obviously still reeling from the pain of her sister's worthless death. I gave her a hug.

'Fuck ...' I cursed under my breath. 'I'm sorry, I didn't know.' Although it was a sunny day, my heart felt suddenly heavy and my head felt tired. In my mind Carol's beautiful laughter was as clear as ever.

We stood outside the library for quite a while talking about Carol's life over the past few years since her release, and the circumstances surrounding her death. Lyndel explained that the police were still uncertain whether it was an accidental overdose. There was an inquest pending. It seemed her boyfriend at the time, a violent dealer/user, had been shot in the knees only a couple of hours before Carol was found overdosed. There was speculation that he may have ripped someone off for some heroin and got shot in the lower legs as a result, but there was no evidence and no-one was talking. After he and Carol had scored their heroin and he'd been shot, a couple of hours elapsed before they were both found slumped in the laundry of some Flemington flats by one of the tenants. They had both overdosed and were unconscious. At first the tenant thought that they were a couple of drunks who had dozed off in a drunken stupor, but when he realised that Carol had no sign of a pulse, he immediately called an ambulance. Although her boyfriend regained consciousness, Carol was already dead when the ambulance and police arrived.

It was shocking news and a shocking story, and even though Lyndel and I talked for quite a while, I had still not recovered my equilibrium by the time I returned home. I'd have to tell Ali eventually, but I dreaded it.

Because Lyndel worked at the local library, I saw her a few times over the followng months and we reminisced about Carol. Lyndel had always been there for Carol, like my brother had for me, but she didn't have the power to change it for her . . . no-one does. Carol's pain belonged to Carol, and although Marg, Lyndel, Carol's mum and probably many others tried to drag her out of the web of violent males and drug use that she'd become caught in, no-one was able to do it for her. Carol had left violent boyfriends so many times. Sometimes she'd hide out at Marg's place swearing that she was leaving them for good, only to return to them a week or two later. There were times when you wished you could take someone's journey for them, when you wished you could take on a bit of their pain in order to make it more bearable for them, but you never can. I began to realise how lucky I was to have escaped that world relatively unscathed.

Much later I found an article on Carol's death at the State Library. It wasn't comforting.

> A man found shot and unconscious next to the body of his girlfriend has discharged himself from hospital and disappeared. Police said yesterday the man checked out of Royal Melbourne Hospital just hours before surgery to

remove shotgun pellets from his legs.

The man and his 30-year-old girlfriend were found slumped on the floor of a communal laundry at a block of flats in Flemington on Saturday. The man, 28, refused to answer police questions when revived. He was taken to hospital but signed himself out in the middle of the night.

A syringe was found next to the woman's body and police believe she died from a drug overdose. No weapon has been found . . .

A resident found [Carol] and her boyfriend in the laundry of the flats in Canterbury St about 6.30 pm on Saturday.

The resident said [Carol] was slumped on her knees with her head on the floor and [her boyfriend] was unconscious on his back. He said he thought the two had collapsed after drinking, but returned minutes later to check if they were breathing. The man then called an ambulance.

Ambulance officers worked on [Carol] for some time, but were unable to revive her. [Carol's boyfriend] was revived and allegedly threatened police and ambulance officers. [Carol's boyfriend] has convictions for armed robbery, burglary, assaults and possessing and using drugs, and has been arrested several times by the police special operations group.

A police spokesman said [Carol's boyfriend] refused to tell police how or where he received the wounds to both lower legs. The spokesman said crude bandages had been wrapped around

the wounds, but [Carol's boyfriend] was still
bleeding profusely when found.

(*The Sun*, 17 April 1990, page 15)

At the inquest into Carol's death months later, no further
information had been gathered and it was concluded that she contributed to her own death by way of an overdose of heroin. On
reading the inquest report, I was astounded at how little investigation had been done. The police never took a statement from
her boyfriend, nor did they get any information from any of her
friends at the time. It seemed like they couldn't be bothered, happy
for the death to be recorded as a drug overdose. Carol had a little
girl who was about four years old when Carol died; she'd been
living with Carol's mum for some months prior to the death.

This was a period during which my life seemed punctuated
by deaths. Not long after Carol's death, I heard more bad news.
This time it was Tammy. On 16 July 1990 Tammy was found
overdosed in a car in East Brunswick, a north-eastern suburb of
Melbourne. A pedestrian found her body slumped across the
front seat of her car, with the passenger side door left hanging
wide open. According to the coroner's report, she may have been
dead for a couple of hours before being discovered. Also found
in the car, underneath her body, were two spoons, a syringe, a
handbag strap (tourniquet), a piece of silver foil, a cigarette lighter
and a tissue showing a small bloodstain. No suicide note, no signs
of violence, no formal statements from any witnesses. One of the
forms from the coronial investigation was titled, 'Death of Criminal'. It brought tears to my eyes. If I'd been writing about
Tammy's death I would have headed it, 'Death of a Very Special
and Beautiful Young Woman'.

As in Carol's case, there seems to have been very little investigation of the circumstances surrounding her death. The autopsy

report gave the cause of death as drug-related: 'The autopsy and toxicological findings are consistent with death following intravenous use of heroin in combination with the use of propoxyphene, ephedrine and benzodiazepines.' In other words, a cocktail of heroin, speed and pills, with a bit of cannabis thrown in.

As had also happened with Carol, it had been some years since I had seen or heard from Tammy, so the loss did not affect me in my daily life. What I did feel, though, was a deep, gut-wrenching sadness, like collective grief from the unconscious. Tammy was twenty-seven when she died. I was unable to find out much about her more recent situation because my only contacts—two of her step-sisters who were also drug users—had already died, one from an overdose, the other by hanging herself in the women's section of Pentridge prison. I knew all of them from drug use and from prison, but Tammy was the one that Vicki and I had become close to. In my later work I was forced to face many more such deaths. You never get used to it.

I was grateful that my own life was moving forward positively. In August 1990 a permanent job became available at the youth refuge where I'd been doing relief work and, in the same week, I noticed a 'counselling' position advertised at Task Force, a community agency in Prahran. I'd already applied and been interviewed for some jobs, but I didn't have any idea how to conduct myself in the interviews and had been unsuccessful so far. I'd walked into a couple of the interviews feeling arrogant, knowing that I could do the job required but unable to understand why I had to sit there for an hour and prove it to them. Needless to say, the outcome was 'don't call us, we'll call you'.

Cliff, a friend of Maud's, gave me some job interview coaching, explaining the questions I'd most likely be asked and how to respond. I had to admit I'd been on the wrong track. Both Task Force and the youth refuge invited me to an interview so, armed with this new information, I approached them with a different attitude. Eventually I was offered the Task Force job and invited back for a second interview at the youth refuge. I ultimately accepted the counselling position. It was the kind of work I was most interested in as I wanted to do long-term rather than crisis counselling. I also knew the manager at the agency, Craig; he'd been a student at Gippsland Institute when I was there, and I liked and respected him. Also, the agency was aware of my 'past' and wasn't fazed by it.

Around this time my relationship with Sarah ran into insurmountable difficulty and, after living together for eight months, we finally separated the weekend before I commenced my new job on Monday, 3 September 1990. I felt sad that it hadn't worked out, but in a way I also felt relieved. We'd been having problems for a few months and the tension and conflict were becoming unbearable.

Maybe it was too soon for me to be in a relationship, but Sarah just didn't understand Ali's and my closeness, even though she had a child herself. She put too much pressure on me to give her more attention and time. In the end I found I wasn't in love with her any more, which she refused to accept. I think she would have been happier if the reason for finishing the relationship had been because I'd met someone else, or had an affair! The straight world baffled me at times, but at least I began to realise that I hadn't ever been as fucked as I once thought I'd been. I found that sometimes people didn't like honesty and that straight people often had as many problems as drug addicts.

Anyway, it was an acrimonious ending to our relationship and Ali and I had to move out. I rang Ron to see whether he'd have us back. I was pretty confident he'd be happy about it because, living on his own since we'd left, he'd had to employ a housekeeper to do his cleaning and ironing. Sure enough, it was fine by him. 'I like your cooking,' he'd said, laughing. He was only half joking, though—the only thing he could cook was bacon and eggs! So Ali, our cat 'Mima and I moved back to Ron's. It didn't take much effort as we didn't own any furniture: we were settled back into our old rooms before I commenced work on the Monday.

On my first day at Task Force, Craig handed me a bunch of keys which allowed me to access not only my office but also the front door, the security room where all the files were kept, and the filing cabinets. It felt so strange to be given this 'privilege' without having to prove anything. I said nothing because I didn't think anyone would understand, but once I was alone in my office, I sat and stared at the keys. Of course they reminded me of prison, but I was astounded to be trusted and respected so implicitly.

I quickly grew to love my job and the people with whom I worked. I threw myself into it heart and soul. Initially, because of my own drug-using past, I thought I'd find working in the specialist area of drug and alcohol treatment a bit boring, but it was one of the few advertised positions for which I received an interview—I guess most organisations weren't interested in a thirty-six-year-old with a criminal history applying for their first counselling job. As I settled into the work, however, I realised that not much time was actually spent talking about substance use. Unless a person presented as being out of control with their using or drinking, the therapy sessions covered an interesting mix of issues, and I found myself on a steep learning curve.

I developed a special interest in working with issues arising from childhood sexual abuse, from which so many substance users have suffered. My office became a sanctuary where people felt safe and, I hope, nurtured. I felt very privileged to have a job where I was witness to the strength and courage that emerged in that meagre space, where daily I could share the miracles of transformation that human beings are capable of. In group sessions I saw such compassion and humility that, at times, it reduced me to tears . . . tears of joy that human beings could care about each other so much. I learned to focus on those things in life that so many other 'normal' people didn't find remarkable.

I have to say that drug addicts and criminals, myself included in that group, have taught me what is vital in life—and my job has taught me not to forget. It also taught me never to think I knew what was going to happen next for someone. There were times as a counsellor that I despaired, thinking that I'd achieved nothing, that someone was never going to make the necessary change to produce anything positive in their life. And so many times, just when I'd felt like giving up, they'd do it—they'd make that big change. I consistently live in awe of the courage individuals possess. Every day my job gave me a lesson in living.

At times it was difficult to contain the sadness it also produced when a person didn't make it and I'd find myself attending funerals, but if I ever felt defeated, it was only momentary. I always maintained a sense of hope. I found my counselling job allowed me to share an intimacy and depth with people, where honesty was a given and trust was developed as journeys were travelled together. My heart was filled with compassion, derived largely from my own suffering, and the suffering of those with whom I worked.

After I'd been at Task Force a couple of years, I approached them for a wage rise to enable Ali and me to live independently of Ron. After a struggle the agency finally agreed, increasing my status to senior counsellor. I knew I was doing a good job and felt that I was worth every cent that I was paid, but I also knew I would never be able to measure my worth in monetary terms. I was more interested in the quality of my work and feeling fulfilled, even though the hours were long and emotionally draining.

While living at Ron's I'd gradually been buying the furniture and appliances that Ali and I would need to live in our own place. Now that I was earning enough money to support us, we started looking for our first 'home'. We could only afford to rent a flat, and Ali threw herself into the task of finding one, excited at the prospect of living independently. She scoured the real estate section of the newspaper every week and we organised to look at several places. I was impressed with her skills! In West St Kilda she found a second storey flat which we both agreed would be our future home, and we became increasingly excited in anticipation of our move. Once again, the piano and 'Mima would be coming with us. Of course, we couldn't afford to pay a removalist, so Ron and a few friends, including Rikki, helped us.

On the day we moved we almost couldn't get the piano up the stairs to the second floor. With patience and persistence, of which Ron and I had very little, we succeeded although at one stage, when the piano hung precariously over the staircase rail as we tried to manoeuvre it around a corner, it looked like we'd have to get a crane to lift it in over the balcony!

'Don't plan on moving for a long time,' Ron said as the piano was finally rolled in through the flat's front door. The only thing left to do was unpack and retrieve 'Mima from Ron's. We opened a bottle of champagne to celebrate: pop! went the cork. 'I declare a toast to me finally attaining independence at the ripe old age of thirty-six! I'm a bit of a late starter.'

'Good on ya, Barny!' said Rikki, clinking our glasses together. She and her partner Carey had been helping us. As our eyes met, I sensed her unspoken respect for me. We both knew how hard and long the journey had been to get where we were.

'Congratulations!' Ron exclaimed, laughing. He was happy for us, although I knew he'd miss us at his house. We'd found it very easy living together as neither of us was intrusive; also as neither of us had married, it also gave us a sense of family. It was a big move for Ali. Now ten, she had lived at Ron's house for a total of six years.

I continued to prosper in the job at Task Force and was totally committed. During my years there I was invited to become a member of several local community agencies' management committees; I became honorary secretary of the Victorian Women's Prisons Council, as well as being invited onto the 'Agenda for Change' committee, which was setting up specific policies for women in prison. Its members had been selected from relevant community and women's organisations and senior staff from Corrections, and its meetings were held in the head office of the Corrections Department. It was weird just going into the building, let alone sitting in the conference room with Corrections staff, and it took me some time not to feel intimidated. For me it was such a role reversal that I wasn't at all sure I could cope with it. When I first walked into the conference room I felt like I had PRISONER stamped on my forehead. It was peculiar being there as a community worker. Sitting around the table were many of the same people who had sat behind a table in Classification Committee meetings in the prison, making important decisions about my life. I had been at the mercy of these people for nearly eight years and, to some degree, would continue to be at their mercy for the remainder of my parole—another five years.

Now I had to try and meet them as an equal—not that I'd ever felt lesser than them, just different. I felt out of place, uncomfortable sharing the room. Maybe I'd never be able to sit on the same side of the table as them. As time passed, though, and because some of the community members were such lovely people, I adjusted and found a way to speak up more openly in meetings. As far as I knew, this was the first time in Victoria that specific policies were being developed for women in prison, so it felt like it was an important thing to be involved in. The outcome was a document called 'The Agenda for Change', and I hoped that it would contribute to creating improvements within the women's prison system.

There were now two prisons specifically for women in Victoria: Fairlea, the maximum security prison where I'd served my sentence, and Tarrengower, which was a minimum security prison in Maldon, about 130 kilometres north-west of Melbourne. Tarrengower wasn't enclosed by a concrete wall and some of the women were able to go out into the community to do voluntary work during the day. Tarrengower opened just after my release. If it had been operational earlier, I may have been able to keep Ali for the duration of my sentence as she would have been able to attend a local school and wouldn't have had to suffer the more severe regimentation of the maximum security prisons. About eight children usually lived with their mums at Tarrengower. Although an improvement on the past, it was still far short of ideal.

My life was branching out from my naive beginnings at Ron's house. I was losing some of that sense of 'innocence', but not my newfound joy. I was able to gradually integrate into the community and feel like I belonged, although I didn't always understand 'life'. I also realised that many people have problems at different times in their lives and that we prisoners/criminals weren't such a strange bunch after all. How I wished we hadn't been so negatively stereotyped. It felt like it would be a lifetime's work to break down some of those community attitudes, but I had the energy for a challenge!

22

The birth of Somebody's Daughter: love, death and vulnerability

M aud and I had often talked of the value of expanding the
work of the Fairlea drama group to the outside community, the main stumbling block being that it was difficult to
find enough women who had left prison, were doing okay, and
who were interested in arts-based workshops. We had already
witnessed the power of our performances in changing people's
attitudes inside the prison.

During 1990, just before I began my work at Task Force,
Maud introduced me to Tracey, who'd recently been released
from Fairlea where she had been involved in the drama activities.
In fact she had been in the same play that Julie had performed
in. Tracey was interested in forming a drama group outside
prison, so eventually a few of us—including Marg and I, who'd
been in prison during the 1980s, and Sam, a woman I'd been
working with at Task Force (Vicki had just moved to New South
Wales so didn't become involved initially)—got together with
Tracey at Maud and Greg's house to discuss the possibilities. All
of us had experienced either the juvenile justice or the adult
prison system and had histories of drug addiction, as well as being
interested in the drama/music aspect of performing. Our
dramatic activities in prison had also taught us how valuable

experience-based performances could be as an educational tool for the community, so we decided to give it a go. We met weekly, with Maud facilitating the drama workshops, and over the next year material began to accumulate. Another group of women who weren't interested in performance also formed, and they met separately as an 'art' group. These sessions were facilitated by Sally, who had also taught visual arts inside prison. As the core group evolved, the need for a name became obvious. A brainstorming session came up with a number of possibilities including 'Fallen Angels', 'Herd of Angels' and 'Somebody's Daughter'. After much debate the name 'Somebody's Daughter' emerged as the favourite, so that's what we called ourselves.

By 1992 we had an abundance of material, more than enough to devise our first 'outside' play, 'Tell Her That I Love Her', based on Tracey's story of leaving prison and facing the difficulties of trying to lead a 'straight' life. For the first time I felt confident enough to step out on stage and perform rather than just sit in the wings singing the occasional song. Another first during the production and performance of this play was that I finally felt disconnected enough from the grief I'd experienced over my separation from Ali to write and sing a beautiful song about what I'd gone through. It was a powerful piece and it was only performing it then, five years after my release from prison, that I could at last unleash my tears. Ali also cried after our first performance, and I was relieved that she'd been able to release her sadness too.

Our two-week season at the Malthouse Theatre in South Melbourne was so successful that we returned for a four-week season in 1993. Vicki hadn't been involved in our 1992 performance, mainly because she was then living in New South Wales, but she returned in time for our second season. She, Marg and I, who'd all been in jail together in the early 1980s, formed three of the five cast members. It was a miracle that the three of us had made it this far. And it was only then, five years after my release, that Vicki and I were finally able to transform our mutual love into friendship.

The play made the schools' list in Victoria, so during the second season hundreds of students attended. We had feedback sessions with them after our performances, and their reactions were amazing. They opened their hearts to us and talked about all kinds of issues from sexual abuse and lack of communication with parents to fears about drug use or their friends' drug use. The teachers from a couple of rural schools were so impressed, they brought their students to Melbourne in a bus for combined drama sessions with people from Somebody's Daughter and Task Force. Many of the issues that came out of these sessions were about drugs, and again we realised the power of this kind of work to inform and educate. I have never witnessed young people so engaged as these students were in the drama sessions. I truly believe they learned lessons about drug use, and life in general, that would remain deep in their hearts for the rest of their lives. I began to think about trying to get funding to run similar sessions for other young people.

During this time some of us began to have singing lessons to help with voice production for our performances. Our teachers were Murray Madardy and his wife, Anna, both of whom I found inspiring. Although the others didn't continue after our performance season was over, I decided to take up regular singing lessons again, for the first time since I was a teenager. I rediscovered my love of classical music as I tackled arias and other beautiful music, and once again my voice and heart sang together. It made me feel strong inside as I worked on breathing exercises, the basis of singing.

Not everything went well at that time, though. During our return season of 'Tell Her that I Love Her' in 1993, a couple of us heard some terrible news on the radio one morning while driving to the theatre in our separate cars. It was about a body that had been pulled from the Yarra River some days earlier, on 8 March. The body had been identified as Julie, our friend from prison who'd participated in the drama group inside. Julie, who used to call me 'mum'. She had been murdered. She was just twenty-nine years old.

As we arrived at the theatre for rehearsal we gathered in the café, not quite knowing what to say or do next. Not everyone had heard the news so we had to break it to them, a painful task. We were all stunned, particularly as the details were so gruesome. Some of us cried, some of us sat there too shocked to do or say anything.

Our play always ended with a tribute to the twenty or so friends who'd died from drug-related causes. As we named each of them we'd toss roses onto the stage in honour of their memory. At the conclusion of that day's performance, we added Julie's name to our growing list. Carol was already on our list and there was a special section in the play which Marg and I performed together which was dedicated to Carol. It included a song called 'Stowaway' which Marg sang during each night's performance, capturing Carol's essence. It was a tribute to the beautiful girl we knew her to be.

As a group we turned to each other for comfort—there was no way to reconcile these violent deaths. We tried not to get lost in our despair, but it was hard. We had to make sure these women's lives had meaning, that our voices spoke for them, so that they wouldn't have lived and died young for nothing. During our warm-up we dedicated that night's performance to Julie.

Months later an article about Julie's death appeared in the newspaper. John Eric 'Buddha' Cuthbertson had been charged and convicted of her murder. He was sentenced to seventeen years in jail. In his summing up the judge had said to the defendant:

> [Julie] had to die after she gave him [the
> murderer] a 'hard time'. You asphyxiated [Julie]
> with Glad Wrap after she was drugged, knocked
> to the ground by [...], stomped on, suffocated
> with a pillow and injected with battery acid.
>
> Afterwards you dumped [Julie's] body,
> rolled in a carpet, in the river. The court heard
> evidence she may have still been alive.

It was a gruesome murder, but what I found almost as upsetting
was the journalist's opening sentence: 'A wicked killer was yesterday jailed for life for the gruesome murder of a prostitute.' I
felt so offended reading it. Julie was so much more than a prostitute and it was such a degrading way to describe her. She was
a beautiful young woman with a wonderful sense of humour,
and she loved children, but none of that was included in the
journalist's description.

Over the next few years our theatre group grasped every
opportunity to try to educate the community by reaching into
their hearts and shattering the myths about drug addicts and criminals so often perpetuated by the media. With each death we
were forced to endure, we became more vocal and more public
in trying to give voice to our friends' lives. We couldn't make
the community value their lives but, with our hearts open, we
could state in our performances and through the media how
much we loved our drug-addicted, prostitute and criminal
friends, and we could only hope that in some way, no matter
how small, we might change some people's perceptions. We had
to hope that people would be willing to take a closer look behind
these destructive social labels we were forced to wear.

Because of our belief in this work, we continued to devise
and perform plays, appear at conferences and provide workshops
for young people as well as community workers such as teachers

and people involved in areas like housing, drugs and alcohol, hospitals and street outreach programs. I did all this in my spare time, utilising my yearly vacation for the performance season and maintaining my full-time job at Task Force.

Later in 1993, not long after Julie's death, the Corrections Department announced that they were thinking of opening a women's section at Pentridge's infamous Jika Jika division, supposedly to ease overcrowding at Fairlea. A protest vigil was immediately set up outside Fairlea as the whole notion was horrific. Jika Jika, a relatively new 'concrete' prison, was purpose-built for the most dangerous male criminals in Victoria. It was an electronic hell in which five men had already died trying to burn it down in protest against its inhumane environment. Even the exercise area consisted of cages. This was where Vicki had been sent for punishment in 1982–83, and her experience there still haunted her. It was hard to believe the department could seriously consider this a suitable environment for women prisoners, most of whom were not violent or dangerous. Another part of the vigil was to campaign against the proposal of turning the maximum security women's prison over to private operators.

While Somebody's Daughter members couldn't involve themselves in the vigil as such—most members found it too difficult emotionally to sit outside the prison for long periods of time, particularly listening to the loudspeaker coming from inside the walls—we did involve ourselves in a concert which took place on the oval right outside the front of the prison, as well as another major event at the Malthouse Theatre where we performed a piece called 'Tell Someone Who Cares'. After eight months of camping outside Fairlea and a lot more public outcry over the plan, the department scrapped the idea and the women remained at Fairlea.

It was during the Jika/Fairlea campaign that I met and fell in love with Amanda. She was a community lawyer who often worked on issues related to women in prison, and our paths had crossed as a result of our work. I'd had my eye on her for a few months and had indicated my interest, but it wasn't returned until one night at the vigil outside Fairlea. Ali and I were there with a few of the people who were 'on duty' for the evening, and so was Amanda. There were about half a dozen of us sitting around a fire, trying to keep warm. We spent the night drinking and talking and generally having a lot of fun. During the course of the night I had to go to a radio interview to promote the vigil. I had intended to return home with Ali after the interview but, as I got ready to leave, Ali decided she wanted to spend the night outside the prison. It meant sleeping in cars and she saw it as a bit of an adventure. Although not so keen myself, I agreed. When I got back from my interview a couple of hours later, I found everyone still around the fire, having drunk much beer, but almost ready for bed.

Amanda invited Ali and me to sleep in her vehicle—it was a panel van and at least promised some comfort by way of a mattress—but when we climbed in we found it too squishy, so Ali decided to sleep in another car where she'd been offered a bed with a bit more space. This left Amanda and me to the privacy of her van. Well ... if I ever had ideas of a romantic night in the back of her van, I could forget it! She was really rude and we actually had a huge argument—trying to talk seriously to someone who is very drunk is futile, of course—but by morning we had managed to talk things through. She couldn't even remember being obnoxious! We were very different people, with very different life experiences, and we were both wary, but it was to be the commencement of a relationship which lasted four years.

The biggest shock came in the morning: 'Muster up! Muster up!' I heard the sound floating on the breeze over the prison walls. What a nightmare! I looked across at Amanda and laughed.

Fancy spending the first night of a new romantic liaison outside the bloody prison! We both had a good laugh at the irony of it . . . I really wonder about myself sometimes!

I climbed out of the van into the early morning mist and took a look around me. The river was not far away, winding through trees and bushes, and we were surrounded by parkland. I'd never really taken much notice before—I guess I'd never hung around *outside* the prison. 'It really is quite beautiful on this side of the concrete wall. I never knew any of this existed. It's so peaceful out here,' I said to Amanda as my eyes feasted on the vivid green of sports grounds, bush tracks, bike tracks, old gum trees—all so different to what lay within that concrete shell. It was like someone had plonked a concrete wall around five acres of land, designating it a container of emotional disaster. It's a wonder they hadn't put a lid on it as well, so the air couldn't mingle with the fresh air outside. I still couldn't understand how a simple, dumb thing like a wall could create such crippling isolation. It's probably no coincidence that right next door was the hospital for infectious diseases—it, too, had quarantine areas. I thought about how some people really believed that things like criminality and homosexuality were genetic or a disease, something that 'normal' people need to be protected from.

It took a few months for Amanda and I to get the relationship happening. For the first six months she wouldn't even tell me she loved me or acknowledge that we were in a relationship. She had this disconcerting ability to seemingly shut her heart off. I had to virtually force her to admit she wanted it. This was the first time I'd taken a risk in an intimate relationship with someone so different from myself. We were opposites in many aspects of our lives: I was only interested in monogamous relationships whereas she'd never had one before; she was very externally focused, depending a great deal on the environment for comfort, whereas I was, at that point at least, almost exclusively internally focused, depending on my meditation and exercise regime for inner contentment. I was very self-contained and self-sufficient, determined I'd never be dependent on another human being ever again. I had only a few close friends with whom I had deep, often intense, conversations, while she had many, many friends. Although our relationship proved challenging, it became the most open and honest one I had ever had, either previously, or since.

It was probably the first time since giving up heroin that I'd felt really vulnerable with someone intimate, but I'd learned how to protect myself by then and I felt safe enough to explore new territory. Amanda's mum had died of breast cancer when Amanda was twelve years old and she seemed hellbent on never letting anyone hurt her that much again. It seemed she wasn't going to let herself love anyone and I had to break my way into her heart. There were times during the first couple of years that I threw my hands in the air and gave up, but she'd always return, asking me to give it another go.

About a year into the relationship, we both really needed a break so we decided to go on a three-week camping trip along the coast of northern New South Wales. Ali, who still had to go to school, would alternate between Ron's, Maud's and Vicki's homes while I was away. Because most of my holidays from my Task Force work had been taken up with Somebody's Daughter performances, I'd not really had much in the way of holiday experiences, so I was very excited as we packed the car with our camping gear.

We drove the whole day, finally stopping, after about fifteen hours, at Hawks Nest, a beautiful coastal village about three hours north of Sydney. We were too tired to look for a suitable place to camp, so we stayed the night at the local caravan park.

The next morning I went for an early jog along the beach, breathing in the wonderful fresh air and absorbing the beautiful surroundings. It was so peaceful, with an endless expanse of water in front of me merging into the sky on the horizon. These sorts of experiences still felt new after all my time in prison. In some way they also felt extravagant, as though they were a sort of luxury or something. We set off early to look for somewhere to camp, quickly finding a remote place a little further north. Surrounded by ocean and sand dunes on one side, and bushland and lakes on the other, it seemed perfect.

We walked through bush for a couple of kilometres until, just off the track, we discovered a small clearing that we immediately decided was 'our' place. There wasn't another person in sight and it felt like we really had found paradise. Because the track wasn't signposted on the main road, we hoped that most people driving by wouldn't notice it, and indeed they didn't— in the three weeks we were there, no-one but us used it. When we'd lugged all our gear in and settled into our little spot, I elected myself the wood collector, my job being to make sure there was enough wood for our campfire in the evenings. Because it was July it was cold during the nights, so it was crucial we had a fire to keep warm. We had to carry our own water two kilometres in from the main road through fairly dense national forest, but the whole experience really was amazing.

After breakfast in bed in the mornings, I loved going off on my own to collect the wood. There was so much to look at and I'd take time to notice everything around me: plants, birds, sky, sea, lakes. Each day we'd walk along the beach and sit in the sand dunes with our binoculars, watching the schools of dolphins surfing on the ocean waves. We'd let ourselves tumble down the side of the huge dunes onto the beach, laughing and squealing, rolling all the way. At night we'd watch the smoke from the fire circling upwards towards the moon, and occasionally animals would poke their heads through the dark trees, as if waiting for an invitation to join us. Sometimes it was a dingo or a fox; another time we were really close to a beautiful, chubby koala. Each night brought a new surprise to our camp site, and we'd make love by the fire, under the stars. In the mornings we bathed, solitary figures, in the clean, salty, ocean water to emerge feeling fresh and revitalised. We'd rinse our dishes on the shore, where the water met the sand. It felt like we owned all this— sea, sky and land—because there was never anyone else as far as you could see—just us.

This was the antithesis of prison and it was here that I could really feel, externally, how free I now was, how in love I was, and how my heart felt like it was overflowing. I began to really appreciate just how much the surrounding environment could affect you. For a long while now I had concentrated so hard on developing internal strength, I had almost forgotten how important external influences could be. My pleasure was tinged with guilt and conflict, though, as I struggled to come to terms with the fact that people in prison couldn't have the wonderful experiences that I was having. If they couldn't have them, perhaps I shouldn't be allowed to either: I should be able to be happy without them ... I am happy without them, but it's so beautiful here ... I want to notice flowers, leaves, the moon, but I don't want to depend on them for my well-being ... I am strong, I can live without these things ... yes, but you don't have to live without these things now. Inside me the questions and answers arose and abated like the tide.

On this trip I shared so much joy with Amanda that I came to accept that it was okay for me to find enjoyment in things that were quite external to me. To do so, I'd had to release the guilt I felt in knowing that people in prison couldn't enjoy the kind of beauty that surrounded me. I started to wonder how different it might be if people could serve their sentences in natural, rural environments instead of concrete institutions. I always felt that concrete sapped your energy; it seems to suck it out of you. In the bush maybe people could learn to nurture themselves, feeling very different on their release to the way they now felt under the current prison system. In the bush it was possible to actually learn something useful about life, about what was important, what was precious.

Of course, total happiness is never possible, for any of us. In the last week of our holiday, I rang Ali from a public phone where we were doing our laundry. She was crying when she answered the phone: 'Rikki's dead,' she said to me. 'She killed herself two days ago.' Ali was sobbing into the phone. 'She's dead, she hung herself.'

'Oh, no . . .' I gasped, 'I wish I was there with you. I'm glad you're with Vicki and Maud. Can you put Vicki on for a moment please, Ali, then we'll talk again?' I asked her.

She handed the phone to Vicki, who explained that Rikki had gotten abusive with her partner, Carey, and eventually Carey had had to leave their home as she was afraid for her own safety. It appeared Rikki had already taken a handful of pills. Carey kept ringing her from a nearby friend's house, but when she still couldn't get an answer after a couple of hours, Carey returned home. She found Rikki already dead. She'd hung herself in their laundry.

Ali's sobbing gradually calmed down when she was put back on the phone. 'It's sad. I don't want Rikki to be dead,' she said to me.

'No, neither do I,' I replied, 'but maybe it just got too hard for her and maybe now she's happier where she is.' We talked a bit longer and then I hung up. I'd be returning for the funeral in a couple of days.

Amanda also knew Rikki through her own prison-related work. Her first reaction was anger at this news which had interrupted our holiday, and she directed some of it towards me. I found it confronting but then she broke down and cried. It was like someone had come and stuck a knife through our hearts.

That night we took some candles and other bits and pieces and walked down to the beach in the moonlight to perform our own ritual for Rikki. And in the hope that her spirit was around, we talked to her. We left a candle burning on the beach and on the long, silent walk back to our camp site, we periodically turned to see the candle still burning in the distance. In the darkness it looked quite beautiful against the vast backdrop of sand, hills and ocean ... a solitary, flickering light that, despite the breeze, didn't blow out.

'She must be around somewhere,' I said to Amanda as we held each other. The fire that had burned inside Rikki for so many years didn't seem to have gone out, and yet I knew that she herself was physically gone. Tears streamed down our faces. It was strange to have to experience Rikki's death in that secluded place where I'd also experienced so much beauty and love.

I knew that Rikki had been unhappy for a few months, perhaps longer. I'd walked along the surf beach near Lorne with her only weeks before. We'd been there for a Somebody's Daughter weekend workshop. Although she'd never performed with the group, she'd contributed artwork and had helped with set design. She had cried and cried, trying to make sense of her feelings, but hadn't seemed any clearer or happier when we'd finished talking. Looking back now, I think she'd been trying to say goodbye. With the benefit of hindsight, it appeared as though she'd given up.

According to Carey, Rikki had started to gamble heavily, moving from one addiction to another in a restless, futile search to rid herself of that nagging emptiness inside. Maybe for some people who've been abused as children, no amount of love can compensate for the lost innocence that such violation and betrayal reaps.

Rikki had been in a relationship with Carey, a beautiful, gentle-spirited woman who'd loved Rikki in a way she'd never experienced before. Carey nurtured and valued Rikki's tortured yet loving soul, and when Rikki became verbally abusive, Carey simply continued to affirm her love for Rikki. She was extraordinary, and finally, I believe Rikki truly did know the meaning of 'love' . . . But it wasn't enough to save her. Rikki turned her anger outward, physically violating the one woman who had loved her so unconditionally. In the end, I don't think Rikki could forgive herself.

Personally I had long since ceased picking up the phone in the middle of the night only to receive verbal abuse from Rikki, out of it on pills, telling me what an arsehole friend I was. It was always followed by deep remorse and apologies days later, but it became too hurtful. Ultimately, after her outward battle, she again turned in on herself, not for the first time in her life, and in her last cry for help no-one could reach her. She wouldn't let anyone, not even Carey.

Two days later Amanda and I commenced the long drive back to Melbourne with mixed emotions, not wanting to leave the solitude of our camping place. By now it felt sacred. Until two days ago we'd felt protected from a world whose reality was sometimes unwelcome; where people sometimes chose to end their tragic lives. Subdued, we arrived in Melbourne early in the morning on the day of Rikki's funeral, which was to be held in the country town where Rikki and Carey had set up their home. Rikki had been a longtime member of Somebody's Daughter, so all our members were there.

It was a very ethereal funeral service, held in an old country hall, and Carey, the theatre group and other friends had placed flowers and eucalyptus branches everywhere. During the ceremony each of us had an opportunity to speak about Rikki—our friendship, our drug use, our shared experiences—and, unlike some funerals where the 'bad' or negative bits of someone's life were kept hidden, we embraced every part of Rikki's life, including the burning anger that she'd inflicted on all of us at some time. Our words felt honest and didn't make her out to be something she wasn't. I sang and played a couple of songs that I'd written for her while I was in prison. My voice choked with the tears I wanted to cry while I was singing, but I held on until the end. It was important to finish her songs.

Although Rikki was dead, I felt happy inside to know that, with Carey, Rikki had finally given and been shown love. A life with no experience of love would be the greatest tragedy.

23

Heeding a warning

After our precious holiday, I returned to work at Task Force, interspersing my work there with committee meetings, theatre group workshops and rehearsals. Ali, who would come to my office after school so she didn't have to be home alone, had also become an active member of the theatre group, performing and devising pieces based on her own experiences. She decided to take up drama and theatre studies subjects at school and was increasingly interested in theatre as a medium.

I was on a roll, getting busier and busier, my day commencing at 6 am when I'd go to the local gym for an aerobics class. After returning home I'd have a shower and get dressed, do my half-hour singing practice (I was preparing for singing exams) and by 9.30 am I'd be in my office. I was rarely home before 7 pm, and that was just my Task Force work. While it was tiring, I felt that there were so many things to do in life that I needed to maintain this pace. In some ways I think I felt I had to make up for lost time.

During 1995 Ali and I decided we wanted to add a dog to our family. Although 'Mima, being a cat, wasn't too enthusiastic, we went ahead anyway. It meant moving from our flat so Ali, with her advanced 'real estate hunting' skills and her friend Cara,

resumed her former enthusiasm. The search proved to be difficult—we had a limited budget and, in the area where we wanted
to live, houses were expensive because it was close to both the
city and the bay. Eventually we settled for a house in South
Melbourne. It was affordable but incredibly rundown, so the
whole theatre group joined in a make-over working bee to
brighten it up. Ali and I didn't really care that much, we just
wanted a place where we could have a dog.

When we had the house organised and had moved in, the
search for the right dog began: according to Ali, it had to be a
dog with some German Shepherd breeding in it. Vicki joined us
(having returned to Melbourne, she was now working as the
administrator at Task Force) along with some other of my colleagues from Task Force—in fact it became quite a community
event over the coming weeks of combing Melbourne's lost
animal shelters. Finally, one of the puppies won Ali's heart, and
when I saw him I could understand why she'd fallen in love—
he was totally gorgeous although, for a twelve-week-old puppy,
he had huge feet. I had to remind Ali that we didn't have a big
back yard. Ali and her friend Cara had long discussions about a
name for our new family member. Eventually Cara (whose own
dog is called Squirrel) came up with Charka, derived from the
word 'chakra'—such spiritual children! Ali and I became besotted
with our little boy, although I could never say the same for
'Mima.

I continued my busy schedule, now adding a dog walk to
the mornings. After a few years of trying to juggle all these commitments, though, my body started to show signs of wanting me
to slow down. Over the following two years I was admitted to
hospital for three operations. The first was minor: a knee operation, necessitated by the wear and tear resulting from years of
netball and aerobics. It only required half a day in hospital, and
my biggest fear was that, for the first time since I gave up heroin

in 1985, I'd be having drugs injected into my system. After I was returned to my hospital bed post-surgery, the anesthetic still wearing off, Amanda, who'd been sitting and waiting, let out a gasp. 'Oh my God!' she exclaimed, wide-eyed, staring at one of my arms.

'What's wrong?' I asked. I tried to see what she was looking at but I was still a bit too hazy from the anesthetic.

'They've left a syringe hanging out of your arm!'

'Great! Now I feel like a real junkie again!' I replied. After we got over the shock we had a bit of a laugh about it before I removed it from the vein in my arm—it was the needle that had been attached to a drip. I was only out of action for a few days, although my return to aerobics had to be gradual.

Only months after this I discovered a lump in my right breast. I immediately had it tested and, although the results were inconclusive, the doctor recommended that I have surgery straight away. I needed to think about it, though. I didn't honestly believe it was malignant but, at the same time, I was aware that the kind of emotional repression I'd experienced in prison was now well accepted as a serious risk factor for developing breast cancer. This, together with my own mother's early death from this disease, created lingering doubts in my mind, so I spent the next few months trying to decide what to do.

Ali's way of dealing with the suspect lump was to totally deny the existence of any problem. I couldn't really blame her, but it meant she wasn't able to be supportive during this uncertain time, and it made it difficult to talk to her. She simply refused to face the fact that anything bad could happen to me. After the years of separation, I guess neither of us could imagine being without the other ever again.

In the end I decided not to take any risks, so I went into hospital to have the lump removed. The operation was a success and there was no bad news, so I continued my more than full-time job at Task Force, my representation on four community committees, my part-time involvement with Somebody's Daughter and my role as a single parent. Life was fulfilling, but busy. In hindsight, too busy.

Only twelve months later, while having a routine pap smear test and internal examination, my doctor found a large group of cysts on my right ovary, confirmed by an ultrasound. Back into hospital for more surgery. On their rounds the morning after, the doctors told me the operation had been successful. The following morning they admitted, slightly embarrassed, that they'd omitted to tell me that they'd removed my right ovary along with the cysts ... the medical profession! It took some weeks to recover from this operation and I stayed at Amanda's place, where she nursed me to health again. This time I resolved to change the pace of my life.

Although I was perhaps more aware than most people of how precious time was, and more determined to get the most out of every hour, I now acknowledged that I needed to reduce my workload and take things a bit easier. Seeing my recent health problems as a warning, I decided to plan for my departure from Task Force. I'd been there for six and a half years and, while I'd miss both my work colleagues and the people who used the service, I needed a rest. The community sector was so under-resourced and the demand for services so great, there was never a moment to reflect or sit back and relax. In my years at Task Force the demand for our counselling service had increased drastically, so that people now had to wait two or three months before we could see them. In reality what this meant was that we would be unlikely to see them at all, the window of opportunity having long since passed or, increasingly likely, an overdose having killed them during the 'waiting' period. Instead of being increased in line with inflation and community need, our funding had remained the same through all my years there. Task Force offered a brilliant service, with wonderful counsellors, but working for so long with so few resources had taken its toll. Burnout was often the price you paid for doing this type of work.

Before I could leave, though, I had to figure out what to do next. I already knew I wanted to write a story, but I had to find a way to earn a wage while I was doing it. I applied to the Australia Council for a Fellowship, which would ensure me two years' 'time out' to restore some enthusiasm and creativity to my thinking while keeping my head above water financially. I desperately wanted to write a book, and I also wanted some time to trial arts and therapy group sessions with young people as a means of looking at issues such as drug use, safe sex, relationships and anything else that was important yet difficult for young people to deal with. In the meantime I continued at Task Force.

Around this time I was scheduled to present a paper and workshop at a week-long international conference on the abolition of prisons in New Zealand. It would be the first time I'd travelled out of Australia since my imprisonment. There were a few community workers, including Amanda, going from Victoria, so we travelled together.

When we arrived in New Zealand and proceeded through the customs area, I was immediately taken aside for questioning. They were quite rude, threatening to strip search me and put me straight back on a plane to Australia. Amanda stuck right beside me, explaining that she was a lawyer. I told them I was due to present a paper at a conference there the following week. The problem seemed to be that I'd been honest filling in the immigration papers: I'd ticked the 'yes' box in reply to the question about whether I'd had any criminal (drug) convictions, even though by then I'd been out of prison for ten years. After holding me in customs for over an hour, they finally let me go—but only on the condition that I attend the conference then immediately leave the country. I asked them whether I'd get the same treatment if I wanted to return to New Zealand when I was sixty years old—the answer was 'yes'. I don't think I'll ever be returning to New Zealand.

There have been many similar situations in my life since leaving prison. About a year later, in 1996, a new maximum security private prison for women opened at Deer Park, replacing Fairlea. It was located on contaminated land which had previously belonged to the defence force. A great deal of the soil had to be removed before the building could commence. After it had opened, I was asked by a lawyer to see a woman who was in need of grief counselling. I hadn't been doing as much work inside prison, and although I no longer knew many staff there, I was able to gain permission from the manager (they're not called 'governors' any more) to see the particular woman and our first counselling session went well.

However, when I arrived at the prison the following week there were a few surprises in store for me. I entered the front foyer section, gave my name to the officer behind the bench and proceeded, as usual, to write my name in the visit book. I then stood behind the counter waiting for the two reception staff to process the necessary information on the computer. There were about half a dozen other people, mostly professionals, also waiting to be processed and escorted to various areas of the prison.

The officer at the computer had typed in my details and the woman officer was leaning over his shoulder, obviously interested in what was showing on the screen. She mumbled something to the man, then looked up at me. 'You have a CRN number,' she said accusingly.

'What's that?' I asked, immediately anxious. The tone of her voice indicated to me that I was going to have some difficulties with her.

'It's a criminal record number,' she replied loudly. I felt she was purposely trying to embarrass me in front of all the other visitors by not being discreet.

'Yes, that's right,' I also replied loudly, trying to be proud.

'You can't go into the prison without a letter from the manager,' she stated, as though that would be the end of it.

'I have approval from the manager. I came in for a professional visit with the same woman last week.'

'No you didn't, not without a letter,' she exclaimed.

'I don't have a letter, but I have come into this prison many times before. Could you please contact the manager?' I asked, trying to remain calm.

'I've never seen you before,' she insisted.

'I came in for a professional visit last week,' I repeated. 'It was approved by the manager. Please ring and ask her.'

Of course, by now everyone in the foyer was watching. I tried again. 'Could you just ring the manager?'

She cut me off mid sentence, replying, 'I'll ring my boss.' She then disappeared into the control room where I could see her on the phone.

When she finally returned she repeated that I needed a letter from the manager granting me permission. I felt like screaming at her, but instead I said, 'If I had such a letter, I would have brought it with me, but I don't have one.'

'What are you?' she then asked.

At first I was puzzled, but then realised she wanted to know what sort of professional I was. 'I'm a psychologist,' I replied.

'Do you have proof?' she asked smugly.

'Yes, in my wallet in the car.'

'Go and get it then.'

'Okay,' I said, pressing the buzzer to get out the door leading to the car park. I was furious—I felt so powerless.

I returned with my registration certificate from the Victorian

Psychologists Registration Board and handed it to her across the bench. I watched her while I did my breathing meditation, trying to calm myself. She was nudging the male officer in the shoulder while shoving my registration card in front of him. Maybe she was going to check to see if I really was a registered psychologist.

After they'd spent a few more minutes at the computer, she walked over to me, returning my registration card and also handing me a locker key. 'Empty everything from your pockets and put it all into the locker,' she demanded.

I stood up and walked towards the locker and she followed, standing right behind me, slightly to one side. I could almost feel her breathing into my ear as she looked over my shoulder. I could feel my hands shaking as I removed everything from my pockets. When I only had a tissue left, I turned towards her, shaking it so that she could see there was nothing hidden in it. 'Can I take this with me? I have hay fever?' I asked.

'No. There's tissues in the visit centre. You can use one of them when you get over there,' she replied.

I locked the locker door and walked towards the metal detector. When I was halfway through she barked. 'Come back here and empty out all of your pockets!' I didn't move. I'd had enough. I stood right where I was and slowly pulled out the inside left-hand pocket of my jeans, then put it back. Then the right-hand pocket and placed it back while she watched. Then my shirt pocket.

'Do you have any other pockets?' she asked.

'No,' I replied and moved on through the metal detector. Then I had to stand and wait at the next door.

'Give me a look,' she demanded, pointing to my manila folder—my confidential file relating to the woman I was there to see. I handed it to her and she flicked through it like she was looking for drugs or other contraband. Behind me were some other professionals waiting to come through. Two male nurses approached the metal detector. 'Do you have anything in your pockets?' she asked them.

'No,' they replied.

'Okay, come through,' she said. They were followed by another couple of people who she didn't even bother to ask.

Once we made it into the visit centre, she immediately escorted the male nurses to a private interview room, even though they'd arrived after me. Then she returned to me and said, pointing into the middle of the room, 'You can sit over there.'

'I need a private interview room, thanks. I'll go in that one,' I said, moving to the one beside the nurses.

'No, you can't use that room. It's a police interview room,' she snapped.

'I used that room last week,' I explained to her.

'No, you're not allowed to use that one.'

'Well, I need a private room to do counselling in,' I said.

'You can use that one,' she said as she pointed to the children's play room. I decided at that point to give up. At least it was better than sitting in full view in the middle of the visit centre.

I saw the woman and somehow tried to focus on her needs instead of my own. Once I was out the front gate and walking towards my car, my feelings began to overwhem me and tears slowly slid down my cheeks. I drove home and immediately tried to phone Amanda to talk to her about my experience, but couldn't locate her. I decided to ring the manager of the prison, who I vaguely knew, having once been a worker at head office of the Corrections Department. But as I began to explain to her what I'd just experienced, I started sobbing, overcome by a feeling best described as hurt.

'I'm sorry,' I sobbed into the phone. 'I'm really upset.' Fortunately she understood and we discussed the incident in detail for some time. As we talked I realised just how deeply this incident had affected me.

'This is why people have so much difficulty in changing their lives,' I said to her. 'It's twelve years since I was in prison, I'm a qualified psychologist, and yet still I'm treated like that.' She agreed, it was abysmal.

After a couple of hours I was back to my normal self and life continued on. I knew it would happen again, somewhere else, with someone else. Although these incidents haven't totally thrown me off balance, it always shocks me that I continue to be treated as a 'criminal'—as though that's all I am, all I ever was, and all I ever will be. I feel like I have so much to offer and yet, whenever I am treated like this, I feel abused, dirty. It's sad that 'straight' people have made their world so exclusive, as though they belong to a different human race than the one I belong to—their's being perfect. It makes it very difficult for us imperfect beings to fit in.

One day some months later, Amanda and I were at Melbourne Women's Correctional Centre, the private women's prison at Deer Park, which had replaced Fairlea in 1996 (our campaigning hadn't been successful in preventing privatisation of the prison). Although we'd driven to the prison together, once we were there we behaved as though we'd arrived separately. Amanda, who'd been instrumental in organising many protests and a lot of media attention around prison conditions, had quite a reputation amongst the paranoid prison administrations. As an ex-prisoner, it was difficult enough for me to gain access without being seen with her!

I had already signed the entry book and been given a permit to go through to the visit centre when suddenly I was stopped.

'You're Helen Barnacle, aren't you?' an officer asked, holding a phone.

'Yes,' I replied, wondering what was going on and trying

not to look across at Amanda to see if she'd noticed.

'There's a phone call for you,' she said as she handed me the phone. I couldn't believe it. I'd never received a phone call at the prison before. I wouldn't even expect them to pass on a message, let alone take a phone call on my behalf!

I took the phone from her, opening my eyes wide in an attempt to signal my confusion to Amanda. I had no idea who was on the other end. 'Hello, Helen speaking,' I said cautiously.

'Hi!' an excited voice exclaimed on the other end. 'It's Maud. Can you hang up and ring me back on the public phone?'

'Okay,' I replied, handing the prison phone back to the officer. Amanda was hanging around in the background, trying to act disinterested while she waited for an escort to take her through to the prison.

'Hi, Maud, it's me,' I said once I'd got through on the public phone.

'I've got some news, but I don't know if I should tell you or whether you'd rather wait until you get home. It'll be in your mailbox,' she said mysteriously.

'Is it about the Fellowship?' I asked her, suddenly intuitive.

'Yes,' she said, bubbling with excitement.

'Is it good news?'

'Yes. You got it!' she almost squealed into the phone.

'You're kidding!' I said, trying to absorb this information. 'Thanks for letting me know. I'll ring you when I get home,' I said to her. Maud had also put in an application for funding for Somebody's Daughter and had received a print-out in the mail which not only included news of her grant, but also the Fellowship winners.

I walked closer to Amanda and whispered to her, 'I got the Fellowship!'

'You're joking!' she said under her breath. She never really thought I stood a chance, although she had assisted me in writing the application.

'Congratulations, Barny,' she said softly, trying not to be too excited in the sterile prison environment. I wanted to dance around the whole reception area, but I knew they might lock me up if I tried! I was overjoyed and could barely believe my success. The Fellowship meant a wage for two years to write this book and to develop my pilot project for young people. It would also give me some time out to reflect on my work and life ... the space to think.

I tried to contain myself and got on with the reason I was there—to visit nineteen-year-old Sharon, who'd requested to see me for counselling. The session had been organised by the prison psychologist, with whom Sharon didn't feel comfortable talking. Because she was in a bad way emotionally but wouldn't talk to him, the psychologist had been quite desperate for me to attend, although his main motivation, in fact, was to get me to try to persuade Sharon to discuss her issues with him in the future. In this new prison it wasn't standard practice to allow outside coun-sellors to work with the women inside.

I'd been seeing Sharon on and off at Task Force since she was fifteen. Unfortunately, she'd never been stable enough to turn up for counselling on a regular basis, so all we could offer was ad hoc support. She was in prison for the second or third time, having already been a client of the juvenile justice system. Did they really think it was going to teach her a lesson? Did society ever seriously think about why this girl was living a life dominated by prostitution and drug addiction? It was difficult for me to accept that this young woman had to be continually punished.

I walked into the visit centre and sat as far away as possible from the three officers who were present. Two of them may be required to do a strip search on Sharon after she'd finished seeing me. The thought of women being strip searched immediately after a counselling session was so unbearable to me that I wasn't able to continue counselling at the prison. At Fairlea I'd been able to see women in the health centre, which meant they didn't have to undergo a strip search afterwards, but this new prison wouldn't allow me that privilege. I felt it was totally irresponsible to subject women to this procedure given that eighty per cent of them had been victims of abuse, usually sexual abuse. It was important for me to see Sharon, though, as she'd told the psychologist that she was desperate to talk to me, so today was an exception.

The door opened at the other end of the room and Sharon walked in, her long, straight, golden hair falling around her face as she glanced around the room. She looked younger than her nineteen years although, with what she'd already endured in her short life, she ought to have looked much older. She seemed healthier than usual—probably the result of a break from drug use, some regular sleep and regular meals. She ignored the officers, a smile spreading across her face.

'Hi,' she said, giving me a big hug.

'Can we sit outside?' she called out to the officers over her shoulder, already walking towards the door that led to a small grassed area. I was relieved when they agreed because at least out there they couldn't hear our conversation, even if they could still watch us.

'There's so much I want to talk about,' Sharon said with a hint of desperation, the smile evaporating from her face. 'So much I need to say. I feel like I'm gonna burst if I don't get some of this stuff out!'

She looked serious and troubled. I could see she was trying hard to rein in her emotions. Under normal circumstances this would have been an ideal time to encourage her to start releasing some of that built-up tension, but the prison psychologist had told me she had to see him in the long term, not me. He'd explained that, because he was paid to see the women, the prison couldn't justify 'outside' counsellors coming in. He wanted me to do a 'handover' session. He must have thought I had some super-human power.

Apart from that, I didn't agree with his handling of the situation, or the way in which he referred to these women, who I saw as special. I didn't get a sense that he respected them. After meeting with him myself, I realised Sharon had made a wise choice in not wanting to discuss issues with him. I wouldn't have felt comfortable either. However, I was in a difficult situation, and I couldn't guarantee that I'd be allowed to see Sharon regularly, so I was forced to try and contain our session. It placed Sharon in a 'no win' situation, too, because what she really needed was to talk to someone she trusted and to release the cork holding in her emotions.

'I can't talk to anyone in here ... it's so fucked and I can't talk to that stupid psychologist. He says I have to talk to him, that I can't see you long-term any more. Is that true? Can't you come here regularly to see me? I need to talk to you. You know me and you understand. I feel like my insides are going to explode, I need to talk so bad!' She lifted her head to look at me, an exasperated expression on her face as she paused to take a breath, the tears making her eyes glisten. She didn't cry, though.

I could guarantee she had a lump in her throat, just like I'd had. The memory of that feeling in my body was still so strong ... It made me feel incredibly helpless trying to work within the prison system. I let out a big sigh, momentarily closed my eyes and drew in a deep breath. Then I reached over and held her, trying to contain her pain. All I could do was to help her hold on—this wasn't a safe enough environment for her to release it—and so, under our current system, the cycle will continue.

Epilogue

1999—12 years after release

The night before last I dreamt I was being released from prison, but I had to be taken into 'protection' so I wasn't really free. I'd said something about someone and some bad men were going to come and get me and kill me. When I awoke I felt anxious as memories of the past came flooding back. A couple of weeks before, I'd also had another dream about prison, and a month before that another one. Just prior to my release from prison a rash formed on a couple of my fingers and under my eyes. Recently, while writing about my release from prison, the same rash reappeared on two of my fingers and under my eyes.

I am free now and I truly feel free inside. My self-assessment would be that I am happier than most people I see around me, yet the dreams still come. They're only occasional, and it's not that they terrorise me or even scare me much, but somewhere in my psyche my imprisonment remains imprinted forever. I notice that, over time, my relationship to the experience of my imprisonment changes. Instead of denial or wanting to wipe it out, I am, in some peculiar way, grateful for my suffering. While in my waking life I have moved on, somewhere in my subconscious the fear of the drug-using life remains; the violence I suffered still surfaces in my dreams; the fear and anxiety of being locked away; the fear of certain people who made my life so unsafe and so undervalued. I can't erase these memories, nor would I necessarily want to—it's part of who I am now, and increasingly these events are integrated with other experiences.

Ali has finished high school, deferring university until later. She is a happy, troubled, selfish, very funny nineteen-year-old. She doesn't like to be away from me for very long and is still jealous whenever I am in a relationship. She likes to have my full attention always. It's as though she believes it could be taken away at any time, even though she is secure in our life together.

Until the end of 1998 I continued to write songs and perform with Somebody's Daughter Theatre outside of prison and this has been important, particularly creatively. Subsequently, though, the time has come for me to move on and explore other things. Hopefully while I was there, we managed to educate many in the community about prisons, drug use and the type of people who end up in prison—you and me.

I often speak or present workshops at conferences, and my professional life feels very rewarding. I enjoy my work, facilitating and observing people discover previously unknown possibilities. I enjoy my garden at home where I watch, with the same joy, a shoot surface from the dirt that I have nourished, to grow leaves from that initial stem, becoming a bud which gradually opens to show its petals to the sun and to anyone who cares enough to notice. Sometimes the seeds I have planted die, unable to make their way to the sun, even though I have nurtured them equally. I feel sad when I see them turn brown, curling under and downward until they finally return to the earth. I still don't know why some live and others die.

Recently our little pussycat, 'Mima, died. She was thirteen. Ali, Vicki and I had rescued her from the lost animal shelter on one of my first day leaves in 1985. At first Ali and I cried and cried, then we laughed as we shared funny stories about 'Mima, especially those times since we'd got our dog, Charka, who 'Mima never really liked. 'Mima and I talked a lot over the years, and even though I couldn't really comprehend her language, it felt like we had a particular understanding. My body was filled with such deep sadness as we brought her lifeless body home from the vet's to bury her. I am now able to cry the tears I was once afraid to let flow and I poured out my grief over the loss of 'Mima.

We laid her on cushions on the table and burned a candle for her while we talked to her little body for the last time and discussed how we'd like to bury her. Ali decided to cut her baby blanket in half, the one she'd had with me in jail and which she took with her when she first went to live at Ron's. When 'Mima was a kitten she used to lie on Ali's baby blanket on top of her bed. Ali has kept half of it, and we wrapped 'Mima in the other half. We also wrapped her in a piece of silk which had been given to me by a special friend, Khalil, and which had been blessed by a Buddhist monk. When we felt ready we carried 'Mima outside. She looked like a little baby cat, even though she was quite old. I dug a hole and we placed her in it. We picked some roses from our garden and sprinkled the petals over her, then I picked a gardenia and placed it on her; finally we covered her with earth.

She lies resting beside the big date palm in our back yard; it's where she would often sit in the morning sun. She lies with her head facing towards the house as Ali had wanted her to be looking towards us. My heart still feels sad when I think about the loss of her, but now when I smell the gardenia at the front of our house, I always think of 'Mima. It is a fresh memory yet. It is hard to let go.

So many of my friends, so many of the people I have worked

with, have died, still so young. When I meditate I often talk to their souls. Although their deaths have at times been overwhelmingly sad, they have also taught me how precious life is. I don't take much for granted although, like anyone, sometimes I forget. When I catch myself, I become conscious again and remember.

I don't have answers, nor can I remove people's emotional pain, nor do I see my work as finding solutions for people—everyone has to find their own way and often it's only through suffering that we discover our most important lessons. I do believe I can walk with people through difficulties and hopefully offer some useful tools along the way. As Thomas Moore states in his book *Care of the Soul*, the major difference between care and cure is that cure implies the end of trouble:

> If you are cured, you don't have to worry about whatever was bothering you any longer. But care has a sense of ongoing attention. There is no end. Conflicts may never be fully resolved. Your character will never change radically, although it may go through some interesting transformations. Awareness can change, of course, but problems may persist and never go away.

I care about humanity and it is the ongoing attention that is so important. While working at Task Force we would often go to court with individuals, trying anything within our professional domain to keep people from being incarcerated. If we were successful in convincing the magistrate or judge of the value of maintaining our support, we would continue to work with people while they served their 'punishment' in the community setting. Because we had established a positive working relationship with the Community Corrections offices in several regions,

the court would order people to attend Task Force for counselling. Interestingly, we found that, even if they were initially
resistant to counselling, once these 'mandatory clients' spent
time with us their attitude would often change as a result of the
'care' offered. In fact in many instances, these 'mandatory clients'
continued their relationship with the agency/counsellor long
after their corrections' order had expired. It's such a simple
concept, I don't understand why governments don't get it.
Prisons, under the current system, will never work, will almost
never rehabilitate people. Their purpose is not to 'care', only to
'humanely contain'.

Seven out of ten people who go to prison return there. If
you have no family or straight friends to pick you up from the
front gate when you are released from prison, you will probably
be faced with two options:

> A drug-using friend will meet you at the gate
> with a syringe full of heroin.
> No-one will meet you at the gate with
> anything.

Maybe this helps to explain the continued high rate of recid-
ivism. The vast majority of people who continue to fill our
prisons are those with 'drug problems'. The system is both
expensive and futile for this group of people. However, with
no change in sight, we continue to try to work around this
system, and hope for something more innovative and
productive.

During the two years of my Australia Council Fellowship, I
have been able to experiment with different ways of working with
people, extending interactions and techniques beyond the usual
one-to-one counselling situation. It has been enlightening and fun,
and I will continue to incorporate the arts and storytelling into my

work. I feel refreshed and invigorated coming out of this precious two-year period.

Like anyone I experience sadness, happiness, sometimes loneliness, but I feel a deep gratitude and humility. I also feel protected—I should have been the one that died so many times. I remember waking sometimes, hours after a hit of heroin, shocked to discover I'd been unconscious for so long, then amazed that I was still breathing, still alive. Maybe even then I knew I had future work to complete.

Now as I write, in May 1999, it's a cold, windy, wet night as autumn turns into winter, but my heart is warm as I sit in the lounge room in front of the open fire at home. It's Saturday night and Ali has gone out with her friends. Even though it's cold and wet, Charki (I call him 'Chucky', which Ali doesn't like—I do it to annoy her sometimes) and I go out for a walk. I've just talked to Sue on the phone—Sue who I worked with at the hairdressing salon when we were so young. Her mum died two days ago and the funeral is on Monday. I have offered to sing a song for her, as I was unable to do at my own mother's funeral. I know Betty (Sue's mum) would have liked that, and would have been proud of me. So would Sue. She has asked me to also have my own mum in my heart as I sing . . .

Charki and I walk down to the canal where I can let him off the lead to sniff around. It's dark and wet, reminding me of those nights at Churchill when I was on weekend leave from the prison. Instead of Ali, I have Charki with me—I tell him every day that he's 'my best friend'. I think he understands. I love him so much . . .

I'm wearing my own jacket now, not a borrowed one, but I notice that it's one I bought from Vicki not long after my release from prison all those years ago. I think it had belonged to her brother before that. It was at a time when we had very little money, and its sale benefited both of us. There was no way

I could have afforded a new jacket, yet I needed something to protect me from the cold Melbourne winter. I still wear it and it still keeps me warm and dry when it's raining.

Connections ... they linger on, and as I breathe in the cold night air and look at the tall gum trees along the canal near our home I feel humble, and yet ever so rich.